The Search for the Perfect Swing

The Search for the Perfect Swing

by Alastair Cochran
and John Stobbs

with assistance from David Noble
and others

Diagrams and design by
John Couper and Peter Kent

the booklegger GRASS VALLEY • CALIFORNIA

The Golf Society of Great Britain

The Golf Society of Great Britain was founded in 1955 with the objects of promoting golfing goodwill both nationally and internationally and for providing funds to further the interests of the game in all its aspects.

Amongst these aspects has been the helping to provide hospitality to Commonwealth and foreign visitors in some way commensurate with that received when our teams are abroad.

The Society has also given large sums of money to the governing bodies of golf in Great Britain towards expenses of International matches.

Members have the great advantage of being able to play on twenty of the greatest golf courses in Great Britain without payment of green fees. They also have the use of the Golfer's Club, with its Restaurant, Bars and residential accommodation, at Whitehall Court, London, S.W.1.

In addition to the foregoing, members receive a quarterly Bulletin dealing with the affairs of the Society and important golf matters in general.

Published in the United States 1986.
Reprinted in 1989 by

the
booklegger

13100 Grass Valley Ave.
Grass Valley, California 95945

ISBN 0-936421-00-2

Dedication

This book is dedicated to the memory of Sir Aynsley Bridgland whose imagination and enthusiasm made the investigation possible

Acknowledgments

The work described in this book would have been impossible without the willing help provided by many individuals and organizations. We thank all of them, though we cannot name them all. A few deserve special mention:

DUNLOP SPORTS COMPANY LIMITED
J. H. ONIONS LIMITED
R. D. SMYTH LIMITED
GORDON CAMERAS LIMITED
THE PROFESSIONAL GOLFER'S ASSOCIATION
THE ROYAL AND ANCIENT GOLF CLUB OF ST ANDREWS

The organizers of the following tournaments, and the officials of the clubs concerned:

1963 WALKER CUP AT TURNBERRY
1964 DUNLOP MASTERS AT ROYAL BIRKDALE
1965 DUNLOP MASTERS AT PORTMARNOCK
1965 SCHWEPPES P.G.A. CHAMPIONSHIP AT PRINCES
1966 SCHWEPPES P.G.A. CHAMPIONSHIP AT SAUNTON
1966 OPEN CHAMPIONSHIP AT MUIRFIELD
1966 ENGLISH LADIES CHAMPIONSHIP AT HAYLING
1966 SWALLOW-PENFOLD TOURNAMENT AT LITTLE ASTON
1966 BERKSHIRE AMATEUR TROPHY AT BERKSHIRE

Many golfers who co-operated in the experiments including: Dai Rees, Neil Coles, Bernard Hunt, Geoffrey Hunt, Guy Wolstenholme, Norman Quigley, Jimmy Hitchcock, Cecil Denny, Eddie Whitcombe, David Snell and David Talbot.

Notes on Illustrations

Throughout the book, photographs in which high speed action is 'frozen' were obtained by means of a very powerful flash lasting only a few millionths of a second. This technique produces a picture without distortion—without, for example, the fictitious and exaggerated bending of the club shaft which commonly appears in photographs taken with a focal plane shutter camera.

The action sequences in the book show, in each case, successive positions in the same swing; they are not *composite* sequences built up from several different swings. They were taken with a Graph-Check Camera, kindly loaned by Gordon Cameras Ltd., Portland Place, London, W.1. This takes eight separate pictures in a time which can be adjusted to anything between 0·1 second and 10 seconds. It has a further advantage for golf swing analysis in that it uses Polaroid film, which can be processed on the spot to give finished pictures in half a minute or so.

The photographs in Chapter 24 illustrating fluid flow round a ball were supplied by Dr C. J. Wood of the Department of Engineering Science, Oxford University; the technique is described in the captions.

The copyright of the high speed flash photographs remains with C. B. Daish. Permission to reproduce any other illustration should in the first place be sought from G.S. Publications Limited, 51 Eastcheap, London, E.C.3.

Contents

Preface

What exactly is this book?

It may seem strange to tee up with a question like that; but the answer is important: especially to the golfer who picks up the book to see what he can find in it to help him to improve his game.

We certainly hope that he will find a great deal. But one thing should be made quite clear from the start. This book in no way claims, or even aims, to be a comprehensive guide to how to play golf. It is not in fact, in the usual sense, even an 'instructional' book at all.

AN EXPLORATION

It is, on the contrary, a very much condensed account of a wide and fascinating exploration, made possible by the imagination and support of Sir Aynsley Bridgland and the Golf Society of Great Britain (G.S.G.B.).

Despite the vast literature of the game, and the scores of new books published every year about it, golf's fundamental principles had remained up till now very largely uncharted territory. From Harry Vardon's *Complete Golfer* (1905) onwards, many excellent attempts had been made to map out parts of the territory in detail. But remarkably little of all the theories and accounts, even in the best and most authoritative of professionals' books, had ever been scientifically investigated, far less proved.

This book does not finally prove all it puts forward either. But it does record, we hope in terms which any keen golfer will be able to follow, the progress of an attempt by a team of British scientists to find out how far golf can be analysed scientifically, and how much can be 'proved' about how it is played: and to see at the same time to what extent their results might throw light upon theories generally accepted up to now about the game's human mechanics, upon the doctrines and practices of teaching professionals, and upon the practical problems of golfers all over the world.

THE MEN AND THE SKILLS

At the back of the book, in Appendix III, the reader will find a brief history of the whole project, and how it was promoted by the Golf Society of Great Britain, together with pen-portraits of the scientists involved, their places of work, their particular interests, and the part each played in the wide programme of research which lies behind this book.

Between them they brought to the service of golf skills and

methods never so variously applied to it before, at least not as parts of a single unified programme of research.

So far as we know, for instance, this is the first time the use of a scientific 'model' of the golf swing has been used as a base for studying its mechanics, and for computer work on exactly how these mechanics work. The ballistics of golf have, of course, been looked at before, but probably never studied so comprehensively as here. Play in tournaments has been analysed before too; but not on the same scale—nor with deductions of the same scope and interest.

The G.S.G.B. programme has used, too, a uniquely wide variety of equipment, ranging from a force analysis platform upon which to study the exact stresses between a golfer's feet and the ground, to a wind-tunnel in which to experiment upon the aerodynamic behaviour of fast-spinning balls.

Much of the work raised more questions than it answered—and by no means all of it has been described or assessed in the book. We have limited our scope here to some of the most interesting of the facts established, plus enough interpretation and fundamental theory to present them as a cohesive whole.

The book is divided into sections. Each deals with a particular aspect of the game, or line of approach to the study of it. The sections are also intended to help the reader see where he is and where each chapter is heading, and to offer him a series of topics, each put as concisely as possible within its own framework.

The lengths of these groups of chapters vary; the scope and length of each section reflects both how much the team felt ready to say with any reasonable certainty about each general topic, and also how much of it seemed to be of practical interest to the non-scientific reader.

THE SCIENTISTS'S POINT OF VIEW

For the scientists involved, the whole programme had itself a special interest and attraction as a general research project. It dealt with a game which is an artificially created human activity (like many industrial activities) in which success in total performance can be very precisely measured—by scores.

Within the game's limits, the scientific problems it offers are extremely challenging. They can only be tackled really effectively, moreover, by very close collaboration between scientists commanding many different subjects, special skills, interests and techniques.

It was because of the pure scientific value of the whole

programme that so many busy scientists were able to give so much of their time to it, by courtesy of their universities or institutes, without direct remuneration by the G.S.G.B.

The need to arrive reasonably quickly at definite results of practical interest to the golfer has meant that many fundamental problems have so far had to be left unanswered. But one very important result of the complex skills involved has been to discover the surprising number of aspects of the mechanical working of the human body which are too complicated to be analysed precisely, even though we now know quite a lot about them. Against this, the team have between them discovered quite a lot of new facts about how human beings work—particularly when they are using a tool or instrument of any kind; and much of this applies very closely to many of man's general activities.

The programme is not yet fully completed. But a halt must be called, and in due course the G.S.G.B. team aims to publish a fully scientific volume, giving the technical results of the research in a form of professional interest to other scientists throughout the world.

This present book then is, to that extent, scientifically an interim report, as well as being a statement of results for the lay golfer.

THE LIMITATIONS OF A BOOK LIKE THIS
Two points of caution about it. First since the research is incomplete, it remains possible that further work, by this team or others, will later bring out facts which throw new light upon the ideas put forward here.

In any case, scientific research never 'proves' anything with one hundred per cent certainty. You can only hope to discover explanations which fit the facts, so far as you can find them out at the time; and although any one explanation may prove to be a very helpful one indeed in its immediate practical applications, only time and experience can give it final authority. Through further discoveries and appreciation of the problems today's best answer may become tomorrow's wrong one.

But this perhaps overemphasizes the uncertainty; scientific theory develops much more often by small steps in the direction of increased accuracy, than by absolute contradictions of previous theories. Some explanations, indeed, last almost for ever—like the one Archimedes discovered in his bath—and we certainly hope that most of what is put forward here will stand the test of time. But if any golfer feels he can improve on

any of it then, such being the nature of science, good luck to him.

Secondly since this book has aimed to interest as many golfers as possible, there has had to be a good deal of simplification in the way some of the results have been put forward. The scientific papers on which it is based, each recording some specific piece of research, would fill several filing cabinets; and many would be incomprehensible to the vast majority of laymen. To put the gist of their conclusions into a book, there has had to be a compromise between the twin ideals of complete scientific truth, and clarity and brevity of exposition for the non-scientific reader.

We hope that we have struck just about the right balance. If the reader feels that we have been a bit too technical here and there, he may have sympathy for those of our scientific contributors who see the results of their often elaborate and painstaking researches summarized with a simplicity which sometimes needs to cast aside strict caution and comprehensiveness in the interests of readability.

HOW WE HOPE THIS BOOK CAN HELP GOLFERS
With these qualifications, what we put forward accurately describes the results of the G.S.G.B. team's researches, as they affect the enthusiastic golfer.

How well any of us plays the game is only part of our enjoyment of it. There's a lot more to being a lover of golf than that. The more any of us can widen our understanding of the game, and the more we can appreciate its subtleties of craftmanship, temperament and psychology alike, the greater the enjoyment we get simply from being golfers, and sharing the same interests with other golfers anywhere. Whether or not this book helps the reader to play better golf, we hope it may add to his general enjoyment of the game.

But of course we hope, too, that it may in fact, offer a great deal of help to any reader who wants either to lower his handicap, or simply to get more pleasure and satisfaction out of hitting a golf ball.

To all golfers the book offers a fairly thorough grasp of the basics of golf. It's only fair here to flourish our own niblicks a bit. What is put forward in it is not just a series of arguments which the golfer can glance through, and then forget until he reads the next lot in the next book. What we say here stands— so far as it goes, and until it is scientifically disproved or more likely improved—as fundamental mechanical, anatomical, physiological and psychological principles of how the game is played.

Everything in it applies to every reader's swing—since his swing is part of the game of golf. It is open to him to apply all or any of it to his own game. At the very least, it should help him to understand the workings of his swing—whatever his personal idiosyncrasies in handling a club.

This can be helpful in a large number of ways—including the working of what he does wrong, even if he prefers to go on doing it (and no one can change the habits of a lifetime overnight). It may also enable any keen player not just to apply what he reads here on his own, but to understand more clearly any advice he takes from his professional. Perhaps even more important, it can help him to see more clearly what sort of troubles he needs to take to the professional, and what sort of questions he needs to ask him about them: in short, to improve the *two-way* understanding between player and professional.

A fuller understanding of the golf swing, intelligently applied, can only be a help to any of us in appreciating, for instance, why professionals tell us to do certain things— 'head still', 'straight left arm', 'don't grip too tightly' and so on—what these points really amount to, and how they work in the swing's fundamental *human* mechanics; and the book examines many of the oldest and best-known of golfing adages —most of which prove to rest on good ground.

There's always the danger, of course, of getting—in Babe Zaharias's immortal phrase—'all fouled up in the mechanics of the game'. But that's always up to any golfer himself or herself—and at least we are offering something pretty reliable to get fouled up in.

To the class player, amateur or professional, the book can be of help, we think, in putting into established mechanics many things he already knows by experience or instinct, but may not fully have understood in their simplest functional form.

For the class player, in fact, there's much confirmation of his own subjective experience and private theories. There's also many a stepping-off point for a new study of the minutae of method, of the kind which can count for quite a lot to the athlete striving to get the very last iota out of his natural ability, and an inch or so nearer perfection.

He may find himself at first strongly disagreeing with a point here and there. Disagreement prompts thought, analysis, experiment and further examination—which is the way any top-class player finds out not just what is best in golf, but what is best *for him*.

To the teaching professional we hope this book will offer a great deal which he can use in his own way in his own teaching. Scientific studies and recommendations are no substitute for human experience in teaching golf. But any experienced teacher who has made his own examination of what is put forward here, understood it, and satisfied himself by his own experience as to how best to apply it in practice, should be able to equip himself to teach even more effectively. Not least, perhaps, in encouraging his pupils to ask the right sort of intelligent and practical questions.

It is the sad experience of many a professional golfer that men and women highly successful in their own business or professional lives often show a sort of built-in resistance against thinking for themselves about what the pro is trying to tell them, and instead expect him to give them infallible simple dogma to sort out their own infallibly complicated methods and temperaments. This book may help him to come nearer doing just that, no matter to what wider and more detailed use he may be able to put the findings laid out in the pages which follow.

We have tried to lay out the book in a way which the golfing reader will find fairly simple to follow, but which is at the same time logical for the scientist. It remains only, on behalf of all those who contributed to it, to wish the reader the best of enjoyment and interest in it.

Anyone who finds any part of it altogether too mind-boggling for the good of his game can always follow the advice given some twenty years ago by Stephen Potter, the golfer and writer: 'Cut it out and show it to your opponent!'

Section 1   Finding the Model Golfer

Chapter 1

When A Player Hits the Ball—
What Exactly Happens?

To look at the golf swing scientifically, to analyse what exactly happens in it and what sort of movement causes what sort of stroke, and then to build up the model of a perfect swing—that was what the Golf Society of Great Britain team was set up to do. From all we know of golf and golfers, a tall order it obviously was from the beginning.

For hundreds of years, the best of players and the most enthusiastic of pundits and instructors had proved, experimented, theorized, looked at things from different angles and stated their theories in different ways. Over different eras, the manner of make and the characteristics in play of both clubs and balls had changed very widely; and with them the outward appearances of the methods most successfully used to grip the club and to swing it at the ball.

In our own times, fashions and theories have repeatedly varied and swung; and as the team set out on their job the air was thick with controversy about, for instance, the 'square method', and the 'long right arm', and the 'long left arm', and 'hitting with the back of the left hand', and 'driving' as opposed to 'flicking'. Although there did perhaps seem to be certain general trends in the development of what was accepted as the ideal game from decade to decade, there remained still almost as many opinions as there were 'professors'; and those who knew most about the game were perhaps the most conscious that today's great new discovery was likely all too soon to become yesterday's exploded theory.

Scientists don't work by arguing speculative, unverifiable theory. They approach a new task or line of investigation in a rather more disciplined way. First, they look at what facts they can find about it, or can fairly quickly discover and prove for themselves. Then, working on the basis of these facts, they think up a hypothesis to explain or, more strictly, to describe the whole operation governing them. They can then usefully go ahead to test the hypothesis by further experiments. Further facts thus established either carry it forward, or force them to modify it. If the original hypothesis is off the mark, in due course some unexpected results show where its weakness lies; and may even compel the scientists to rethink it again from scratch.

First of all, then, scientists need facts. They need to step back, look carefully and decide what exactly it is they are talking about anyway. That applied to this investigation just as fully as to any other line of research.

The first thing the team had to do was to ask themselves what exactly happens when the club strikes the ball; then what is going on while the player swings at it.

It would have been possible, of course, to have set off on the opposite tack by analysing the game at large: the nature of a 'golf course', the structure of the ball and of the clubs used to strike it, and the different flights and trajectories the golfer imparts to it (a gloriously wide field of research in itself, incidentally). All this, of course, comes into a full study of the game, and some of it is reported in the latter part of this book.

But whatever else may be involved in it, or has developed around it, golf still consists in essence of a man or woman making a ball fly through the air by hitting it with a club. Everything else hinges upon that, and has developed, however imperfectly, to suit the possibilities it offers. You can change course, clubs, balls, the rules—at least in theory—as much and as widely as you like. But you cannot change the structure nor the human nature of the player.

Golf begins and ends with a man hitting a ball with a club.

The team, then, first set themselves to answer two questions, phrased simply but carefully like this:
1. What are the essential things a player is trying to do with his club when he swings at a golf ball?
2. What is the essential structure of the physical movement he develops to do them?

What makes a good golf shot?
The first question they could answer immediately from existing knowledge about golf and about physical science. The subject is dealt with in some detail in Chapters 19, 20, 22 and 23, but what it boils down to is that, to hit any full-length straight shot, the golfer has to:
—swing the clubface straight through the ball towards his aiming point,
—make the clubface aim square towards his target as he does so—or at least during that part of the swing when it is in contact with the ball,
—swing the clubhead through impact as fast as he can manage to while still achieving both the first two prerequisites of a straight shot,
—hit the ball more or less in the middle of the clubface.

This really is all that is involved. The fact that the good golfer may swing slightly up at the full drive with the ball perched on a high tee, or slightly down at the ball he is forcing out of a divot-hole with a six-iron, does not really affect the essentials of striking a straight shot. Variations of this kind, like variations of swing-direction and clubface alignment to produce draw or fade (or, come to that, quick hooks or wild slices) are only modifications of emphasis he may apply, intentionally or unintentionally, to particular strokes within a round. All he is trying to do, on typical shots, is to hit the ball hard, straight and square.

That much is common ground amongst all golfers. So far, so good.

But even the above simple and obvious requirements begin to show faint undertones of assumption. And the second question, about the working of the swing itself, cannot begin to be answered by mere surface appearances, or by the subjective sensations which we all experience as we play the game.

Before they went any further, then, the team had to establish a good deal more in the way of quantitative fact about what exactly happens while a man swings a club and strikes a ball. The experiments put in train to do this produced the most thorough collection of basic established facts about the game of golf ever obtained in one exercise.

Since these facts formed the sure basis upon which the first stages of constructive analysis and thesis could go ahead, it may be of interest to the reader, before we go any further into the account of the team's work, to set some of them out, at least in their bare detail.

Here, then, in outline, is what the team established about some of the main points in the structure of the golf swing, as it works on the course, and as it strikes the ball.

Power

During his downswing, a good golfer can generate up to four horse-power. This is a surprisingly high power; and must need at least thirty pounds of muscles, working flat-out, to produce it. This figure excludes those muscles which merely stabilize his joints in action; and it leaves no doubt that the big muscles of the legs and trunk must play a greater part in the top-class player's striking of the ball than those of his arms and hands.

Impact

Time: During a full drive, the face of the driver is in contact with the ball for only half a thousandth of a second. (For convenience, a thousandth of a second is commonly called a 'millisecond'. We shall call it that from now on. Contact in a drive thus lasts 'half a millisecond'.)

1:1 *Impact in a drive. After travelling only three-quarters of an inch in contact with the clubface, the ball leaps into clear flight (bottom drawing). By this time the sound of the first contact (top drawing) has travelled only six inches or so towards the player's ears.*

Distance: From the moment it first touches the ball until the moment the ball springs clear of it, the face of the club in a full drive travels forward only three-quarters of an inch.

Force: The force applied to the ball by the clubhead during impact in a full drive rises to a *peak* of about 2000 pounds—nearly a ton. The *average* force applied at all stages during the half millisecond contact, that is to say during the compression and springing away again of the ball, is around 1400 pounds. The time, distance and force involved are very much the same for either the British size of ball or the American size.

'Feel' reaction time

It takes about two-thirds of a millisecond for the shock of impact to travel up the shaft from the clubface to the hands. By this time the ball is about half an inch *clear* of the clubface, and already in flight; but the hands have still not yet 'felt' the stroke. At least a further ten milliseconds must elapse before the message gets to the golfer's brain and he can be said to 'feel' the reaction. By this time the ball is a foot or more clear of the clubhead. It would be at least another fifth of a second (200 milliseconds) before orders from the golfer's brain could cause his hands to take any action to modify the stroke. Certainly nothing could be done to affect the ball, which by this time would be fifteen yards away.

Speeds

During the downswing, the top-class golfer may accelerate his clubhead about one hundred times as fast as the fastest sports car can accelerate: from rest at the top of the backswing, to 100 miles per hour at impact, all in as little as one-fifth of a second!

Travelling at 100 miles per hour, a driver head of the usual weight, seven ounces, sends a top-class ball away at about 135 miles per hour. If the head could be swung at 200 miles per hour, it would send the ball away almost twice as fast, at 250 miles per hour. (Not quite twice as fast, because with all golf balls the faster the impact the less resilient the ball.)

Weight

The principles of mechanics tell us that a heavier head swinging at the same speed of 100 miles per hour will not send the ball away proportionately faster. One of fourteen ounces, twice the normal weight, would send the ball away at 149 miles per hour. A hugely heavy one of sixteen pounds would push the speed up only to 165 miles per hour. Even one weighing 10,000 tons travelling at the same 100 miles per hour would only send the ball away at 166 miles per hour.

Reducing weight, on the other hand does not add proportionately to the speed at which the head can be swung either. Since the golfer has to swing the club shaft, his arms, and other parts of his body, as well as the clubhead, a 10% reduction in clubhead weight usually only enables him to swing it about 2% faster; and consequently gains him little, if any, distance. There is, in fact, a very wide range of clubhead weights which will give any player much the same length from the tee if he strikes the ball squarely. What weight of clubhead he should choose is thus much more a matter of what combination of weight and swinging speed best suits his own individual characteristics and abilities in the practical matter of swinging consistently at the ball.

Long hitting

Outstandingly long drivers get their length simply by being able to swing the clubhead faster than the majority. For instance, to carry 280 yards before the ball hits the ground, a player has to send the ball off at 175 miles per hour. To do this he would have to swing:

> a 6-ounce clubhead at 134 miles per hour;
> a 7-ounce clubhead at 130 miles per hour;
> an 8-ounce clubhead at 127 miles per hour.

Temperature

A warm golf ball is more lively than a cold one. A drive which carries 200 yards through the air with the ball at 70°F (21°C), would carry only 185 yards if the ball were at freezing point.

Loft and spin

A seven-ounce driver head with a loft of 11° or 12°, swung at 100 miles per hour, normally sends the ball away at 9° or 10° above the horizontal, with a backspin of sixty revolutions per second. A good player's stroke with a typical seven-iron, which has a loft of 39°, sends the ball away at about 26° elevation, with a backspin speed of about 130 revs per second.

1:2 *Thinks, 'That felt good'. At this point Max Faulkner will have just 'felt' the impact of clubhead on ball. The reaction travels fast, but not infinitely fast, up the shaft and along the golfer's sensory nerves; so he doesn't feel it instantaneously, but a short time after it actually happens.*

These are examples. The actual elevation and spin-speed from any stroke with any club will depend very much upon the precise manner in which the player makes the stroke. 'Chopping' or 'hitting down' increases spin. 'Hooding'—that is playing the stroke with the hands ahead of the ball—tends to start the ball off at a lower angle.

Crooked shots

Pulls and pushes are straight shots in the wrong direction. They fly straight because at impact the clubface is at right angles to the direction in which it is being swung. They go off in the wrong direction because the clubhead is being swung in that direction, instead of straight on target.

For every 1° the swing itself is off-line, the pull or push will pitch only $3\frac{1}{2}$ yards from the intended line, at 200 yards from the tee. To pitch the ball into the rough, which usually means about twenty yards off-line, the player's direction of swing in a pull or push must thus be nearly 6° off-line—quite a big error of swing in fact.

Hooks and slices, are curving shots caused by the clubface aiming, at impact, in a different direction from that in which it is being swung. They go more than twice as far off the correct line as pulls or pushes for the same amount of basic striking error at impact. If, for instance, the clubface points only 1° off the direction in which it is swung, then by the time the ball carries 200 yards through the air it will have curved enough in its flight to end up seven to eight yards off the line it set out on. To hit the rough, twenty yards off-line, needs an error in clubface alignment of less than 3°. The effects of hooking and slicing, moreover, are more spectacularly magnified by long hitting.

The implication of golf's basic facts

Some of the facts above are quite surprising in themselves, and may easily be new to many golfers. To the team they had some pretty obvious, if important, practical implications. The more you look at them, the clearer it becomes that they cast a great deal of light on the real nature of the good golf swing; and even make it quite clear that it doesn't by any means work in a number of ways most golfers have always assumed it did.

Take first that odd fact about impact: that the ball is in contact with the club for less than half a millisecond, that it takes longer than that for the clubhead's reaction to the blow to travel up the club shaft to the hands, and another twenty times

the total length of impact before the player becomes aware of the 'feel' in his fingers.

This means, in plain language, that what we all feel while making a stroke is not how we are hitting the ball, but how we have already hit it. This in its turn can only mean that, in hitting a full drive, the player in effect puts his clubhead into orbit at 100 miles per hour around him and—perforce, because he can't do anything else—leaves the clubhead to hit the ball

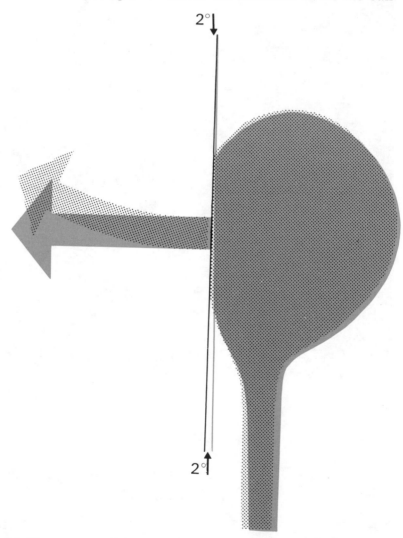

1:3 *The tiny margin of error in a drive. A 2° misalignment of the clubface imparts enough slicing or hooking spin to bend the shot into the rough at 200 yards from the tee.*

entirely on its own, in the path and at the speed he has already given it.

The clubhead's orbit is then settled by the plane and method of the player's whole downswing, its speed by the power he puts into it, together with how effectively he has applied it. *At the moment of impact*, the clubhead might just as well be connected to his hands by a number of strings holding it to the rough circle of its orbit, for all the effect he can have on it.

Another point of interest is the remarkable accuracy achieved by any top-class player in his swinging of a club. To play the sort of golf he does play most of the time, he must consistently manage to align his clubface at impact within 2° of the direction of his swing. If he didn't, he'd never drive the ball within fifteen yards or so of the middle of the fairway, nor strike it on to some part of the putting surface, in the way most good players do.

He achieves, in fact, outstandingly consistent accuracy in alignment and striking, as the illustration of his 2° margin of clubface error shows.

Pretty narrow bounds within which to confine natural human errors in swinging for a full-length shot.

We can also take note that, in order to apply as accurately as this the four horse-power which he may generate in accelerating his clubhead to 100 miles per hour in a fifth of a second, the golfer is not only going to have to use the strength of pretty well his whole body, but also to apply it through a very effective system of mechanical leverage of limbs and joints.

To achieve the accuracy required, any such system just has to be as simple as possible. If it isn't, no player can begin to control it consistently enough to produce anything like championship-standard golf.

One key to the perfect golf swing, then—and, in all probability, to the differences between top-class players and duffers —must be the maximum possible simplicity in operation compatible with generating full power from almost all the active muscles the human body has at its call.

This is the starting-off point for the analysis of the perfect swing.

Chapter 2

There are two ways in which you can set about the business of finding the best sort of swing to play golf with. One is to analyse the swings of the best players, find out what they have in common, and then build up, from that, a swing combining the features which all their individual swings seem to share. We call this the *empirical* method.

No man, of course, has achieved, or ever will achieve, the absolutely perfect swing. If he did, his golf would be infallible —at least up to the greens! But the length of time for which golf has been played, and the very many variations in style which have been tried, together suggest that the methods used by the most successful players are likely to come pretty close to the best method possible: allowing, of course, for all those individual variations of physique, muscle structure, suppleness and—not least important—temperament, which together prevent everybody ending up with precisely the same swing.

If you now ask yourself, 'What are the common features of all the most effective individual methods of swinging and striking the ball?', the answer can be expected to give at least the skeleton of a very sound golf swing. You can then ask yourself, 'Why do these common movements and muscle actions make for the most successful golf?', and go on from there.

It is at this stage that the empirical approach begins to run into difficulties. For one thing, in its pure unaided form, it is basically a trial and error approach and therefore a slow one. What is much more limiting, however, is that before you can answer questions like the second one above you must have some understanding of the basic mechanics of the movements involved; and this the empirical approach cannot really provide. To speed things up then, and also to provide this basic understanding of what is really going on and why, you bring in pure inventive science and tackle the whole problem simultaneously from the opposite end, by what might be called the *fundamental* approach.

Since the human being is a very complicated machine, and a human being swinging a golf club is more complicated still, you need to find some comparatively *simple* way of examining what goes on when a man swings his club at a ball. To do this you have first to define what a good golf swing has to do. Here the experimental results already summarized in the last chapter provide something to work on.

The next thing you do is to take a close look at the sort of movements and leverages a human being has at his command. From the two you can then set out to build up a concept of the

ideal golf swing, looked at from considerations of pure science.

Although, in this method, you regard the human being simply as a machine, with certain characteristics of structure and certain capabilities of leverage and generation of power, you are at liberty to relate pure theory to what you are finding out by observation and experiment.

This combination of both methods, indeed, offers the quickest and most realistic way of going ahead with the whole programme of research; comparing as you go along the results from the two approaches. So long as they make sense with each other, you can use them jointly to expand your understanding of the golf swing.

It was along these general lines that the G.S.G.B. scientists planned their efforts to build up a scientific concept of the ideal golf swing. In their fundamental approach the more detailed process of reasoning worked roughly as set down below.

A fundamental theory of the swing

A good golf swing must have:
- —speed,
- —accuracy,
- —the ability to repeat itself consistently.

In order to repeat itself consistently, the swing must be simple. All possible sources of human error, liable to cause variations from swing to swing, must be reduced to a minimum. Any very complicated forms of movement are therefore to be avoided.

What, then, is the simplest possible movement? In the purely mechanical sense, it is straight-line motion. Look, though, at the human being's collection of fixed length levers (bones) moving about pivots (joints) which may or may not be fixed, and you can see at once that he is not by any means well adapted to produce straight-line motion. A golf swing in which the clubhead was swung in a straight line would therefore not be simple at all, but on the contrary would involve very complicated compensating movements of joints, bones and muscles.

On the other hand, you can see that, if he can fix his pivots, then his 'fixed length levers'—and the club is one too—enable him to produce *circular* swings. For example, fixing his elbow by resting it on a table enables him to move his hand in a circle. In purely mechanical terms, a circular movement is about the next simplest to a straight-line one.

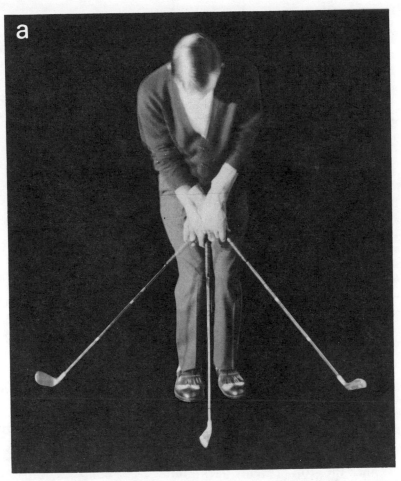

swing the club from his wrists and hands, he would never begin to generate the full power he's capable of, and which he needs to hit a ball as far as he can.

(*b*) can't be the answer either. To swing the arm and club as one, with no break at the wrists, would indeed enable him to use most of the power of his body; but analyse a fixed-spoke movement like this mechanically and you can soon prove that it could never deliver into the clubhead at impact more than a quarter of the energy a golfer's legs and body are capable of generating, let alone that of his arms and hands.

It could not do so because, in hitting the ball that way, he would have to move the whole spoke—shoulders, arms, grip, shaft and clubhead—at the same angular speed around him. Too much energy would go to the upper parts, and not enough to the clubhead. In fact he could never swing the clubhead anything like as fast as a good golfer actually does.

Moreover, although the movement of arm and club as a rigid unit would, in theory, make a very simple swing—a sort of massive spoke of a wheel—it would not, in practice, be quite so simple. To begin with, the wrist is not naturally a fixed joint; and for a club to be swung like this, it would have to be forced to behave like one.

The fundamental importance of the hands and wrists
Thus neither of the two most obvious and mechanically simple ways in which first principles might suggest a human being could swing a clubhead can provide the most effective method of playing golf. As will already be obvious to any

2:1 Two ways of moving the clubhead in a simple circular arc: (a) by movement at the wrists only, or (b) by keeping the wrist and arms rigid and rotating the shoulders. Neither, on its own, can provide enough power for a golf swing.

Still leaving aside what you actually see a man doing when he swings a club, and just working out what you could expect him to do from the way he is built and put together, you now ask yourself: 'What simple circular movements of this kind are possible for him?'

Two obvious answers are:

(*a*) He can swing the club around his wrists.

(*b*) He can swing his arms and a club together around his body like a rigid spoke.

Neither of these can be the answer on its own. (*a*) can't be the answer because, just using the muscles of his arms to

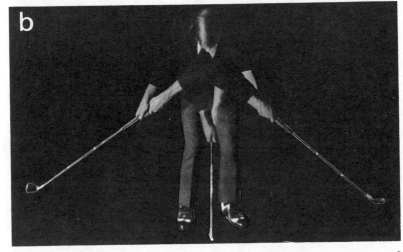

golfer, though, these two simplest possible swinging methods can be made to fit the observed facts much better by introducing a single complication, which combines them into one.

Suppose we see what happens if we now treat the wrist as a free hinge, in the middle of the massive spoke of arm and club?

Straightaway, this radically changes the potential of the

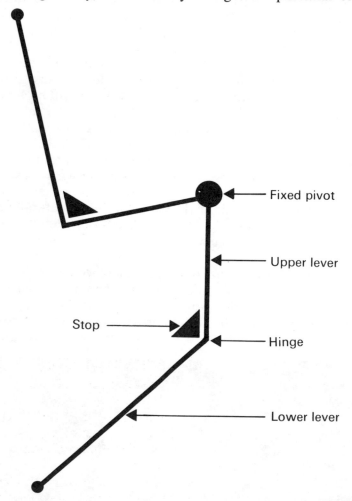

mechanical system we are looking at. Instead of the whole spoke having to be swung around its centre at the same speed all through, the hinge at the wrists makes it possible, in theory at least, for the top half of the spoke (representing the arms) to come to rest at impact and transfer most of its energy into the bottom half (representing the club, though we are still thinking in terms of a simple mechanism, not of an actual golfer).

We now have a system of two levers, hinged in the middle. The 'upper lever', as we'll call it, roughly corresponds to the golfer's shoulders and arms, while the 'lower lever' corresponds to the club, and the 'hinge' between them corresponds to the golfer's wrists and hands.

This hinge works 'free' in all but two respects. First, it works only in a single plane, that in which the upper lever is swung about its 'fixed pivot' at the top (which will be at a spot roughly corresponding to the middle of the golfer's upper chest). Second, it has a built-in 'stop' which prevents it from opening out to more than about 90° either way. This simply represents, in the actual golfer, his inability to bend his wrists back more than 90° or so at the top of the backswing (or anywhere else). From now on, we will always assume the presence of this stop, in any further discussion of the two-lever system.

How does the system work, precisely? If we start from a general position of the two levers which roughly corresponds to the top of a golfer's backswing, with the lower lever hinged back at about 90° to the upper, and we then swing the whole system in a plane around the upper lever's fixed pivot, things happen as follows:

Since the stop prevents 'jack-knifing', but holds the hinge fully open at around 90°, to begin with the lower lever follows the swing of the upper lever and stays at a constant angle to it.

Very soon, though, centrifugal force begins to throw the lower lever outwards, so that it begins to catch up with the upper lever. While this is happening, momentum is effectively being fed outwards from the upper lever to the lower lever, and most particularly to the extreme bottom end of it, which corresponds in an actual golfer to the clubhead.

As part of the reaction between the two levers, this process automatically slows down the swing of the upper lever, as it speeds up still further the swinging-out of the lower lever.

Fig. 2:3 shows how and why this happens. It makes, in fact, a good example of a law well known in physics, the Conservation of Angular Momentum.

A large proportion of the total energy generated by the

2:2 The two-lever system shown in two positions. A model like this can swing efficiently, in a manner very similar to a good golfer. The fixed pivot corresponds to a point between the golfer's shoulders and is 'fixed' only in so far as it stays in one plane; the upper lever corresponding to the arms and shoulders swings around on the fixed pivot. The lower lever (club) swings around the hinge (wrists). You can think of the stop as a wedge of slightly yielding material which prevents the two levers from jack-knifing on each other. It represents the golfer's inability to cock his wrists by more than 90° or so.

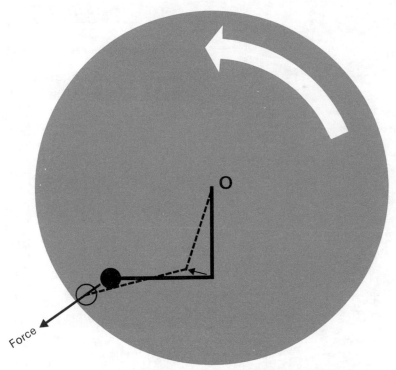

2:3 Why the upper lever slows down as the lower one speeds up. Imagine the two-lever system lying static (i.e. not rotating) in the position indicated by the heavy lines. Then any force which pulls the head outwards will also tend to straighten the hinge out and move it 'backwards' as shown. Now think of the whole system rotating in the direction of the white arrow. The force pulling the head outwards is now centrifugal *force; and the 'backward' movement of the hinge (due to its straightening out) is now superposed on the general forward rotation of the whole system, and so becomes merely a slowing down of the upper lever.*

swinging of the whole two-lever system around the fixed pivot at the top of the upper lever is thus channelled into speeding up the swinging-through of the extreme end of the lower lever.

It is clear, then, that a system like this—two levers, hinged together, being swung around a fixed point in a single inclined plane—will produce a more efficient application of energy than either of the single-lever systems. It is capable, in principle, of delivering into the clubhead at impact up to four-fifths of the total energy generated in the whole swing, and thus of making the clubhead travel almost twice as fast as could a fixed-spoke swing for the same total energy generated.

From the point of view of pure scientific theory, this is, in fact, an almost startlingly successful first step forward: how-ever obvious it looks to the golfer, once he gets there.

The fundamental approach thus offers the simplest possible skeleton of a good swing: a circular movement of the hands around a fixed centre, swinging within a single plane, with the club hinging in the same plane from the hands as it goes, and with the hands not necessarily applying any force themselves.

More fundamentals: rhythm, timing and 'hitting late'
If the hands serve simply as a free hinge and apply no force at it, then the system is working almost exactly as does one of man's oldest inventions—the threshing flail. But the question at once poses itself whether power applied at the hinge would enable an even greater proportion of the total energy to be applied to the clubhead.

On mechanical grounds, this looks likely. It looks even more likely—and the whole system looks even more realistic—when you relate it to what actually does happen in the swings of good golfers.

The first point of major interest here is that the flail-like system above, especially if it is powered at the wrist-hinge as well as at the centre-point of rotation of the whole system, will need to be 'timed', if it is to work at its maximum efficiency both of striking and alignment, and thus to transfer the maxi-mum possible amount of total energy to the clubhead at impact, in the required direction.

Reassuringly, this straightaway implies fundamental scien-tific importance for one of the best-known traditional concepts of top-class golf: 'timing'.

Moreover, it is clear that, unless the system is 'timed' in operation, the lower lever (the club) might swing outwards too soon, and thus reach its maximum speed *before* instead of *at* impact; and that it might even be desirable to hold it back for the first part of the downswing. However it is done, it is clear that circumstances could easily exist in which the swinging-out of the clubhead would have to be delayed—in relation to the rest of the swing—so that it reached its maximum speed only at, or just before, impact; 'hitting late', in fact: another of golf's traditional key phrases.

Another hinge?
At this point we might ask ourselves whether the system might not work even more efficiently if we inserted into it an extra hinge—making it a kind of three-lever flail, instead of only a two-lever one.

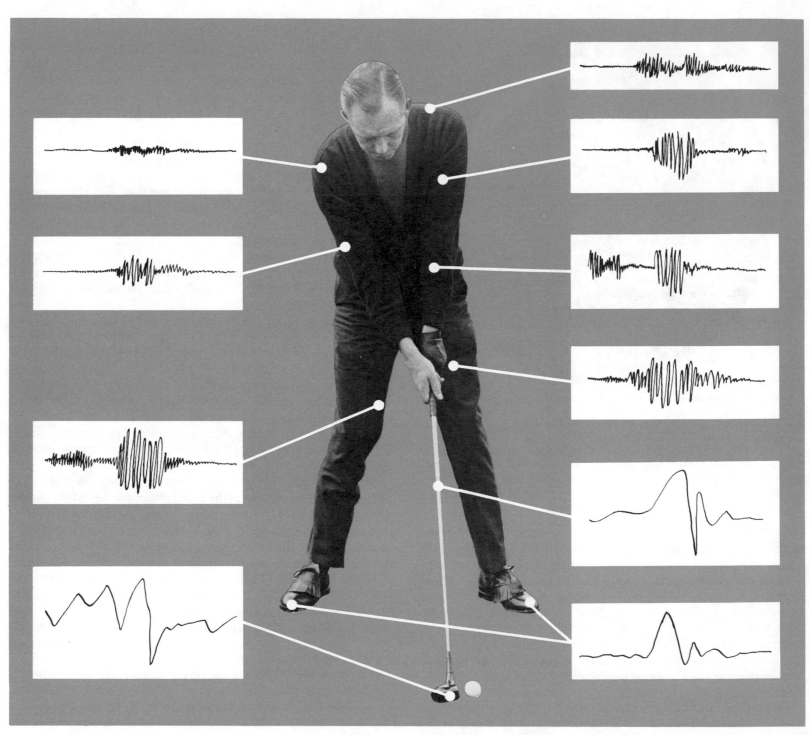

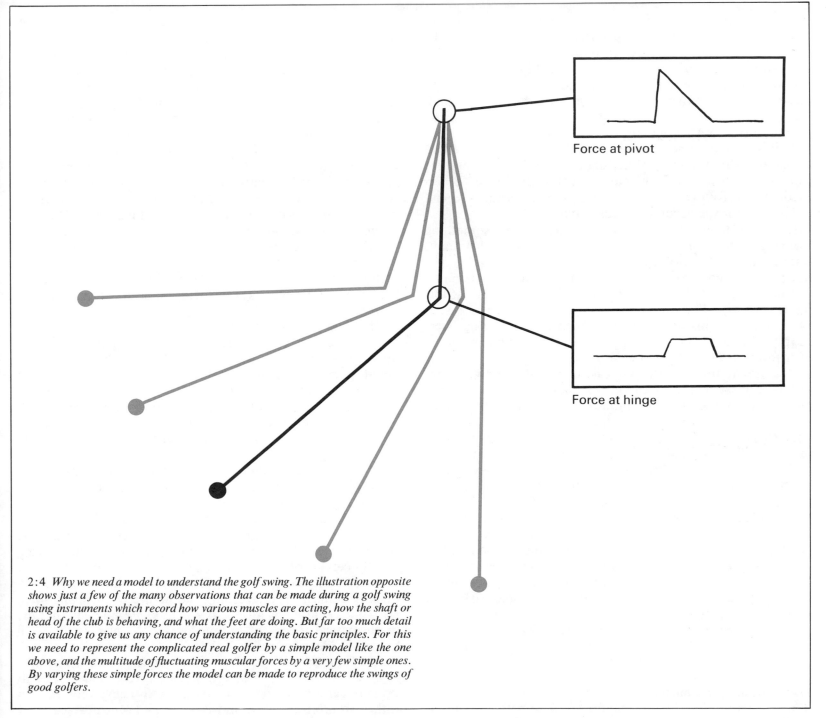

Force at pivot

Force at hinge

2:4 *Why we need a model to understand the golf swing. The illustration opposite shows just a few of the many observations that can be made during a golf swing using instruments which record how various muscles are acting, how the shaft or head of the club is behaving, and what the feet are doing. But far too much detail is available to give us any chance of understanding the basic principles. For this we need to represent the complicated real golfer by a simple model like the one above, and the multitude of fluctuating muscular forces by a very few simple ones. By varying these simple forces the model can be made to reproduce the swings of good golfers.*

The answer to that is yes: a second hinge could indeed increase the proportion of the total energy transferred to the clubhead. Only very slightly, though; and it would be much more difficult to 'time' the simultaneous action of two hinges. The system would seem likely, in fact, to lose more in accuracy than it would gain in clubhead speed; and—as our first analysis showed—in golf, clubhead speed is not much use without both accuracy of striking and consistency.

This is no doubt one reason why the bent-left-elbow method of playing—another way of adding an extra hinge—does not work too well for most people, even though Harry Vardon used it to win four Open Championships, and became a legend in his time for the accuracy of his driving.

It's as well to note here that the golfer already has something working instead of a hinge in the springiness of his shaft. Imagine all the bending in the shaft to occur at a single point (it doesn't, of course) and it's clear how during the beginning of the downswing the golfer could bend back the club at this point, storing a little energy in doing so, and then release it even later than his hand action: which is just putting over-simply what actually does happen, but with the effect spread over most of the shaft below the grip.

Reaction to this little extra release of stored-up power slows up his hands an extra bit and may actually aid the transfer of momentum outward to the clubhead. In any shaft, the degree of 'whip' is really a measure of the delay between the storing and releasing of energy; and this is why it is generally found that whippy shafts offer more practical advantages to slow-swinging short-hitters, than to those who swing faster and hit harder. There is, in fact, quite a bit more to it than that, though (as the reader will learn in Chapter 32).

It's clear already how quickly the mechanical system derived from fundamentals seems almost eager to merge into the picture we already have of the working of the golf swing. Yet what has been constructed here is—in mechanical terms—simply a 'double compound pendulum driven by couples at the two pivots'. (A 'couple' just means a force making it swing on its pivot.)

Can we now use this system as a 'model' for continuing the study of the swing? Before we go further here, we must first take a look at what a scientist means by a 'model'.

The usefulness of a model

In science a model is a representation of something compli-

cated or ill-understood by something simple or familiar. A scientist can actually build such a model with wood, metal, plastic etc., and carry out tests to show in detail how it works; or else, and more commonly in point of fact, he can just describe his model mathematically, and work out on paper all he wants to find out about its behaviour.

Before it is going to be any use to him—or to anyone else—a model must, in the first place, faithfully represent the observable outward effects of whatever it is he is using it to study. Obviously, too, any model is more to the point if its parts can readily be identified with parts of the system under study. If they can't, the model isn't going to say very much about the internal workings of the real system; and it's desirable that it *should* say as much as possible in this way. Unless it does, and can thus help the scientist to understand how the system he is studying works, the model may not enable him to make predictions about effects not yet observed in the real system.

How much it predicts is the acid test of how much a model is worth in practice.

The model need not look like the original, though. Electrical circuits, for instance, are often used as models or 'analogues' of mechanical systems. It must, however, be as simple as possible. If it isn't, the large numbers of variables it introduces only obscure and confuse things. Just because of this need for simplicity the scientist does not expect the model to represent every feature of the original system being studied; and because of this it may in time have to be modified, or even replaced.

The 'solar system' model of the atom makes a good example of many of these points. In it, 'planetary' electrons are imagined to move in orbits round a tiny 'sun' nucleus. Nowadays we know that the interior of an atom certainly does not look like a small-scale version of the solar system. Nevertheless, when this model was first proposed, it did reproduce very exactly certain observable and hitherto puzzling facts about atoms; furthermore, it made predictions, which were subsequently confirmed, concerning the nature of then unknown radiations emitted by atoms. It was a *simple* model in that the mathematical theory of the motion of the planets was well known; it identified parts of the model (planets and sun) with parts of the original (electrons and nucleus); and it was able to make predictions. It was found, in the end, inadequate to explain certain observed facts without being modified in rather an arbitrary way, and it has now been superseded by another model entirely mathematical in character. It was, nevertheless, very useful in its time.

All we can yet say about our model of the golf swing is that it looks very promising at this stage. And we shall see, as we go on, that the early promise is to a large extent fulfilled.

Explaining all that 'violent effort'

For one thing, the model still looks, too, as if it may satisfactorily explain how the human body manages to generate a four horse-power swing at the ball. Quite early in the investigation, it was able to explain something which puzzled one of the non-golfing members of the panel very much. From his study of the power generated to strike a golf ball as hard as a golfer does strike it, he was surprised at the violent effort which it appeared to him must be involved. This so coloured his expectation of what a golf swing looked like, that he was very startled indeed when he saw for the first time how

smoothly and gently a professional seemed to be swinging at the ball, yet still producing the power he himself had predicted.

Since the correct working of the model, for the maximum energy to be delivered to the clubhead at the right moment, depends directly upon the timing of the swing, the model in itself goes a long way towards explaining what might seem as surprising to any non-golfer as it did to the professor.

First step: test the model

Building of the model and analysis of actual golf swings—fundamental and empirical approach—did, in fact, go on hand in hand. But it does no harm, and it may help the reader, to pretend, as we have done in this chapter, that the model was dreamed up from considerations of pure mechanics, and now has to be tested to see how well it fits those facts about the swing which the team discovered by analysing the methods of professional golfers.

Chapter 3

The Model Golfer

3:1 *The idea of the hub of the swing. In addition to its physical reality it is an invaluable mental image to have. The golfer is Brian Barnes.*

How closely does the two-lever model tally with what actually happens when a professional swings a club?

What, in fact, does the working of this model mean in terms of a man playing golf?

To fit the model, his swing has to have certain definite characteristics, as follows:

1. He'll swing both hands and clubhead around himself in such a way that the clubhead travels in a single plane.
2. The centre-hub of the whole swinging movement will be somewhere in the middle of his neck or chest. Although his neck and chest move, this point will remain fixed in space; and some point on his hands—probably near his left wrist—will be swung in a roughly circular arc around it.
3. During the swing, the clubhead will also be swung around the hands; and the arc through which it travels will thus be determined by the timing of this swinging of the clubhead around that point near the left wrist, which is itself being swung around the centre-hub of the swing as a whole.
4. As the swing approaches impact, angular momentum is transferred from the arms to the club, so that the clubhead is accelerated and the hands slowed down.
5. Of the points above, which all refer to the forward swing at the ball, the first three may also apply to the backswing as well.

Let's look at these key points and see to what extent they feature in an ordinary professional golf swing.

The plane of the swing

Look at the diagrams (Fig. 3:2) of the swings of four professional golfers: C. S. Denny, J. Hitchcock, Dai Rees and E. E. Whitcombe. They were constructed from high speed film taken from straight behind the ball (not the player), with the result that they all show the plane of the swing as if it were looked at slightly from one side. But they leave little doubt at all that the good golfer does indeed swing his clubhead in an inclined plane, in the manner of the model, at least for the major part of his downswing.

They show also that there are differences between one man and another in the exact aim and angle of the swing plane; and that there can be even bigger differences in how the upswing plane compares with the downswing plane.

Both Whitcombe's club and his hands swing back and then

3:2 *Tracings from high speed films of the upswings and downswings to the moment of impact of four professional golfers viewed from almost directly behind the line of flight. You can see how the downswings of both clubhead and hands lie in planes (inclined slightly to each other); how also the backswings vary quite a lot, with Denny (below) and Rees (overleaf) going back well 'inside', with Whitcombe (p. 20) almost tracing out the downswing plane, and with Hitchcock (overleaf) going back a little outside the downswing plane and 'looping' the clubhead at the top.*

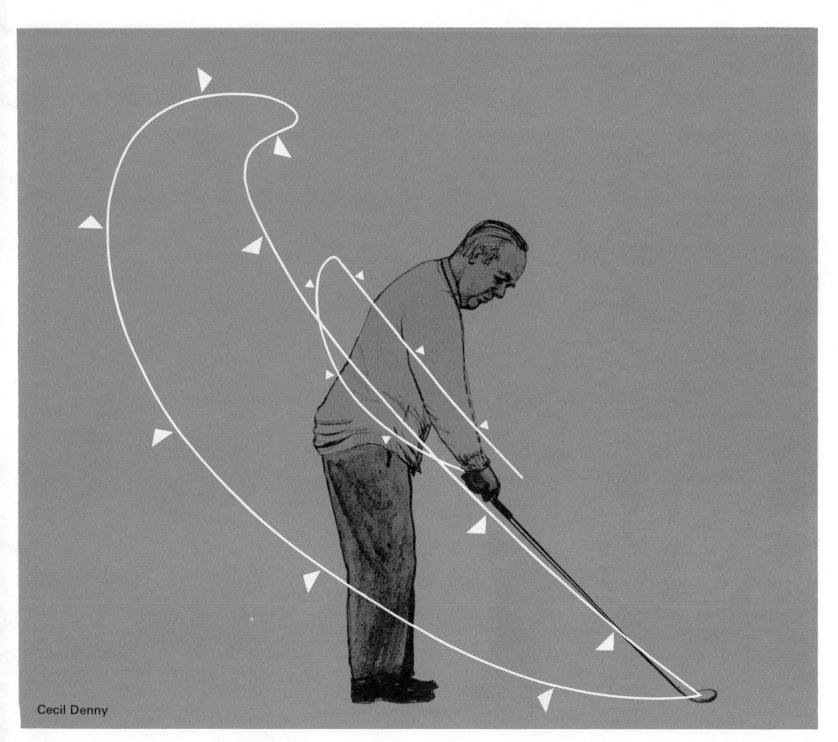

Cecil Denny

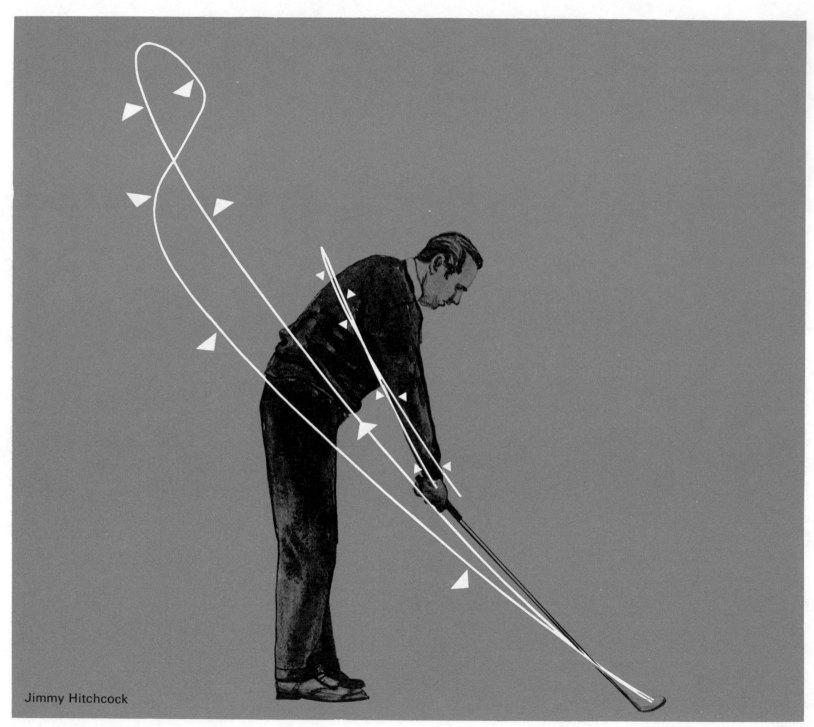

Jimmy Hitchcock

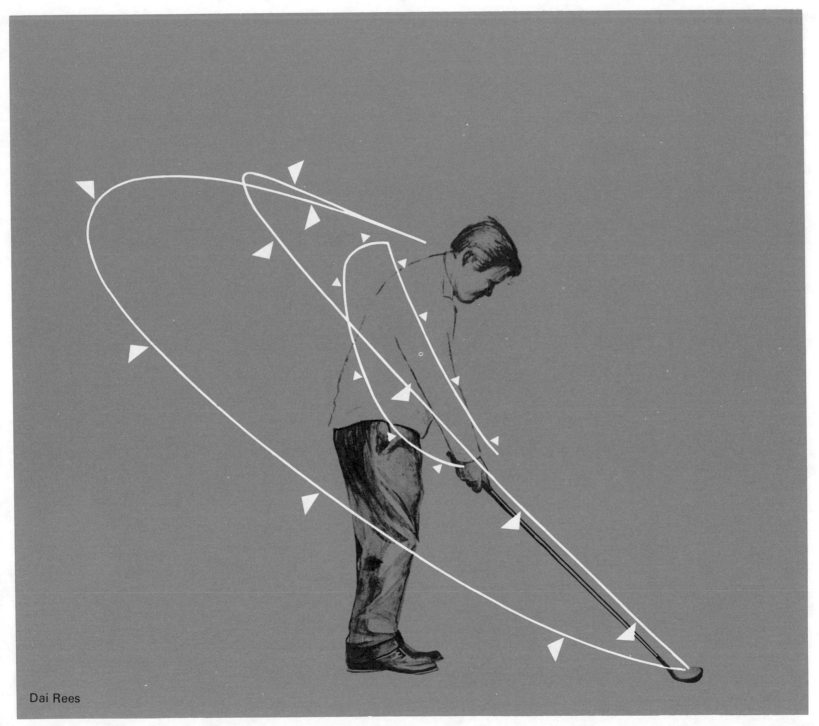

Dai Rees

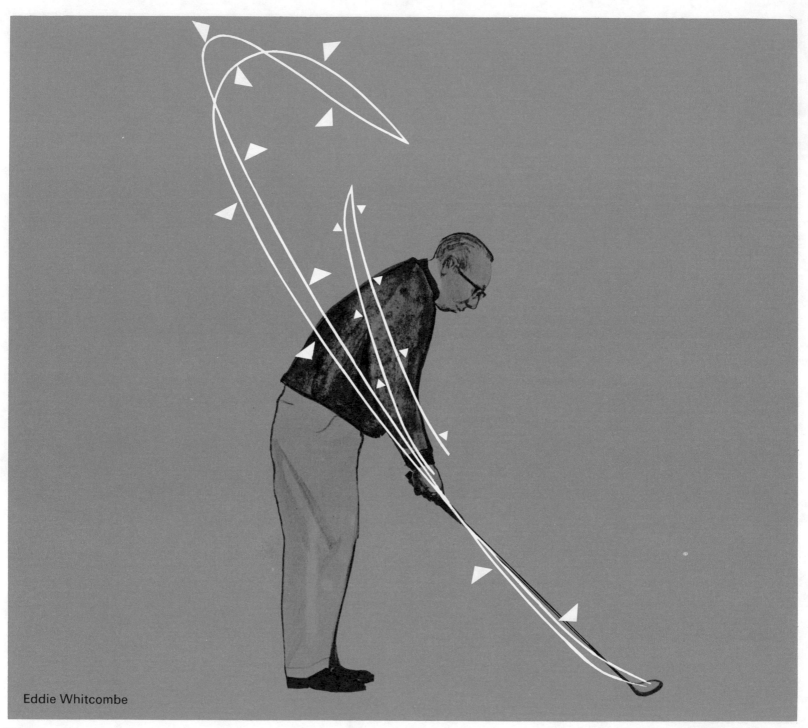

Eddie Whitcombe

swing down again very much in the same plane. Hitchcock's hands trace much the same plane up and down, but the club-head goes back slightly wider and flatter, and is then looped into a different plane for its swing down again. In the cases of Denny and Rees, the clubhead swings back on a flatter, wider plane than that in which it swings down again towards the ball.

There were obviously far too many factors which could account for these differences for the team to attempt any detailed analysis of them at that stage of the investigation: among the simplest factors being differences in build, grip (which both reflects natural hand-action and also in its turn affects how the clubhead travels), length of swing, and how each man thinks about what he is doing.

Despite these differences, however, all the swings fit the prediction of the model that a good golfer's forward swing at the ball, and much of his follow-through as well, will be made in a single inclined plane. (The follow-through has not been shown in these diagrams but it does lie in the same plane as the downswing.)

The diagrams in Fig. 3:2 suggest that the backswing also takes place in a plane, if not necessarily the same one as that of the downswing. There are differences in plane between hands and clubhead certainly; but we should not be too sur-prised at this, if only because a golfer's club is not a straight extension of his arms.

The circle of the hands

Look at the diagrams in Figs. 3:3 to 3:5. They are based on film taken from an elevated position in front of the player, with the camera looking roughly at right angles to the plane in which each golfer was swinging.

The swings of all three players here, Ryder Cup players Bernard and Geoffrey Hunt, and Guy Wolstenholme, show very clearly the way the hands are swung in a circle about a point somewhere in the upper part of the chest.

They also show, if you examine them closely, that at about the top of the backswing this centre-point of the circle moves from the player's right to left; so that the hands describe one near-circular arc on the way up, and a different one on the way down.

The reasons for this shift are not yet entirely clear, or at least not yet scientifically substantiated. Allowing for the shift, though, it is clear that the upper lever of the model system does fairly represent a golfer's left shoulder, arm and hand, and

that he does swing them in the way the model predicts.

The reader, unrestrained by strict scientific responsibility, is of course free to conjecture here. It may seem to him that the shift-effect these diagrams show is very much what he might have expected to see in a first-class swing. The golfer, as many knew subjectively and as now appears scientifically proven as well, must find the most effective way of using the big muscles in his hips and legs to generate swinging momentum. To do so he must move his hips laterally (whatever else he may also do with them); and it is quite likely that, to allow the fullest use of this movement, he has to shift his centre of rotation also. Provided the shift of both hips and central pivot is completed early in the downswing, his swing will not lose efficiency, and complication of the simple up and down circle of the model swing will be kept to a minimum.

The swing of the clubhead around the hands

From the same diagram, three further things are clear:
1. That the clubhead does swing around the pivot of the hands, as implied by the model, and as you might expect.
2. That the hands do accelerate at the beginning of the downswing, and then, as they approach impact, are slowed by the transfer of momentum to the clubhead. To what extent this is due to the effects of centrifugal force upon the clubhead and to what extent also to force applied to the club from the muscles of the shoulders and arms by the hands it is impossible to tell from the evidence of these diagrams alone.
3. That there is a good deal of variation in the extent to which the hands slow down as they approach impact, between one top-class player and another.

At one extreme we have Bernard Hunt whose method is usually described as a 'pushing' one rather than a 'flicking' one. Here the hands neither hinge back at the top of the up-swing so far as they do in the case of his brother Geoffrey, who represents the other extreme, nor are they slowed down so much as they approach impact; while Guy Wolstenholme's action seems to offer a middle case between the two Hunt brothers.

These variations perhaps represent a difference in the extent and manner to which each player employs a conscious or instinctively acquired control of the wrist action in the swing, or—conversely—a positive hitting-action with the hands. Obviously, too, different degrees of strength and natural flexi-

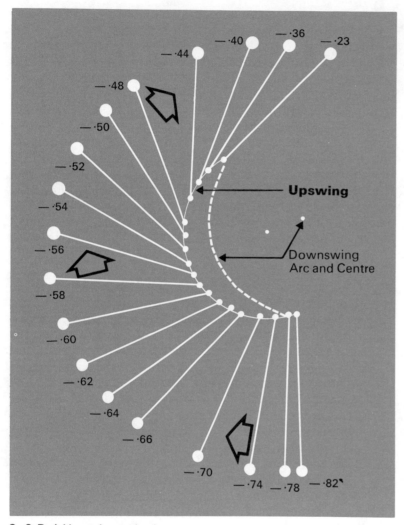

3:3 B J Hunt (upswing)

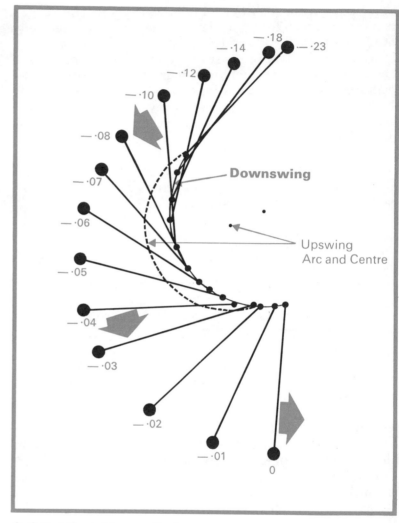

3:3 B J Hunt (downswing)

3:3–3:5 The simple circularity of a good swing. These drawings are based on high speed cine-films of three tournament professionals taken by a camera looking straight at the swing plane from an elevated position.

The smaller blobs are the actual positions of the left hand; they are not faked in any way. They lie almost exactly on two circles, one for the upswing, one for the downswing. The time, in seconds, before impact is given for each position. For example, Bernard Hunt's backswing starts 0·82 seconds before impact, and his club reverses direction at the top of his backswing 0·23 seconds before impact. Notice that the time interval between successive positions shown in the illustrations is not the same throughout.

bility in different players' wrist joints will tend to affect both the length and the internal working and timing of their swings.

All three of these successful professionals, though, show the flailing effect very clearly indeed, which means that timing is every bit as crucial as the mathematics of the model predicted it must be.

It seems that, despite deviations which occur because of the complexity of the human golfer and the vast range of move-

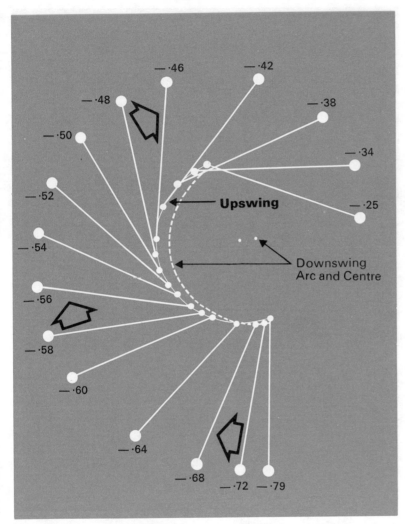

3:4 G M Hunt (upswing)

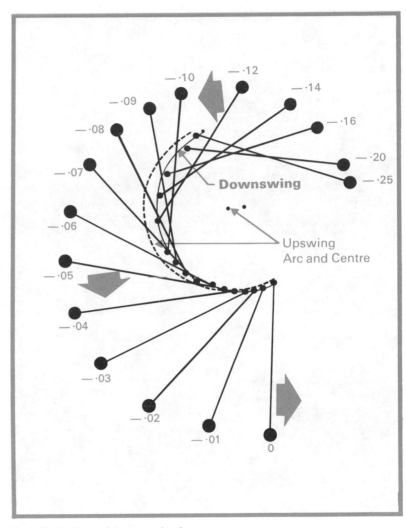

3:4 G M Hunt (downswing)

ments available to him, the two-lever model fits the swings of good golfers pretty well. It is certainly worth pursuing further, and considering such questions as: how the complicated golfer can best approximate to the simple model; where he must deviate from it; and what will be the consequences of such deviation. We'll look at all these points and many others in the next nine chapters.

Readers might first care to look at the action sequence photographs on the following pages. These show both good golfers and bad and they pinpoint some of the basic model movements. In addition, many of the detailed points of technique illustrate refinements of the model swing discussed later in the book, and readers may find it worth while, from time to time, to turn back and look at these sequences again.

But do not let the search for detail obscure the overall sense of rhythm.

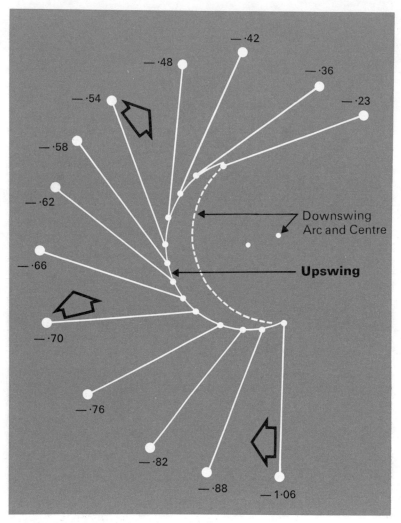

3:5 G B Wolstenholme (upswing)

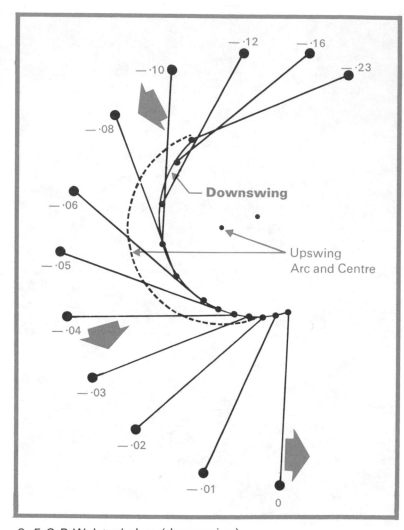

3:5 G B Wolstenholme (downswing)

3:6 *The conservation of angular momentum at work. As centrifugal force and positive hand action throw the clubhead outwards and speed it up, the reaction slows down the speed of rotation of the upper parts. Angular momentum has gone from the upper to the lower lever. In the photograph you can see the hands are moving appreciably slower in region B than in region A.*

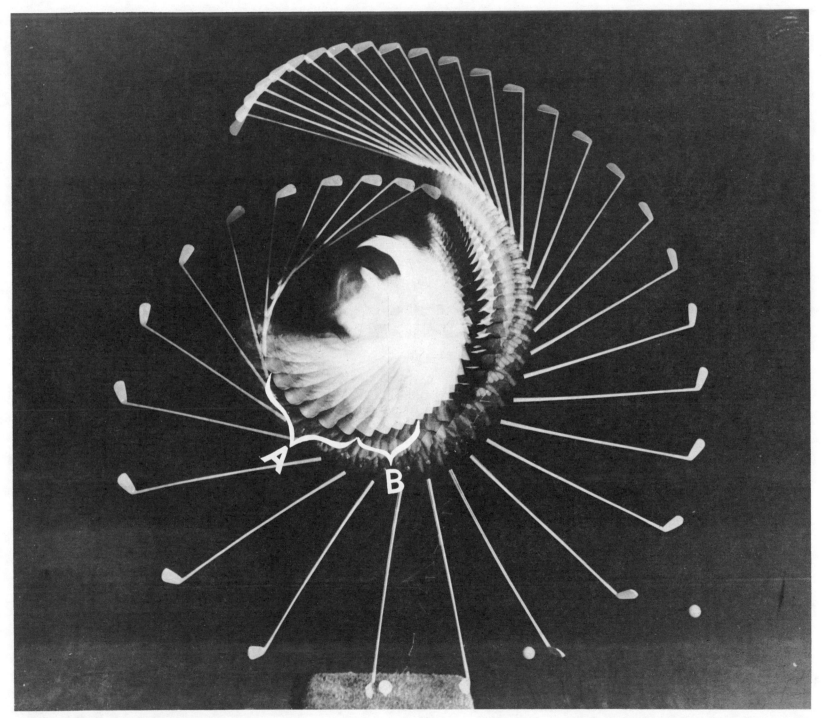

Guy Wolstenholme

Billy Casper

Neil Coles

Bruce Devlin

Hugh Boyle

Doug Sanders

Bill Collins

3:7 *Backswings of the experts. Although there is quite a wide variety of styles—compare, for example, Bill Collins's quick break of the wrists with Doug Sanders's one-piece takeaway—they all wind up round a fixed central hub to an in-plane top-of-the-backswing position. These sequences illustrate many other points discussed later in the book and it will be well worth the reader's while to turn back to them from time to time—particularly after Chapters 6 and 15.*

Bruce Devlin

Billy Casper

Hugh Boyle

Bill Collins

Doug Sanders

Dean Reefram

Chi-Chi Rodriguez

3:8 *Downswings of the experts. The way they use their hips and their hands may differ a bit, but the essential model characteristics are present in all these downswings: in-plane (not clearly shown here), no sideways or up-and-down movement of the hub, hands moving in a circular arc, and momentum transferred from the body and arms to the club late in the downswing. These sequences illustrate many other points discussed later in the book and it will be well worth the reader's while to turn back to them from time to time—particularly after Chapters 7, 13 and 15.*

3:9 *Some rather less-expert backswings. Readers can play 'spot the deviation from the model' with these.*

Section 2

What the Model Tells Us

How can the golfer apply the working of the model to his own game? And how can he benefit by doing so?

The first thing he has to do is to begin to think in terms of the model's two-lever swinging action; and see how closely he can reproduce that in the method he himself uses to hit the ball.

The model itself is very simple indeed, both in its structure and in its operation. Partly by this very simplicity, it is also very versatile. It can be made to allow for all kinds of individual variations which result from different players' different characteristics. It can cover, in a general way, all sorts of factors like the variations in build, suppleness of joints, speed of action and reaction, and consequently in timing, which top-class golfers show between one and another.

The team have indeed used the model to work out by computer the effects on a golf swing of combinations of these common variations, like different lengths of backswing coupled with different times of completing the whole swing. There are so many things which can vary that, even with a computer, it takes a long time to work out and then interpret the answers. (They prove to be interesting, though; and we go into some of them in Chapter 35.) For the moment, all we need say is that the computer studies do confirm what we already suspected: that the two-lever model can throw a good deal of light on the general problems any ordinary golfer has with his game.

Aiming the primary action

Anyone can see at a glance that there are two main parts to the model's action. There is the primary action of the swing of the upper lever about the central pivot; and there is the secondary action of the freer swinging of the lower lever from the hinge between the two levers. These two swinging actions are interdependent and equally important for the effective hitting of the ball; but it must obviously be the aiming of the swinging action of the upper lever which will primarily determine the aim of the final swinging action of the clubhead.

Before dealing with the problem of aiming a human golfer, let's first think how we should set up a driving machine, built like the model, to hit shots at a target. It is really quite easy. Since the machine swings in a plane, and the face of the club always points along a line lying within this plane, all we need to do is to line the machine up with its plane aimed at the target, and then let fly. Once it has been set up like this, there's

no reason why it should change either its aim or its 'stance'. (If we had a wobbly machine though, we should have to take steps to make sure it stayed put.) The essential thing remains the same: to get the swing of the upper lever properly centred and directed; so long as we do this, the lower lever will follow it, and crack ball after ball straight on the target.

When we come to lining up the golfer, in essence just the same thing applies. But the problem is unfortunately not so simple. The trouble is that the golfer is a very wobbly machine indeed, which makes it difficult not merely to fix the axis of the plane, but even to identify it. He will not necessarily succeed in swinging straight just by aligning his stance, hips and shoulders sideways on to the target as he addresses the ball. As all golfers know all too well, it is the easiest thing in the world to aim straight and swing crooked; and the most perfect address alignment will never *guarantee* a straight swing.

The converse proposition is also true: within fairly wide limits, it is quite possible to stand crooked and swing straight. This is illustrated by the way good golfers overcome the difficulties of sloping lies or other awkward stances. Even on level ground, experiments in which professional golfers were made to adopt unnaturally open or closed stances showed they could hit the ball almost as consistently as from their normal stances.

Nevertheless, addressing the ball with the shoulders or feet aimed markedly to the left or right of the target is likely to make it much more difficult for most golfers to swing the upper lever straight at the target, at least for full shots.

How then can a golfer 'aim the model', as it were, for his own swing? First, clearly then, by standing reasonably square to the ball, and avoiding extreme stances. Professionals often tell us to 'aim your left shoulder at the target', and that does seem to put the emphasis in the right place, in that the line of the shoulders—containing, as it does, the central pivot of the two-lever swing—is more important than the line of the hips or the toes, although there is no obvious reason, at least for a full shot, why all these lines should not aim at the target together.

As we saw, however, this is only a start. It gives the golfer a good chance of swinging in the correct plane, but he must complete the picture in a way which fixes his swing's alignment to the target much more decisively. This he can do by thinking not just of lining up his hub with the target; but by thinking in terms of lining up the whole swinging action of his hands

4:1 *The hub in the mind. A vivid mental image of the hub of the swing lined up to turn in a plane through the target is a great help to swinging in-plane.*

around that hub. He is then not just lining up the model's centre, and fixing that, but mentally lining up also the whole path through which he is going to swing his hands: round and up in the backswing and down and through again in the forward swing.

For shortness, we'll talk from now on about the place of the hub in the golf swing; but whenever we do, it should be understood to stand for this process of aiming the whole plane of the swinging action of the upper lever towards the target, and

for the mental picture which goes with it. It will depend very much on the individual golfer whether he thinks primarily of the hub keeping the swing aligned; or of the swing of the hands keeping the hub aligned.

Keeping the hub still, and swinging in plane around it
While working on aligning his swing towards the target, and then on working the swinging action of his hands around the hub within that set alignment, what else must the golfer concentrate on in order to reproduce the primary upper-lever action of the simple model?

The other main point to stress is that he must keep the

33

centre of the whole action firmly fixed, as the central pivot is fixed in the model, if the swing is to work in its simplest and most powerful form, which alone can make it a consistent and repeating one. He must do so from at least the very beginning of the forward swing up to the moment of striking the ball.

This is a fact which can be derived from the mechanics of the model. A golf swing *can* work effectively, after a fashion, even if the central pivot *is* moved forward towards the hole during the downswing—so long as the whole action of the two-lever system is timed to flow with this movement of the pivot. But moving the pivot (which, in effect, means the whole body), during the forward swing inevitably reduces any player's ability to generate the greatest possible clubhead speed into impact, for the very simple reason that it uses up, wastefully, energy which might have gone into the clubhead. It also makes the swing's working more complicated in a way which most men and women could very well do without.

Even in the case of those few players blessed with intuitive timing of a swaying swing, it is still probably true that in a full drive the head, shoulders and upper chest (where the hub of the whole swing will be somewhere located) do 'stay back behind the shot', and never actually sway past the ball before the clubhead strikes it.

Most of what we customarily call a 'sway' in any top-class player's golf swing takes place, when you examine it closely, not during the downswing at all, but at two fixed stages: laterally to the right at the very start of the backswing; then sharply back again at the point where the swing reverses direction before the stroke.

The photo-analysis in Chapter 3 showed how, in the swings of top professionals, any sudden shift forward in the position of the fixed centre-point of the swinging action appears to take place only at this stage of reversal of swing direction at the top of the backswing. During the actual down, forward, and through swing, the centre-point stays still. Once the forward swing gets going, the action works just like the model, around a fixed central pivot.

What shift there may be at the top of the backswing results, it would seem, partly from the way a golfer has to use the weight of his whole body, and the power of all the big muscles in his legs and hips, to generate the turning power he applies to swing the upper lever around the central pivot. The model just assumes that power is applied there, and does not say anything about the means whereby that power is generated. The ap-

parent shift in a human golfer's swing also results partly from the precise working of the more versatile bodily movement of chest, shoulders and arms which he has to use to reproduce the very simple fixed upper-lever action in the model.

Both these points we'll be coming back to in a later chapter. At this stage, let's just concentrate on the model's action from the moment the whole body shifts into position to begin the forward swing of the clubhead through the ball.

The hub in common terms

During the whole forward-swinging action by the whole body, the central pivot remains perfectly still until the ball is hit. The hinge between the two levers—that is, the hands—thus moves in a circle around the central pivot. The hub thus acts as a fixed centre for the swinging of the upper lever around it, and

4:2 *The head need not stay still. A big hip-movement in the downswing will require the head to move back and down if the central pivot is to remain fixed. Most good players do this—but not, of course, by conscious effort.*

Table 4:1 *Average head movement for* 31 *American pros hitting three drives each (as reported in Golf Digest December* 1962*).*

Head Position	Address	Top of Backswing	Impact	Finish of Swing	Movement during Downswing
Left or Right* of ball	3·1″ right	5·2″ right	6·1″ right	1·1″ left	0·9″ to right
Above or below address position	0	1·1″ below	2·2″ below	6·9″ above	1·1″ down

* 'left' or 'right' refers to the player's left or right.

for the swinging of the clubhead through the ball by the secondary action of the lower lever.

Thousands of professionals have told millions of golfers since the game began to 'Keep your eye on the ball' or 'Keep your head still'. The model shows that it is not really his head which the golfer needs to keep still, but the hub of his swinging action. This actually lies, for most players, somewhere in the middle of the chest just below the shoulders. To tell any golfer to 'Keep your head still' is just the simplest way of getting him to keep his hub still.

In fact, the best players' heads do not stay quite still. But they do move only in a way which is quite consistent with keeping the hub of their swings still. In fact, as the hips are swung forward, with the hub held still, the good player's head may move slightly back and downwards. In any normal shot though, it will never move *forward*, and that is what the pro rightly teaches his pupils to avoid. 'Hit past your chin,' he often puts it.

Difficulties in maintaining the plane

As we noted before, the golf swing is not a fixed-spoke thing like a huge cartwheel: in which, so long as the hub turns at the correct angle, the whole wheel must exactly follow it. On the contrary, as we all know, the moving parts of the golf swing are thrown out of line very easily indeed.

One essential move in fitting any golf swing to the model—or, if you like, in basing your own swing on the model—is to get all the movements to work consistently within whatever plane best follows the model for the player's own build and characteristics. To do this, the hub has not just to be correctly lined up in the first place; but it has to stay lined up. The whole swing has to follow its aim in the plane it is working on until the ball is struck.

Merely thinking hard about swinging the hands in plane

may not be enough to make sure of this. There are one or two specific points in the swing, particularly where the system is moving slowly and thus has not yet enough momentum to keep things in plane, where things can very easily still swing out of alignment.

The most obvious of these is the very first movement into the backswing—the takeaway as it is usually called. Even after lining up the whole swinging action of the stroke around a mental hub aimed at the target, the player has still to *start his swinging action off* in that alignment; and in practice it is all too easy to swing the club out of plane instead. This need not be too serious, since backswings can vary quite widely without too much disaster. Indeed, there's many a good golfer who 'loops' at the top of his swing; which is another way of saying that the plane of his backswing is different from the plane of his downswing. Other things being equal, though, there is a lot to be said for starting the clubhead back in the plane for which he has physically and mentally aligned himself.

The other main point in the swing at which the golfer can very easily shift his swinging action away from the alignment he chose for it at the address is in the first movement of the downswing. This is much more serious, because from then on he has no chance to swing it back into correct alignment again before he hits the ball.

The clubhead's momentum on the backswing will have tended to take the clubhead back to whatever position the takeaway started it towards. But as it slows up and comes to rest, and as the player then begins to accelerate it down again into the forward swing, it once again has little momentum, and can thus easily be diverted into a new path. In short, a correct in-plane top of the backswing position is not enough, on its own, to ensure a properly directed downswing.

The most common way a player throws his swinging action out of the alignment he has chosen for it, at this stage, is by rolling the right shoulder up and outwards at the start of the forward swing, while the clubhead is still moving slowly. The moment he does that, he throws his hub out of alignment *and* throws the path of his clubhead outside the correct plane for the shot he is trying to play. Then, in order to hit the ball at all, he has to bring the clubhead back across the correct line through impact from out-to-in. This can only cause either a pull (straight to the left), or a slice, or a combination of them, depending on where the clubface is aiming at impact. (See Chapters 19 and 20.)

Nearly all the traditional cries about 'Keeping your left shoulder on target', 'Rolling the right shoulder under not round', and even 'Hitting against a firm left side' are more or less closely to do with maintaining on-target alignment of the model-swing's hub at the beginning of, and thus right through, the forward swing.

One very important thing to realize is that, once the swing has got properly under way, it will always tend to follow the plane it has set off in. If the golfer starts his swing off in plane to target, then at least it will tend naturally to stay in plane through impact—though, of course, he may still sway sideways or get his clubface out of alignment at impact.

The model action in human terms

Once we begin to look more closely at the way in which the human golfer reproduces the swing of the two-lever model, though, we begin to run into complications.

A golfer is not built like the model. If he were, it would make his golf a great deal easier. But it would also make nearly everything else he does in life a great deal more difficult than it is at present. As it is, his structure is an extremely versatile one. It can be made to fit pretty well any action or activity he requires of it, within obvious limits. It manages to do this by means of a complicated system of bones, joints, muscles and linkages.

A man playing golf is no exception. The good golfer has already instinctively himself discovered that the two-lever model action is the mechanically most effective one in golf. Whether he recognizes it or not, he has shaped his whole swinging action to work like the model. But he has only been able to do so by adapting the natural working of all his limbs, muscles and joints to this specific task.

In golf, it can certainly help him a great deal to have in his mind all the time a clear, uncomplicated picture of the basically simple movement he is using to govern all the complications of limbs, muscles and joints. This, we feel, is where the idea of the whole swing working around a central hub may be very useful to him. Whether he thinks of the central pivot as fixing the arc and plane of the hands, or of the arc of the hands as fixing the central pivot, the idea of a hub governing the swing from a position somewhere between his shoulders can make an excellent practical basis for trying to swing the club as nearly as possible in the pattern of the model.

The following chapters analyse in some detail how he can set about this, and how he can fit his own swing to the model in the simplest way possible.

Chapter 5

Swinging the Clubhead to Match the Model

The model doesn't need a backswing. Being a rigidly hinged structure, working in a fixed plane around a fixed pivot, its action can start quite simply from its 'top of backswing' position; and thence work perfectly in its forward swing through the ball.

The human golfer is not a rigid structure. His mechanism can bend and hinge in all manner of directions entirely irrelevant to golf. He has also to provide his own central pivot round which to work his swing, and has then, moreover, to support that pivot against all the forces he generates during the whole stroke at the ball.

Further, where the model can be driven by a single simple turning force applied to swing the upper lever around the central pivot, the human golfer needs to use all the bones and joints of his legs, hips and trunk, and all the big muscles of his body to generate the greatest power he can command to drive his swing around his hub.

Working the swing by swinging the clubhead

From these differences, it follows in practical mechanics that the easiest way for the human golfer to get into the model's top-of-backswing position, from which to set off his forward swing through the ball, will be by swinging himself back into it by means of a backward swinging of his clubhead.

By this simple action of swinging, he can fix and settle his central pivot, and simultaneously align his whole hub action in the correct plane of aim for the shot he wants to make. By swinging his clubhead back in this same plane, he can then align it in plane towards the hole at the top of his backswing; so that he is then 'wound up' in an 'on-target' position exactly paralleling that of the model, from which he can then begin his 'model action' forward swing at the ball.

In the course of his backswing, he generates considerable swinging momentum in his clubhead. This itself helps to guide his whole action, winding up his body into a top-of-backswing position naturally and accurately aligned to the target, whence it can most simply set about generating—in-plane to target— the power he is going to apply to his hub action as it reverses direction to drive his forward swing through the ball.

The human golfer, in sum, uses the backswing to position and align his hub, to position and align his clubhead, and to position and align himself; all three into the best practical human position from which to reproduce most closely the in-plane-to-target action of the model in his forward swing.

There is another, perhaps even more important, reason for having a backswing, which we shall discuss in detail in Chapter 13. All we need say at present is that it makes possible a more powerful as well as a better-aligned downswing.

Looking at a left-arm swing

To any reasonably cynical golfer, which means just about any golfer at all, the above summing up of the backswing may sound little short of a wholly unscrupulous simplification.

In fact it isn't, as this chapter aims to show before it is finished.

For an immediate illustration of how the whole backswing process works, and how it can lead naturally into a near-perfect reproduction of the forward-swinging action of the model, look at the sequences in Fig. 5:1.

These compare with the model action the swings of two men who achieve admirable golf swings despite a considerable physical handicap. Both Alec Wilmott of Carnoustie and Bobby Reid of St Andrews had the misfortune to lose the right arm early in life. Yet they drive the ball up to 250 yards, and play to handicaps of 8 and 4 respectively.

The action sequences of them show how very closely they illustrate the main movements of the two-lever model in the whole method they use. Reid's greater strength permits him a 'tighter', less floppy hinge at the wrist than Wilmott, but with this slight variation, they both reproduce the timing sequence of the model's swing. Here, in fact, we have the essence of the model golf swing shown in its basic human form: that of the swing with the left arm only.

There is at once a lesson here. It is upon the action of his left arm that the golfer can build a swing nearest in practical terms to the perfect swing of the model. In structure, plane, working sequence and timing, the action of the left arm can— and must—very closely reproduce that of the model.

How close to the model?

These two players show how well this can be done. But even in this simplest possible example of the top-class one-armed backhand swing, the identity in action between man and model is by no means so close as it looks at first glance.

For one thing, the model's hinge bends back and then swings forward again exactly within the plane of the swing. The golfer's wrist, on the other hand, even when swinging with one arm only, has to turn through about 90° within the

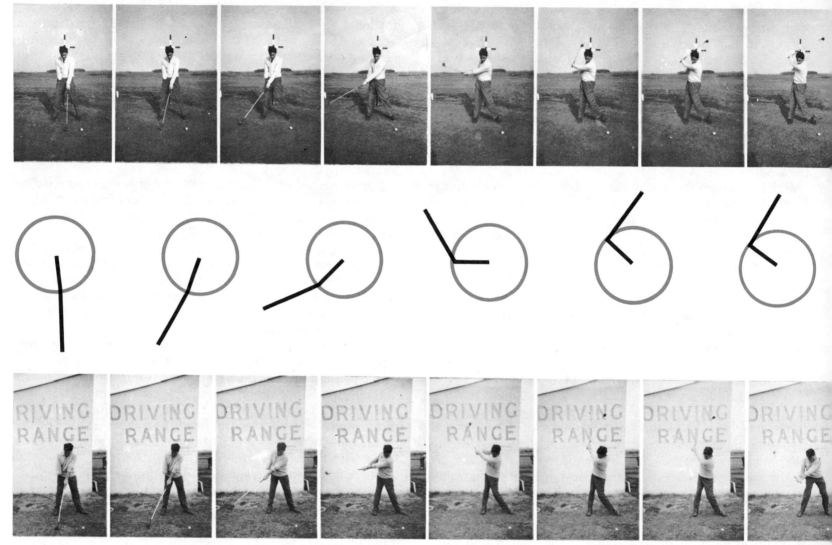

5:1 *Two near-perfect swings. Alec Wilmott (top) and Bobby Reid, probably the two best one-armed golfers in Britain. Their swings represent the nearest approach to the two-lever model that is humanly possible. They have no strong right hand to help out a complicated swing, so to get consistently good results they just* have *to swing smoothly and simply in the manner of the model. How successfully they do so can be judged by the comparison with a typical model sequence and by their handicaps of 8 and 4 respectively. Notice how both golfers keep their 'fixed pivot' absolutely still. Wilmott's swing is very like that of the free-hinging model. Reid, with his greater strength, achieves some measure of 'delayed hit'. This enables him to hit the ball further than most two-armed golfers, and he nearly always wins the one-armed golfers' long-driving competition—once with a drive of 283 yards.*

(These photographs were taken with a 'Graph-Check' sequence camera. Each sequence is really two sequences of eight pictures and the time interval between pictures on the right-hand page is considerably shorter than between those on the left-hand page.)

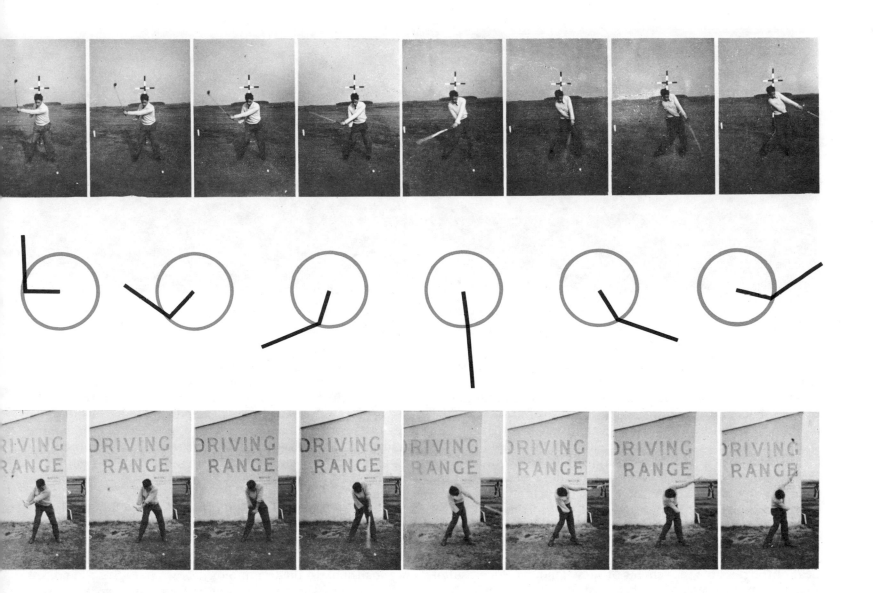

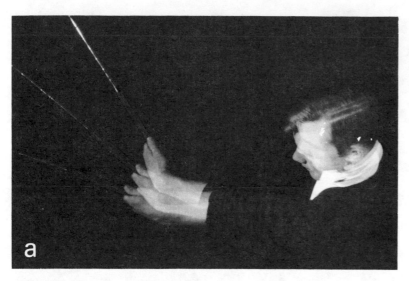

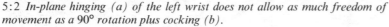

5:2 *In-plane hinging (a) of the left wrist does not allow as much freedom of movement as a 90° rotation plus cocking (b).*

plane before it can reproduce the model's lower-lever swing with an in-plane action of the club.

Any golfer, in truth, has only to try to reproduce the action of the model exactly, in the swing of his own arm, wrist and club, to find that he quite simply cannot do so.

In the way he is put together, he's quite incapable of it. He has only to grip the club and address the ball with it to find that he cannot hinge back the left wrist along the plane of the swing in anything like the same way as the model does. The backward hinging of his wrist, in that plane from the address position, is controlled by tendons. These run from high up in the forearm to the tips of the fingers. As he bends his fingers round the shaft to grip the club, he at once takes up a great deal of the possible movement of these tendons. The result is that he can then only hinge his wrist back, in that plane and from that position, awkwardly and rather weakly.

Instead of the strong free hinge of the model, he finds he has one which can only work in the same way uncertainly; and cannot open out to more than around 75° which is not enough to get the greatest practical power from the two-lever system. Nor can his wrist, when bent at this angle, be anything like strong enough to take the strain of the sudden reversal of club-head momentum which occurs as the player goes from back-swing into downswing.

We shall be discussing wrist movements quite a lot in sub-sequent chapters, so it might be as well, at this stage, to give names to the basic wrist movements and stick to them. They have, of course, got anatomical names, but they are unfamiliar to most people and might be confusing. We shall use 'cocking' and 'uncocking' to mean movement in the plane thumb to little finger, and 'hinging' to mean movement at right angles to the palm. Figs. 5:3 and 5:4 show these, and give the anatomical terms also.

'Cocking' and 'uncocking' are used loosely among golfers to mean any sort of bending and straightening of the wrists, and we shall occasionally use them in this way where no ambiguity arises. But in any detailed analysis of wrist action we shall stick to the terminology shown in Figs. 5:3 and 5:4.

Using these terms then, the golfer cannot work his two-lever system within the plane in the prime mechanical simpli-city of the model, simply because his wrist cannot 'hinge' back either far enough or strongly enough.

Another obvious complication arises from the structure of his hub. The model's is just a pivot fixed at the correct angle to set the plane of the model's whole swing. The golfer doesn't have any such simple hub in himself. He cannot even use a swinging of his shoulders at right angles around his spine. To do so he would have to bend so far forward as to limit severely

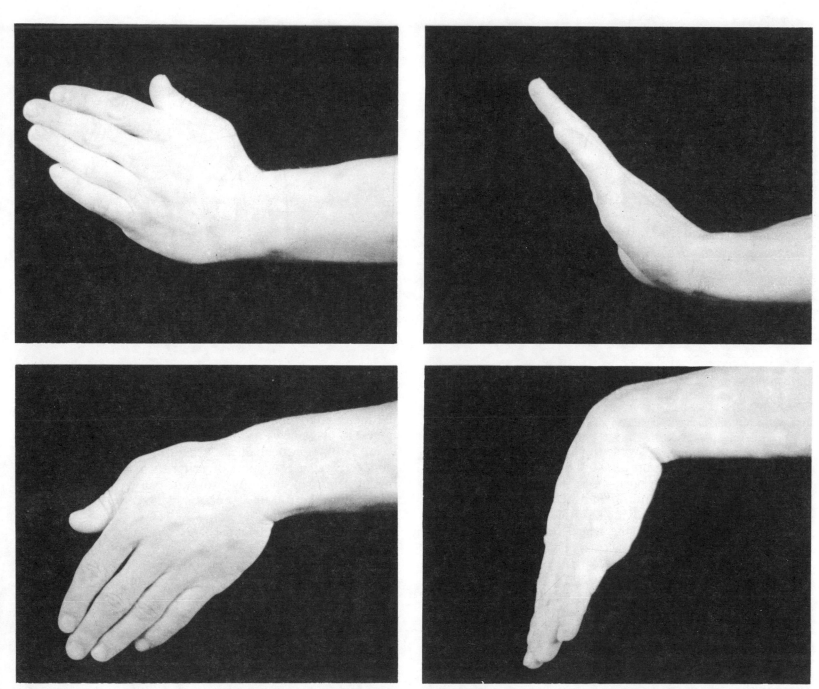

5:3 'Cocking' and 'uncocking.' We use these terms to refer specifically to this movement in the plane of the hand. Anatomically the two positions are called 'radial' and 'ulnar deviation'.

5:4 'Hinging.' This movement is at right angles to 'cocking' and 'uncocking'. Anatomically known as 'hyperextension' (or 'dorsi-flexion') and 'flexion' (or 'palmar-flexion').

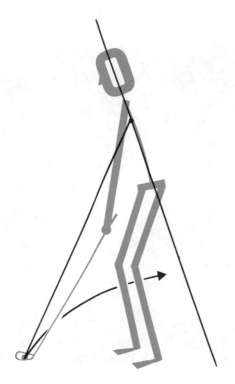

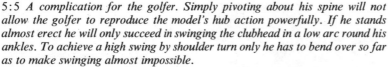

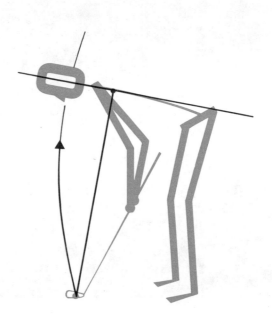

5:5 A complication for the golfer. Simply pivoting about his spine will not allow the golfer to reproduce the model's hub action powerfully. If he stands almost erect he will only succeed in swinging the clubhead in a low arc round his ankles. To achieve a high swing by shoulder turn only he has to bend over so far as to make swinging almost impossible.

his freedom of action to swing the club most effectively. In practice he cannot take up the sort of stance the model requires of him in order to position his hub for the swing, and still incline his spine at more than a few degrees from the vertical. He thus cannot provide a simple hub like the model's by turning his shoulders, like a wheel's hub, directly around his spine.

The two basic movements of the swing

Accordingly, to provide his basic hub action he has to combine something else with the simple turn of his shoulders: so that the two movements together make a form of 'universal joint'.

This second movement he uses is the raising and lowering of his arms from the shoulders. Tacked on to the basic turn of his shoulders about his spine, this straightaway enables him to swing his left arm back at any angle to suit any plane of swing he chooses.

The golfer is thus at once departing slightly from the basic action of the two-lever model; and the further he goes in reproducing the model's swing, the more he is going to have to use increasingly complicated combinations of movements of bones, joints, sinews and muscles, to reproduce its action in terms of human mechanical structure. The reader may then wonder what is the point of using such a simple two-lever model if human anatomy proves so very much more complicated in practical operation.

The model as a guide to movements

The answer to that question is the key to the use of the model.

Any sort of swinging momentum of a fairly heavy-headed golf club will try to move in the smoothest and simplest possible way. So, although the actual movements taking place at all the joints which the golfer uses are together quite complicated, the constant overall tendency will be for the swinging action itself to smooth out most of the complications of its own accord.

Apart from ensuring that our swing is basically a two-lever one, we do not in any way have to *force* it to fit the model. On the contrary, the art of golf lies in *allowing* our swing to follow the model.

Chapter 6

The Basic Movements of the Model Backswing

We have admitted that the structural movements the golfer has to make in order to follow the model can be made to look quite complicated if taken bit by bit; and even more so if analysed scientifically in terms of joints and muscles!

We now want to demonstrate the exact opposite: that, in the sort of terms in which we all, as laymen, talk about the human body, and in which we think as we play golf, the movements we need to make in order to reproduce the model swing are really unexpectedly few and simple.

Even so, a word of warning would not be out of place here. Detailed analysis of a rapid movement like the golf swing must be applied sensibly if it is not to do more harm than good. It can be, and we sincerely hope, will be of great interest and value in clarifying any golfer's ideas about his own swing, and thereby pointing the way to possible improvements; but analysis of this kind should not, perhaps, be uppermost in his mind when he is playing a serious round of golf.

The left is the master arm

Let us first look closely at that simplest of all golf swings, the left-arm backhand one, as used by Reid and Wilmott; for it is this which must form the essence of any normal two-armed golf swing.

We can say quite emphatically, here and now, that the perfect golf swing in the pattern of the two-lever model can only be based upon the action of the backhand arm. The function of the other arm, though equally important and even of greater power in its muscular contribution to the striking of the ball, must follow the pattern of action set by the backhand arm.

For any normal right-handed golfer, in fact, the left arm is the master in setting the plane of the swing and in reproducing the action of the two-lever model in it.

The two main movements—plus a third

We said in Chapter 5 that, in setting the hub action of the model, the golfer uses a combination of two movements: the turning of the shoulders about the spine, and the raising and lowering of the left arm. It is the correct combination by the player of these two simple movements which is the key to following the swing of the model. Between them, they provide him with the central and vital hub action for his whole swing.

Let's therefore just look at these two basic movements a little more closely. In what follows we are assuming a straight-faced club is being used, so that, for example, at the address position, its face 'points' *horizontally* towards the hole. It will probably help the reader to have such a club, or a ruler (or anything of that sort with a 'face') in his hand.

We're looking here only at the left arm. We go into the part played by the right arm in Chapters 9 to 12. If the reader carries out the movements described here, he can use his right arm to support his left if necessary; but it is the action of the left arm and hand we are interested in at this stage.

Movement 1: Simple turning of the upper chest

If the golfer stands *upright*, holding his left arm and club straight out directly in front of him at right angles to his body, he can turn his shoulders and upper chest to the right through about 90°. This movement points the club directly away from the target, with the clubface pointing roughly horizontal.

Let him then take up his normal address position, *inclining* his body forward from the hips as far as feels comfortable and powerful, and dropping his arm and club together to address the ball, and then repeat the movement by rotating his shoulders at right angles around his now inclined spine, from the normal golf position.

Again he will be able to swing the club round through about 90°; but this time its face will end up pointing slightly below the horizontal, downwards towards the ground, and the club will end up rather lower than it did before. This is as far as the club can be taken by that movement alone: a very tight and restricted backswing indeed.

Movement 2: Simple raising and lowering of the arm

What the golfer now needs is a second movement to widen the arc of his upper-lever swing to let it go more freely and widely up and around his hub.

If he addresses the ball, holding his club in his left arm only, in a normal address position, and then, without moving his shoulders or turning his arm, he raises his arm to about head height, then he has carried out the second component of movement which he needs.

Movement 3: Wrist cocking

If, as he carries out Movement 2, he allows the momentum of the club to cock his wrist back until the angle between club and arm is about 90°, he will have, without trying, combined Movements 2 and 3.

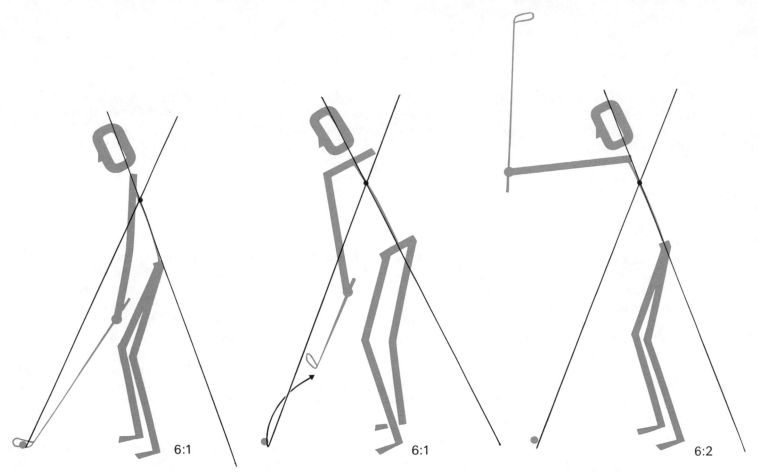

6:1 *Reproducing the model backswing—Movement 1: Turn of the shoulders around the spine as axis.*

6:2 *Reproducing the model backswing—Movements 2 and 3: Raising the arm vertically from the shoulder and cocking the wrist.*

6:3 *Reproducing the model backswing—Movements 1, 2 and 3: Shoulder turn plus arm raising and wrist cocking.*

6:4 *Reproducing the model backswing—Movement 4 added: Arm swung slightly across chest putting the hand into plane.*

6:5 *Reproducing the model backswing—Movement 5 added: Roll of the left forearm putting clubhead into plane; backswing complete.*

If he then combines the three movements exactly as described, he ends up in the position illustrated in Fig. 6:3.

You can try getting into this position by carrying out the movements in two sequences. 1 then 2 and 3; or 2 and 3 followed by 1. There are, of course, other sequences, but these are the only ones in which 3 follows directly on top of 2 as it does naturally.

The position achieved is still not the model's. It has moved outside the plane. To give this action freedom to follow the plane to the top of the backswing, the golfer needs a further movement.

Movements 4 and 5: Rolling the hand and clubhead into plane
This is the simplest possible roll of the left forearm across the upper chest from the left shoulder. It is needed only as a *passive* movement, to enable the backswing of the left arm to follow the plane of the model.

This slight movement has two components:
Movement 4 *:* A simple movement of the arm across the chest to point slightly to the right of wherever the player's chest is

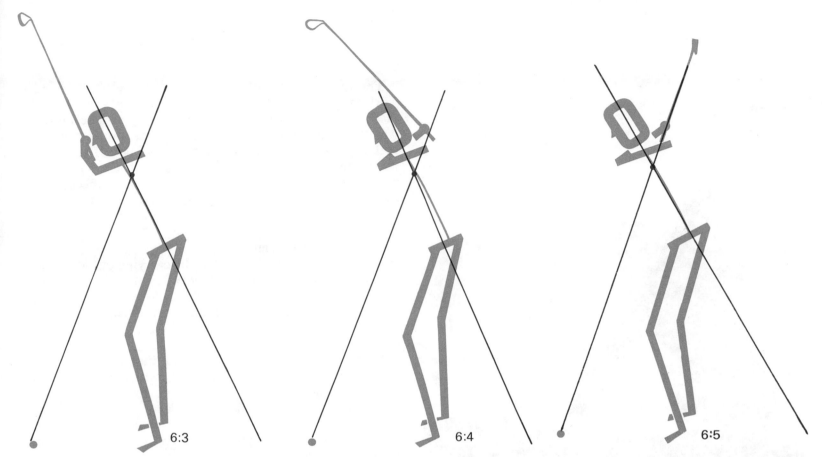

6:3   6:4   6:5

facing. This brings the hand into plane, but still leaves the clubhead above the plane, unless the wrist has bent by hinging backwards (arching) as well as cocking. Some people can do this but most golfers find it at best a very weak position and it is better to preserve the straight up and down cocking by adding

Movement 5: A turn of the forearm and hand together on the axis of the whole arm from the shoulder, so that the back of the left wrist, instead of facing slightly down towards the ground as it did at the end of Movements 1 and 2, now faces slightly upward above the horizontal, and can thus allow straightforward wrist cocking to take place in the model's plane of swing.

We called these passive movements, because their function is simply to allow the other main movements to follow the plane of the model swing as they take the left arm round and up in the backswing. They result from swinging the clubhead in the pattern of movement which best reproduces the model's backswing.

In the anatomical sense they might almost be regarded as a single movement because of the way the versatile joint of the left shoulder usually tends to roll the arm slightly towards the palm downward position as it moves the arm across the chest. However, since this 'natural roll' will not always get the clubhead exactly in plane, and since some increase in roll is going to be needed in the forward swing, we shall continue to talk of two separate movements—arm across chest, and forearm rotation.

A difference from the model

One effect of these five movements together—and this is quite an important point to note—is that the back of the left wrist has turned through about 90° in relation to the plane of the swing. It began at the address facing straight towards the target and exactly *along* the plane of aim. It ends up lying flat *within* the plane, and *facing at* 90° to it, at the top-of-back-swing position.

Only a small part of this change of alignment results from Movements 4 and 5, the roll across of the arm on its own axis from the shoulder joint. By far the greater part of it is a

45

6:6 *Kel Nagle in a perfect in-plane top-of-the-backswing position with flat left wrist and clubface in plane.*

structural effect of using a combination of Movements 1 and 2 to swing the whole arm back from the ball.

It's worth repeating here, perhaps, that the 90° turning of the hinge at the left wrist, in relation to the plane, is one of the main fundamental structural differences between the working of the human golf swing and that of the two-lever model.

The model could, of course, quite easily be modified to work this way as well. But since this turning of the hinge takes place quite naturally in the human swing, as a result of the way the body reproduces the action of the model, there is no real need to complicate the model by adding it. The model, in its simple form, still represents the essential action in what the golfer is trying to achieve, no matter how he is affected by his own structural differences from the model's simple in-plane hinge.

Some permissible variations

If you get the left hand into plane by carrying out Movements 1, 2 and 4 first, and then follow with Movements 5 and 3 (forearm rotation and wrist cocking) to put the clubhead in plane, you will see that there is quite some scope for variation in these two movements, but that these variations are interdependent.

In particular, it should be noted that there is nothing 'magic' about the position with the wrist lying flat within the plane. By increasing the amount of forearm rotation in Movement 5, you can make it necessary to 'cup' the left wrist slightly in Movement 3 (hinge it forward as well as cock it, in the terminology of Chapter 5) to keep the clubhead in plane. In that case, the toe of the club points to the ground, rather than along the plane of the swing, in what professionals call an 'open' position. Though mechanically this position is more complicated and more error prone than the 'square' position, with the back of the wrist and clubface lying in plane, many people find it easier to achieve, and it thus certainly cannot be said to be 'wrong'.

Indeed the precise manner in which a golfer reproduces the model's simple hinge by his wrist action is to a large extent an individual compromise between what is, in the purely mechanical sense, least liable to error and what is anatomically most comfortable and effective *for him*. It is probably true that years ago the dictates of comfort prevailed, though perhaps the equipment used had also something to do with it. Nowadays, with so many golfers reading books by professionals, the pendulum may have swung the other way; certainly, many club golfers are to be seen persevering with wrist actions which look impossibly uncomfortable and for that reason probably inefficient.

We return to this question in detail in Chapter 16, but meantime we shall regard the flat wrist, clubface-in-plane position demonstrated by Kel Nagle in the photograph as being a good compromise to be going on with.

Everything follows the takeaway
The reader may, perhaps, at this stage begin to wonder whether the situation is, after all, a bit too complicated to be of practical use to him. But describing these movements is very much more complicated than carrying them out. They will happen quite naturally if they are given the chance to.

The simple in-plane cocking of the wrist, for instance, is merely the natural conclusion, caused by the backswinging momentum of the club, of the swinging up of the arm.

The left arm will be carried automatically across the chest towards the end of the backswing, simply because the clubhead will want to move in a plane once its speed is high enough to make its momentum felt. For the same reason the arm rotation will happen automatically and align the hand so that the clubhead can continue to swing in plane as it cocks the wrist, also in plane.

Only at the very beginning of the backswing will the momentum of the arms and clubhead be so small that there will be no natural tendency to stay in plane. This is why the takeaway is so important in getting the backswing going in the right plane.

It is basically not a natural move; for it is a combination of arm raising and shoulder turning which people don't often have occasion to use. There is nothing to guide it except the player's intentions. He has to teach himself to combine the movements to work in plane together. If, instead, he swings the clubhead out of plane right from the start of the backswing, even the natural mechanical correction which will take effect once the momentum of the clubhead is appreciable may not put things right. It will probably be hampered, too, by his own conscious or subconscious attempts to correct a swing he can already feel is going off on the wrong tack.

It thus seems certain that the key move in getting to the correct top-of-backswing position is the successful co-ordination of Movements 1 and 2 in the first foot or so of the backswing. If this is achieved, the rest of the backswing will tend to follow naturally. If this is *not* achieved—or if any of the other moves are deliberately or excessively used at this stage—the whole backswing is likely to be made much more difficult to complete correctly.

This is why professionals so often advise a 'one-piece

takeaway' or a 'wide arc'. The essential is to get a full shoulder turn plus correct arm raising; and this becomes more difficult and complicated if other movements are brought in too early in the downswing.

Summing up: a dominant unifying principle
To sum up, the human body in a left-arm-only backswing can be fitted to the model very simply, using only the following simultaneous or consecutive movements. Looked at separately:

1. A 90° turn of the shoulder and upper chest.
2. A straight vertical lift-up of the left arm, from the shoulder joint.
3. A pure cocking of the left wrist; working, in practice, in plane with the action and usually the last move to be completed.
4. A slight swing of the upper arm across the chest to the right.
5. A slight roll of the arm on its own axis, to the right—perhaps 30°.

It is probably worth the trouble at this stage for the reader to study the diagrams in this chapter and carry out the five movements, one by one, in a variety of sequences, just to get clear what they are; and to satisfy himself that any combination of them will achieve the desired in-plane top-of-the-swing position.

He can also demonstrate to himself that too much, or too little, of any of the movements will call for some compensating movement which will complicate the backswing.

Thus, although we can look at these movements separately, and even make them separately for purposes of illustration and personal experiment, they must all serve one dominant unifying central principle implied by the model, and must obey it exactly.

This central principle is the swinging back of the clubhead within a planned, controlled plane all the way from the address to the top of the backswing, in such a way as to end up with the whole action set in a plane aimed at the target, ready to flow rhythmically and powerfully into the model's two-lever in-plane action in the forward swing through the ball.

As this chapter shows, the movements involved are, separately, quite simple ones. It is in combining them into a smooth in-plane backswing that golfers run into practical difficulties.

It is also where the art of golf begins.

We now come to consider how the golfer can best reproduce the action of the model in his swing through the ball.

First, let us look at how the model itself works, remembering that although it is very much simpler in structure than the human golfer, it does still say pretty well all there is to say about the basic mechanical action he is trying to use in order to hit the ball as far and as straight as is physically possible for him.

Fig. 7:1 shows an action sequence of a typical swing of the model, from top of backswing to just after impact.

The exact timing of that sequence will depend on the size and pattern of the forces applied to drive the upper lever around the central pivot, and to drive the lower lever around the hinge at the end of the upper lever.

For instance, by applying a very powerful and accelerating drive to the upper lever speeding it around the central pivot, and none at all around the lower hinge (except for the previously mentioned stop, to prevent jack-knifing), you might get a sequence more like Fig. 7:2.

Or, by applying a weak drive to the upper lever, but a very strong and fast-acting one around the hinge between the two levers, you might get one like Fig. 7:3.

Both these actions are quite obviously mechanically ineffective in producing clubhead speed in the model itself; and even more unnatural and awkward in terms of a human golf swing.

They are, though, in truth, only extreme exaggerations of two common faulty swinging actions which golfers use every week on countless courses all over the world. We'll be coming back to that in Chapter 19. For the moment, let's just follow the logic of the model.

The model's natural sequence

Any natural sequence of the model is going to work roughly midway between these two extremes. We do not want to get involved here in a lengthy philosophical discussion on what exactly we mean by a 'natural' sequence. Let us merely say that a sequence is intuitively recognized as 'natural' if it is produced by the action of forces which remain constant, or at least do not change abruptly, during the movement, and which are familiar to us in some way.

For instance, what might be regarded as the most 'natural' sequence of all is that of the model swinging freely around the central pivot under the drive of gravity alone, and with its

48

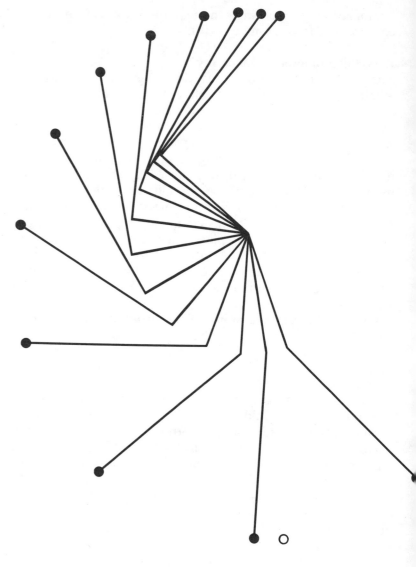

7:1 *A 'well-timed' model sequence.*

lower lever swinging freely from its upper lever.

As you can see from the photograph, a small model actually constructed and working like this does, in fact, produce an action immediately recognizable as a good-looking golf swing. And if we add a bit of independent power to drive the central pivot, the effect is not substantially changed. The swing remains of a type which any of us can recognize as a

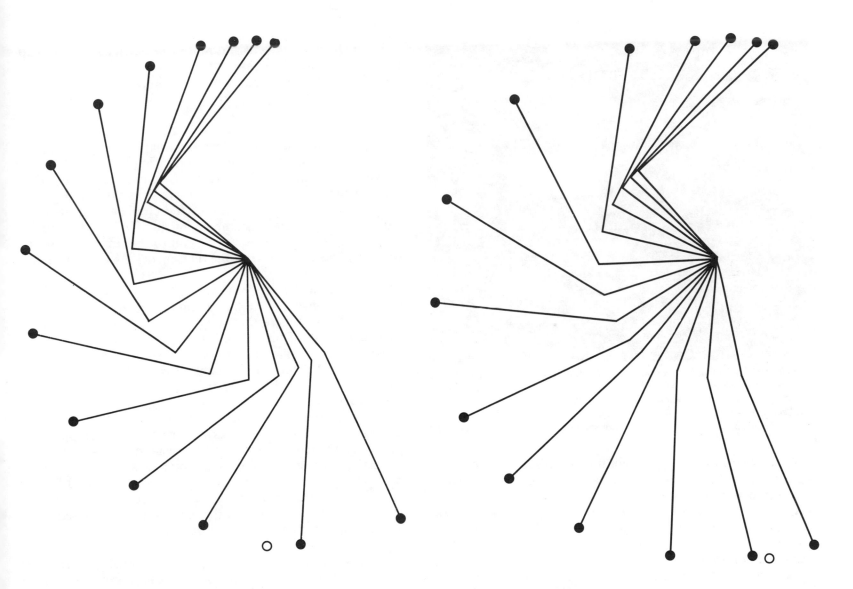

7:2 *A badly timed model sequence, with a powerful drive at the upper pivot, and a weak action at the hinge between the two levers.*

7:3 *Another badly timed sequence, with the action at the hinge too powerful and too early.*

'natural' one, speaking purely mechanically now, in terms of the structure and action of the model.

It looks too, immediately attractive to the human golfer: the sort of swinging action which many of us might feel quite keen to have a go at ourselves. This is good instinct on our part; because it is, in fact, the sort of swinging action which is bound to produce the best results in terms of golf.

A 'natural' sequence generates most power

To investigate its working scientifically, you can build actual models, apply different forces to them, and then measure the results. But you can do the same thing more easily, and very much more quickly and comprehensively, by feeding all the information into a computer; and thus carrying out all the experiments you want to in terms of mathematics alone. This

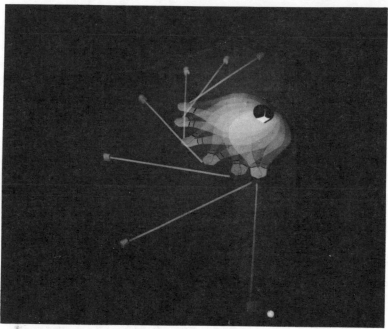

7:4 The two-lever model at its simplest. This little model has a completely free and unpowered hinge and is driven by gravity alone. Yet it produces a recognizable golf swing. Note particularly how, as momentum goes to speed up the 'clubhead', the arms are slowed down. Indeed with this particular model they are brought to rest at impact (the hands haven't moved between the last two club positions).

way, you can work out the exact motion of any sort of model moving under the influence of any sort of forces whose effects you want to test out on it.

This the team did. What they found—put broadly—was that it is the sort of action most natural-looking in the model which will most effectively use the power available to get the clubhead moving.

To be a bit more precise about it, to get the lower end of the lower lever moving at the greatest possible speed for the total power available, the most efficient general pattern of movement will be achieved:

—by driving the upper lever smoothly and strongly at the central pivot, and then

—by actively applying force to the lower lever only at the stage of the action when it is trying to fly outwards of its own accord: as it does when you allow the model to work under gravity alone.

Jerky, unnatural sequences, such as those in Figs. 7:2 and

7:3, which are inefficient and moreover when carried over to the human golfer are intuitively 'wrong', arise out of gross violation of the above principles. The final 'clubhead' speed is low in relation to the effort expended and errors in 'clubhead' position are very likely.

A 'sequence' for the golfer's forward swing
What does all this imply for the golf swing?

Well, first, that if a golfer succeeds in uncocking his wrists early in the downswing, at best it will drastically reduce the speed at which he finally swings the clubhead through the ball. It can also mean a complete mishit. The right place for him to apply whatever power he can to the uncocking of his wrists will be about at the time that uncocking will take place of its own accord.

The left-armed golfer has very little power he can apply at this hinge anyway, since he has only one wrist to cock and uncock. He must therefore base his whole swing on letting the wrist uncock itself; and time his whole action so that the uncocking will take place naturally at the stage needed to get the most effective results. Look back at the action sequences of Reid and Wilmott (Fig. 5:1), particularly the latter, and you can clearly see the results of their doing just this.

The sequence of movements in the downswing is really much simpler than in the backswing, where, for example at the takeaway, the hands must actively resist the tendency either to leave the clubhead behind as the hub turns, or to snatch it back—where, in fact, two actions may be required simultaneously. In the downswing the hub action leads and the hinge action follows, so that the basic timing of the sequence is: hub, hinge, clubhead; or in directly human terms: body, hands, clubhead.

We say 'body' rather than 'upper chest and shoulders' for a good reason here. To generate the greatest power he is capable of, and thus to drive the hub of his swing as strongly as possible, the golfer must use all the big muscles of his whole body; and the sequence in which he uses them has to begin well before he brings in that part of him which is serving as the 'upper lever' of his golf swing.

He will actually generate power roughly in the sequence: legs, hips, trunk, upper chest and shoulders. It might appear from this that he is only really swinging his hub action fourth in the whole sequence of movements; but in fact, what we really mean by the hub action is the whole sequential build-up

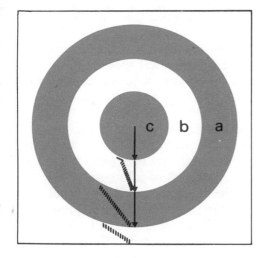 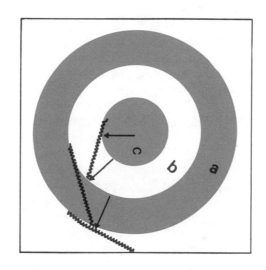 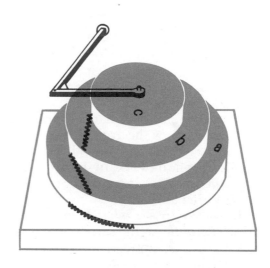

7:5 *A mechanical model driven by springs which illustrates the principles of body rotation, and the importance of maintaining tension during the downswing in golf. From the 'wound-up' position (centre), with all springs fully stretched, the top-most cylinder (C) can ultimately be given the greatest speed of rotation if the springs are released in sequence from the bottom upwards. Adding an 'arm' and a 'club' (right) completes the analogy with the golf swing, and the principle of maintaining the tension can be continued. The hinge between arm and club should not be released until all the springs driving the cylinders have done their work.*

of speed into a powerful rotation of the shoulders and arms. That is to say our model, at this stage, is concerned only with how fast and how powerfully the hub is turned, not with *how* it is turned.

A sequence of maintained tension

There is, however, one very important general point in the build-up of the hub action which ought to be mentioned here. In the whole action which the golfer uses to power his forward swing of the clubhead through the ball, *there is never any unnecessary slack.* From his toes to his clubhead everything happens or should happen—in *tight* sequence. This becomes very clear when you analyse mechanically the working of models like the one in Fig. 7:5.

The three cylinders, A, B and C can all turn about a central pivot and each is driven by a spring connecting it to the one immediately below. Cylinder A's spring is fixed to a firm base. The cylinders decrease in size and the springs decrease in

strength as you go upwards. The first diagram shows the system with the springs unstretched.

Suppose we now stretch each spring to its limit, by winding C back clockwise (looking downwards) on B, then winding B and C back together on A, then finally A, B and C together on the base; and suppose, further, that the system can be locked with the springs in these stretched positions. Although muscles should not be thought of as springs, the analogy with a golfer wound up at the top of his backswing is fairly clear; even more so if the cylinders can turn through only 30° or so relative to each other before the springs are stretched to their limit. In that case the upper cylinder will have turned through 90°—as a golfer's shoulders do approximately.

The question now is: in what order should the springs be released to impart the greatest possible rotational speed to the topmost cylinder C, when it passes its original starting point?

Well, the answer is that they should operate in sequence from the bottom upwards. The spring joining cylinder A to the base is released first, and since the other two springs are stretched to their limit, it drives the whole system A, B and C together as a single unit. When all, or most, of the energy of the first spring has been imparted to the system (calculation of the *exact* point depends on the precise nature of the springs and the size of the cylinders), the spring joining B and A is released. This drives the unit, B+C, a bit faster, and at the same time the reaction slows down A. Ideal matching of the springs and cylinders would reduce A to rest again, but we cannot expect this in general. When all, or most, of the energy of the second spring has been used up, the spring connecting C and B is released. This drives C still faster and the reaction slows down B.

We are therefore left with C rotating rapidly; and B and A slowly. If you care to pursue the analogy with the golf swing, and add an arm rigidly fixed to cylinder C with a club hinged back at the end of it hard against the stop (Fig. 7:5), then you can see how the argument can be continued.

Release of the hinge should be delayed until the spring driving C has done its work. In short, at any given time there should never be any slack between the clubhead and the spring which is operating at that time.

It is easy to see what happens if slack does appear; or, which amounts to the same thing, if the springs operate in the wrong order. Suppose, for example, cylinder C were set in motion first by releasing the spring joining it to B; then at some later stage when B itself were driven either integrally with A, or on its own, it would merely rotate under C without adding anything to C's speed, at least until it started to stretch the spring between them once more. This might not happen in the time available before C reached its original starting position so that C would have been driven by the energy in its own spring only.

Thus a 'tight' sequence working from the bottom, upwards and outwards, will transfer a considerable amount of energy from the lower (and more powerful) springs into the final movement at the top; a 'slack' sequence will do so much less

successfully, and in the worst circumstances will waste all of that energy in moving the lower cylinders.

Even with idealized cylinders and springs, calculation of the precise timing of events to achieve greatest speed in the uppermost, or outermost part of the system is quite a complicated problem. And when we come to the human golfer the situation is enormously more complicated.

Nevertheless the general conclusion holds: that every part of the rotating and swinging system must be pulled round by the part nearer to the ground, until that part can no longer apply useful effort. That is, in terms of a human golfer, the legs pull round the hips, the hips the trunk, the trunk the upper chest and shoulders, the shoulders the arms, the arms the hands, the hands the shaft, and the shaft the clubhead. You can see all this in the Hogan sequence in Chapter 11.

The last part of the body where tension is released in the forward swing through the ball is through the wrists. As they uncock a considerable part of the energy generated from the swing of the whole body is passed into the club, as it is allowed to swing away freely at and through the ball. Throughout the forward swing up to that point, though, tension is maintained as it is generated, throughout the body; with each part finally unleashing its power in sequence.

This is the essence of what is involved in 'swinging the clubhead' down, forward and through the ball. Which brings us back to the point we had reached at the end of Chapter 6; and from which we can now continue in the next chapter.

Chapter 8

The Left Arm Forward Swing Through the Ball

We can now continue with the analysis of the forward swing of the club, as it is seen in the left-arm only player: that is, in the simplest essential structure by which the golfer can reproduce the model's basic two-lever swing through the ball.

As the last chapter explained, the primary power for this swing is going to come, in sequence, from the legs, hips, trunk and big muscles of the chest and back. They will all combine to drive that part of the human swing which the model represents: that is the 'upper lever' action of the player's shoulders, arm and hand, and the 'lower lever' action of his club. The model, on the other hand, takes as given the primary power, driving the upper lever around the central pivot, and goes on from there; so that is what we are going to do in describing how the golfer fits his basic left-arm action to the working of the model.

Reproducing the model

In order to reproduce the model's action in his forward swing through the ball, the golfer must do the following things:

1. He must start his upper-lever structure swinging in plane towards the target right from the ending of his backswing; and must then accelerate it around his 'central pivot' through that same plane as powerfully as he can towards the target.

    Put this in simplest human terms and what does it amount to? It means swinging his hands around his 'central pivot' in a plane aimed at the target.

    In a left-arm-only swing, it is just a swinging of the left hand alone in plane, with the left arm and shoulder structure acting as a simple upper lever, not very different from the model's.

2. He has then to allow the clubhead to swing out and through the ball, also in a plane aimed at the target.

    It will not be quite the same plane as that through which the hand swings, since the way a golfer grips the club will not comfortably allow the arm and club to make a perfectly straight line, looked at from behind the shot, as the clubhead hits the ball. But the two planes through which the hand and clubhead swing towards the target are separated only slightly in angle, and not at all in direction of aim; so that, for most of the argument, we can usefully think of them as coinciding within a single plane, as they do in the model itself.

3. He must so apply any power he can to the hinge of his

8:1 *The club shaft and arms do not usually lie in a straight line, so the plane in which the clubhead is swung will be inclined at a slightly different angle from that in which the hands move. For much of the argument, though, it is simpler and permissible to think of a single plane. The golfer here is Tony Grubb.*

left wrist as merely to assist the natural swinging-out of the lower lever, in its 'natural' timing sequences. In a left-arm-only swing, the power he can apply to the hinge at the left hand on its own is negligible, so that the one-armed golfer's swinging action must be very near the very simplest possible action of the model; that in which only the swing of the upper lever is powered.

4. He must put the whole action to work in the sequence of maintained tension indicated by the model, and time his whole swinging action accordingly.

5. He must use whatever simplest possible human modifications of the model's action his own individual structure may dictate in order to reproduce the action summarized in 1–4 above.

Getting the hub action going in plane

The first four points above need little further explanation or elaboration. They all follow quite directly and straightforwardly from what has been said and examined in previous chapters.

The main point the player will need to concentrate upon, in reproducing the mechanics of the model, is to start the upper lever down and through the swing *in plane*. In this, it will be the swinging turn back of his shoulders, from their position with his back to the target at the top of the backswing, which will primarily determine both the power of his forward swing and whether or not it works in plane to the target.

Although he will at the same time be applying some force to the lowering of his arm again, gravity will be helping him here all the way; and it will be the shoulder swing which will play the main part in getting his whole forward swing under way in plane, and then in accelerating it towards impact.

His aim, in following the model, will be to let his clubhead merely follow the whole hub action during the early stages of his down and forward swing. It will be the hub action, as we analysed it in Chapter 4, which will set the plane, pattern and timing of the swing at the ball.

It will thus be during this first stage, before the clubhead has been given enough momentum to follow the plane set for it in the downswing, that the shoulder action *must* work in such a way as to get the whole action moving in the plane required. In fact, doing this may be even more difficult in a two-armed swing than in a left-arm-only swing, because of the tendency for the 'strong right arm'—and side—to take over control too soon.

Swinging out the lower lever

It will be the fifth of the points given at the beginning of this chapter, which presents the golfer with complications; when he has to modify the simple action of the model to fit his own structure.

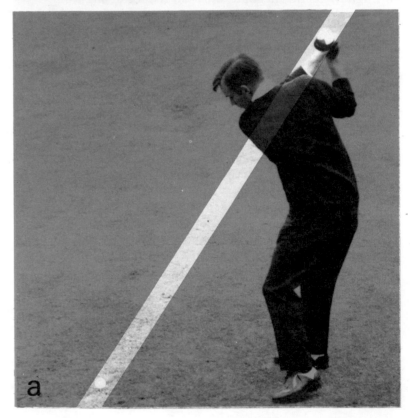

8:2 *The final roll of the forearm. For the golfer to get from position (a) to position (b) at impact his left forearm must roll through almost 90°, while simultaneously his wrist uncocks. All this happens in about a fiftieth of a second, during which time his hands move forward only a very short distance.*

8:3 *These photographs demonstrate the need to allow the roll of the left forearm, which begins in the upswing, to continue into the downswing. If the hands are swung down without further forearm roll from the in-plane top-of-the-backswing position (a), then the clubhead is thrown well outside the plane by the time position (b) is reached (try it). In order to bring it back into plane (c) forearm roll is required. Of course in practice the roll occurs gradually during the first half of the downswing, and then is suddenly reversed as the wrists uncock and the clubhead is brought squarely to the ball.*

In discussing the backswing, we have already noted one very important structural complication which a golfer has to introduce into the basic sequence of his own movements in order to reproduce the action of the model. It arises because he uses the strong 'up-and-down' cocking movement of his wrist to provide the model's hinge-action. This is just as true in the forward swing, as in the backswing.

The fact that the wrist has to stay cocked until late in the downswing, and that the clubhead has also to stay in plane, means that the slight rotation (30° or so) of the left forearm, which we saw was needed to let the clubhead follow the plane all the way on the backswing, will not just be maintained into the downswing, but will actually *increase* until it reaches a peak of nearly 90° of roll, just before the clubhead is unleashed into impact. This is clearly shown in the photographs (Fig. 8:2) and in picture 9 of the sequence of Hogan in Chapter 11, where the hands are not far from their impact position, but

the back of the left hand is still facing out at right angles to the swing plane.

The precise mechanical reasons for this are best explained pictorially (Fig. 8:3), although they may be self-evident to readers.

A human advantage in 'rolling the left wrist'

The need to roll the forearm back very rapidly to a 'square on' position at impact can, in fact, be used in a positive way by the golfer, since the wrist movement involved is quite well suited to helping him speed up the clubhead into and through impact.

To perceive this, the reader has only to roll his left forearm 90° to the right on its own axis (anatomically, 'pronate' it); and then roll it back again to the thumb-upright position in which it will be when hitting the ball with the blade square to the line ('supinate' it). He will recognize the latter movement as the one he uses—though with his right arm if he is normally right-handed—to drive in a screw with a screwdriver.

As human movements of the hand and arm go, this is a very well-adapted and strong one indeed; and it is precisely this movement which a golfer has to use in combination with the simpler one of straightforward vertical uncocking of the wrist, to unleash the clubhead out and through the ball during the final stage of the natural sequence of the forward swing.

He can, in fact, let the clubhead swing in the 'natural' mechanical plane of the model only by using a combination of these two movements. The in-plane momentum of the clubhead will itself determine how they work together; and how they add whatever extra power they can to the whole action of the forward swing.

The 'screwdriver' effect can, of course, speed up the clubhead only so long as there is an angle between the club shaft and the left arm. When they lie in a straight line it merely rotates the club about the shaft. We must, therefore, beware of giving an exaggerated impression of how much clubhead speed is increased by positive wrist action.

In the left-arm-only swing, which we are discussing, the wrist probably behaves more like a completely free, unpowered universal joint (except, as always, for the 'stop' at the top of the backswing). And remember—even when power is added by wrist action, whether uncocking or 'screwdriver', it is merely as a help to the natural outswinging action of the clubhead.

Bringing the clubface through impact in the pattern of the model

The final movement of the forward swing sequence up to the moment the golfer hits the ball, then, will be a combined straightforward uncocking and rotary 'screwdriver' movement with his left wrist—or, more strictly, forearm.

With it, he will:

1. Allow the natural swinging-out of the lower lever to take place, and possibly add speed to it by positive muscle action.
2. Swing the clubface through 90° in relation to the plane upon which he is swinging it; thus bringing it from a position where it lies aligned heel-down *within* the plane through most of the down and forward swing, to a position square to the target, and at 90° to the plane, as he swings it through the ball.
3. Time this whole movement, together with any power which he is able to put into the hinging-out action resulting from it, to fit the 'natural' sequence of the model forward swing, as explained in the previous chapter.

An essential point in the pattern

There is only one essential point for us to add now to sum up the forward swing through the ball: and this itself is a finer point of the basic sequence of swinging and uncocking action already examined. It is, though, one of the essential structural secrets of all good golf.

When the model is made to swing under the action of forces similar to those developed by a golfer, it suggests that a swinging action of this kind works to best effect if the hinge action through impact works as in Fig. 8:4; and not as in Fig. 8:5.

The position shown in the first photograph (Fig. 8:6), with the line of the left arm pointing well behind the clubhead should never be reached at (or, worse still, before) impact in a normal full-power shot.

It appears that, at impact, the line of the left arm should point at least to the clubhead, and possibly even ahead of it; as in Fig. 8:7.

There will, of course, be occasions when the clubhead-in-front-of-hands position is desirable; but these will be in special recovery shots or high-cut pitches or flicks; where the aim is not primarily to drive the ball forward, but rather to coax it over an obstacle, or 'finesse' a stroke to stop quickly by the hole.

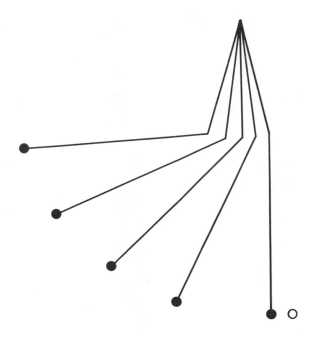

8:4 *A good hinge position at impact.*

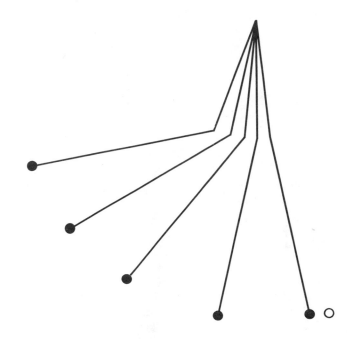

8:5 *A weak hinge position at impact.*

We ought to stress that these are not deductions from the model, merely possibilities suggested by it; but photographs of first-class players at impact bear out abundantly that the position illustrated in Fig. 8:7 is one of the 'secrets' of good golf. Look, for example, at Dai Rees (Fig. 8:8) or Ben Hogan in Chapter 11.

'Free-wheeling' into the follow-through
We cannot conclude this chapter without mentioning what happens after the ball has been struck.

The model itself does not require a follow-through; it could work perfectly well without one, simply by 'hitting stops' directly after impact. The human golfer, on the other hand, needs to make the whole forward swing through the ball and up into the follow-through a smooth continuous movement. For him the follow-through is an inevitable continuation of the swinging action through the ball, which serves the purpose of absorbing the momentum of his body, arms and club left over after impact.

The primary power during the follow-through will be, of course, the momentum in the clubhead itself. The aim of the whole model-type swinging action is to transfer as much as possible of the momentum generated in the swinging action of the body and arms out into the clubhead at impact. The momentum of the body itself after impact should thus have very much less effect in continuing the whole swinging action into the follow-through than that by now concentrated in the clubhead.

Some of this is, of course, carried off by the ball (over a quarter, as a matter of fact); but the remainder must be absorbed in the follow-through. It is so absorbed by the work the clubhead now does in pulling the whole action around the hub against the resistances of the arms, body and legs: that is, their increasing inability to go on turning much farther.

In the simplest model-type swing, the whole body is drawn freely into this action, as the player relaxes. It is a free-wheeling action which carries the golfer up to a follow-through position closely reflecting the action he used to swing the clubhead through the ball.

The left wrist through impact
As far as the left wrist is concerned, the action into the follow-

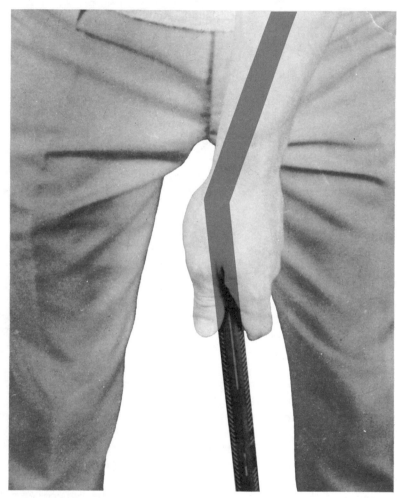

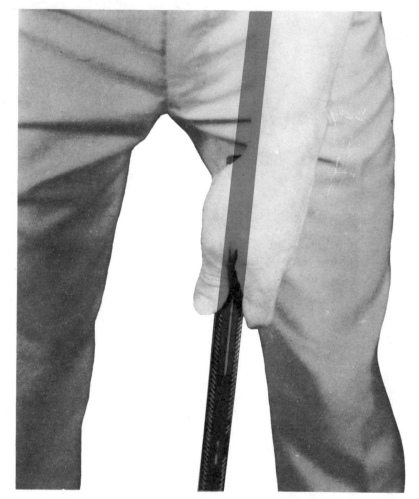

8:6 *A bad impact position. Compare Fig. 8:7.*

8:7 *A good impact position. Computer studies of the two-lever model and observation of good golfers suggest that the clubhead is moving fastest at, or possibly just before, the point where it catches up with the hands.*

through continues in direct sequence to the action into impact.

First the 90° turn of the forearm into impact continues freely through impact, so that the forearm begins to roll the other way, with the back of the hand turning now towards the ground ('supinating').

Secondly, and as a direct result of this, the momentum of the clubhead, as it takes the clubhead onwards beyond the point where it struck the ball, begins naturally to cock the left wrist again, as it draws the left arm behind it up into the follow-through.

To what extent the clubhead carries the wrist from the 'square' uncocked position at impact into a supinating and recocking sequence in the follow-through will depend upon how freely the player allows this to happen. Like any other movement in the swing, it can be allowed to happen quite freely as part of the natural swinging action, or it can be helped along, or it can be resisted and even slowed up.

As far as the implications of the model go, the simplest action is the natural or 'free-wheeling' one. It follows that if a lot of 'wrist roll' has been employed in the downswing then a lot will be used in the follow-through.

Note again, though, that the hinged-forward wrist position illustrated in Fig. 8:6 should still not be reached in the early stages of the follow-through. If it is, it means that forearm rotation has been abruptly and therefore undesirably halted, and the clubhead momentum has hinged the wrist into this cupped position.

Summing up the forward swing

We can sum up the human forward swing through the ball most nearly reproducing that of the model, then, as follows:

1. A swinging back and through of the hub action, in plane to target.
2. A swinging back and through of the clubhead, in plane to target.
3. A timing of the uncocking of the left wrist, and of any force applied to it by the player, to fit the 'natural' swing sequence of the model.
4. A further roll to the right (or 'pronation') of the left wrist during the early part of the downswing; this is needed in order to allow the clubhead to follow its direct plane towards the target through the earlier stages of the downswing.
5. A 90° roll back again of the left wrist, acting simultaneously with the uncocking of the wrist, as the clubhead is swung out, still in plane to the target, and through the ball.
6. A governing of this whole action so that the back of the left wrist is aimed at the target as the clubhead swings into and through impact. For most efficient striking the wrist will be fractionally ahead, at impact, of a line from the clubhead to the centre of the player's chest.
7. The left wrist continues to roll, supinating into the follow-through, and begins to be cocked again by the forward momentum of the clubhead, as the residual momentum of the clubhead is absorbed by the body in the follow-through. The follow-through will then take a shape directly reflecting the player's whole swinging action through impact.

8:8 *Dai Rees at impact. This clearly shows the clubhead just catching up with the hands. In terms of the two-lever model, the lower lever (club) has still not caught up with the upper lever (line from left hand to about tie-knot).*

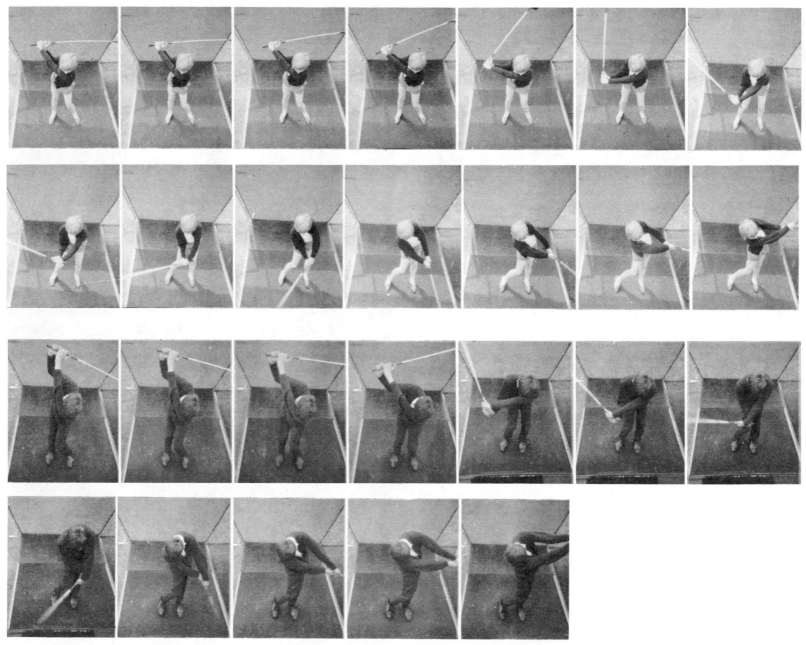

8:9 *Two junior golfers, showing beautiful model downswings photographed from above. The club is a little long for the girl, aged 10. Notice the left below the right grip of the boy (aged 12). It is quite possible to reproduce the model action with this grip, but it does pose problems at certain stages of the swing—for example at the top of the backswing.*

Section 3

How the Right Arm Fits the Model

Chapter 9

How the Right Arm Strengthens the Swing

The previous chapters showed how the swing of a golfer using his left arm by itself could be made to reproduce the swinging action of the model quite simply and comfortably. They showed how human joints and leverages prove to be quite well adapted to the slightly more complicated mechanical action which the golfer has to use to reproduce the essential working of the model.

He uses, for instance, a swinging action which includes a turning of the clubface through 90° in the backswing in relation to the plane of the swing, and then a swinging-turn of it back again at the final stage of the downswing. The wrist movement by which he achieves this swinging of the blade of the club, first open, and then square again through impact, is a strong and well-controlled movement. So is the up-and-down cocking movement of the wrist which he uses to supply the hinge required by the model.

The left-arm-action forward swing we described *is* the basic golf swing.

Upon it must be founded the more powerful and more effectively controlled two-handed swing of the ordinary golfer.

It is the basic model-type left-arm-only action which sets up the skeleton for the best swing possible for the ordinary golfer.

The weak points of the left-arm swing
How does the right hand then come into it all?

Before answering this question, we ask the reader to look first at the inevitable weaknesses of the left-arm-only swing. They are, in fact, fairly obvious; and those most obvious of all will serve very well to illustrate at once what the right arm can do to strengthen and to add striking power to the swing.

(i) At the takeaway
As we saw earlier in the book, the first takeaway of the club-head from the address position is one of the danger points in any golfer's swing. It is there that he has to start the clubhead moving away in the right plane; and then, as he goes, generate in this plane sufficient clubhead momentum to help him to continue the rest of his backswing action in the same plane, right up to its fullest extension at the top.

It is thus a stage of things where he can very easily get the action going away from the plane he intended, and put himself into trouble right away.

In getting the clubhead going in plane and with the action 'in one piece' right from the start, the left-arm-only player is

up against special physical difficulties. He needs, to start with, a considerable firmness of the wrist if he is to avoid 'leaving the clubhead behind' as he goes away into the backswing, and thus then having to make it catch up again later in the back-swing. Unless he uses the full power of his wrist to do this— and even if he does—he is liable to get the clubhead going in a somewhat wobbly and uncertain plane and sequence.

Here is a point, obviously, where the right hand can be of great assistance in the swing.

(ii) At the top of the backswing
Again, once he has successfully got the clubhead to accelerate in plane on his backswing, he has to absorb its momentum again, bring it to rest in the same plane aimed on-target at the top, and then to start it swinging down again in the right on-target plane for the forward swing through the ball.

Here, again, his left hand, wrist and arm have to work very hard indeed to prevent the clubhead from getting out of control. The force of momentum which the clubhead applies to his hand—as he slows it up, halts it, and then begins to pull it down again in the opposite direction—will be trying all the time to loosen his grip by prising open the fourth and third and even second fingers of his left hand, to bend his elbow, and even to swing his arm too close against his chest and thus drag the whole action out of plane. In resisting and controlling this natural force, the right arm and hand can obviously come very effectively to the aid of the left.

(iii) At the unleashing of the clubhead through the ball
We said in the last chapter that the left-arm-only golfer will have to swing almost exactly to the pattern of the model's action when it works without any secondary power applied to the hinge action between the upper and lower levers.

This he can do perfectly well; but always with limitations on both control and power. Wrist action near impact has to com-bine uncocking with forearm rotation; both added to the upper-lever swing. And the left-arm-only golfer must do this almost wholly by a free-swinging action of the wrist. This is bound to be a comparatively weak action, difficult to apply accurately and consistently, and inadequate for the variations needed to cope with practical difficulties like having to play out of a divot-hole, off a downhill lie, or from thick rough.

In this, the right hand can again bring invaluable help.

It can also enable the player to apply a definite positive

force to his uncocking of the wrists. And although this force is not indispensable to a model-action type swing, adding power to the hinge action in this way can increase the speed the player generates in the clubhead itself; and thus the distance he can hit the ball.

How much this can contribute is fairly measured by the fact that Reid and Wilmott, who can drive a ball a very good distance of around 250 yards, are exceptions. The average one-armed back-handed player gets nothing like so far, nor does the first-class two-armed player who has trained himself to play with left arm only. About 200 yards is the limit for most, which means that using two arms will add an extra 25% or so to the distance most people would be able to hit the ball swinging back-handed with one arm alone.

In sum, to play golf effectively through all kinds of lies and conditions, the left-arm-only player is going to have to put in some very hard work indeed with the muscles directly involved in operating his swing and in keeping it under control. Even then, the swing will retain several especially weak points, which even the best left-arm player in the world can never wholly overcome.

What the right arm has to do
These inevitable weaknesses of the left-arm-only player at once suggest the main ways in which the right arm can most effectively contribute to the whole golf swing.

They are as follows:

1. To reinforce and brace the swinging action of the upper lever of the model by converting it into a more rigid composite lever of both arms working together from the whole structure of the player's shoulders and upper chest.
2. To provide additional clubhead speed into impact, by enabling the player to power his wrist action as well as the primary hub action around the centre of his swing.
3. To add both control and sensitivity to his clubhead action through the ball.

All three of these depend upon one paramount condition for their most effective operation. It is so important that it can be put as a fourth function of the right arm in the swing:

4. To do what is required in 1, 2 and 3 without upsetting the pattern of the basic left-arm swing. To serve it, reinforce it, and add extra power, control and sensitivity to it; but not to change it, or impose any right-arm-based pattern upon it.

Reinforcing the swing
Let's take these basic points in the order given above.

The mechanical cause of the weaknesses already described at takeaway can be summed up as the inability of the single wrist to stand up to the strain put upon it by the inertia of the club, as the player begins to accelerate it into the backswing, slow it down at the top, and accelerate it again in the down-swing.

Yet, as we saw in Chapter 6, getting the action to go back 'in one piece' and in plane from the very start is of crucial importance in reproducing the swing of the model.

To recapitulate in detail, a man swinging with the left arm alone can, for a start, very easily either leave the clubhead behind, or leave the whole arm behind his shoulder turn, or even overcompensate for this danger by raising his arm too sharply and closely across his chest, and then leaving the clubhead floating away from the plane.

Against all these primary faults in trying to reproduce the model's swinging action, the help of the right arm and hand in bracing both the hinge at the wrist and the upper lever as a whole can at once make a world of difference.

With the adding of the right arm, the upper lever becomes at once a framework rather than a simple lever. It is not, of course, a rigid framework; but even if all the joints are held loose (and in practice they are not), it at once increases the ease with which the player can get his backswing going in a one-piece takeaway in direct combination with the pivoting of his shoulders. As the reader can see from the diagrams (Figs. 9:1 and 9:2), the structure of his hub action at once becomes much more firm and reliable.

We'll go later into what may decide exactly what sort of a grip may be best for golf, and where the right hand should be placed upon the grip; for the moment let us just accept that the conventional position here shown is about right for what the right arm has to do.

After the takeaway, momentum generated by the clubhead as it is accelerated round and up in the plane of the backswing helps to wind up the player's muscles from his toes to his fingers. As the momentum generated in the backswing is thus transferred into stretching the player's muscles to a state of full 'wound-up-ness', the backswing is naturally slowed down and brought to a halt.

As this begins to happen, though, the clubhead is still travelling at some speed and will again throw its inertia

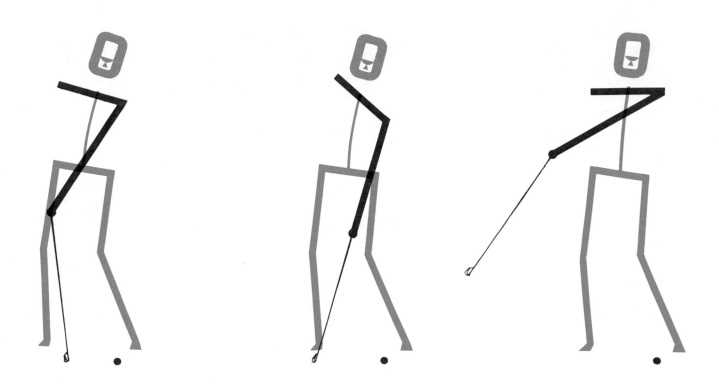

9:1 *Some of the weaknesses at the takeaway of a left-arm-only swing.*

against the efforts the left hand will be making to control its slowing down. Here again having the right hand to help vastly strengthens the player's control of the action.

The right arm gives to action of the left
One thing is clear at once in the mechanics of the swing. The way the left arm works as a straight upper-lever spoke in reproducing the action of the model makes it quite clear that, holding the club where it does, the right arm cannot work in anything like the same way.

Both the left arm's rolling move across the upper chest, and its cocking at the wrist will bring the lower part of the club's grip very much nearer the right shoulder than it was at the address. It follows that somewhere during the backswing the right arm must bend at the elbow, in order to allow this basic-model-like left-arm action to take place at all.

Despite its having to bend like this, though, it is quite

obvious that the mere presence of the right arm, attaching itself to the grip beside the left, considerably strengthens the system.

The top-of-backswing stresses on the left hand, wrist and elbow obviously continue forcefully into the downswing itself, as the hub action begins to drive the whole system forward again towards the ball. Again the right arm equally obviously adds to the player's control of the system as it goes into forceful operation.

But as the downswing develops into the main area of the forward acceleration of the clubhead through the ball, and the clubhead is speeded up very quickly, the right arm can do much more than just strengthen the system.

Speeding up the clubhead
Let's look briefly at the mechanics of the forward swing with the left arm alone.

64

9:2 *How the right arm braces the framework at takeaway.*

The driving force for it comes from the turning forward of the whole hub action, as it is driven by the body. This pulls first the upper lever, and then in its turn the lower lever, back then down, around and forward towards the ball. So long as a player overcomes the weaknesses inherent in a one-armed swing, and gets his swing started in timing and in plane from the top of the backswing, it will continue more or less naturally to strike the ball a reasonably good blow.

It will do no harm to summarize how this works again: As the shoulder and arm swing round towards the ball, they will try to leave the clubhead behind. This tendency will be firmly resisted alike by the player's control of his left wrist and by its physical inability to cock-back any further without losing control. Much the same factors will be at work also in controlling the extent to which the left arm is allowed to move to the right across the upper chest.

The result will be that in the forward swing the whole

system will begin to swing around as a single unit, with the wrist in its fully cocked position; just as the model does when it is hard against its stop.

As the movement speeds up, however, and the driving force at the hub begins to expend itself, centrifugal force will start to throw the clubhead outwards. It will thus begin to draw the left arm away from the chest again, on its pivot from the left shoulder; and simultaneously, or very soon after that, it will begin to uncock the wrist again as well.

As this swinging out of upper and lower lever in sequence together gets under way, the whole power of the action will begin to be flung out by centrifugal force into an acceleration of the clubhead into impact.

Owing to the way the golfer uses structural movements of his left wrist and forearm to bring the clubhead back in plane all the way, this outward-swinging acceleration of the clubhead will, naturally and without effort, simultaneously uncock the left wrist and at the same time roll it back through the 90° or so needed to bring the face of the club square to the line of aim as it is swung through the ball.

This happens because the system tries of its own accord naturally to behave like the free-swinging model.

The only way this can happen with the human hinge (the left wrist) replacing the model hinge, is for the forearm to roll as the wrist uncocks. If there were no roll, only a straight-forward uncocking, the player would bring the club into the ball heel first—and probably sprain his wrist as well.

There's no question, of course, of this combination of free uncocking of the wrist and free 90° roll back automatically producing *exactly* the right clubface position at impact. But there *will* be a natural mechanical tendency for the two movements to combine in roughly the right proportions without

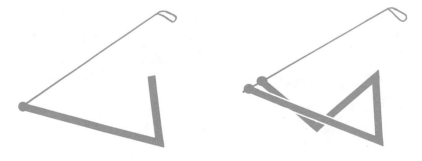

9:3 *How the right arm braces the framework at the top of the backswing.*

9:4 Uncocking with no forearm roll. This would bring the clubhead heel-first into the ball, and might sprain the golfer's wrist on the follow-through. About 90° of forearm roll is necessary to square up the clubface in the last stages of the downswing just before impact.

any violent effort on the part of the player. Even a right-handed player, if he trains himself to swing with the left arm alone, will be likely to find not that he slices with it, as he would probably expect, but that he tends rather to hook. The rolling movement, in fact, does tend, more or less, to match the uncocking movement quite automatically.

The right hand gives positive assistance to the left
Where now does the right hand come into all this in such a way as to add the maximum power it can to the stroke?

In addition to bracing the whole upper-lever framework against all tendencies to buckle under the strain of the swing, it can add speed to the clubhead at impact by giving *positive assistance* to some of these naturally occurring movements of the left-arm swing.

Look at it in terms of the model itself. The obvious way to add speed to the clubhead is by applying some effort at the hinge, instead of merely leaving the lower lever to swing outwards of its own accord. In terms of the left arm alone, this will mean a deliberately forceful uncocking and unrolling of the wrist into impact.

There is little muscular power the left wrist can command on its own to do anything like this. Even in a two-handed swing, the action of the left wrist is virtually one of free-hinging; although some players apply a certain amount of effective effort through the 'screwdriver' action previously mentioned.

The two-handed player can easily test for himself, though, how comparatively little power he can apply through un-cocking alone: just by 'waggling' the club in his left hand only. Once he lays the right hand on the club as well, though, a few waggles tell him at once that two hands give very much greater purchase; and he can also feel how that purchase may be used to speed up the straightening-out of the hinge in the uncocking of the wrist.

To do this, the right arm has simply in the first place to *push*: that is to try to straighten out at the elbow, as in Fig. 9:5.

Pushing like this with the right arm from the shoulder is a very strong human movement; and because of this it can lead

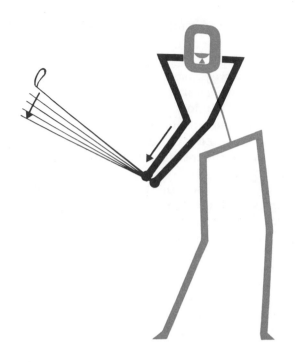

9:5 *How the right arm speeds up the straightening of the hinge—by pushing.*

wards within the plane of the forward swing, the right hand thus simultaneously pushes across the top of the left hand as it lies on the grip, and applies power also to the roll back of the clubface square to the line.

As with the left, the right arm's action in the swing into impact can be thought of as combining these two as separate movements. In practice, though, they occur quite naturally together.

Here again, according to the example of the model, the golfer needs to make no conscious effort to 'hold the clubface square through impact'. Good timing of the whole hand action, according to the pattern of the model, when powered at both hub and at hinge, will alone bring the clubface square through impact. Without that, nothing else will.

The hands will then swing together into the follow-through in automatic sequence to these movements into and through impact, just as the left did when it was swinging on its own.

How much forearm rotation has been involved, as the player leads the clubhead round through the plane in the forward swing up to impact, will tend naturally to determine how the roll over of the hands continues in the follow-through.

If a lot of forearm rotation has been involved, then there ought—by the precept of the model—to be a marked crossing of the right hand over the left shortly after impact. Conversely, if comparatively little forearm rotation has been needed, the crossing of the right hand over the left will take place more gradually, and will become noticeable to the eye a bit later in the follow-through.

to complications in the timing of the basic free-hinge left-arm action.

Speeding up the roll of the blade

In the basic swing, the left arm more or less automatically rolls the clubhead round square to the line of aim at impact, in synchrony with the free uncocking of the wrist. It follows that any extra speed imparted to the uncocking movement by the right arm must be matched by a corresponding speeding up of the rolling movement; or else the blade of the club will still be pointing to the right of the line of aim as the ball is struck.

Here again, though, there is a quite natural mechanical tendency for things to sort themselves correctly. The orthodox position of the right hand on the grip, coupled with the direction in which the right arm exerts its push in speeding up the uncocking movement, makes sure that the right will automatically assist the left in swinging the clubface back square to the line through the target as the club hits the ball.

At the angle in which a golfer holds the club, the right hand lies naturally on top of the left. As it pushes the clubhead out-

The fundamental practical rule for the right arm

These are the main structural ways in which the right arm joins in the golf swing in harmony with the left, both to reinforce the action of the basic left-arm swing into the ball, and to add speed and snap to the final unleashing of the clubhead.

In serving these functions the right arm must never be allowed to alter the basic left-arm pattern of the swing; the more so as there is a very natural tendency for it to do just that, on account of its superior strength.

It is at the very beginning of the downswing that this tendency is most difficult to resist and at the same time most disastrous in its consequences.

What happens, all too often, is that the golfer, having swung back in model-like fashion to a good on-target top-of-the-swing position, allows his right hand to take control as he

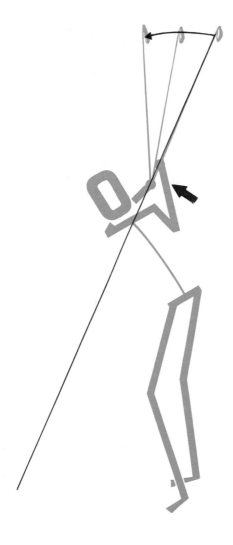

starts the downswing. This will almost certainly produce a badly timed forward swing as we shall discuss in the next chapter.

But it nearly always has another, more serious, result: it puts the whole swing out of plane. The strong push of the right forearm—which does not lie in the plane of the swing—moves the hand (and with it the clubhead) outside and above the on-target plane; and, of course, it is especially easy for it to do so at that moment since the clubhead has little or no momentum to keep it on course.

From this position outside the plane, the clubhead cannot be swung back to the ball and still make a square straight hit at the target. It has to come back 'across the line': thus producing either a slice or a straight-flying pull to the left, depending on how the face is aligned at impact. This sort of action is graphically described by some professionals as 'over and round' in contrast with the more desirable, yet somehow more elusive, 'down and through'. The latter phrase, in fact, fairly describes the model's action.

The professional's warning to his pupil to beware the 'strong right arm' at this stage of the swing thus makes very good sense scientifically. The right-arm action is—and must be—governed by the sequence described in Chapter 7: legs, trunk, shoulders, arms, hands, club. The right arm strengthens the whole golf swing: not by overpowering, but by assisting the basic left-arm action.

That is a fundamental practical rule of good golf.

9:6 *One danger of the right hand—the push from the top sending the clubhead out of plane.*

Chapter 10

The Timing of the Two-handed Swing

The timing of the two-handed swing has to be modified slightly, from that of the free-hinging left-arm-only swing, to get the greatest advantage out of the force the right arm can supply. If it isn't the player will tend to accelerate the club-head to its maximum speed too early in the swing, so that it will actually be slowing down again before it strikes the ball.

The way this happens (and it *can* happen in practice) is best explained by looking again at the basic free-hinge action of the model.

The first swing series in Fig. 10:1 represents an effective free-hinging action of the model; where it is driven at the fixed pivot (O) (i.e. at the centre of the hub action) in such a way that the clubhead reaches the greatest possible speed through impact.

Suppose now that a large straightening-out force were to be applied at the pivot between the two levers as the clubhead comes through the position marked 'X'. The effect would be to produce a series something like that in the next diagram (10:1B), with the clubhead reaching its greatest speed too soon (between *a* and *b*), and then slowing up (*b* to *c*) as it goes through the ball.

To get the greatest additional clubhead speed from the extra force applied at the hinge, the player thus needs to apply the maximum 'push' *later* in the swing than position X. He needs to apply it at some stage more around position Y, as in the third series in the diagram; and it will be even more effective if he can hold the angle of position X until position Y is reached.

As the reader can see, the angle between the two levers (the extent of cocking of the wrists) then stays close to 90° for longer in the downswing. The extra push from the right arm can then combine with the natural uncocking forces generated in the swing to throw the lower lever out late enough in the action to generate its maximum clubhead speed through impact, instead of well before impact.

Delaying the wrist action

In sum, to modify the timing of the model action, from that most effective for a *free* hinge to that most effective for a *powered* hinge, the uncocking of the wrist—being now a faster and more powerful movement—thus needs to be delayed until a later stage in the swing towards the ball. To do this may even involve making a positive muscular effort to hold back the out-swinging of the lower lever. In human terms, it may in-

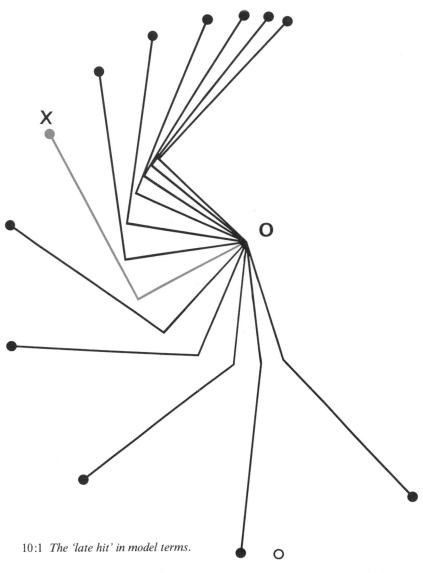

10:1 *The 'late hit' in model terms.*

(A) *A well-timed free-hinging model action, with no force applied at the hinge.*

volve the golfer in consciously *holding back* his wrist action, which now includes the pushing action of his right arm, until the right moment.

Here we find ourselves once more on familiar golfing ground: that usually signposted 'hitting late' or 'delayed wrist-action'.

Many golfers have in fact a tendency—not themselves 'feel-

69

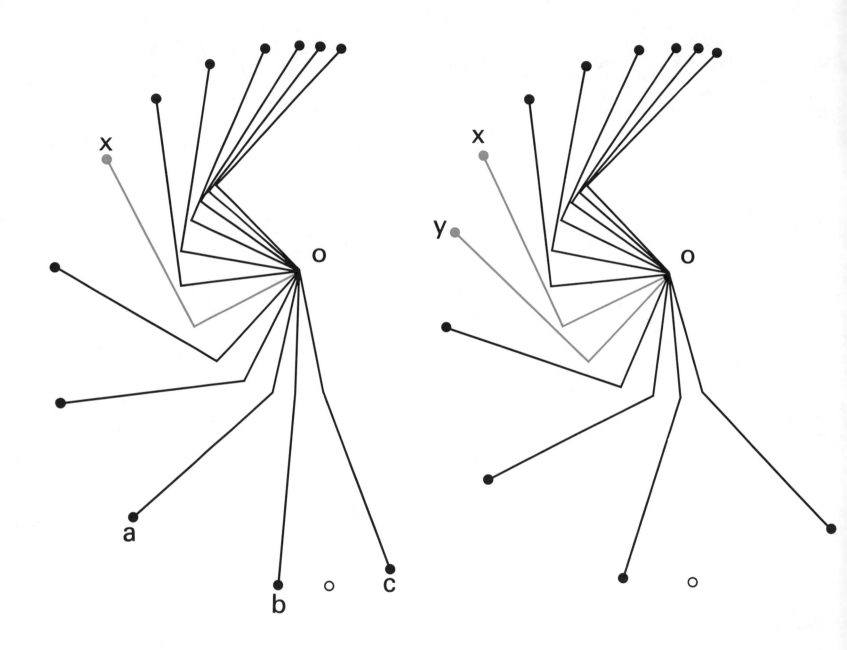

(B) *The same action but with a strong hinge action applied at X. The hinge opens out too quickly and the clubhead reaches its greatest speed too early.*

(C) *By holding position X until Y, and then applying the strong hinge action, the hinge still opens out rapidly, but maximum clubhead speed occurs once again near impact, and is even greater than the free-hinging speed at impact.*

ing' the swing pattern of the model—to try and 'hit' with the right arm too early in the downswing. All they usually succeed in doing is swinging the club out through and *past* its maximum speed before impact.

The remedy for this kind of fault in the swing is often for the golfer quite simply to work to keep his wrists fully cocked beyond the point where he feels it natural for them to begin to let rip.

The fault arises, usually, from his thinking of his whole swing in terms of a wrong timing-sequence. A study of the model's sequences may help him to rethink his own objectives.

It is worth mentioning that the delays we have been talking about are of very short duration; for instance the time between position X and position Y in the diagram is *no more than a fiftieth of a second*. It is an indication of the good golfer's sensitivity that such differences in timing make two swings 'feel' quite different to him.

Timing depends on how a golfer swings

The most effective timing for the right-arm push and wrist action in any player's swing depends on the length of his backswing of both upper and lower lever and on how fast he naturally swings the club. It will also obviously depend upon how strongly he can supply power to the hinge. The weaker his right-arm push, the earlier it needs to start uncocking the wrist; the stronger, the later. Analysis of the working patterns of the model makes this quite clear, as indeed any experienced golfer might expect it to.

For instance, the man with a long, supple backswing will usually have to delay his wrist action longer than the man of equal strength but with a very short, tight backswing. In common golfing terms, the man with a short backswing can start 'hitting' earlier in the downswing; and this is why golfers who tend to 'hit too early' often find that they can actually hit the ball further by shortening the backswing. An uncocking action which comes too early in a long swing can come just right in a shorter one.

There are also many top-class golfers (Bernard Hunt, for instance) who automatically delay their right-arm action and wrist action by beginning the forward turning of their hub, and with it the pulling down of their hands, quite noticeably *before* the clubhead has completed its backswing. By doing this they delay their maximum cocking of the left wrist until the early stages of the forward swing, and thus also delay their usually

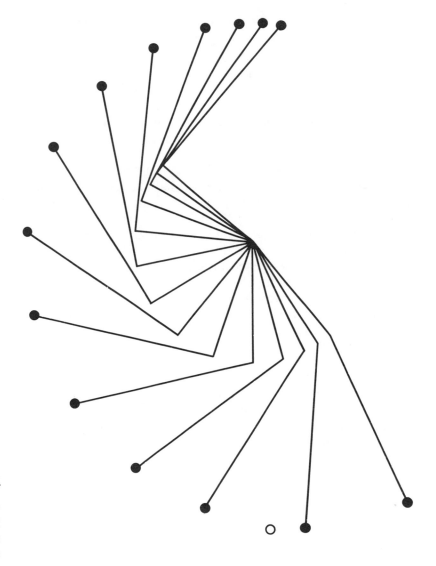

10:2 *A too late hit by the model.*

71

very powerful uncocking action until the latest possible stage. They thus guard against any tendency to 'hit early'.

Experimenting from the model

Generalizations like this are always interesting, and may be useful. But, as we have already said, the precise timing of the uncocking action most effective for any individual player's swing will depend on the overall characteristics of his swing as a whole.

The best way for any player to find out whether he hits too early is simply by seeing whether the ball flies better for him if he makes a special effort to hit later; or alternatively—if this proves difficult—by trying the effect of shortening his backswing. If a shorter backswing gives him greater length from the tee, then it is a pretty safe bet that he was uncocking his wrists too early to get the best results from his previous swing.

If this was happening, then he may be amused to learn what good company he was in. Of those first-class professionals whose swings the team analysed during their researches, more than half were generating their maximum clubhead speed too early and were already actually slowing down as they made contact with the ball.

In the case of professionals there may be other factors operating here (overcompensation against a fear of hooking, for instance—an error much more serious for a tournament professional than losing a few yards in length). And it is also just as true that it is perfectly possible to hit 'too late'—as illustrated by the sequence in Fig. 10:2 on page 71.

Amongst ordinary golfers, observations rather suggest, quite a fair proportion are so obsessed by the idea of 'hitting late', which they have read about, heard about and even been lectured to upon, that quite as many of *their* bad or feeble strokes are caused by restricting or distorting their wrist action in an attempt to unleash it late, as are ever caused by unleashing it too soon.

The reader—especially if he is of a fairly low handicap—may therefore quite sensibly experiment with an attempt to unleash his wrist action earlier in his swing than he is accustomed to. He can usually best achieve this by making a conscious effort to apply that push with his right arm earlier in the downswing.

For a player with a true swing *absolutely in plane to target*, 'hitting too early' will tend to cause a high hook; and 'hitting too late' a low slice.

This, though, soon begins to be dangerous ground for self-analysis—simply because other swing variations will often much more radically affect the outcome. Many habitual slicers, for instance, hit too early all the time; but since they also hit across the ball, the outcome is a chronic high slice.

If your game develops complications like this, it isn't a bad idea to head for the club professional. He may not be an expert on the theory of the two-lever model, but he certainly has plenty of experience in dealing with habitual slicers. Above all he can *see* your swing; you can't.

Chapter 11

The characteristics of a man's shots can also be radically affected by variations in that other complication which the right-arm push brings to the free-hinge left-arm swing, and which we were discussing earlier: the speeding up of the roll back of the clubface through about 90°, working in combination with the uncocking of the left wrist, to unleash the clubhead through the ball.

There have been theories, for instance, that you can play golf without any forearm roll at all. This is true if it means without any *consciously directed* roll; because the basic pronation-roll of the left wrist in the backswing and early downswing, and the corresponding supination roll through impact, both result directly from the most natural human mechanics of swinging the clubhead in plane.

The various degrees of roll possible—conscious and unconscious—we go into later, in Chapter 16. But it might as well be made quite clear, at this stage, that it is virtually impossible to play good golf without any rotation of the left forearm at all. All top-class golfers employ it in some degree as an automatic factor in the mechanism of their swings.

Any idea, for instance, that a player can follow-through to a position like the one shown in Fig. 11:1, without introducing enormous complications into the mechanically natural model-type swing, is doomed to disillusion from the start. To try to do so would not only put great strain on a number of joints—particularly those of the spine—but would also make it very much harder work to achieve any sort of consistency of striking. It would almost certainly require pre-corrections to the natural swing into the ball, and thus make the whole forward swing more complicated and less simple to control consistently.

The position shown is, admittedly, an extreme one. Lesser varieties of it are possible, as part of a balanced swing. How they can work is discussed in Chapter 16.

Wrists through the ball: a law from the model

We should note, too, that it is always true that in any normal full-length stroke, there should never be any question of either the right wrist or the left wrist *hinging* appreciably towards the target, either at or just after impact. (We use 'hinging' here in the sense carefully defined in Chapter 5.)

The swing of the model's lower lever past the upper lever, after impact in the follow-through, is allowed (and powered) automatically by the two hands working together in the right

11:1 *An almost impossible position, at least in a full shot. To hold the clubface square to the line like this needs a sudden change, from impact onwards, in the way the wrist joint and forearm behave. Up to impact, left wrist uncocking and left forearm rolling (both assisted by the right hand) combine to reproduce the hinge action of the simple two-lever model. These movements are rapid, and to a large extent free; and they will therefore naturally tend to continue through and beyond impact.*

73

1   2   3   4

9   10   11   12

11:2 *Near perfection. This sequence of Ben Hogan illustrates so many features of the 'model swing' that it was difficult to know in what chapter to use it! Two particular points from this chapter which Hogan demonstrates: first, the left arm remains straight well into the follow-through (pictures 14 and 15); and second, the left forearm rotation is allowed to continue naturally after impact (pictures 13 and 14), no attempt being made to hold the face square to the clubhead arc. Other points mentioned elsewhere in the book: one-piece take-away (pictures 1 and 2); the sequence of maintained tension in the downswing with the legs, hips, torso, shoulders, arms, wrists acting in that order, and no 'slack' being allowed to develop (pictures 4 to 11); the turn and sideways thrust of the hips starting the downswing and setting the whole upper structure in motion as one unit with little or no relative movement of the shoulders and club (pictures 4 to 7); the fixed pivot throughout the downswing (pictures 4 to 11);*

the 90° roll of the left forearm into impact (pictures 9 to 11) accomplished while the hands travel a relatively short distance; the slightly arched left wrist at impact (picture 11). Warning note: beware of making false deductions about the relative timing of the backswing and downswing. The pictures are not all taken at equal intervals of time (though 9 to 14 probably are); so the backswing (pictures 1 to 4) does not take half the time the downswing takes, as a first glance at the sequence might seem to suggest. In fact it takes more than twice the downswing time.

5   6   7   8

13   14   15   16

combination of continuing left forearm rotation and re-cocking of the left wrist, with the recocking of the right wrist following it along.

If this is done in the simplest way consistent with a model-type swing, there is no need for the left elbow to bend in the early stages of the follow-through. The crossing-over of the right hand, coupled with the natural recocking of the wrists, will enable both arms to remain stretched-out-straight to-gether right until the stage when the whole follow-through begins to be checked by the inability of the back, shoulders and upper arms to follow the swinging action through in the same

plane any further. The sequence of Ben Hogan (Fig. 11:2) illustrates this perfectly.

This will automatically put the brakes on the whole hub action, as it slows in the follow-through; and when this hap-pens the left elbow *has* to bend to allow the clubhead to con-tinue to swing on through the plane to its own natural halting position at the 'top' of the follow-through. Again, suppleness, length of swing, and strength of wrist-action all affect the result here. So does natural flexibility of the player's spine, chest and shoulder structures.

It remains, at the least, very likely that any player who finds

75

himself unable to maintain a straight left arm in the follow-through up to the stage where his hands swing through to shoulder level again, is restricting some other movement which would otherwise be a natural and simple outcome of his whole forward swing into the ball.

Simplicity paramount in the follow-through

The basis of the follow-through is simply that of a natural free-wheeling continuation of the whole action of the forward swing into and through the ball.

The player thus cannot easily modify his follow-through without previously affecting the simplicity of his whole forward swing.

The rule of greatest possible mechanical simplicity, in re-producing as powerfully and consistently as possible the two-lever forward swing of the model, thus weighs heavily against

11:3 *Crossing over the right hand. This photograph exaggerates it a little, but on any full shot it will tend naturally to happen soon after impact to an extent which depends on the amount of forearm roll just before impact. Any attempt to restrict it, especially on full shots, complicates the swing unnecessarily.*

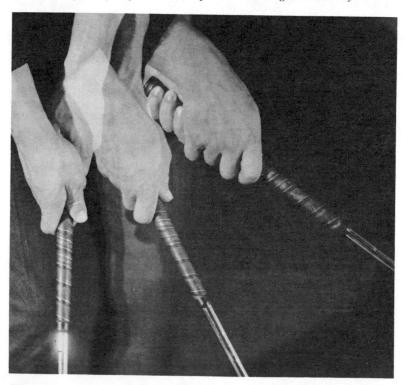

11:4 *Arnold Palmer shows quite marked crossing over of his right hand early in the follow-through with a three-wood. With a half shot or less it is often possible to hold the blade of the club and the hands square to the line of flight after the ball has been hit. But in a full shot any roll into impact (and even the most shut-faced players have some) is mirrored by a corresponding roll after impact.*

any artificial modifications to the follow-through which do not serve some special practical purpose in the whole swing.

This possibility most certainly can arise in play. For instance, it is the whole reason for applying modifications in order to draw or fade a ball, strike it high or low, cut it up with extra spin, or project it forward with reduced spin. Where any player's basic method of striking a golf ball is concerned, though, the prime case must lie strongly in favour of the greatest possible simplicity, making for the greatest possible consistency in striking.

This, indeed, is one of the major lessons in the game which the example of the model has to offer.

Chapter 12

The Right Hand—Sensitivity, Control and Learning

It's all very well, some readers may feel at this stage, to talk about aiming at the simplest mechanical reproduction of the model action, and to say flatly that uncocking of the wrists and squaring up of the blade to the line of aim will tend to go together automatically in the right proportions to produce a straight and powerful golf shot.

This, any man may feel, may be scientifically true; but it is not true in practice—not for him, anyway. If he just lets rip like this, he slices all the time, or hooks all the time—or even does both more or less alternately.

This would be an entirely fair comment, but it still does not affect the truth of the proposition it disputes. All it means is that, even if the player is swinging with a roughly model-like action—which he possibly isn't anyway—then he has simply not yet succeeded in adapting his swing to hitting a golf ball consistently.

All human movements require some learning; many only a little, some a great deal. You have only to watch a very young child's first few attempts to lift a mug to its mouth without spilling the milk, or to watch a beginner on a bicycle (or a learner in a car, come to that) to see that the human being teaches itself to do things accurately and consistently by a straightforward process of trial and error.

This involves the ability to learn from experience, to make experiments in method until effective combinations of movements are found, and finally to adjust accurately the movements made to the job to be done. It is a process of learning to co-ordinate a number of movements into the simplest and most effective way to do the job.

Applying learning to golf

This goes for hitting a golf ball accurately just as for any other human movements which require 'feel', 'touch', and the ability to learn by experience. Mastering the final acquired skill also requires the ability to 'correct' it almost without thinking if anything goes wrong.

It is the ability to learn by experience, coupled with the study of what he is trying to do, which enables the golfer to develop a sound simple swing; and it is the ability to learn to apply instinctively automatic corrections when anything interferes with the learnt method, or goes wrong with it, or, much more commonly, when any special problem of lie or aim demands some slight variation of it, which enables him to control each individual stroke in the game.

The right hand's part in learning golf

In all this, the right hand and arm have a primary part to play.

For normal right-handers, the right is the more skilled and sense-reactive hand. During the backswing, especially, it is almost certainly the main route for information to the brain about the position and movement of the clubhead.

The brain hasn't time to take into account, and apply corrections for, any information it receives once the downswing has begun. (More of this in Chapter 17.) In that case, it can only use the information it has received as experience upon which it can base modifications of the swinging action for future shots.

It *can*, however, react to information it receives early enough—and react in time to make an instinctive attempt to get the swing back on course before it hits the ball.

This is the sort of process which enables a player to strike the ball fairly well, despite beginning to overbalance at the beginning of his backswing—though experience of playing from similar stances may well have alerted him to be ready with the appropriate correction in any case, or even to modify his stance and control of balance to allow for it.

In this way, the right hand is at work all the time transmitting impressions of the swing to the brain, which then relates them to the success or failure of the shot and 'files' the information for future reference. Swinging the clubhead through the ball is, of course, a whole-heartedly two-handed operation. But learning the 'feel' of it, particularly for the short shots, depends more upon the right.

Its job in this is made the more important by the nature of the grip the golfer uses to reproduce the most model-like action possible to him. He holds the club more in the fingers of the right hand; more against the solid palm of his left. With this grip the right hand is well placed, not only to exert physical control over the club, but also to sense its position.

This is probably why many golfers use the reverse overlap grip when putting; why also, among one-armed golfers, those who play forehanded are generally considered to have the better short games; why, indeed, a normal golfer, asked to play one-handed, would almost certainly choose to pitch and putt forehanded, however he chose to play his long shots. The skilled and sensitive hand, obtaining information and controlling the stroke through the fingers, can do better in all of these operations where precise knowledge of, and sensitivity to, clubhead speed and position is required.

77

Even the least successful amongst golfers has, in fact, acquired no little skill in interpreting 'touch' and 'feel' messages from the right hand, and in applying effective corrections to anything going wrong at the beginning of the backswing; the more especially if it is, as it often is, much the same thing going wrong every time.

This is why hopelessly un-model-like methods of swinging a golf club can produce a proportion of quite admirable actual shots. The player may be trying to play golf in a consistently difficult way—but the sense and touch of his right hand, allied to his skill in learning from experience, enable him to enjoy his game, and hit an occasional glorious stroke, every bit as accurate as an Open Champion.

His right hand and his brain have done together the best they can do with the material offered to them; and made as good a job of it all as possible. But what this player has failed to do is to ask himself the right questions and make the right experiments.

One of the things the whole examination of the model-type swing may do is to enable the less successful golfer to ask himself a lot of new questions, make a few quite new experiments, and thus discover through his own experience a rather easier way of playing the game.

We all correct all the time
It's only fair to point out here, though, that to the very extent that his right hand and brain have been successful in applying corrections to faults in his method, and have built them firmly into his manner of striking the ball, he will—if he now wishes to simplify his swing—have to teach himself to eliminate these corrections at the same time as he eliminates any faults which called them into being in the first place.

The world's golf courses are at least three-quarters full of players applying built-in corrections to built-in faults; and it may even be the lower handicap man, who has built in his corrections most successfully, consistently and accurately, who has most difficulty in getting rid of them when he needs them no longer.

However, we must not think of this need and ability to make corrections as an unmitigated evil, which masks faults in the golfer's attempt to attain perfection. It is far from that. Indeed it is the very essence of *playing golf*, as distinct from hitting golf shots.

The man whose swing reproduced exactly the model swing *every time* would no doubt be world champion at driving from a perfectly level tee; but he would be a hopeless duffer at *playing golf*, because practically every shot he would meet in a round of golf would differ in some small way from the next. He would be forced to make adjustments to his swing, for even if one foot were as little as half an inch higher than the other, his brain would have to perceive this and issue instructions (based on previous experience) to modify the swing accordingly.

The best that human golfers can aim to do is, as far as possible, to eliminate unnecessary complications from their method, and thus the need to build *permanent* corrections into their swings. The more closely a man can base his method on the model, the easier a job he'll have in hitting a golf ball to his best possible ability—even though he'll always need to make *ad hoc* adjustments.

Section 4

Human Factors in Model Type Golf

Up to this point analysis of the swing in the pattern of the model has been able to carry us directly.

Once we begin to work back through the golfer's hub action, and thus back past the central pivot of the model, to look at how the rest of the body plays its part in the swing, we would seem to be leaving the model's world behind.

In a direct sense, we are. But, as we saw in the later sections of Chapter 7, this does not mean that we cease to be governed by the model's working. On the contrary, the very way the model swing works makes a fundamental statement about the way the whole body works in the golf swing.

A timed sequence from feet to clubhead

This is: that it must generate power in such a way as to be able to discharge it in timed sequence into the hub action, just as the hub action will then pass it on in timed sequence into the clubhead at impact.

The action of the model may seem to start off at its central pivot. But the fact that it is taken to have a massive rotary power built into it there implies that, in terms of the human body, the action of the golfer in 'swinging the model', as it were, must start off at his feet—the only fixed point that he has. The whole momentum effect of his swing is thus applying itself via his feet against the ground. (If any golfer doubts this, let him try a full swing while standing on smooth ice.)

In fact, when a golfer hits the ball he changes the speed and/or angle of the earth's rotation. If all the world's golfers lined up on all the world's eastward going fairways and simultaneously hit 300-yard drives, the speed of the earth's rotation would drop by an amount that would lose it one second in about twenty billion years (British size billion!). But by the time air resistance had slowed each ball down, and the stopping effect of the ground had finally brought it to rest, the reaction of these forces on the earth itself would have restored the speed of rotation to its original value. The effect of each drive, in fact, is both miniscule and transitory.

Nevertheless, the effect is there; and even in a practice swing, where there is no ball, any player moves the earth to and fro as he accelerates his club one way then the other.

As we said in Chapter 7, from the golfer's toes to his clubhead, everything needs to happen in a tight co-ordinated sequence, with each part of the whole swinging system being pulled round upon the prior-moving part below it. In any good golf swing, this must be true. But how it is achieved in

each individual golfer's swing will depend to some extent upon how he is put together, and upon the way in which his own individual muscles work. His whole nervous system, even his temperament, will come into it.

A little about the action of the muscles

The common attempt to represent him doing this by winding up a big spring in his trunk—however vivid the colours of the drawing—is really very wide of the mark.

In the first place it is untrue simply because a man's muscles are not themselves elastic. When stretched, they just stay stretched, until they are told to contract. Sinews and tendons can provide just a little elasticity at the top of the backswing; and this may indeed make some small contribution to the power of the forward swing. But the main power of the forward swing must come from *positive* muscle action.

Another important property of muscles is that they can only pull, not push. They work by using the bones as levers with which to move the body about. They are thus necessarily arranged in 'antagonistic' pairs, to balance and stabilize each other's action. To make any movement, muscles nearly always work together in groups or sets; and it's a fairly safe bet that in any apparently simple limb movement you care to think of, there will be many more muscles at work than you would ever imagine.

All of them are singly and jointly controlled by co-ordinated electrical impulses sent down nerves from the brain, and they also send back continuous and equally highly co-ordinated information to the brain describing their position and state of tension at any moment. Singly and together they thus function as a highly co-ordinated, versatile and delicately controlled engine to produce force and power.

One other characteristic of the muscles is relevant. The power they give depends on the speed at which they are able to contract. In general, big muscles work at their greatest efficiency, and thus give their greatest power, when working comparatively slowly; whereas small muscles give their peak performance when moving fast.

For all of them, efficient power output depends upon moving the sort of loads at the sort of speeds best suited to them.

Co-ordinating muscles in the right gears

A good example of a man consciously giving his muscles the

best sort of loading is a cyclist using his three-speed gear. On the level, where he can bowl along at a reasonable speed, he'll find it costs him least effort to ride in top gear. As he hits a slope, the load increases, his speed falls off, and he finds it less effort to keep up the speed of his leg action by changing to middle gear; and as the hill gets steeper still, down he comes to low gear. Finally, he may find it easier to get off and walk.

Part of the art of the good golfer is that he uses sequences of muscle action so balanced that they enable him to use all the various muscles involved each in the best gear for the job. He will train his central nervous system—his brain and all the nerves in his body together, that is—to co-ordinate all these gearings together in the best possible way to do the job.

All skilled human operations involve and depend on this. The sequence and practicability of the co-ordination in which the muscles work determines power, accuracy and delicacy of control alike.

Which muscles supply the power?

The power required in the golf swing can be calculated, starting from some fairly simple observed facts. We know that the head of a driver weighs about seven ounces; we also know, from film and other measurements, that in a good drive it is accelerated from rest, at the top of the backswing, to just over 100 miles per hour at impact, in a time which can be as short as a fifth of a second. From these figures you can calculate that the average power supplied to the clubhead is about one and a half horse-power.

Of course, when you reach impact the clubhead is not the only thing that is moving; the shaft is, and so are the arms. Indeed the whole body is still turning. This means that power has been supplied to them also. It is not so easy to calculate this power, because we don't know exactly how heavy any given part of the body is, or how fast it is moving at impact; but it is fairly safe to say that at least an equal amount of power, a further one and a half horse-power, is used in this way, giving a total of three horse-power, and probably more, for the whole downswing.

This power must come from muscles; and we can calculate how much muscle is involved. Working at their best possible loading (in the 'right gear' as we put it earlier) muscles are known to produce a maximum of about an eighth of a horse-power per pound of muscle. In the average man the total weight of all the muscles acting in and on the arms is about twenty pounds, of which only about half can produce useful power at a given instant, on account of their arrangement in opposing pairs.

Roughly speaking, therefore, the power available from the arms amounts at most to one and a quarter horse-power, and is probably less, since loading cannot be optimal throughout the whole duration of the downswing. Clearly, if we are looking for three to four horse-power, we must go to our biggest muscles, those of the legs and lower body, for the main supply of power. In fact, the muscles acting in and on the legs weigh about forty pounds and can produce two and a half horse-power or so.

Thus, without even considering the detailed movements in a golf swing, we can make a fundamental and far-reaching statement about it: that the muscles of the legs and hips constitute the main source of power in long driving.

This is not to deny the importance of hands, arms, shoulders, or any other specific part; but *they* are important primarily because any sequence of linked movements is only as good as its weakest point. Make no mistake: **the legs and hips are the 'engine' of the swing; the arms and hands are the transmission system**—albeit one in which a certain amount of extra power can be added. Strong hands may be *needed* for big hitting, but they are not the primary power source.

Getting the power to the clubhead

We have, in Chapter 7, already discussed the broad principle involved in transferring the energy produced by the muscles of the legs and hips to the clubhead. Thinking in terms of a stack of co-axial cylinders, we saw that the most efficient energy transfer took place when we worked upwards and outwards in tight sequence from the bottom-most cylinder, allowing no slack to develop in the system.

We can carry this principle virtually straight over to the human golfer. It may or may not help him to identify cylinder A, in Fig. 7:5, with his thighs, cylinder B with his hips and trunk, and cylinder C with his shoulders; or to introduce more cylinders and further subdivisions of his body. It will almost certainly do his golf positive harm to go a step further and consciously think of using muscle groups X, Y and Z to get cylinder A going, then muscle groups P, Q and R to get cylinder B going, and so on—though doubtless these groups could be scientifically identified. Carrying things that far could only end up as the sort of golfing illustration which

13:1 *Bruce Devlin and Neil Coles near the top of the backswing. The hips have already begun the forward swing before the club reaches the limit of its backswing. This helps maintain for as long as possible the tension in all the muscles which drive the forward swing, and the extra load it puts on the large muscles of the legs allows them to work at their most efficient.*

Stephen Potter labelled: 'Don't look at this. Cut it out and show it to your opponent.'*

What *does* matter in carrying over the model's principles is for the golfer to feel that each part of his body is being pulled round by the rotary action of the part immediately below, until this action has largely spent itself, at which time the part higher up in the sequence takes over the driving function.

It's worth noting too, that, by doing things this way, we not only *transfer* energy efficiently, but actually ensure that the large muscles *produce* something near their maximum amount of power. This is a direct consequence of the fact already mentioned that these muscles are most effective when moving large loads. By acting early in the tight sequence the thigh muscles have to move virtually the whole system.

We can carry this argument even further—and arrive at an important practical conclusion. The load on the large muscles of the legs and hips can be effectively increased if we use them to arrest the backward movement of the upper parts; that is, in golfing terms, if we start the forward swing of the hips before

* *The Theory and Practice of Gamesmanship*

the backswing of the club is complete. Besides giving these muscles a large load to work on, this also prevents 'slack' developing at the top of the backswing—a distinct possibility if all parts of the system came to rest simultaneously.

All good golfers, in fact, do start their hips forward before the clubhead reaches the limit of its backswing—by over a tenth of a second in most cases. The sequences of Bruce Devlin and Neil Coles in this chapter (Fig. 13:1) and of Ben Hogan in Chapter 11 show this 'hips before clubhead' effect very clearly. In fact, it is true to say that to allow this to happen is one of the two main purposes of having a backswing, the other being the need to aim the plane of the swing, which we mentioned in Chapter 5.

Any reader can easily demonstrate the dual purpose of the backswing to himself. Hit some shots with a driver (three-wood, or long iron will also do) using the following swings:

1. Normal backswing.
2. No backswing at all; that is, pose yourself as nearly as possible in your normal top of the backswing position, and from that static position swing at the ball.
3. Same as 2 except allow yourself to relax a little, with the clubhead perhaps six inches from the top-of-the-swing position; then take that six inches of backswing before moving into your downswing at the ball.

You will find, compared with your normal swing, that both 2 and 3 impair your accuracy of striking; which establishes the aiming function of the *complete* backswing. If you discount the mishits, however, and measure the distance of the best shots, you will find that, with Method 2, no backswing what-

ever, you lose considerable distance; but with Method 3, the six-inch swing to the top, you can achieve virtually the same distance as with the normal swing. The reason is simply that the short swing of the club to the top provides sufficient time for the hips to start forward ahead of the club, with all the benefits that entails.

Incidentally this experiment is quite instructive in another way. Using Method 2, no backswing whatever, most people can actually feel 'slack' developing in the downswing.

13:2 *How two different rotations can produce the same forward movement of the 'hand'. Readers will easily identify the rotation around the vertical axis with the turning of the upper body, and the rotation around the horizontal axis with the sideways thrust of the hips shown in more detail in Fig. 13:3.*

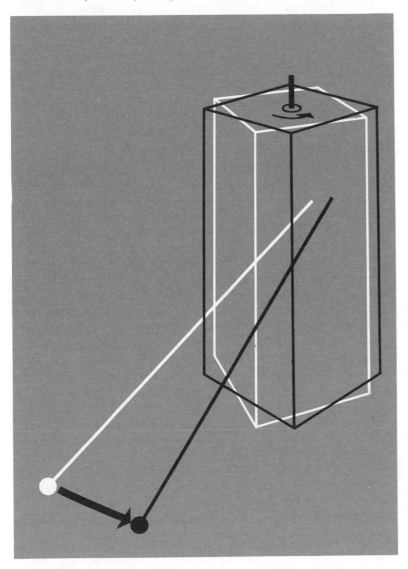

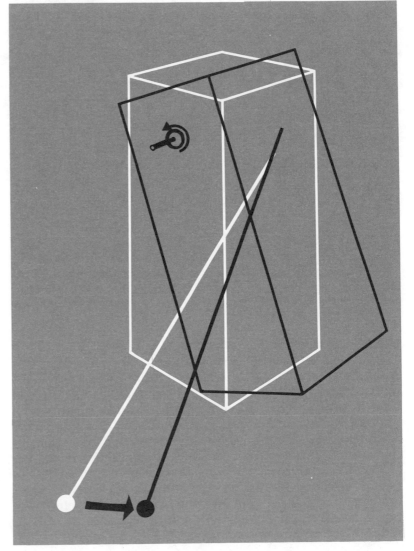

13:3 *Power from the hips. Beginning the downswing with a turn back and sideways thrust of the hips sets the whole upper structure in rotation without releasing any of the tension in it. The relative positions of shoulders, arms and clubhead remain almost unchanged.*

Storage of energy in the backswing

We have already said that you do not wind up a golfer like a spring; for the most part the energy for the downswing is thus not 'stored up' in the backswing. Nevertheless there are two ways in which a small amount of energy can be so stored.

The first is against gravity. For example, by raising a sledge-hammer, a man stores energy which is later used to supplement the power he produces in the downward stroke of the hammer. (If you doubt this, try knocking something into a *downward* facing surface, by hitting up at it with a sledge-hammer.) In a golf swing, similarly, a man swings up not just a clubhead, but his arms and hands as well; and then makes use of their weight to assist him in the forward swing into impact.

84

This use of weight, however, in alliance with gravity, although it undoubtedly has its part to play in the smooth well-timed sequence of a good golf swing, contributes only a small fraction of the total of three or four horse-power required to drive the swing. In fact, using the two-lever model with real-istic values of weights and lengths of parts of the human body, you can calculate that a 'swing' under gravity alone would send the ball off at only fifty or sixty feet per second—scarcely enough to get it off the ground with a driver.

The other way in which energy can be stored is in elastic stretching of the tendons which connect the muscles to the skeleton. Again this cannot amount to much on its own, but is worth having, when added to the energy produced by active muscular contraction; another reason for having a backswing, you might say, though, in truth, it is scarcely a separate reason, being very closely bound up with the need to preserve tension already discussed.

Lateral hip movement

If the club were swung around a vertical axis, there would be little more to say about the general pattern of muscular action required to produce the driving power for the model's hub, from the complicated structure lying below. But, in fact, the axis is inclined, and any movements producing rotation about a horizontal axis may well also make a useful contribution.

Fig. 13:3 illustrates one such movement and a very powerful one too, originating as it does from the legs. Provided there is no slack higher up, an early tilting thrust of the hips towards the hole (without, let it be stressed, any lateral movement of the hub) will set the whole massive upper part of the system rotating as one unit about a horizontal axis through the pivot. Incidentally, you can see from Fig. 13:3 that this will cause the head to move back and down during the downswing—as most good players' heads do. The combination of this rotation with rotation about the vertical axis produced by the 'un-winding' of the hips turns the massive hub powerfully around an inclined axis; this is the ideal movement with which to set the downswing going.

The movement of the hips is therefore neither a simple rotation, nor a simple lateral movement, but a combination of both. It is a very powerful movement indeed; and one that must be fully and correctly accomplished by anyone aspiring to hit the ball long distances.

If there is a secret of long driving, this is it.

Chapter 14

Rhythm, Timing, Balance and Stance

The words 'rhythm' and 'timing' are often used in describing a golf swing—particularly a good one; we have, indeed, used them ourselves in this book. It might be as well, therefore, if we clear up exactly what we mean by them.

'Timing' means co-ordinating the sequence of actions in the downswing in such a way as to get the greatest possible clubhead speed from the total effort put into them. Bad timing means that this has not been done effectively; the sequence has gone wrong, and effort has been wasted either because 'slack' has appeared somewhere in the chain or, less commonly, the wrist action has been held back too long. In either event the clubhead is not made to move as fast as it might—or at least, not at the right point in the swing.

The difference between bad and good timing shows more clearly in the hand action—the 'hinge' in the model—than in any other part of the system; but wherever it arises bad timing will make any swing less effective to play golf with.

'Rhythm' is a rather more vague term. It is closely connected with timing; in fact it includes timing. But rhythm refers, more specifically, to the overall to-and-fro, metronome-like pattern of the backswing and forward swing; to the smooth and measured way in which the backswing builds up and flows into a well-timed forward swing.

It is, at least in part, a matter of subjective experience; and is therefore of limited value in trying to describe the golf swing objectively. Nevertheless just because each man has a pretty good idea of its meaning to him, it can be a useful concept in conveying something about the broad outline of the swing.

For example, handicap golfers often show improvement for a time after watching a professional tournament, not because they have learned to grip better, or stand better, or keep their left arm straighter, but because they have come away with a firm mental image of the overall rhythm of a good swing.

Balance and centrifugal force

The rhythmic swing, however difficult it may be to define, will always contain certain ingredients. One of these we haven't yet mentioned is balance. Not just static balance, but the dynamic balance of the whole swinging system.

'Action and reaction are equal and opposite,' says Newton's Third Law of Motion; and that applies just as surely to the body, limbs and club of a golfer as it does to the weights, springs and trolleys on the school laboratory bench. For example, the push with the right arm required (Chapter 9) to speed up the clubhead is achieved by straightening the elbow joint by the action of muscles in the upper arm; but this will either cause the shoulder to move as well, or will require the action of further muscles to stabilize it; in either event something else will move or have to be stabilized; and so on. The whole complex system of force and reaction, movement and countermovement, must be finally balanced up at the golfer's feet.

One of the most important forces he has to deal with is the centrifugal force which he uses to help him sling out, into the clubhead, the accumulated momentum of his body action. In accordance with the principles stated above, if you swing anything you generate a counterbalancing force in whatever you are swinging. Just as the moon swings round the earth, so the earth swings round the moon; the smaller object always swings wider and further (relative to their joint centre of gravity).

This is happening all the time with a golfer and his clubhead. As it is swung, the clubhead generates centrifugal force; that is, force pulling out against the golfer's hands as the clubhead tries to fly straight ahead on whatever line it is pursuing at any split second, instead of being held to the curved arc of the swing by the shaft and the golfer's grip upon it. This force rises to a peak of over a hundred pounds near the bottom of the swing for about a tenth of a second; quite enough to make it perceptible to the golfer who has to pull with his hands, arms and whole body to resist it.

He is thus simultaneously, in truth, swinging himself round the clubhead just as he is swinging the clubhead round himself. The centre of their joint balanced movement will still be somewhere in the golfer's upper chest; so that to all visual intents and purposes only the clubhead is being swung.

(To underline the point, it is perhaps worth contrasting the golfer with the hammer-thrower in this respect. As you can see when you watch him in action, the thrower and his hammer rotate about a point well outside his body, somewhere between his outstretched elbows, in fact.)

A golfer is a swinging counterbalance

The counterbalancing effect upon the golfer's body, though, of this swinging centrifugal force applied to him enables a good golfer to balance and stabilize his swinging action.

This is undoubtedly a part of good co-ordination and a firm base of rhythm and timing. It is really what the word 'swing', in the golfing sense, itself means. It must imply two masses pulling on each other.

In golf, in fact, you do not swing the club around you as, for instance, you swing a gate on its hinges. A golfer is not a gate-post, rigid and immovable. He is himself a balancing part of the general movement, a free-swinging entity: perfectly able at any time either to fall flat on his face or lean over too far backwards.

The centrifugal pull of the club is just one of the many forces to which the golfer must react, so that in reality there is much more to rhythm and timing than merely getting an efficient transfer of energy in the narrowest sense. Where any transfer of energy or momentum takes place, by the interaction of forces between parts of the body, balancing forces and movements must come into play. The efficiency with which a man co-ordinates these things—greatest power generation on an effectively balanced, but far from rigid, base—determines, to a large extent, how well he will play golf.

Stance serves the hub action

We said that the whole sequence of movement which a golfer uses rests upon his feet. This means that all his problems of stance—how he places his feet—are closely linked with the way he generates power to swing the club.

The purpose of stance, on any shot, is to swing the hub action as surely as possible from the footholds available, in the light of what sort of angle of approach and timing of the two-lever action is going to provide the most practical and effective means of swinging the clubhead through the ball.

There is not a great deal of ground for dogmatic assertions about particular details of the stance. For instance, a good player can drive a ball over 200 yards when standing with his feet together, or even with his legs crossed, or indeed when standing only on one leg.

There are, though, a number of elementary general principles which—other things being equal—govern all players all the time

One is that extreme stances make the game more difficult. Legs placed too wide apart restrict the freedom with which the player can use his hips in the power generation sequence—both in stopping him from turning them fully and in stopping him from making the best use of the strong up-and-down pushing action of his legs, to tilt and retilt them. So can stances with the toes turned markedly in or out.

Stances with the feet too close together prevent the full use of the leg drive as a source of power to produce lateral movement of the hips and lower torso, which, if the pivot remains fixed, can be turned into a powerful rotational movement of the arms and club.

Stances with one foot or the other drawn a long way back can make it more difficult for the golfer to swing his hub in line to the target; though lesser amendments of this kind can be of practical help to him as an individual—either in helping him to get the full pivot any player needs to keep his hub action in line and in plane at the top of the backswing, or in restricting the freedom of that pivot in order to keep his whole action still in tight sequence for a 100-yard pitch.

Here again the angle of the foot can suit different players differently. The right foot at right angles to the line to the target served Ben Hogan very well in preserving tightness of sequence on his backswing and forward swing into the ball. But someone with slightly differently jointed legs and hips, or whose muscle structure is either more or less supple than Hogan's, will clearly need to start from a different angle. However a man or a woman walks will give a first indication of the angle of foot placement likely to work best for them.

Stances make the model swing versatile

Another universal point is that the stance for any particular shot must depend upon the lie, and upon the type of stroke the player wishes to play.

To play the game at all, the golfer must be extremely versatile in how he adapts both stance and swing to the needs of each different stroke and lie. An automaton, swinging perfectly, but inflexibly, in any sort of completely uniform working of the model, would only be able to hit shots off the type of lie it was designed for. It could not cope with golf's continual practical variations in problem and approach, which are the breath of enjoyment and interest to the golfer, and which provide the practical challenge and fascination of the game.

Summing up the stance

In sum, all science can lay down emphatically about the stance is that it must serve the purpose of tight, balanced, co-ordinated sequence of generation of power, and of aligned swinging of hub action, for the final product—the unleashing of the two-lever system through the ball.

We could, of course, analyse statistically all the stances used on all shots by the world's best golfers. This would give an accurate abstract of usage; but again it would be an average picture applying accurately to only about one golfer in ten.

For what it is worth, the results of such an analysis of fourteen top professional golfers showed that on average, they stood, for drives, with toes 24½ inches apart, with the line between toes square to the hole (i.e. stance not open or shut) and with the ball 33 inches from this line and about 3½ inches inside the left toe. There were no relationships found between the height of the golfer and the width of his stance, nor between height and distance from the ball, nor between openness or closedness and slicing or hooking.

The really important conclusion of these studies on stances used by expert players—and similar ones on poor players—is that the main difference in stance between good and bad players is that the good player takes up his stance much more consistently. His feet come down in almost exactly the same spot every time he repeats the shot.

Stance, range and tightness of sequence

How does all this tie up with customary teaching? For instance, why have the stance slightly more open and the right foot slightly nearer both the left foot and the ball, for each club down the range from driver to wedge? Why do this particularly as the length of shot drops down into the short approach category?

Well, for one thing, this doctrine exactly fits the scientific deductions about keeping the sequence of body-movements tight, as the clubhead's swing is timed into the ball. By continually slightly opening the stance, the player is slightly tightening his back- and downswing sequence. This goes hand in hand with a steady reduction in the need for a full-power backswing, and a steady increase in the need for consistency and precision of aim and striking as the range of each stroke gets shorter.

Again, as the club gets shorter, the clubhead needs to be timed to come into the ball later and more steeply, for purely practical reasons of striking the ball crisply from the turf with increasingly lofted clubfaces. This too would seem to tie in both with tightness of sequence, foot placing, and the fact that, with stance open and feet closer together, the player is enabled to swing through the ball more freely and directly towards the hole.

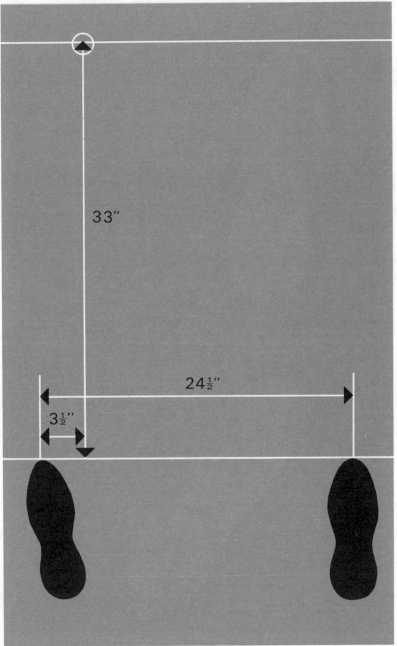

14:1 *The 'average' stance of fourteen tournament professionals, each hitting ten drives. The line of the toes is exactly parallel to the line to the hole, though individuals varied in this respect from about 2½ inches 'open' to about 1½ inches 'closed'.*

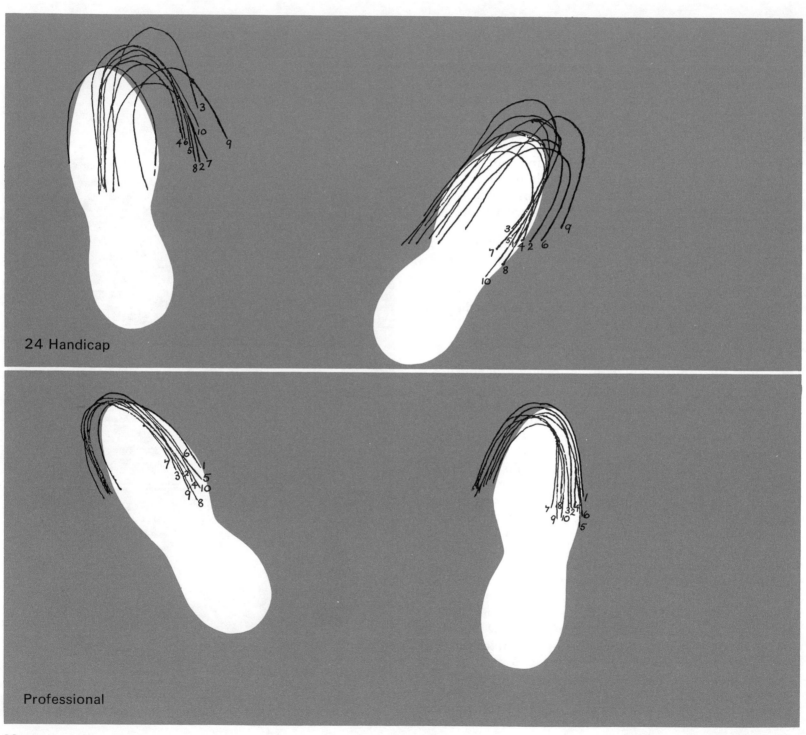

24 Handicap

Professional

A basic guide for standing open or closed would seem to be:

An open stance gives the player a tighter sequence on the backswing and downswing, but a greater freedom to swing through more directly towards the hole.

A closed stance gives him greater freedom to pivot on the backswing and thus to generate maximum power; but at the same time reduces the freedom of his body action on the follow-through. And if the stance is very closed this lack of freedom will have its effect before the ball is reached. Together with excessive freedom on the backswing this may well introduce 'slack' into the system and cause loss of power.

Anyone can get a very good idea of this sensation of slack by trying to play a twenty-yard pitch from an exaggeratedly closed stance. There's quite a marked feeling of arms swinging freely and powerlessly with no resistance from the body going back, nor help from it coming down.

Most golfers believe that standing open will make them slice and standing closed will make them hook. There is a lot of sound logic behind this. If the line of the shoulders, and with it the whole hub action, follows the line of the feet, then as the clubhead comes to the ball it will certainly be moving across the line to the target—out-to-in from an open stance and in-to-out from a closed one. The expected slice or hook will then materialize if the clubface has remained square to the hole.

There are, however, a lot of 'ifs' in that argument; and, in practice, any drastic alteration in stance can so alter the way we think of the shot and thereby the way we actually go about it, that the hub action may *not* follow the line of the feet, and

the clubface may *not* stay square to the hole. In short, it is virtually impossible to predict the overall effect of standing open or closed.

The only experiments which the team were able to carry out seemed to confirm this: among golfers whose foot positions were carefully observed, those with open stances showed no more tendency to slice than those with closed.

It is quite likely, in fact, that standing more open than usual may merely give the golfer a somewhat better chance of doing other things (with his hands for example) which may be necessary to produce a slice; it certainly does not automatically guarantee one. The same applies to a closed stance and hooking.

All we can recommend then is: avoid extreme stances, whether in openness, width or distance from the ball, for they will lead to loss of power and consistency. Apart from that, though, golfers should not be afraid to experiment. It is only really by practical experience that any player can find his best stance and the effects on him (and him alone) of variations from it; especially which variations will aid him in coping with particular shots.

In ordinary circumstances the stance which most positively encourages the hub action to take place in an on-target plane is the best one for any individual golfer. Once he has found this he should take special care to take it up consistently, at least on all the straightforward, uncomplicated shots. There are many such shots to be played in a round of golf (nearly all tee shots, for example) and it is very often with just those that the average golfer is most careless, or can become so without knowing it—and then wonder why he is off his game.

14:2 *The consistency of a professional golfer's stance. These are traces from an actual experiment in which golfers' feet were photographed without their knowledge on ten successive drives. The 24-handicapper took up his stance much less consistently than the tournament professional, thereby making consistent swinging more difficult before he even started.*

Chapter 15

Wrist Action: Structure and Grip

We have not so far suggested any scientifically based dogma about grip and specific wrist, hand and knuckle alignments.

This may have surprised readers of conventional golf books, which as often as not begin: 'Chapter I: The Grip.' But this book cannot conceivably do this. The whole implication of the model for any individual golfer is that the wrists and hands should serve as an adaptable and obedient hinge between the upper and lower levers, in whatever way may be best for him; they *allow* the action to happen. So however complicated are the movements of bones, muscles and tendons he uses to reproduce the hinge action, they are the *result* not the cause of the action. His grip will be the logical consequence of his swing.

Wrist action must fit the needs of the model

Any grip and wrist action, then, will violate the model—and thus, in our terms, be a 'wrong' action—only if it does any of the following things:

1. Throws the club out of plane, particularly at the take-away and/or the beginning of the forward swing.
2. Makes it necessary to add further complicated movements to the swing in order to stay in plane.

3. Prevents proper timing of the clubhead, by introducing slack into the sequence of actions.
4. Fails to give the player the best possible service in bringing in the clubhead square to his line of aim and accurately aligned to both ball and lie.
5. Prevents him from making the most of the sensitivity, touch and feel which we described in Chapter 12.

Among obviously 'wrong' grips and actions under these headings are those extremes of unorthodoxy which restrict the wrist's freedom to react to the swing, which throw the application of their own strength out of balance, or which, by introducing off-true alignments of clubface, force the player to make compensating movements in the working of the whole action, which complicate and weaken it.

A complicated joint for a simple result

Before going on to discuss the grip it would be as well to be aware how extremely complicated and versatile a joint the wrist really is. An arrangement of mobile small bones in the wrist enables it to bend in any direction by anything up to about 90°. This is in addition to the simple rolling action ('pronating' and 'supinating') of the hand supplied from the

15:1 *The anatomy of rolling the left forearm. The diagrams show how a man with 'X-ray eyes' would see a golfer's left forearm sometime before impact and then sometime after impact. The forearm roll necessary to square up the clubface is achieved by uncrossing the two bones in the forearm.*

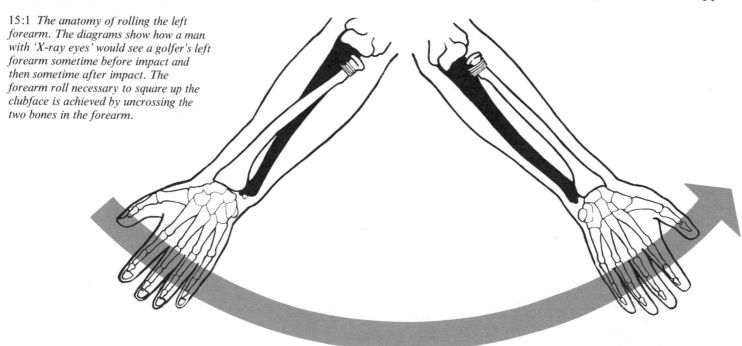

elbow through the mobility around each other of the two bones of the forearm.

There is no way in which a player can hold a club securely as a dead straight continuation of his left forearm. He can get as near as possible to it by gripping the club transversely across his hand and fingers and then bending the wrist also around the assembly of mobile small bones.

This movement puts the wrist into its extreme 'uncocked' position, and thus leaves the action around the small bones free to provide the basic cocking-action for the swing, with the rotation of the forearm from the elbow allowing whatever degree of roll and unroll may be needed at any moment in the whole action.

Grip and mobility

All movements of the wrist are restricted in range and freedom if anything is gripped tightly in the hand. This is because the tendons which close the fingers around any object are worked from the forearm, as are those which bend the wrist either way in any plane. They are so arranged as mutually to restrict each other's working. (Though the 'cocking-uncocking' movement is less restricted by gripping than backward and forward hinging is.)

In golf, thus, tension of grip and strength of muscle-action in the wrist and hand closely affect the wrist's freedom of mobility; and each player must find his own most effective combination of mobility and tightness of grip to serve the needs of his own swing. Some players' muscles are much stronger than others', and some have much suppler joints at the wrist than others.

Whatever happens, all the power generated by the legs, body and arms must be passed on, in the simplest possible action, through this quite complicated linkage at the human wrist, into swinging the clubhead through the ball.

Wrist work cannot—or at least should not—dominate any player's action. The swing is worked by swinging the clubhead from the hub, and the wrists simply serve this essential as best they may.

The grip is a compromise

How successfully the wrist action reproduces the lower pivot, or hinge, in the model, depends, among other things, on the way the hands are laid on the club—on the grip employed. We cannot, as we have said, be dogmatic about details of the

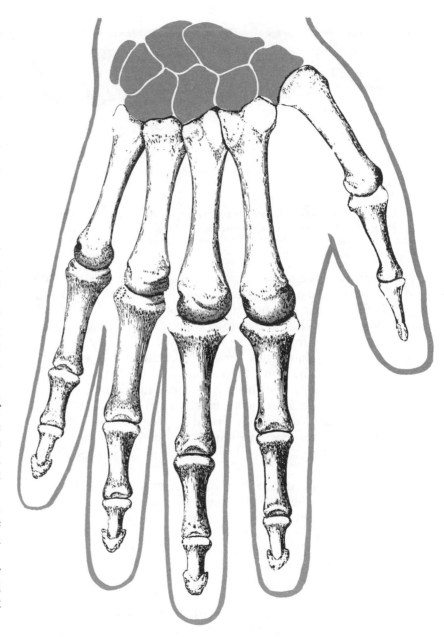

15:2 *The wrist is not a simple joint. It consists of eight small* carpal *bones arranged in two rows of four, and bound together by strong ligaments. Although the relative movement between any two of these bones is small, the sum total of their composite movement gives the wrist its full range of flexibility in cocking and uncocking, and in backward and forward hinging.*

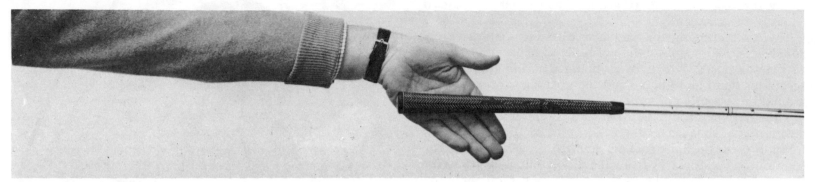

15:3 The left-hand grip. The position of the grip of the club across the palm of the left-hand is to a large extent dictated by the need to get the shaft to form as nearly as possible a straight continuation of the left arm when the wrist is in its extreme uncocked position.

grip, but there are some general pointers if the swing is to be given the best possible chance to reproduce the model's.

It is fairly clear that any grip is a compromise between the best ways of serving the various functions of the hands. The model demands free hinging for part of the swing; and this will most easily happen if the club is held loosely in the left hand only, or if the right hand is placed directly on top of the left. But for bracing the shoulders-arms-club framework, and also for maximum leverage in speeding up the natural opening out of the hinge, the hands would be best placed some way apart. There are other considerations too; hands placed far apart, for instance, make for extreme awkwardness in the backswing.

The best compromise certainly seems to be to have the hands close together without being on top of each other, as in the grip recommended by every professional and every golf book; for which reason we shall not describe it in detail here.

Whether one of the finer variations of this grip is better than another we certainly cannot say. In general the more the right hand overlaps the left the more freely will hinging take place; the farther apart the hands are, as in the two-handed grip, the better able will they be to strengthen the weak points in the swing and speed up the clubhead by right arm action. As both free hinging and right arm action are required for greatest clubhead speed, any individual must find his own best compromise position, both for speed and accuracy. His professional can assist him in this, but ultimately the player himself must experiment on his own to experience the 'feel' of all the variations in grip, from which he must select the best one.

The fact that most of the world's best golfers use the overlapping grip suggests that it is the best compromise for those with the physical make-up of first-class players. It doesn't necessarily follow that it is best for their weaker brethren, though it is probably a good starting point from which to try variations. Recent American experiments on a group of golfers, who hit shots with the overlapping, the interlocking and the two-handed grip, could not find any one grip to be superior to the others in either power or accuracy.

Much the same can be said about how much the hands should be rotated on the shaft; or, as golfing terminology puts it, how many knuckles should show. The orthodox position with the v's of both hands (formed by the forefinger and thumb) pointing somewhere between chin and right shoulder

Table 15:1 How gripping hard affects wrist mobility.

Strength of gripping	Range of cocking-uncocking movement at wrist	
	In degrees	(As % of maximum range)
Maximum (72 lbs)	0°	—
¾ maximum	26°	32%
½ maximum	57°	74%
¼ maximum	70°	91%
Zero	77°	100%

Table 15:1 How gripping affects freedom of wrist movement. The table averages some of the results from a series of experiments which measures the range of wrist movement of ten people gripping at various fractions of their 'strongest possible grip'.

seems a good place to start from, and very few good players' grips lie outside that range; but only the golfer himself can feel which of the slight variations is going to be best for him.

A word of warning

A word of warning, though, before experimenting with grips. Beware of preconceived ideas. We have all read, or been told, that turning the hands to the right—i.e. right hand under, left hand over—will make us hook, and that turning them to the left will make us slice. It's as well not to take this too literally. *If* your basic swing remains unchanged by these variations in grip, then they will have the effects usually stated, since the 'hooker's grip' will tend to bring the face of the club back closed (i.e. turned left) at impact; and conversely for the 'slicer's grip'. That will in all probability happen with a left-arm-only swing.

When the right arm is added, however, a change of grip will often alter the way in which the right hand works, and so alter the swing itself that it may produce the opposite effect from the one expected. For example, when the right hand is very much under the shaft, it tends to work not by driving out over the top of the left, but by uncocking alongside the left. The result can be failure to square up the clubface; that is to say, a slice rather than a hook.

Conversely with the right hand round on top of the shaft there may be a tendency towards a wristy, rolling swing, and depending on how quickly the roll back to impact is accomplished, a hook can result.

Thus the traditional 'hooker's grip' can produce a slice, and the traditional 'slicer's grip' can produce a hook; it depends very much on the individual and how he feels these grip variations.

There's another favourite parrot-cry connected with this, which is also of dubious authenticity. 'Too much right hand' is often the diagnosis (sometimes self-diagnosis) made after a hook. In many cases the reverse is almost certainly true—'not enough right hand'. Many people, perhaps most people, who can train themselves to hit the ball with either arm alone find that it is the left arm (backhanded) swing that tends to hook, and the right arm (forehanded) swing that tends to slice. Of course the two-armed swing is not just a simple sum or average of the separate components; but the fact remains that, to put it no more strongly, the right hand is by no means always the villain of the piece when it comes to hooking.

Chapter 16

Wrist Action: Squares and Rollers

Through the early 1960's golf theory was enlivened by an almost passionate controversy between 'squares' and 'rollers'. Since it involved factors in the swing which affect any player we discuss it in some detail. Readers may still skip this chapter without interrupting the continuity of the book.

As we said, in any good golf swing the clubface must be rolled through something like a right angle, within the plane of the swing, by the way the player uses his body, shoulders, arms and forearms to reproduce as closely and simply as possible the mechanical action of the model.

All golfers, in fact, 'roll the clubhead'. They have to, in order to swing it from a position where it lies at about 90° to the swing's plane and arc as it faces the hole at the address, to a position where it lies end to end within, or parallel to, the plane at the top of the backswing; and then again in order to swing it back again through that 90° angle during the final stages of the downswing, in order to drive the ball straight off towards the hole.

As we saw earlier, only about 30° of the clubhead roll to the top of the backswing comes directly from 'wrist roll', or more accurately, rotation of the left forearm. The other 60° or so results from the combination of arm raising and shoulder turning which the golfer must use to reproduce the model action.

It is, nevertheless, convenient to talk and think simply of a 90° roll of the clubface, particularly as this angle between clubface aim and swing-plane lasts until late in the downswing; by which stage the back of the left wrist lies, similarly, at a position of about 90° of 'roll' from its impact position. It is thus true to say that both left arm and clubhead have to 'roll' back together through nearly 90° in the hitting area; and we'll continue to talk of 90° of 'roll' of the clubhead at the top of the swing, even though about 60° of it is not really true roll.

All 'squares' roll

This does not for a moment mean that protagonists of what they call the 'square method' of swinging a golf club are talking nonsense. On the contrary. It is all really very much a matter of terminology; and one in which the looseness of the terms used on both sides of the 'squares *v.* rollers' controversy has tended wonderfully to confuse the issue, and to obscure the truth of what is really meant on either side.

There always is roll; but the amount, and timing, of roll which a player uses can vary widely. This is really what the argument is all about.

A meaning for 'square method'

Let's start by saying then that the 'square' method is—or ought to be—one which reproduces the model's action in the simplest shape mechanically possible to the average human being; one, that is, in which the amount of roll is about 90°, just sufficient to align the face of the club and the back of the left wrist neatly within the plane at the top of the backswing; and one, moreover, in which that roll takes place fairly evenly all through the backswing, then unleashes again, according to the timing of the whole sequence, in the later stages of the downswing, as the lower lever is swung out to fly the clubhead through the ball.

We think this is probably the simplest way to play golf, and thus by basic supposition potentially best for most people in reproducing the same action time and again.

Individual golfers, though, may easily gain—within the scope and ambitions of their own game—by using more or less roll either on any particular shot, or even on all shots all the time.

The free 'roller'—open at the top

Mechanically the essence of it is as follows. If the player rolls his blade through more than 90°, say up to even 120°, then he has also to roll it back again more quickly during the final stage into impact. This, of course, will make his timing and accuracy of striking that much more critical and difficult to bring off precisely and consistently time after time.

On the other hand, by increasing the scope of the 'screwdriver action' he uses into impact, and thus making it more powerful, the extra 30° of roll may well make it easier for him to hit the ball a good blow, and to get the clubhead travelling really fast (for him) through impact.

There will, in fact, be a freer discharge of the whole action into the clubhead—*past* the body. The player will have the feeling of hitting the ball freely with his hands rather than his body; and this will be at least a partially correct impression of the reality of what will be happening (although the total body swing is always the main source of power). Especially for a weaker player, extra roll like this may easily give him much more of a sensation (and reality) of being able to lash the clubhead through.

It would seem, in sum, to be quite a good way for the one-round-a-week man to get maximum clubhead speed from a body not in tip-top muscular trim.

But he has always to be on guard not just against the danger of inaccuracy by mistiming, but also against the tendency to hit too soon; for if he does this, he loses clubhead speed into impact and with it most of the advantages of the method.

Another common (and almost opposite) fault which may assail him is 'quitting' on the shot—or rather on the roll—perhaps through fear of hooking. A player who rolls a lot going back must fearlessly roll a lot coming through—or, strictly, he must fearlessly allow the full roll to happen.

This sort of player will have the left wrist 'cupped' at the top of his backswing. That is to say the wrist will be hinged in the direction of the back of the hand, as well as cocked, and the toe of the club will point almost vertically downwards instead of parallel to the plane.

This is usually known as 'open at the top'; you could equally well call it a 'cup-wristed' position. The precise clubface position will, of course, also depend on the grip he has adopted.

The methodical 'pusher'—shut at the top

The opposite variation is 'shut at the top' or 'convex-wristed'. 'Shut' because the toe of the clubface points outward above the plane and rather towards the horizontal at the top, having been rolled through less than 90° on the backswing. 'Convex-wristed' because the player's left wrist will, if anything, be hinged in the direction of the palm of the hand, as well as cocked.

This action is based on the entirely reasonable idea that the faster the angle of aim of the clubface is changing as it approaches and swings through the ball, then the more any small error in timing must be likely to bring the clubhead through impact with its face off-line to target, and thus cause a crooked shot.

The man who swings in this way tries, therefore, to cut down the rate at which his clubface swings round near impact. He does this by cutting down the total amount of roll and roll-back he uses in his swing as far below the 90° of the 'square' player as he can manage. By rolling the clubface round through less than 90° on the backswing, he reduces the angle through which he has to roll the blade back during the final stage of his downswing. He thus slows the rate of change of

16:1 *An open or cup-wristed position. At the top of Christy O'Connor's backswing both his clubface and the back of his left hand lie in a vertical plane. This means that his clubface has rolled through an angle of about 130° in relation to the plane of his swing. From this position a lot of forearm roll will be required up to and beyond impact. Notice two other points of interest: (i) that O'Connor has gripped his club a few inches from the end of the shaft, and (ii) that his left hand has opened a little at the top. A number of good players do this, and they probably add a little speed to the hinge action by closing the fingers and pulling the club back into the palm of the hand again at the right time in the downswing. But it's a complication that most golfers could do without.*

95

16:2 *A shut or convex-wristed position. At the top of David Thomas's back-swing his clubface lies in a horizontal plane and the back of his left hand very nearly so. His clubface has therefore turned through an angle of only 40° or so in relation to the plane of his swing, so only a little forearm roll will be required up to and beyond impact. Notice the huge shoulder turn which is necessary (and which he achieves) to get this far back with an action as convex-wristed as this.*

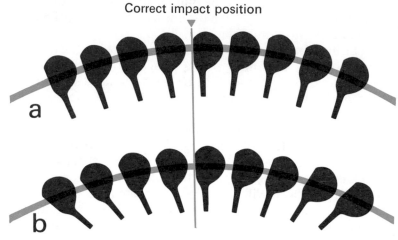

Correct impact position

16:3 *The theory behind the 'shut-faced' method. The smaller the angle the club-face has to turn through, as it goes through the ball, the less serious an error in timing will be. You can see this, if you think of an error of timing as being equivalent to taking the ball too early or too late in the sequences illustrated. For example in sequence (b), at three clubhead positions to the right of the true impact position the clubface is wide open. If the ball were to be struck from that point a wild slice would result. The same error in sequence (a) would merely push the shot a bit to the right. This, of course, is a purely mechanical argument, which takes no account of the greater difficulty most golfers have in swinging in the way represented by sequence (a).*

angle of his clubface through the area of impact, making it— at least in theory—mechanically easier to get it consistently square to the target as he hits the ball.

He still has to roll his clubface through 60° or 70° but his swing is coming as near as a human being's can to that of the ideal machine swinging the clubhead *square to the plane* all the way and using virtually no independent conscious wrist action.

He achieves this, though, at the cost of throwing away part of the mechanical advantages of the 'screwdriver action' and the whole wrist movement feels, and *is*, weaker and more restricted. To balance this he has to use more obvious body action into impact, which gives his swing its 'pushing' appearance.

A question of choice of advantages

A golfer's choice of wrist action is not, of course, restricted to one of three quite distinct methods: open, square and shut. He can use any variation anywhere between 'extreme open' and 'extreme shut'. But the choice is hardly ever just a straight compromise between easier speeding up of the clubhead at the 'open' end of the range, and greater consistency at the 'shut' end. Things are by no means as simple as that.

For one thing, the shut method minimizes the chance of error only in the *mechanical* sense. The fact that the wrist movements involved are, to many people, unnatural and uncomfortable, may itself give rise to *human* errors which would be less likely in a more open wrist action. Thus some golfers may find that, for them, the shut method is *more* rather than less productive of errors, and so of inconsistency, than the *mechanically* less reliable open method.

Another complication is that the type of wrist action you use affects the body action that must go with it. Thus some golfers may find that a shut method, by virtue of its association with a stronger body action, will produce greater clubhead speed than an open method.

For somewhat complicated reasons it does seem that you cannot easily combine the desirable features of these two extreme methods. That is you cannot superimpose the extreme rolling, wristy lash which extracts most power from the lower pivot, upon the leg, hip and body action which extracts most power from the body. And though most 'rollers' would be surprised how much their body *does* come into the shot, and most shut-faced body-heavers would be equally surprised how much their wrists *do* roll into the shot, some degree of incompatibility does seem to remain. The golfer can only work out by trial and error what balance between the advantages and disadvantages is best for him.

The essential point is that there is nothing wrong in either one of these methods, nor in the continuous range between them—which of course, includes the 'square' method. The 'shut' end of the range is perhaps best suited to professionals in the peak of athletic trim and muscular strength. It may well enable them to knock the ball more closely on the right line, time and again than a more open action, if at the expense of extra muscular effort from the body and perhaps a greater strain upon the structure and muscles of the back. The 'open' end of the range may recommend itself to golfers who are neither athletic nor strong, and who play only occasionally.

But these are generalizations. It is really up to each individual to find the point in the range which gives him the best balance of advantages and disadvantages, either for his general method or for his approach to any particular shot; and always depending on the sort of game he plays, and how ambitiously—and often—he plays it.

Address position and roll
One other factor might be noted. To use an excess-roll swing, it helps to lower the hands slightly at the address, thus reducing the total angle between left arm and club shaft. The 'reduced roll' player, on the other hand, will probably hold his hands high, so that at the address left arm and clubhead make almost a straight line—looked at from directly *behind* the shot.

The crossover
Again, other things being equal, excess roll into impact is matched by a quick crossover of the wrists as the ball is hit, and a balancingly quick roll of the clubhead to lead the hands into the follow-through. Reduced roll into impact will mean reduced roll into the follow-through, and a slower crossover after impact, slowing the clubhead's tendency to lead the rest of the body into the follow-through. This will match the greater body action and more 'pushing' hand action, as opposed to the more 'lashing' or 'flicking' action of the opposite style.

But here again, any man can build minor variations even on to the mechanically easiest forms of major variations, like these we are describing. Each extra variation from the simplest plane action absorbs extra effort, though; and the less simple any man's swing becomes, the harder he is likely to have to work at the game.

Takeaway and roll: points of analysis
Before we leave this topic, it may be helpful to take a look at the structural effects upon a player's swing which can result from—or occasion—the amount of forearm roll he uses, and how early he brings it in.

As we have seen, the 'square swing' will have the clubface lying approximately flat within the plane of the swing at the beginning of the forward swing. 'Square' most certainly cannot mean keeping the clubface aligned at right angles to the plane, like a simple driving machine—which is humanly impossible. The anatomical complication of this would be indescribable.

It can mean that for the first foot or so of the backswing, the player makes little or no forearm rotation to open the face of the club. He takes it back instead by means of a simple rotation about the central pivot at the hub, together with a raising of his left arm—the basic in-plane takeaway we described in Chapter 6. As we noted then, because of this *combination of*

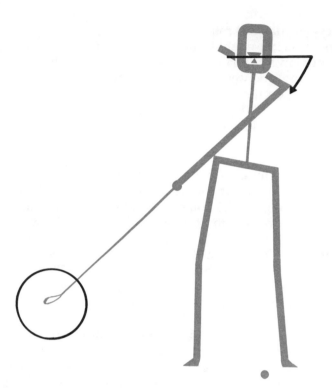
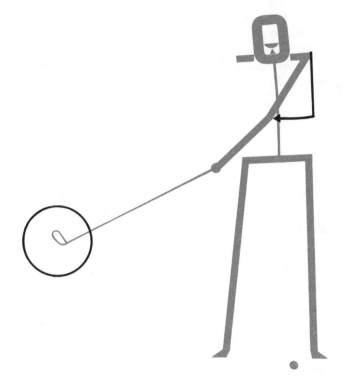

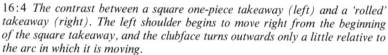

16:4 The contrast between a square one-piece takeaway (left) and a 'rolled' takeaway (right). The left shoulder begins to move right from the beginning of the square takeaway, and the clubface turns outwards only a little relative to the arc in which it is moving.

two movements the face of the club will start to turn 'out-wards', decreasing from 90° its angle to the plane—but not so quickly as it does when taken away with a marked roll of the left forearm.

Such a roll of the forearm is usually needed by a player who takes the club away from the address position mainly with the arms and hands; whereas the 'square' takeaway occurs when he takes it back with a 'one-piece' movement of club, arms and shoulders.

Thus one characteristic of the simple 'square' takeaway is that the left shoulder begins to move round under the chin right from the start, whereas in the 'roller' takeaway the main movement is usually in the arms.

Their respective positions, exaggerated slightly and showing left arm only, are shown in Fig. 16:4.

When we add the right arm we see one reason why the

'arms only' takeaway usually goes with rolling—there just isn't anywhere for the right arm to go. In the first drawing the shoulders-arms triangle is unchanged, but in the second draw-ing the distance from right shoulder to right hand must decrease, so that the right elbow must bend.

If you try to hold the clubface or the back of the left hand in the 'square' position, the tendency will be for the right elbow to bend outwards—leading you into a highly un-desirable position at the top of the backswing: that known as the 'flying right elbow'. Rolling the left forearm 'open', on the other hand, enables the right elbow to remain close to the side. In any case, when the left arm is swung close across the chest like that, the simplest movement anatomically is for it to rotate slightly towards the palm-downwards position, thus rolling the clubface open.

With this early arm-across-chest and forearm roll there will also be a tendency to cock the wrist earlier—partly in order to get the clubhead into plane (or perhaps we should say because of its tendency to fly into plane), and also because the wrist will be in a position in which it can very readily cock early.

When the left shoulder eventually begins to turn under, the

16:5 *Shut, square and open at the takeaway. These are relative terms but F. Ishii (top) appears to be making a deliberate effort to hold the blade of the club shut, while Bill Collins (bottom), a U.S. Ryder Cup player, is allowing it to roll open. Sebastian Miguel (middle) is intermediate between the two, in what we can call a 'square' takeaway. The third picture in each sequence shows up the differences particularly well.*

player has to let his forearm roll even further, simply in order to keep the club in plane. His wrist then cocks in the characteristic 'cupped' position of the roller, with the clubface very open: i.e. with the toe pointing below the plane of the swing, corresponding to a total rotation of 120° or so of the clubface, through which he has to roll it back again during the forward swing.

A rolling action like this does not always go with an early wrist-cock. It is quite possible, in fact, to 'cock early' with little rolling. In that case, however, the wrist cock must be by a palmward hinging (arching) of the left wrist—in the manner recommended, for instance, by Dante and Elliott in *Four Magic Moves to Winning Golf**—if the clubhead is to stay in plane. Dante and Elliott claim certain advantages for this method, some of which certainly make sense; but generally speaking it adds a complication in that you still have to turn your shoulders and raise your arms, making, in all, three conscious movements, whereas, with the swing we have been recommending as the simplest, the momentum of the swing will itself cock the wrist automatically.

The 'one-piece' square takeaway also leads more naturally into a wide arc on the backswing. Let it be said straightaway that a wide arc of the clubhead on the backswing has no merit whatsoever in itself. But it does help to make sure that the club is swung to the top of the backswing with a full turn of the shoulders, not just by pulling the left arm across the chest. It pulls the whole body into a true swing *around* a still hub or central pivot.

Wrist action and the model

There is a limit, though, to the advantages to be gained by analysing too many possible variations of individual wrist action. They are all governed by the one basic rule—that the action of the wrists should serve the swing as a whole, and should do so in the simplest and most effective way for any individual player.

What is the best way for any individual can depend on very many factors: his power, suppleness, build, natural strength and make-up of wrists and hands, his age, and even his temperament.

It is impossible to be dogmatic. Whatever grip and wrist action enables him to swing most easily and powerfully and consistently, in the general pattern, sequence and timing of the model, is a good grip and wrist action for him.

* Published by Heinemann, 1963

Chapter 17

Programming the Swing: Some of the Mental Aspects of Golf

The early chapters of this book described the mechanical principles of the perfect golf swing. To do so it was necessary to simplify the extremely complex structure of bones, joints and muscles, controlled by an even more complex network of nerves, and regard the body as a simple system of levers, pivots and power supplies.

The shoulder and wrist joints, for example, are capable of movement in virtually any direction and the problem is to restrict their movement to the mechanically simple ones implied by the model.

There are many points in the swing like this, where 'wrong' movements are anatomically quite possible; and when it comes to attempting the complete swing, remembering all the individual items makes the task appear impossible to the beginner.

He shouldn't be too discouraged though. Everyone has this feeling at the start. The most learned brains and the most successful athletes from other sports find the golf swing an extremely difficult skill to master.

There are several reasons for this. For a start the golf club-head is so far from the hand of the player, and both the ball and the clubhead he is trying to hit it with are so small, that he has difficulty in making any sort of contact at all. Furthermore, to produce an acceptable shot, the area on the face of the club within which the ball must be struck is only the size of a sixpence. Indeed, purely in terms of the stroke itself, golf is the most difficult of all hitting games.

The facts presented earlier in this book will probably have already made that clear. Of course, in most other games the ball or other object to be hit is moving, so that you have to anticipate its flight as you prepare to hit it; and often tactics and strategy are part of the overall skill of playing these games. So you can't really compare golf with other games in degree of difficulty. But purely in terms of the difficulty of accurate striking, golf is unequalled.

The need for great accuracy is not the only thing which makes golf so difficult. But before we look at the other reasons, let us first try to explain why the golf swing will always give rise to controversy.

Why is the golf swing so controversial?

Learning a golf swing, or anything else, involves the brain. The fact that we are, to quite a large extent, ignorant of how the brain actually works leaves anyone free to voice an opinion about how it should be used with little fear of being proved wrong. For example, until concrete evidence is available on the subject, everyone will have his own ideas on how best to educate children. The same applies to the golf swing.

In addition to this, the swing is over so quickly that details of the movement escape the eye of even the most skilful observer. To avoid appearing ignorant, experts often claim to see more than is actually possible; and a mystique is built up surrounding the events, both physical and mental, which take place during a swing.

This is perpetuated in countless books and magazine articles and endless conversations between golfers. Indeed it probably adds to the popularity of the game. Even where facts are available, golfers often prefer to listen to subjective feelings and to opinions which cannot be substantiated. (Of course, knowledge of the facts will not necessarily solve the golfer's problems; but it nearly always helps to clarify complicated situations and enable them to be discussed in more realistic terms.)

The eyes-brain-muscle chain in most skills

Skills like golf, which involve the manipulation of objects, are known as sensori-motor skills. In everyday life they vary in complexity. Driving a motor-car is a complex skill; handling a spoon is a simple one: but both have to be learned. Of course, we are so accustomed to using a spoon that we are inclined to forget that as children we had to learn how; and we now regard the action as automatic, though in fact this may not always be the case. Expert golfers experience the same feelings in swinging a golf club; but, as we hope to show, their swings are not so 'grooved' as they imagine; and it is the brain, not the hands, which really controls the golf club.

Car driving illustrates the inseparable part played by the three sections of the body in all skills. The eyes receive information about the speed and position of the car on the road, and about possible dangers which lie ahead. Information may also be received through other sense organs: the ears may hear a danger signal, or the sense of balance may warn that the car is cornering too quickly.

This information is passed to the brain and used, together with memories stored from the results of previous experience, to come to a decision. This decision is coded in the form of nervous impulses and passed to the appropriate muscles which carry out the tasks required of them.

100

All of these stages are equally important. It is not the eyes which make any reactions to control the car, but the muscles. However, the muscles do not contract unless they are instructed to do so by the brain; and the brain must have information from the eyes on which to base its decisions. In other words, it is a chain reaction of sense organs, brain and muscles; and all skills, whatever their outward form, involve all three processes to a greater or lesser extent.

Chess, at one extreme, requires little of the muscles but a lot of the eyes and brain in observing and planning strategic manoeuvres involved. Golf lies at the other extreme. After he has taken up a position to hit the ball, the player's eyes have very little information to send to his brain (unless, for example, the ball falls off the tee), but his muscles still have to carry out an extremely complicated movement based on instructions from his brain.

Accurate movements require continuous correction
During skills which involve moving an object under control to a target, the eyes provide a continuous supply of information on the relationship between the object and the target. When great accuracy is required, the muscles make finer and finer adjustments as the distance between object and target decreases, and the results of each adjustment are referred to the brain before another correction is made. This takes time; so movements calling for great accuracy are usually done slowly.

When accuracy is less important, on the other hand, the brain usually instructs the limbs to carry out the entire movement, without waiting for further information from the eyes to allow corrections to be made.

In the golf swing, however, it is important to move the clubhead not only as accurately as possible but also as fast as possible. During the swing the eyes send information about the position of the ball, and the sense organs in the muscles and joints (called proprioceptors) continually send information about the movements and position of the various parts of the body.

We are not so aware of the proprioceptors as we are of the more obvious sense organs like the eyes and ears; but it is easy to demonstrate that they are there, and are providing information about movements and positions of the limbs. Simply close your eyes and move your arms about. Although your eyes are telling you nothing, you are aware of the position of your arms, and can carry out movements reasonably accurately. Not too accurately, however, as you may demonstrate by trying to bring the tips of your index fingers together with your eyes closed.

With information coming in from all these sources during a golf swing, we might think that perfect control should be maintained over the club. But in order to show the relatively small value of this information during the golf swing, let us describe an experiment.

An experiment in reaction time
A golfer is hitting drives into a net in a room, from which all daylight has been excluded, and which is lit by a single artificial light. It is rather a special one, because when it is switched off the light decays very rapidly indeed; for all practical purposes the room is instantly plunged into darkness. The golfer goes on hitting shot after shot, and, as a measure of how good each shot is, the speed of the ball and the point on the clubface where contact is made are recorded.

During some swings, however, the light is switched off. The golfer knows this is sometimes going to happen; but he doesn't know in which swing. When it does happen, he is to do whatever he can to stop his swing; or, if he can't do that, at least to change it by slowing down, by swinging over the top of the ball, or by mishitting it.

The object of the experiment is to find out, by switching off the light at different points in the swing, at what stage the golfer is totally committed to his shot and quite unable to alter it in any way.

Well, where would you say was the point of no return? Clubhead a foot from the ball? Or two feet? Or halfway through the downswing? In fact, much earlier than any of these. Of all the many golfers tested, not one could in any way alter his stroke when the light went off after a point just barely into the downswing. Nearly all could actually stop the shot if the light went out during the backswing.

What this implies is that once any of us has fairly begun the forward swing, we can't correct or alter it in any way.

This may surprise golfers. It didn't surprise the scientists carrying out the tests too much, because the time the downswing takes (0·2 to 0·25 seconds) is just about the minimum time required for the brain to perceive external signals, to give orders for the appropriate action, and for the muscles concerned to do something about it.

101

Correcting an error—only on the backswing

Now, of course, when he is playing golf, the player's brain is not likely to receive messages by means of flashing lights. Indeed, while he is actually swinging, only a limited amount of useful information can reach him via his eyes; but his brain is continually receiving messages from the proprioceptors which tell him the position of his limbs and joints, and the state of contraction of his muscles. It is unlikely that the times involved in that process differ much from those in the visual process.

The results of the experiment mean that although the brain is receiving information from the sense organs, it does not have time to make use of it. Should a golfer feel he has 'gone wrong' at any stage after his downswing has started, there is absolutely nothing he can do about it.

This is not to say that a shot which starts wrongly cannot be saved; but, to be saved, it must have gone wrong, and the news of this must have been passed to the brain rather earlier, sometime during the backswing. So, when you see a professional hit the ball with an exaggerated last second roll over of the right hand, transforming an embryonic slice into an acceptable drive, you can be pretty sure the information that his swing was going off course was sent to his brain early in the backswing.

He may not know this. He may well imagine that the whole process occurred in the downswing; but this is an illusion. The 'lights-out' experiment showed this up quite clearly. The golfers tested were asked to say when they thought the light had been switched off; and, without exception, they said it had gone out later than it actually did. For example, if the light went out at the beginning of the downswing, most thought it went out at about impact.

Clicking cameras and overhanging branches

This has some bearing on a problem sometimes encountered at professional tournaments: clicking cameras. Players often complain that a photographer, by taking a picture during their downswing, has distracted their concentration and spoiled their shot. Well, in those terms, it just couldn't happen. According to this experiment, any click during the downswing could not possibly affect the shot, and would probably not even register in the player's mind until the ball had gone. However, if the camera clicked during the backswing, then the player might be aware of it in time for it to upset his con-

centration; and he might imagine he heard it happen during the downswing.

The click of the camera is, of course, usually unexpected, whereas, in the experiment, the golfer knew that on each shot there was at least a possibility of the light going off. This may make it dangerous to draw firm conclusions about clicking cameras from the test results. But, in fact, when he began the test, each golfer thought it was merely his clubhead speed that was being measured. He was given no warning that the light was going to be switched off; and it was just as unexpected as the click of a camera.

Of course, only one test on each person could be done like this, so there were fewer results to go on, but they did suggest that being taken by surprise in this way certainly did not improve the chance of taking late action on a shot; if anything it reduced it. That is to say, the point in the swing beyond which an interfering agency can neither have any effect, nor be remedied, may well be earlier if the interference comes as a surprise than if it is expected.

This is something readers may be familiar with. If you are playing from under a tree and you are aware of the possibility of hitting a branch near the top of your backswing, it is relatively easy, should you actually hit the branch, to stop your swing, and try again. However, if you haven't noticed the branch, or if the possibility of hitting it has not occurred to you, you will find it difficult or impossible to stop.

The whole swing is programmed in advance

All we have said so far concerns the point beyond which no alteration of the swing is possible. But what happens in the experiment if the light is switched off before that point? The player will be able to alter his shot if he tries to; but if he chooses to continue with his swing at the ball, can he do so quite unaffected? If so, how early in the swing must he be deprived of visual information before it begins to affect his shot?

The experiment answered these questions. If the light was switched off at the very beginning of the backswing, when the clubhead was only a few inches away from the ball, nearly all the players were able, in total darkness, to carry on to the top of the swing, and come down and through the ball in a perfectly normal way. (They could, of course, stop if they chose to.)

On the other hand if the light was switched off just before

the clubhead was drawn away from the ball, very few could hit the shot consistently. This is an experiment you can try yourself, just by shutting your eyes at the appropriate time.

Now what does all this mean? It means that the golf swing is fundamentally different from most other skills which demand great accuracy. As we described earlier, precise movements are usually made in a series of ever-decreasing steps with the eyes informing the brain of the result of the previous step before the next one is started. In the golf swing there is no time for this, so the brain programmes the whole series of events in advance. It sends pretty well all the necessary instructions to the muscles before the movement actually starts. Once the operation is under way it is very difficult, and, after a certain stage, impossible, to break into the system and alter it. And this, of course, is just what getting set up, concentrating, waiting for the right moment to swing is all about.

In many ways the brain might be compared to a general before a battle. But this general has to make a plan of action before the battle begins, based on his intelligence reports and on his own judgment; and he will not be able to modify the plan throughout the subsequent action because he is not going to obtain any progress reports as the battle proceeds. Similarly the golfer must marshal all his thoughts before he swings; and to do this he will probably need to have *one* positive thought in his mind about what he is going to do during the swing.

A few checks before the swing; only one during it

It is not really possible to think of more than one or two things in any single swing—which is why beginners find it so difficult to learn, particularly if given too much instruction at once. It is also one reason why pros teach grip and stance first. The pupil can take as long as he likes to get them right before actually setting the whole process in motion. It is doubtful whether a correct grip and stance are quite as important as some people would have us believe; but they are very easy to get right and standardize, and it does the beginner's morale a lot of good to hear that he stands up to the ball like an accomplished golfer.

The first movement of the backswing, or the way you feel it, is also something that you can take time to prepare for; and this *is* important. So all golfers, good or bad, should take advantage of the time available to get these things right; then concentrate on one further thought for the swing.

The first-class golfer may have a problem here because he can probably swing well without thinking. This may be all right when playing 'for fun', but in competition some *positive* thought should be in his mind for every shot, if only to block out negative ones.

These positive thoughts can be almost anything. Interpreted literally, they may even be quite nonsensical. Yet in so far as their object is to achieve some real practical effect by getting the player to aim at a 'feeling' of something imaginary or even impossible, they may make very good sense. They may just be an exact mental picture of the intended flight of the shot, but more often they concern some particular point in the swing.

The follow-through can be quite a good source of key thoughts, even though, in the strict mechanical sense, it cannot affect the shot. Thus a man who concentrates on driving the clubhead along the ground straight towards the hole for at least a foot beyond the ball is, in a sense, deluding himself. He cannot do it; even if he could, the shot would be no better than one with a normal clubhead arc, and anyway, he'd probably do himself an injury. *But,* having the thought in his mind, having *one* simple objective, may help that particular man to bring the clubhead fast, square and true through the ball; and that does make for a good shot.

Henry Cotton has many of these key thoughts (see his book, *Henry Cotton Says**) which he calls 'pegs to hang your hat on', and Dave Marr writing in *Golf Digest,* May 1966, also has a number of points and a very graphic way of picturing them. These key thoughts will often change; indeed it may be that they *must* change, otherwise they become exaggerated movements which actually change the swing. Properly applied key thoughts, gimmicks if you like, help to *retain* the swing, not change it.

Always, though, the player must have his key thought absolutely clear in his mind before he begins his swing.

Building up the beginner's programme

All of this is of value to someone who has some idea how to swing the golf club; but it doesn't help the novice very much. In essence, we have been saying that before every golf shot the player has to make up his mind exactly what sort of stroke he needs to play, take up his position to hit the ball and then by making a decision in his brain, switch on the programmed sequence of instructions to the muscles. The novice, of course, has no programme to switch on, and his problem is to build one in his brain—to 'learn the golf swing'.

The precise way in which this occurs within the brain is still unknown, but research on other skills reveals a fairly consistent pattern. A good example is learning the Morse code.

When an operator begins to learn Morse code he first recognizes the dots and dashes which indicate the individual letters of the alphabet. As he becomes more proficient, he copes with larger groups of symbols representing whole words, and later even entire phrases. The units with which he is dealing become larger and larger. The same thing applies to typists and pianists—and very likely to golfers.

When the budding golfer starts to learn, he is aware of many separate feelings from various parts of his body, and as he begins to move he has to check them individually: to make sure that his left elbow doesn't bend, that his wrists cock in the right direction, that his head doesn't move, that his shoulders pivot correctly and so on. But gradually, after repeating the moves of, say, the backswing a few thousand times, he becomes less aware of feelings from individual parts of the body and begins to gain a much more general impression of the whole movement. The size of this movement has probably then been increased to include the downswing; and again over a long period, and after many repetitions, he 'feels' the swing as a unified movement.

Once a pupil has become reasonably competent, he must guard against giving too much consideration to movements of isolated parts of the body and too little to the continuity and rhythm of the whole movement. For this reason a visit to a professional tournament often helps golfers of all abilities. It isn't that you need look for particular technical points on the grip, the stance or anything else, but that a general sense of timing and flow may rub off on to your own swing, at least for a time.

Seeing yourself on film has a similar effect, particularly if the film can be compared with one of an expert golfer. Glaring technical faults will, of course, show up; but the main benefit is to obtain an impression of the timing and rhythm of your swing, which no professional can easily describe to you.

In a sense the expert golfer is the worst person to analyse a swing in detail for the beginner, just because he does not himself feel it as a series of movements but as a complete unit. It all follows so smoothly and quickly that, when he comes to describe it, he can often only talk in vague terms, which have little meaning to the pupil. In that case demonstration is better than explanation.

The really expert teaching professional, though, does in the long run learn by experience which sort of phrases get home most effectively to his pupils. To him, this chapter may be of special interest.

Chapter 18

Teaching, Learning and Practice

The previous chapter may have made some readers wonder how on earth anyone ever manages to learn the golf swing. The scientific answer to the question is that we don't really know. The fact remains, however, that professionals regularly hit the ball up to 300 yards with remarkable consistency; so it is possible. Somehow people do learn.

In teaching beginners the professional is faced with several problems. One is that, if the pupil makes no progress at the first or second lesson, he may not come back. To satisfy him in this respect, professionals often have to abandon their teaching ideals, at least for part of the lesson. Learning to play golf is a long and frustrating procedure, in which the desire to see progress is only natural; but if a beginner can somehow be patient enough to build a sound technique right from the start, without demanding instant progress on the golf course, he will achieve more in the long run.

How the beginner should set about things

How should the beginner set out to become a competent golfer?

First, he should know exactly what he is trying to do with the clubhead: he should know that it must be brought through the ball (a) in a straight line to the target, (b) square to the intended line of flight and (c) as fast as possible.

Second, it may help him to know, in a general way, how he is going to attempt to do it. For example, the model could be explained to him in simple terms, or, better still, shown to him as a simple mechanical man. Then he should see as many experts as possible to get a general impression of the timing and co-ordination of the good player.

After all this he may begin to handle a golf club! Unless there are good reasons for not doing so, he should at first use the standard grip and stance; but later in his golfing career, when he has attained a reasonable standard, he should try other grips and stances.

During the early stages of learning it is important to have the advice of an expert. Studies on other skills have shown that early attempts to perform a movement have a considerable influence on later progress. In particular, if the first attempts are incorrect, it is difficult to 'un-learn' the resulting method, the more so since it may be only slightly different from the correct method. Until considerable skill has been acquired, it is easier to learn a movement totally different from a habitual movement than one only slightly different.

Children—a different approach?

Taking expert advice and tuition, as described above, is probably the best way for adults to learn a sound technique as quickly as possible. But it may be best to allow those who have plenty of time—especially children—to play with a golf club and ball without formal tuition. By a process of trial and error each individual will find for himself the method which suits him; and, provided he sees enough good players during this period, it is unlikely that excessive variations in style will occur.

This would appear to be the method that has produced several of the outstanding players in Britain at the moment. Each has been exposed to golf from a tender age; and through constant practice and play, handling a golf club has become as simple to them as handling a knife and fork is to most people.

Problems of teaching and learning

Let's now look at the problem the professional has in teaching the beginner.

Most professional teachers know a good swing when they see it, though they may not know exactly what is happening at all stages of it. This is not a criticism of golf teachers, merely a way of saying that things move too fast for the human eye to do more than gather an overall impression of the movement.

Moreover, as we explained in the previous chapter, the professional feels his own swing as a complete unit and finds it very difficult to explain to a beginner what *he* should feel. The pupil has to build, through experience, the feeling of a good golf swing; the professional can only do his best to help him in this process. It is a mark of a really good teacher that he can put what he is trying to say in different ways, one of which finally 'clicks' with the pupil. This, incidentally, is the source of a lot of apparent contradictions in golf teaching.

When one professional says that the first movement of the downswing is to put the left heel back on the ground, and another says it is to pull with the left hand, they are not necessarily contradicting each other. They may well just be suggesting to their respective pupils that it would be worth trying to *feel* that the left heel, or the left hand, initiated the downswing. The end product—a correct downswing—would be the same in either case.

Some teachers of the game believe in the literal truth of what they teach; for example, that the first movement of the downswing really *is* a pull with the left hand. They are, generally speaking, the ones who try to teach their own golf swing to their pupils. Of course, some of the time they will be right, since there must *be* a first movement of the downswing (probably movement of the hips, in fact); but it is not always helpful for the pupil to know this.

Teaching golf is an art

The better professional teacher recognizes that, in order to convey the right feeling, he may have to exaggerate, or even to say something which he knows not only to be untrue, but to be the exact opposite of what he said to the previous pupil. He may even, with one and the same pupil, contradict something he said five minutes before—though if he does this without explanation, the pupil may lose confidence in him.

Of course, all this does not just apply to the first movement of the downswing. At many points in the swing, there may be a difference between what actually happens and what the player feels he is doing.

At all these points the first-class teacher has several ways of suggesting the right feeling to his pupil, and probably has a pretty good idea about which ways are likely to be most successful with any individual pupil. In fact, golf teaching is an art, and no amount of scientific investigation or apparatus is likely in the foreseeable future to take the place of a good professional, though it can undoubtedly help him in his work.

Too much detail confuses

Instructions are best given in the form of general feelings rather than specific details as to what any particular part of the body should be doing, unless the pupil asks for advice on the position or movement of any specific part. Normally, detailed instructions serve to confuse rather than help a beginner, so advice should involve only general principles.

In order that the feeling of a golf swing may be developed, it is important that large units of the movement are taught as one. For example, an entire backswing should be taught as the first movement and later the downswing should be added. To make more than one break in the swing is adding unnecessary complications and should be avoided.

Hit hard from the beginning

One general point in learning the swing, about which there is some controversy, is whether you should hit hard from the

start and let accuracy come, or hit gently and gradually build up the ability to hit hard. Most of the evidence from other physical activities favours hitting hard; and theory suggests it too.

Certainly to practise a swing so slow that the movement is no longer 'ballistic' (i.e. so slow that the club can be guided) is a waste of time, as the muscles and nervous system will have to act in quite a different way from the way they do in a normal golf swing. But even a lesser reduction in speed, which still retains the ballistic nature of the swing, changes the dynamic relationship between one part of the system and the other.

In terms of the simple two-lever model, if the turning force at the top pivot is reduced, then the turning force necessary at the hinge to bring the two-lever system to the same impact position, is not just reduced in proportion but is changed in pattern and timing also. In other words a gentle, slow, full-length swing does not work the same way as a normal one; and practising it may only upset the timing of the player's next game.

If you want to learn by hitting more gently, then it would seem to make more sense to do so by using a shorter swing instead, and still hitting hard (or as hard as you comfortably can). The relationship between the forces at the pivots is more closely preserved in that case and 'slack' is kept out of the system. It is plausible to generalize on this and say that the 'secret' of playing all shots which demand less than a full swing—even a ten-yard run up—is to avoid slack in the system. In that way you can carry over something of the timing of one shot to another provided you keep the basic pattern similar.

Make things easier for beginners

Most competent golfers will have forgotten the immensely frustrating experiences of the beginner. He reaches a stage where he can grip the club correctly, stand to the ball correctly and even swing smoothly and elegantly; but on a proportion of swings he completely misses the ball. Even the professional's reassurance that the swing was basically a good one cannot stem the feeling of anger which rapidly rises as successive attempts fail to make contact. Eventually in the obsessive desire simply to hit the ball, he completely forgets style and makes a wild—and sometimes successful—lunge at the ball. This, in the long run, can have a disastrous effect on his progress.

But when we look at the situation logically, it is perfectly obvious that the beginner will miss the ball. He is asked to hit a tiny target with a very small clubhead by means of a complicated movement carried out as fast as possible, and therefore without guidance. Furthermore, as we have said, it is important to start with a swing which is fast and which is complete. How can it be made easier?

One obvious answer would be to start off with a larger target: not a golf ball but perhaps a rubber ball about four inches in diameter. This would enable the beginner to perfect the gross body movements without demanding so much accuracy. Once he had mastered swiping this outsize ball, he could go on to successively smaller balls until he could deal with the ordinary golf ball. This simple progression could eliminate some of the earlier frustrations of learning to play golf and make progress in the long term more rapid.

Knowledge of results and learning

One essential requirement for learning is knowledge of the results of our efforts; and the more complete this knowledge is, the more it will help progress. There is ample experimental evidence to prove this. In scientific terminology, using our knowledge of results in this way is known as 'feedback', since the results of previous attempts are 'fed back' to the brain and used to correct later ones.

All golfers, of course, have their own private feedback loop, which almost invariably judges each swing by the success of the resulting shot. But, particularly for beginners, this is rather unreliable, since there are so many ways of producing any given poor shot. A complete top, which dives into a bush in front of the tee, may result from a swing nearer to a good one than that producing a heeled slice which finishes 160 yards up the fairway. The expert golfer may realize this, but the beginner will not. What the beginner wants is some means of knowing that his swing has gone wrong as soon as it happens. If, for example, a machine could be devised which would give the golfer an electric shock as soon as it detected an error in the backswing, the rate of progress of beginners, and others, would be enormously increased.

Of course, the teacher serves this purpose to some extent by making comments on the swing, regardless of the result of the shot. Though this is much more helpful to a beginner than trying to provide his own feedback, it suffers from two great deficiencies compared with our hypothetical machine. In the

first place comments from the pro almost certainly have to wait until the shot is complete; and secondly they are subject to the pro's own personal, and probably biased, interpretation. In fact, one of the dangers teaching professionals must guard against is thinking they perceive more than they actually do. Many would find it both arresting and helpful to check their own powers of observation, from time to time, against some accurate objective method—such as a high-speed camera.

The main value of feedback in a golf swing is in the way it can be used to improve the swings which follow; and the more immediately it can be applied after any bad shot, the better— particularly for the beginner. If he is playing with only one golf ball and has to walk to collect it after each hit, this just isn't possible because by the time he has reached it, he has probably forgotten what he did or didn't do last time. It is therefore essential, when learning golf, to give some time to practice with several balls (preferably about twenty) and to repeat any shot many times to make immediate use of feedback.

It may also help to have someone else there to provide still more information about the swing. He doesn't have to be an expert; any willing friend will do. All he has to do is to concentrate on one particular point in the swing, or one particular part of your body, and tell you what happens. You might ask him, for instance, to see if your head moves, or if your left heel comes off the ground, or if your club goes back beyond the horizontal.

Practice: How much and how often?

This is a whole field which has never been seriously studied in relation to golf. Yet it is very important to practise not only in the right way, but for the right length of time and with the right interval between practice sessions.

Studies of other skilled activities suggest that one thing which retards a learner's progress is going on too long in practice sessions, or not having a long enough interval between sessions. Proper spacing of practice gives the learner a chance to forget bad habits he has built up.

Ideally, therefore, people learning to play golf should take short lessons at frequent, but not too frequent, intervals. Daily lessons lasting half to three-quarters of an hour are probably about right for a complete beginner. He's unlikely to get too tired during the lesson, and the twenty-four-hour interval between lessons allows mistakes to be forgotten, without being long enough to disrupt the continuity of learning. When lessons can only be arranged once a week, the first part of the lesson is normally spent in returning to the standard where the previous lesson ended and this inevitably slows progress.

Getting all this right when learning golf may be an academic matter for most people, who have neither the time nor the opportunity to practise or take lessons just as they'd like. But with golf being taught in more and more schools and in colleges of physical education, it could be important; and in training schemes for young professionals it may be vital.

Learning involves repetition

We all know that in order to learn anything we have to do it again and again in the early stages. Without this kind of repetition we can remember a telephone number long enough to dial it immediately after reading it in the directory, but if we need to memorize it for future use, we have to repeat it many times before it sticks. How well we remember it from then on will depend on how often we use it. If we dial it regularly we remember it easily; otherwise we don't.

It is as though the brain has two compartments for the memory: one for the short-term memory, the other for the long-term memory. When someone reads a telephone number in the directory, it is stored in the short-term memory and recalled when the number is dialled. If anything delays or distracts us between first reading the number and actually using it, we may forget it.

To store the number, or anything else for that matter, in the long-term memory involves repeating it regularly. Similarly in the early stages of learning the golf swing, the player needs constantly to repeat the correct movements. Later, it is important to play and practise regularly, purely from a memory point of view and quite apart from the need to keep the appropriate muscles in trim.

Swing is not 'grooved' mentally or physically

Although we have stressed the need for repetition, we must now make it clear that the learner is not striving for a single unique swing to be repeated identically time after time—a swing set in motion by just one memory trace (or 'circuit'), with instructions sent along just one nervous pathway, and executed by a unique set of muscle fibres.

That just wouldn't work. For a start, no two swings ever

have exactly the same demanded of them. The very nature of a golf course, with its variations in slopes, lies, grass texture and ground hardness ensures this; but even when playing from exactly the same position no golfer can set himself up to the ball in *exactly* the same way in successive swings.

Good players do set themselves up very consistently, much more so than poor players, but they never achieve *perfect* consistency even though at times the resulting shots may suggest they do. The golfer's brain is, in fact, always being presented with a situation which differs slightly from the previous one, and neither mentally nor physically can he use exactly the same swing every time—though, of course, the overall mechanical properties will be the same.

And it's not only a question of *having* to employ slight variations in the nervous pathways and muscle fibres; it is physiologically desirable too. Constant repetition of *exactly* the same process would fatigue and perhaps eventually wear out the parts involved.

Thus, variations necessarily occur in all three elements involved in making a golf swing: memory circuits (indeed there may be a separate circuit for every possible situation), nervous pathways and muscle fibres. Plenty of scope, in fact, for the large variety of golf shots which we know are possible; but also plenty of scope for developing alternative ways, differing only slightly in outward appearance, of producing the same shot.

Why practise?

This brings us to the essential purpose of practice. This may surprise some readers. It *isn't* to 'groove' a swing, but to build up a series of alternative 'routes' whereby almost identical swings can be produced—swings that result in acceptable, though not in every case perfect, golf shots. When a professional goes round in 65 and afterwards claims that he felt only four or five shots to be 100%, he is not being falsely modest; he is just summing up, in everyday terms, what we have been saying in the last few paragraphs.

This sort of theoretical exposition cannot, of course, lay down whether a man should show three knuckles or two when he grips the club; but together with results from research on other skills it does help to formulate a general approach to practising.

Once a golfer has reached the stage of having, in the loose golfing terminology, 'a swing', he should deliberately introduce variations and extra difficulty into practice sessions. By so doing he broadens his experience (increases the variety of memory traces) and develops alternative nerve and muscle routes for producing acceptable shots.

He might try, for instance, hitting one-handed shots. This gives the additional benefit of building up the muscles of the hand and arm. He might try 'splash' bunker shots with a six-iron; or hitting full shots while standing on one leg or with feet together. Practice from bad lies and sloping stances is useful; so too are deliberate attempts to hit hooks, slices, high shots and low shots. Even a chronic slicer will be surprised to find how difficult it is to produce a big slice intentionally; and it is said by at least one well-known teaching professional that once a golfer learns to shank on purpose he'll never do it accidentally again.

Another useful form of this sort of practice is to go to a short-hole tee, where, say, a six-iron is usually required, and try to hit shots on to the green with a five-, four-, three- and two-iron and even a three-wood.

Readers can no doubt think of more exercises like this. Remember, though, they are not for beginners—only for those who have a well-established swing already; or, to put it more strictly, for those who can already produce near identical results by means of a series of similar mental and physiological processes. Beginners will merely confuse themselves if they introduce this amount of variation into their learning.

Set yourself targets when practising

None of this is meant to suggest that practising conventional golf strokes is of no value. On the contrary, it is; but you must know exactly what you are trying to achieve. Without a precise aim practice may do *harm*, at least to your swing, though it may still help strengthen your muscles.

All this, again, may seem very obvious; but lots of people do practise with no particular object in mind. Compared with the unconventional practice we have been describing, ordinary practice offers nothing startlingly clear to aim at, and all too easily it becomes a matter of merely slogging your way aimlessly through a bag of practice balls.

Not only should you know what you are trying to do in any practice session, but you should have some definite goal to aim at; that is, an actual numerical target which you set yourself. If you are happy that your swing is working on the right lines, the goal can be quite a simple one. For example, practis-

ing with a five-iron and aiming at a flagstick, you can try to get 50% of shots within fifteen yards, say. At the least you can check your progress in this way. Elsewhere in the book (Chapters 28–31) we report the standard achieved by professionals in various departments of the game. Any reader can modify these to suit his own game.

When practising drives, it is useful to record both the average length and the 'spread' in length of, say, the middle 50%, and the 'spread' in direction of the middle 50% too. That is, out of twenty drives, ignore the five farthest left and the five farthest right, and pace out the distance left to right covering the remaining ten. This 50% 'spread' makes a better rough measure of playing accuracy than the total spread of all shots which can be unduly affected by one freak bad shot.

The reason for doing all this is not just to make practice more interesting—though it does that—but to provide the necessary motivation and satisfaction which, experiments on learning other skills suggest, make it more effective also.

There are, of course, times when this sort of thing doesn't really help. When you are trying to eradicate a fault in your swing, you may at first hit shots worse than before; and the urge to reach your target may tempt you to go back to the old method, or to make temporary adjustments. Even on occasions like this, though, it is still possible to have a numerical standard of *something* to aim at, if only the times you overcome the fault you are working on. This may call for a helper; and it is, in any case, often quite a good idea to practise with somebody. He doesn't have to be an expert, so long as he does not try to offer advice, but just gives simple 'yes' or 'no' answers to any questions you put to him about your swing.

He can, for example, very easily say if your head moves forward during the downswing (by sighting on a tree behind your head); but he mustn't be tempted to look at *anything* else. You can try to hit first twenty ordinary drives, then twenty really hard drives, without moving your head forward. You can swop roles—good training for both of you.

Why practise putting?

The same principles apply to practising the short game and putting.

If you have some definite fault in method, practice can undoubtedly help to eradicate it and to build up a sound technique; but otherwise it seems likely that the main benefit is in increasing and widening your store of experience of the behaviour of the ball rolling on a green, or pitching on to a green, or of playing shots out of different types of grass.

No two run-of-play approaches or putts are ever exactly alike. The wider the player's range of experience, the better he can cope with any shot as it arises. In putting, a wide range of experience will include fast greens, slow greens, sloping greens, undulating greens, large greens etc. It's even worth trying putters of various weights and designs, and going against common practice by trying heavy putters on fast greens and light putters on slow greens. Experimenting with situations quite outside normal golf can sometimes help. Putting with any smallish ball (a tennis ball even) on any reasonably smooth surface, for instance, widens any player's experience of a rolling ball, and may thus help to improve his putting.

Of course we don't recommend this immediately before the monthly medal; but putting experiments like this are probably of greater value than aimlessly knocking a ball round the practice putting green.

Conventional practice is useful too, of course, particularly in promoting confidence, but again it will be most effective if the practiser sets himself targets all the time against which to measure his performance and so provide the motivation and satisfaction necessary for the development of skill.

Exercises for golf
When we come to the question of training and exercises for golf, as distinct from practice, we are on rather insecure ground. Little is really known about how effective particular exercises are, though many prominent golfers believe very strongly in their own favourites; and from time to time the golf magazines describe a course of exercises.

There is no doubt that exercises, particularly progressive resistance exercises (or weight training), do help to increase muscular strength. Most golfers, however, are not convinced that strength is necessary for golf. They are well aware that, in terms of total energy expenditure, walking round the course is the main physical effort involved. This investigation has shown, however, that for the brief duration of the swing, the muscles have to work very hard. If anyone doubts this, let him put twenty balls down in a line and hit them in rapid succession with a fairway wood or long iron.

Golf uses nearly all the muscles in the body; so almost any sort of exercise will be of value; and the prime aim of any course of exercises should be to develop overall strength.

110

Some professional golfers say that, since the hands play such an important part in the swing, the golfer should give special attention to strengthening them. The G.S.G.B. team wouldn't quarrel with that. In the earlier reports in the Press, there was some misunderstanding over what this investigation revealed about the importance of the hands, so let us now state it quite clearly:

1. The hands are the most important link between the main source of power and the clubhead.
2. The greater that main source of power, the stronger the hands must be in order to cope with the faster movement, and the greater forces involved in it.
3. To maintain a firm enough hold of the club strong hands need to grip relatively less tightly than weak hands, and therefore allow freer wrist movement.
4. The man with strong, 'educated' hands can often play reasonable golf with a considerably less than perfect swing.

BUT

5. The hands and arms can never *be* the main source of power.

So there is a lot to be said for strengthening your hands by exercise; the effect on your golf, however, seems likely to show up as greater accuracy and consistency rather than greater length (although the latter may follow from the former). Any player striving specifically for greater length by exercising, should aim first at overall muscular strength, particularly in the legs. Incidentally, the use of weights to exercise the arms, trunk and legs also strengthens the hands more successfully than exercises solely intended for grip strength.

The other form of fitness which may be useful for golf is endurance. This is not developed best by weight training, but by running. Cross-country running, especially on undulating ground, is the best form of exercise to take to develop endurance of the heart and circulation. Games involving running, such as football, basketball or hockey are good alternatives. Skipping, squash, cycling and even swimming will also help.

There is, by the way, absolutely no truth in the theory that developing the muscles in one sport adversely affects performance in another. Most of these other games also help to strengthen the leg muscles and thus make particularly good training for golf. But obviously there are common-sense limits too. Running a marathon in the morning is not going to improve anyone's medal score in the afternoon.

Section 5 The Player and His Problems

Chapter 19

Golf's Crooked Shots: Hitting on the Wrong Part of the Club

If the ability to produce the goods is an indication of expertise and understanding of the underlying processes involved, then few golfers should need to read a chapter on crooked shots. We all produce them. With great ease. Yet many golfers have only a hazy idea of the mechanical effects which lie behind bad shots.

There are only three basic causes of a ball not flying where it is meant to. Each can operate on its own, or—more commonly—in combination with the others.

The three causes are:

1. *Off-centre impact*. Hitting the ball at a point other than the centre of the clubface.
2. *Off-line swing*. Swinging the clubhead through the ball in a direction other than along the chosen line of aim.
3. *Face off-line to swing*. Hitting the ball with the club*face* aiming along a different line from that through which the club*head* is being swung.

There is no other way of hitting a crooked shot: no matter what any of us may fancy ourselves capable of.

The ultimate horrors: complete mishits

Let's take the extreme examples of off-centre impact first: the air-shot, the sclaff, the full-blooded top, the shank, the ones that fly tangentially off the outside of the toe, the inside of the heel, or the top edge of the clubhead. They are all so straightforward and wholly calamitous as to need no too precise investigation; and their permutations, combinations and variations would in any case baffle a computer.

All of them are simply the result of the player swinging the clubhead through the ball so far from the position from which he drew it away into his backswing, that contact with the ball is not merely off-centre, but not even wholly on the face of the club.

In terms of the two-lever model, the most common cause of all these shots is moving the hub during the swing, so that the club is led outside (heeled or shanked), inside (toed), above (topped or missed) or below (skied or sclaffed) the position of the ball.

Fig. 19:1 shows what can happen when the hub is lifted upwards during the downswing. Result: a complete miss (or 'air-shot') or possibly a full-blooded top. In a similar way ducking the hub will produce a 'sclaff'; and swaying it forward and outward a shank.

Of course, this grossly oversimplifies the situation and

generally the man who plays these shots will be deviating from the model swing in several respects, as well, very likely, as mistiming the outward swing of his lower lever—his club, that is. Nevertheless it remains true that, whatever else has happened, you can point to an unwanted movement of the hub as a major cause of those horrors.

The photographs (Figs. 19:2, 19:3 and 19:4) show some of these shots at the moment of birth. They are of some intrinsic interest, if only to show what a golf ball has to put up with.

Off-centre impact: a simple twist effect

One of the most interesting and important discoveries of the G.S.G.B. research programme is that, at impact, the clubhead behaves as though it were freely moving and not connected at all to the player. The reasons for this, and the full significance of it, are discussed in Chapter 22. What it means for us at the moment is that to study the effect of striking the ball off-centre with the clubface, we need consider only the reactions that take place between the clubface and ball. We can forget the shaft.

At impact the ball very strongly resists the clubhead's attempt to send it into instantaneous flight at 150 miles per hour. It resists strongly enough to flatten itself out against the face of the club before reacting into flight. The force involved —as the reader can easily imagine from the normal hardness of a ball to his hand—is very great. On a long drive it averages over half a ton for the period of contact between ball and club.

If this force is applied to the middle of the clubface, in line with its centre of gravity, it will slow the whole clubhead up quite appreciably, but without twisting it or throwing it off balance in any way. That is precisely what happens during impact in a perfectly struck golf shot.

Suppose, though, that the force of impact is aimed, instead, through a point on the clubface wide of the centre of gravity. It will then not just slow up the clubface but will knock it round at an angle as well; and this, indeed, is what happens when the ball is struck off-centre.

Let's take an example: the common 'thinned' shot; the one which stings the hands as it flies low and catches the hazard we meant to carry. What has happened is that the ball has struck the clubface below the centre of gravity, and turned it downwards during the course of impact. This has, in effect, reduced its loft, and thus both the angle above the horizontal at which the ball is dispatched and the backspin imparted to it.

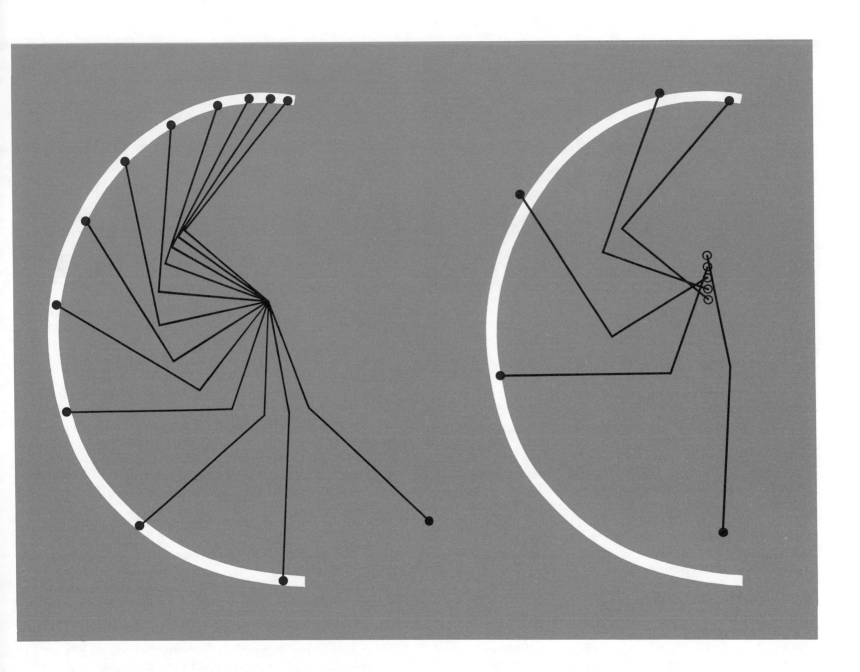

19:1 *An 'air shot' in model terms. One of the most common causes of the complete miss (or the less extreme form of it, the full-blooded top), is raising the whole hub of the swing during the downswing. This lifts the arc of the club-head over the top of the ball as it approaches the ball. The golfer knows this fault as 'head-up'.*

19:2 *A full-blooded top with a driver. The bottom edge of the clubface has sunk into the top half of the ball driving it into the ground just in front of the tee-peg.*

19:3 *Another topped shot. This is a 'double flash' photograph showing two stages of the shot. The ball will never be the same again after this treatment.*

These effects, even on their own, will tend to give the ball a lower flight. But they are nearly always assisted by another effect. The area of contact between ball and clubface in a full shot, with a reasonably straight-faced club, is roughly circular and an inch to an inch and a quarter in diameter. Since the depth of the clubface from top to bottom is only about an inch and a half, any shot in which first contact with the ball is made more than a quarter of an inch or so below the middle of the face will squeeze part of the ball round the bottom edge of the club at maximum compression. This also contributes to a lower flight. The more of the ball 'wrapped round' the bottom edge, the 'thinner' the shot is. If more than half is wrapped round you have a complete top.

Any stroke off-centre wastes power

An off-centre blow turns the clubhead around its centre of gravity. That is to say, the part of the clubface which strikes the ball 'gives' rather easily to it, and the ball leaves the clubface with less speed than the shot struck from the centre of the clubface. Thus, in the case of a 'thinned' drive, length is lost on this account as well as the lower elevation.

With a lofted iron most golfers know that a thinned shot will often travel farther than a properly hit one. This is because the loss in speed may be more than balanced by the lower eleva-

tion; or it may even happen that speed will actually be gained by getting just the right amount of ball squeezed over the edge of the club, so that, in effect, the blow is made less oblique.

The reader will be able to perceive for himself how the equivalent forces will work in an exactly similar way if the ball is struck too high upon the clubface, instead of too low. The result will be a higher shot, with more backspin and less power, with again the probability that part of the ball will be squeezed over the *top* edge of the clubface.

In contrast with the corresponding effect in the thinned shot, squeezing the ball over the top edge will always still further reduce the power of the shot, because it can only make the blow, in effect, more oblique, never less.

Hit high on the face the ball is, in fact, slightly 'shovelled', and this is why the common 'skied' shot always feels a weak one at impact, even before the player can see it begin to fly ineffectively up into the air.

One point may be worth mentioning here as an illustration of how off-centre blows can affect the game all the time, often without the player noticing it.

On a seaside course with very firm thin turf, some golfers have wondered why even their well-hit shots seem to travel lower in the air than usual, and have accordingly suspected that they weren't striking them properly. In a way, this is true.

114

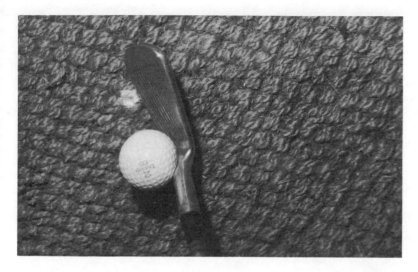

19:4 *Golfer's eye view of a shank. The ball has missed the face of the club altogether, and will scuttle off to the right.*

The cause of the inland player's low-flying seaside shot may be that his game is adjusted to grassier fairways; so that his normal stroke at the ball tends, on seaside turf, to make contact lower on the clubface than usual.

Conversely, the high-flying shot a man often gets from a very grassy patch of fairway or from a good lie in semi-rough, results quite simply from making contact with the ball at a point in its face slightly above that opposite to the clubhead's centre of gravity.

To understand how these two characteristic strokes arise may be to go at least halfway towards being able to correct them, guard against, or allow for them. So here is one factor which any golfer may take into account in assessing a stroke from any patch of unusually bare, thin or lushly thick turf.

This applies not least, of course, if he is trying to send the ball really close to the pin. As we mentioned earlier, the shot hit high on the face will nearly always lose distance, whereas the shot hit low on the face, or even slightly 'thin', may gain or lose distance depending on the club used and the precise nature of the blow. Most 'thinned' approaches go rocketing through the back of the green; but some stop short of the green, particularly if the grass is long; and the odd one or two, by a complex balancing of unpredictable factors, finish up six inches from the hole.

The player can only anticipate the likely effect on any shot in the light of the exact lie, and the type and run of the ground around where the ball must pitch to reach its target. But, where the lie is in any way unusual, the wise golfer will decide what sort of shot to play and with what club, at least partly on the basis of the kind of mishit which *might* be produced, and the possible results of it.

By far the most important factor here is going to be the player's experience. But understanding the effect of striking the ball high or low on the clubface will help him to make the best use of it.

Heel turns left, toe turns right

What applies to balls struck above or below centre applies in exactly the same way to balls struck left or right of centre.

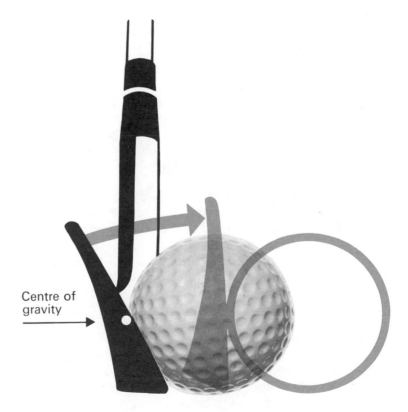

Centre of gravity

19:5 *Striking the ball below the centre of gravity of the clubhead. The clubhead is turned downwards by the blow, giving a lower trajectory than usual.*

19:6 *A 'thin' drive. Contact has been made low on the face of the club, and at maximum compression a little of the ball will be 'wrapped round' the bottom edge. The shot will fly low and be less powerful than one off the centre, though into wind and on fast fairways it may not lose distance.*

19:7 *A skied drive. Contact is mainly high on the face of the club, but part of the ball is wrapped over the top edge. The shot will fly high and lack power.*

In this case the results may be even more obvious to the player himself.

A ball struck towards the heel of the clubhead will turn the face to the left of the line, and thus send the ball to the left. One struck on the toe side will similarly send the ball away to the right of the line.

It is when we come to look into precisely how the ball's spin will be affected in either case, and thus how its flight through the air will be affected also, that we come to the more subtle ground in the matter.

We won't yet go into the technical details of the way spin is applied during the impact between clubface and ball, but put it, for the time being, in non-scientific terms. If the ball is struck on the toe side and the clubface is thus 'opened'—i.e. turned to the right—during impact, clockwise spin will be imparted to the ball (looking down on it).

This is the kind of spin which causes the ball to slice (curve to the right), during flight. Anticipating Chapter 24 for a moment, the rule of spin in golfing ballistics is that a golf ball flying through the air always tends to curve in the direction in which the front of the ball is moving by virtue of its spin. You could say it tries to 'follow its nose'.

Thus, at least with an iron club, a shot hit towards the toe will tend not just to set off to the right of the intended line, but to curve to the right as well. Conversely, one hit towards the heel will start off to the left and also curve to the left—provided, of course, it is not so badly heeled as to be a 'shank'.

Neither curve effect, though, is as great as you might expect it to be from the angle at which the ball is sent off by the shock-turned blow; and it is here that we must introduce a further subtlety of the mechanics of clubhead behaviour during off-centre impact with the ball.

With woods the 'gear effect' counters simple sidespin
The heads of most iron clubs are fairly thin from front to back. But wooden clubheads are not; and, in particular, their centres of gravity are usually some distance behind the striking face.

So when the clubhead is turned clockwise, for example, about its centre of gravity, by the force of an off-centre blow towards the toe, the point on the face with which the ball first made contact, as well as moving back, is also swung to the right, across the back of the ball.

To the extent that this happens it will spin the back of the

19:8 *Off the toe. Notice how the clubface which was square to the line of the white tape at impact, has been violently twisted open by the blow. The ball starts out to the right, but provided the club-ball contact didn't miss the face of the club altogether the shot may curve back part way towards the intended line (see 'gear effect' in this chapter). In any event it will lose a lot of power.*

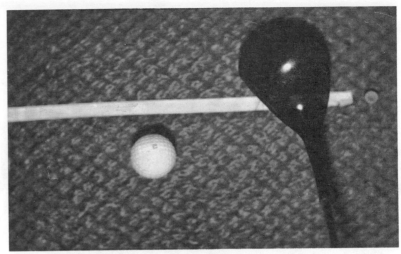

19:9 *Off the heel. Here the clubface is twisted shut by the force of the blow and the ball starts to the left, but may curve part way back towards the intended line. Like the shot off the toe, the heeled shot lacks power.*

ball to the right, the front (i.e. the part nearest the hole) to the left. This is sometimes called the 'gear effect' since the clubhead and ball are working upon each other like two enmeshed gear-wheels.

The effect is a small one in an iron clubhead whose centre of gravity is close to the face, but it is still there; and that is why shots struck on the heel or toe on iron clubs of thicker-bladed sets do not hook or slice quite so strongly as you might expect them to from the other forces involved.

It is when we come to look at off-centre impact with wooden clubs that the gear effect comes to the fore.

As with irons, the clubface is turned at an angle to the intended direction of flight, making a heeled shot start to the left and a toed shot start to the right. But this time the simple spin effect of 'opening' or 'closing' the face will be more than just *reduced* by the gear effect; it will be completely over-ridden by it. This is a direct result of the point of contact being well ahead, and not merely to the side, of the centre of gravity. Fig. 19:10 shows this.

The result is that if the ball were to be struck near the heel of a driver with a completely flat face, it would start left but *slice* (instead of hooking), and if struck near the toe would

start right but *hook* (instead of slicing). These effects would be so pronounced as to swing the shot completely off the fairway. A toed shot, for instance, would start off slightly to the right and then curve across to the rough on the left.

The reader will have noticed a tendency for a heeled drive to slice and a toed drive to hook, but not to the extent described. The reason is that wooden clubheads are made with a very slight convex curve outwards in all directions from the best striking part in the middle of the clubface. This convexity increases the angle-spin effect, without increasing the gear effect, until the two are more or less matched up.

Not completely matched, though. The gear effect is always left slightly in the ascendancy; so that a shot struck off the heel, and thus starting off to the left of the line, will still tend to curve a little back towards the middle of the fairway; and one struck off the toe, and thus starting off to the right, will tend to draw back towards the middle. In both cases, this is preferable to exactly matching sidespin and gear effect so that the ball flies straight off on any line the twist of the clubhead sends it on.

There is, of course, no simple answer here, which can give a player a clubface that automatically sends the ball straight, no

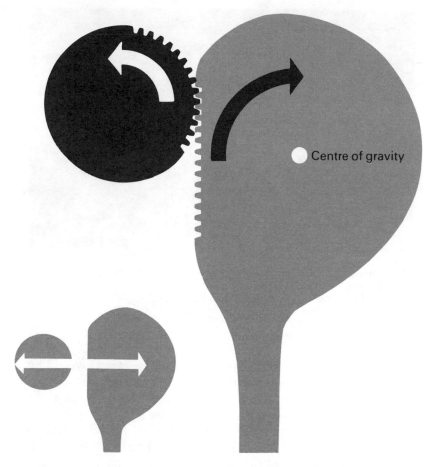

matter whereabouts on the clubface he hits it. In the case of irons—in which simple sidespin overrides gear effect—a slightly concave clubface might help to reduce the ill-effects of off-centre striking, but is expressly forbidden by the Rules of Golf.

In the case of woods, the precise balance of effects will depend upon all manner of variations in the player's individual striking. The best that clubmakers can do to help players in general is to give them wooden clubfaces which make sure a heeled shot *tends* to come back from the left, and a toed shot *tends* to come back from the right. And this is what they do.

Off-centre shots always lose length

The thing to remember above all, though, about any shot struck *off-centre* to the clubface is that, apart from the thinned shot with the lofted irons, whatever else may happen it will *always* lose length, through losing that part of the power of the stroke wasted in turning the clubface.

Thus the only way both to produce maximum length—especially from a drive—and to range all the clubs in the bag to a consistent and reliable distance of striking, is to hit the ball in the 'sweet spot' of the clubface all the time.

The latitude allowed a player in this respect depends on the design of the clubhead; but, typically, a scratch player's drive will lose three yards in carry when struck a quarter of an inch away from the sweet spot, twelve yards when struck half an inch away, and nearly thirty yards when the error is three-quarters of an inch.

These figures refer to shots hit towards the toe or heel of the club. The latitude for hitting high or low on the face is even smaller. The overall margin for error, in fact, is about a quarter of an inch from the sweet spot; or a circle smaller than a sixpence.

An effect on the golfer's hands

Steel shafts have high torsional rigidity; that is, they twist very much less easily than they bend. This means that, in an off-centre blow which twists the clubface open or closed, the twist effect is passed up the shaft very rapidly and sharply to the player's hands.

So if you find after you have played a shot, that the club has twisted in your hands, do not necessarily blame weak hands or a poor grip. More often than not it will have been caused by failing to hit the ball on the centre of the clubface.

19:10 *Why a heeled drive usually slices, and a toed one hooks: the 'gear effect'. This is most easily understood if we imagine the clubhead to be stationary and the ball projected at it. If it strikes the clubface opposite the centre of gravity of the clubhead, it just knocks the clubhead straight back; but if it strikes the face near the toe it not only knocks the clubhead back, but in addition sets it turning around its centre of gravity. This effectively 'opens' the clubface a little during the period of contact with the ball, which in the absence of any other effect would then take on the slicing spin normally caused by an open face. However, if the centre of gravity of the clubhead lies some distance back from the clubface, as it does in a driver for example, the rotation set up by the off-centre blow causes the point of contact between clubface and ball to move sideways (towards the top of the page in the case illustrated) as well as back. This pushes the clubface across the back of the ball, and so imparts, in the case of a toed shot, hooking spin, which, with a perfectly flat-faced driver is more than enough to counteract the slight opening of the clubface. The same argument holds for heeled shots, which will tend to take on slicing spin. The effect has been called the 'gear effect' since ball and clubface behave like two enmeshed gear wheels, with the clubface rotating in one direction and the ball in the other.*

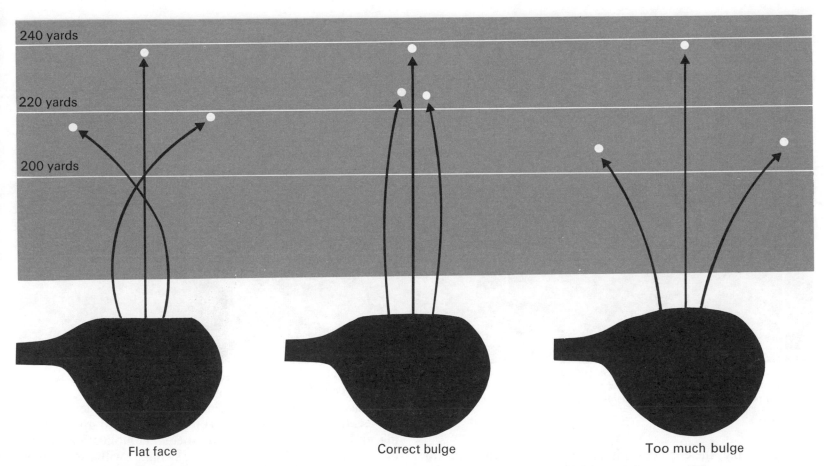

240 yards

220 yards

200 yards

Flat face   Correct bulge   Too much bulge

19:11 *Getting the right amount of 'bulge' on a driver. When the ball is hit near the toe of a driver two opposing effects come into play. First, the force of the blow 'opens' the face, thus sending the ball off a little to the right of the intended line, and tending also to impart slicing spin to it; and second, the 'gear effect' (see text and Fig. 19:10) imparts hooking spin. With a perfectly flat-faced driver (left) the gear effect predominates and a 'toed' shot sets off to the right but hooks violently back across the intended line to the rough on the other side. A convex bulge on the face of the driver can help restore a balance, simply because it makes the toe of the club a little open (and the heel a little shut). The correct amount of bulge (middle diagram) leaves the gear effect very slightly in the ascendant, and imparts just enough hooking spin to a toed shot to bring it back to the middle of the fairway. Too much bulge (right) gives the gear effect no chance to counteract the extreme openness of the toe of the club-face. Heeled shots are affected in a similar way by bulging the clubface.*

The crooked shots which fly straight

No, there is no contradiction in this heading. It merely stresses the point that a shot which finishes to the right or left of the target may still have been a perfectly straight golf shot; at least in the sense that it did not curve in flight. This is true whether it ends five yards from the target or twenty yards into the rough, or even way out into the fairway of a different hole. Such a shot, hit to the right is usually called a 'push'; hit to the left, a 'pull'.

It flies straight off on the wrong line simply because the player has struck it fairly and squarely in the wrong direction. No complicated error in impact ballistics is involved. The clubface is closely aligned to the direction of swing, as it should be. The trouble has started earlier than that by the player somehow getting his whole hub action aligned towards the point the ball's flight reveals, instead of towards the target.

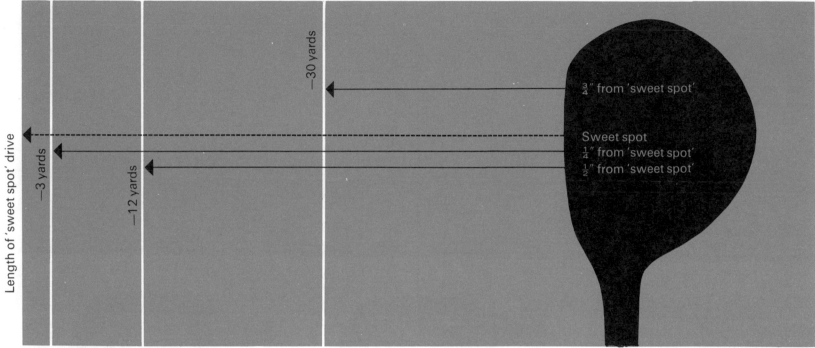

Length of 'sweet spot' drive

—3 yards

—12 yards

—30 yards

¾" from 'sweet spot'

Sweet spot
¼" from 'sweet spot'
½" from 'sweet spot'

19:12 *How much distance you lose by missing the 'sweet spot'. The exact amounts will vary from club to club and from player to player, but these are typical of the yardage lost by a scratch golfer when he hits the ball off-centre by varying amounts.*

In principle, the correction is the simplest possible one: to stop swinging off-line to target and start swinging on-line. And that is really all there is to be said about it.

Unfortunately, in practice things are not always as simple as that. The player may, for instance (as many week-end golfers do all the time), have fallen into the habit of using a bad grip or a shut or open face, and then of shifting his stance around in order to 'swing across himself', thus making some sort of square contact and getting the ball to fly reasonably straight most of the time.

The result can very often be a perfectly straight drive bang up the middle of the fairway. Whether it may be better for any individual player to try to correct both faults, or to go on working to adjust them to each other so that they cancel each other out, is a matter for a professional's judgment and the player's preference in any individual case.

One thing is certain, though. Using two balancing errors

like this will always tend to make it more difficult for any player to produce his best form consistently.

It may, moreover, lose him a certain amount of length from the tee, through the extra effort likely to be used up in adjusting and controlling two simultaneous complications to the basic simplest possible model-type swing. It will also be likely to cost him greater effort in concentration throughout his round, especially in stroke-play competition, and he will carry with him all the time a potent source of breakdown under pressure.

The fact that the ball is flying straight through the air, then, in whatever direction it takes from impact, should not make any player too cocksure that all his professional needs to tell him is how to realign his swing.

Even for the most extreme example of a double-correction player, however, it remains true to say that in making the ball fly in a straight line through the air and with a normal trajectory, he is making near perfect contact between the clubhead and the ball, in relation to whatever line he is swinging the club upon; and this is true no matter how awkward and complicated may be his method of swinging the club upon that line.

Chapter 20

Golf's Crooked Shots: The Practical Mechanics of Slicing and Hooking

Here we begin to touch upon the aerodynamics of golf. The science of spin, of golf ball trajectories and of a ball's curving in the air during its flight, is a complicated, if fascinating, field of research. Chapters 24 and 25 report something of what has been discovered about it.

At this stage, in order to help make clear the practical side of it as it affects the ball's behaviour upon the course, the reader is asked to accept three fairly straightforward propositions, each put in a simplified form, but none the less true in practice.

1. A ball will always tend to curve in its flight through the air if it is spinning upon its own axis; and, unless other forces interfere, it will curve in whatever direction its front surface is spinning.

2. A player is able to make his ball carry the distance it does through the air only because he puts 'backspin' on it. The club actually does this for him, by hitting the ball a slightly glancing blow as a result of the face being set back according to its degree of loft.

Even a driver's face is set back at 10° or so; and this is enough to set the ball spinning at about sixty revolutions per second as it flies away at 150 miles per hour for a drive of 250 yards. In every stroke in golf (apart from some complete mishits and some putts) backspin is applied to the ball. The ball thus tries all the way to curve upwards in flight. Gravity, of course, prevents it doing so to any appreciable extent; nevertheless it carries much further through the air than it would do without spin.

3. Shots which curve to one side or the other in their flight through the air do so because sidespin has been applied as well. It is applied in exactly the same way as backspin —by the clubface not being at right angles to the direction in which it is travelling as it hits the ball.

A ball cannot, of course, spin in two directions at once. What happens is that, when sidespin is applied, instead of spinning around a horizontal axis, it spins about a slightly inclined axis, as Fig. 20:2 shows. Thus a ball hardly ever curves simply to right or left, but is nearly always making a lifting effort as well.

The simplest curve effect: loft at an angle

This is something the golfer is perfectly familiar with. The simplest way it arises is when he is playing an iron shot off ground which is not level. If the ball is *below* his feet at the address, he can expect the shot to curve to the right in the air; while if it lies *above* his feet he can expect it to curve to the left.

You can easily see how this happens if you imagine yourself trying to use a lofted iron to hit a ball, somehow stuck on to the side of a wall at about head height.

It's not any effect these lies have upon weight, balance, or wrist action that produces the curved flight, but simply the way the player has to apply the club with its bottom edge more or less parallel to the surface of the turf. The sidespin, in this sort of situation, thus comes simply from the angle of lie at which he has to make contact; and it comes even if he swings the clubface perfectly straight and square through the ball in relation to the lie. It is not really 'sidespin' at all, but loft at an angle.

There are several methods of dealing with the difficulty posed by sidehill lies. You can simply aim off and allow the curved shot to take place; or you can try to open or close the clubface at impact to counteract the effect of the slope (open, when the ball is above the feet). If sidehill lies are common on your home course, it may even be worth having clubs with a rounder sole than usual to allow you to use something like your usual plane of swing on these lies, without fear of digging the heel or toe of the club into the ground.

20:1 *Even a drive has backspin. Here two 'flash' exposures on the one picture show the ball to have turned through 30° in 1·2 milliseconds, corresponding to a backspin rate of 70 revs per second.*

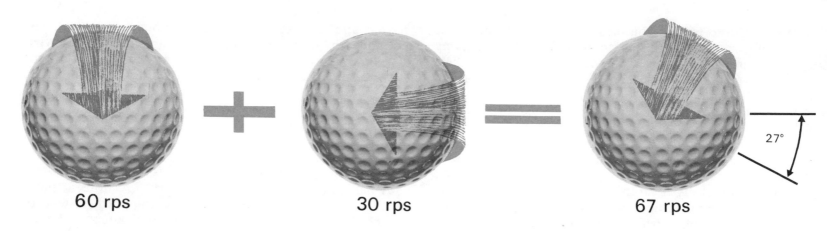

60 rps + **30 rps** = **67 rps** 27°

20:2 *Combining spins in two directions. Pure backspin (around a horizontal axis) and pure sideways spin (around a vertical axis) combine to give spin around a tilted axis between the two. The greater the sidespin (for a given amount of backspin) the more the resultant axis of spin will be inclined to the horizontal. The revs per second (rps) are typical values for a badly sliced drive*

True sidespin: the basic rule

All the other curved shots of golf arise from a quite different cause: the clubface not being swung through the ball square to the line of swing. By 'square', in this context, we do not mean exactly aimed at the line to the hole; but exactly aligned at 90° to the direction in which the clubhead is travelling at impact.

A straight-flying on-target shot, of course, will be 'square' in both these senses. Both the aim of the clubface, and the aim of the swing, will be correctly aligned towards the target. In curving-flight shots, though, the clubface and line of swing point in different directions at impact, whether either is aligned to the intended line to the hole or not.

Applying sidespin: how hooks and slices begin

We have already seen how sidespin can result from not hitting the ball in the middle of the clubface. We now look at how it can be produced when the ball *is* struck in the middle of the clubface.

In practice, of course, the two effects can and do occur together. But for the rest of this chapter we are going to consider only true sidespin effects from impact in the middle of the clubface. These are responsible, in the main, for most of the ordinary golfer's hooks and slices. They are all the result of an oblique blow between clubface and ball, which makes the ball move across the face of the club during impact, thus

20:3 *Loft at an angle produces sidespin. If the golfer simply swings normally through the ball from this sort of lie, his nine-iron shot will hook violently, since, with the sole of the club fairly grounded, the loft will point the face to the left of the line. He can counteract this in several ways, for example by deliberately holding the blade of the club open, or simply by aiming well to the right and letting the hook happen, or more likely by a combination of both.*

spinning the front of the ball towards the left or the right.

To make discussion of the 'benders' of golf as clear as possible, we ask the reader to forget backspin for the time being; and consider only what will happen if the ball is struck in the centre of its face with a driver with no loft on the face at all.

There is a general rule which governs all shots hit in this way. The more sidespin effect, the less speed off the clubface, and usually the less carry through the air. This is true for any shot with any club of any degree of loft: simply because of the glancing nature of the blow which produces the spin.

In scientific terminology, only a *component* of the clubhead's momentum is being used to propel the ball forward on its way. That is to say, whether a blow is oblique by virtue of the loft on the club, or by misalignment of the clubface relative to the swing direction, the speed imparted to the ball will be reduced compared with the absolutely square-on impact; and the more oblique the blow, the less will be the forward speed of the ball.

Golfers recognize two main groups of curving shots: the spin-to-the-left family of draw, hook, quick-hook and duck-hook; and the spin-to-the-right family of fade, cut, slice and what we might call the 'push-and-slice'.

The draw and the fade are the respectable members of each family; the ones which curve only slightly and which the golfer may play intentionally (or, at least, after the shot, claim to have played intentionally). In truth, though, the boundaries between the territories of the different members of each family are never very clearly marked; and the golfer's terminology for them reflects more the direction of starting off and degree of spin applied to them than anything else.

All those in Fig. 20:5, for instance, are 'hooks' of a kind: in that the direction of the blow is obliquely to the right of the direction in which the clubface is pointing. Thus all of them will spin to the left, and as a result curve to the left in flight. But where some will curve the ball only a little in the air, a really shut face as in (a) will send the ball off to the left of the line, even when the clubhead is being swung towards the right of it; and will correspondingly make the ball curve in the air very sharply indeed.

The amount of curve in the air is the direct result, of course, of the size of the angle at impact between the aim of the swing and the aim of the clubface. This, for instance, is why, although the clubface points in exactly the same direction in either case,

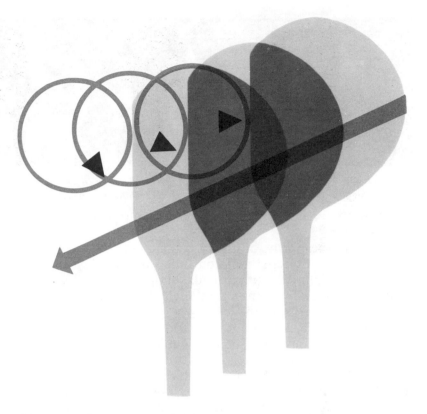

20:4 *How sidespin is imparted if the swing direction and the direction in which the clubface is pointing are not the same. The ball tends to slide and roll along the clubface, and, in the case illustrated, takes on slicing spin.*

(a) will end up further into the rough on the left than (b), even though the swing into impact (b) is to the left to begin with, and that into (a) is actually to the right.

The intentional 'draw' is only a slight hook started off a little to the right of the target, and then brought back towards it by the sidespin arising from the comparatively small difference of angle between the line of swing and the line of aim of the clubface. Both will be aimed slightly to the right of the intended line; but the face less so than the swing, so producing the slight sidespin needed to bring the ball back, while still starting it off to the right of target. Something like (c) in the diagram.

The draw is thus in no way different in kind from all the other members of the hook family: any more than is that maximum-curve full-blooded hook which an expert may use

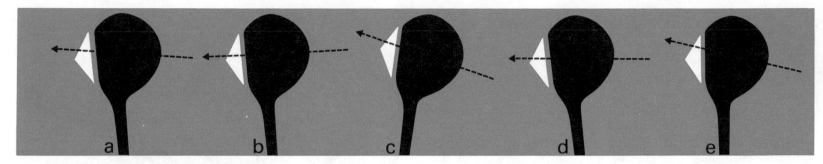

20:5 *Five hooking impacts. In each of them the swing-direction (dotted arrow) is to the right of the clubface direction of aim (broad white arrowhead).*

to bring the ball around a clump of trees to a green hidden behind them.

Like all other forms of intentional spin-effects, both these trajectories are selected and controlled by the player as the best sort of flight for that particular shot; maybe to bring the ball into a green from the safest angle despite having driven too far to the left from the tee.

What we have said about the various forms of hook goes also for the various forms of slice, cut, fade etc.; but with the mechanics of them reversed. For a true right-hand sidespin of any kind, the clubface aims to the right of the direction in which the clubhead is being swung; and sidespin is thus imparted in the same way as for a hook, but in the opposite direction.

The direction the ball starts off in

Which is more important in determining the direction the ball starts off on: the direction in which the clubface is pointing or the direction of clubhead travel?

A ball will always leave a clubface somewhere between these directions; but usually nearer the direction along which the clubface is pointing than that along which it is being swung.

In the case illustrated (Fig. 20:6), the angle between these two is 20° and in a full shot an average golf ball would go off at perhaps 7° to the right of the perpendicular to the clubface. (If the face of the club were perfectly smooth it would leave exactly at right angles to the clubface; in a putt the angle would be 4° or 5°.)

Diagnosing the fault from the way the ball flies

A lot of sidespin can be put on the ball, either way, by quite

small misalignments of clubface to swing line. If the two differ by only 1°, the impact will put several hundred revolutions per minute of sidespin on the ball: quite enough to make it swerve seven or eight yards off the line it sets out upon by the time it travels 200 yards from the tee.

Thus, if a fairway is forty yards wide, and the clubface at impact points directly up the middle of it, a swing only 3° off line to either side at impact will be more than enough to put the ball into the rough. Exactly the same will apply if the *clubhead* is swung dead straight through impact towards the middle of the fairway, but the *clubface* is 3° out of alignment with it, again either way.

How much more dangerous this is in play than a push or pull can be illustrated by the comparison: hitting a straight square shot 3° off the intended line will land it only ten yards off course at 200 yards from the tee—an acceptable error in most drives.

The player can usually tell which error is responsible for a curving shot of this kind by observing the flight of the ball.

If it is only the swing which is off line to the target, the ball will start off slightly to one side of the line up the middle of the fairway, but then curve back and away towards the rough on the *other* side.

If the swing is straight, and it is the clubface which is out of true to it, then the ball will again start off to one side of the centre-line but will this time curve further away into the rough on the *same* side.

Very often both the swing and the clubface are misaligned to the target. Under these circumstances almost any result is possible: ranging from the banana shot which starts off towards the deep rough, but arrives back and finishes in the middle of the fairway, to the unbelievably curving slice, which starts towards the right and soars farther and farther off line.

It is very depressing, too, for the man who keeps hitting that

124

sort of shot to find that the harder he tries to keep the ball up the left of the fairway, the more viciously it curves away to the right. But the explanation is quite simple once he knows it. As his original slice came from aiming the clubface to the right of the line he was swinging on, the more he tries to keep the ball left by swinging still further to the left, the more disastrous becomes the angle at which he swings his clubhead across the line upon which he is aiming his clubface.

Here is a situation where a man should head for his club professional, who should be able to see what is happening a

lot more clearly than the player can himself. Failing that, a friend should at least be able to tell him whether he is swinging the clubhead across the line or not.

It would seem, from general observation of long-handicap golfers, that of the two errors causing unwanted hooks and slices, swinging the club off-line to target tends to become an ingrained habit, while misaligning the clubface tends to fluctuate erratically. A habitual slicer is thus nearly always a habitual out-to-in swinger, while a very erratic player is more likely to be suffering from inability to control the clubface

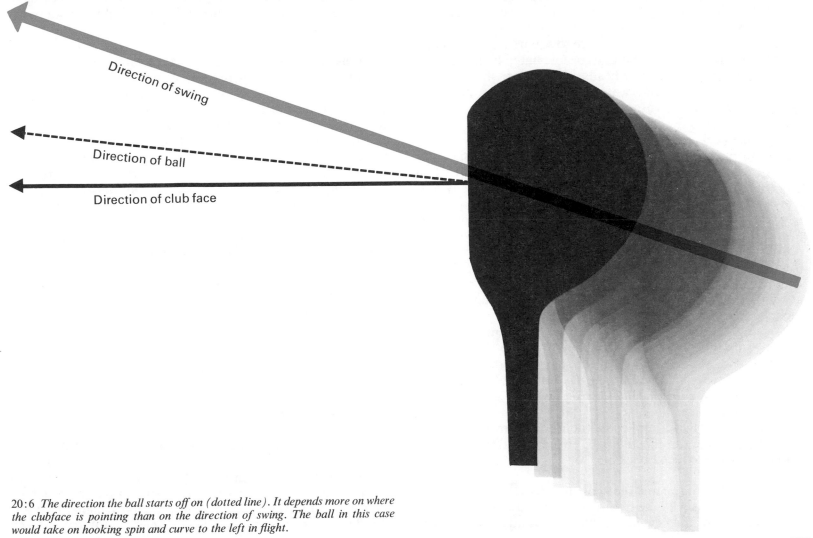

Direction of swing

Direction of ball

Direction of club face

20:6 *The direction the ball starts off on (dotted line). It depends more on where the clubface is pointing than on the direction of swing. The ball in this case would take on hooking spin and curve to the left in flight.*

alignment rather than from variations in the swing direction.

Of course, the two are connected, both mechanically and mentally. If the habitual slicer is content to aim down the left and let his slice take the ball back, he will probably develop a fairly consistent swing and clubface control will not be so difficult. If, however, he is dissatisfied with his slice he may well experiment with his grip and hand action in order to 'cure' it. These are easier to change than the swing direction and produce a greater variety of results; so that after a few attempts he can often achieve his object—a straight shot. In doing it this way, though, he may entirely lose the feeling of consistency in his swing, and is liable, moreover, to make his clubface alignment very erratic.

The kind of slice caused by failure to square up the clubface in time for impact, can sometimes be alleviated by using clubs with thinner grips, or lighter heads, or whippier shafts—all of which, in slightly different ways, tend to speed up the rate at which the clubhead turns into impact.

Why hooks duck and slices soar

So far we have talked as if, spin for spin, hooks and slices behave in much the same way. But every golfer knows that they don't: that, by and large, hooked shots tend to fly low, sometimes extremely low, and run when they hit the ground, whereas slices tend to fly high and stop quickly when they pitch.

Why should this be? The answer lies in the asymmetry of the golf swing and so, of the club. The shaft comes into the head at about 55° from the horizontal as it lies upon the ground, and the golfer swings the clubhead through a plane inclined at anything from 45° to 60°.

Turning the face of the club to the right thus, in effect, *increases* its loft (try it) and consequently both the height at which it sends the ball off and at the same time the amount of backspin it gives it. It doesn't take a great deal of this effect to produce the characteristically soaring flight we associate with a full-blooded slice.

Exactly the reverse applies to the hook. Turning the face to the left *reduces* the effective loft, and thus starts the ball off lower and with reduced backspin too.

Keeping the fade down and the hook up

This, of course, is why the expert player aiming to play a fade will often 'hood' the face of the club, by standing a bit ahead

126

of the normal stance position and then carrying his hands through well ahead of the clubhead as it strikes the ball. This effectively keeps the loft down to normal, despite having the clubface slightly open to the line of his swing.

It is correspondingly why, when aiming to play a big high hook round a tree, the expert will be very likely to play the ball more forward in his stance than usual and whip the head through ahead of his hands, so far as the lie permits. By so doing he maintains or even increases the effective loft, despite the turning of the clubface to the left. If he does not do something like this, the aiming of the face to the left of the line of his swing will tend to produce a ducking flight instead of the trajectory he needs.

The pros and cons of the intentional fade or draw

It is often said that a method of swinging which attempts to fade or draw long shots is more reliable than one which attempts to hit them dead straight; and there is considerable argument about which of these two shots makes for better scoring. Several professional golfers—for example, Hogan, Alliss and Palmer—are said to have altered their swings more than once in order to use one or other as their basic long shot.

The 'faders' claim that their shot rarely *runs* into trouble, whereas the draw can; and that if the fade degenerates into a slice it will at least get off the ground, and therefore travel a respectable distance albeit into the rough, whereas the quick hook simply dives to earth a short distance from the tee.

The 'drawers', on the other hand, point to the extra distance gained by their shot due to its more lively run up the fairway, and to the fact that really bad slices usually go farther off the line than really bad hooks.

Both have substance in their arguments, so there is no firm 'answer' on the point. A lot, though, must depend on the particular course. The only low-handicap man we ever heard of to retire from a match play competition through running out of golf balls before actually being beaten, was at the time using what he called the 'Hogan fade'—on a course lined with gorse all the way.

Except where an obstacle makes a curving shot desirable, the whole business of deliberately playing with fade or draw can too easily be based on fallacious argument. It may be that psychologically a player feels 'safer' aiming for the rough on the right and trying to draw (or for the left rough and trying to fade) rather than aiming down the middle and trying to hit the ball straight; but it is a fact that, in the mechanics of the thing, he leaves himself no more room for error whatsoever.

If he aims to start the ball off for the left rough (say twenty yards left of the centre of the fairway) and 'fade' it back to the middle, then the degree of error which will produce instead a pull which flies straight into the rough on the left, or a slice which curves right across into the rough on the right, is almost exactly that which will produce a hook or slice to the rough either side for a man aiming to hit a straight shot down the middle of the fairway.

There is also the fact that the man aiming to draw or fade, in order to bring the stroke off consistently each time, needs to make at least two adjustments to his simplest action (swing-line, and clubface-aim). He is thus giving himself more work to do, both physically and mentally, than the man who just tries to hit the ball along in the simplest possible way.

Summing up the benders

To sum up, there are four factors which can make a ball fly off the line intended for it.

1. Using a perfect 'level stance' swing from a sideways sloping lie.
2. Hitting the ball off-centre upon the clubface.
3. Swinging the clubhead towards the left or the right of the true line towards the target at impact.
4. Having the clubface pointing at impact to the left or to the right of the direction along which the clubhead is being swung through the ball.

Pulls and pushes, caused as in 3 above, will travel just as far through the air as ordinary straight shots. True sidespin strokes, as in 4 above, will tend to lose length of carry mainly because the blow will have been an oblique one, but also, at least in the case of the drive, through soaring above, or ducking below the best flight path through the air. (Hooks, though, may sometimes gain enough in run to make up for this, especially on hard ground with a wind from the right.)

Off-centre blows, as in 2 above, will tend to lose both carry and total length every time, through the waste of energy at impact in turning the clubhead.

Thus the purely practical arguments for aiming to make the ball fly straight from the centre of the clubface whenever possible are by no means negligible; and, of course, in terms of approximating most closely to the simplicity of the model, the straight-flying shot has the advantage every time.

Chapter 21

Can we, indeed dare we, say anything about putting, that part of the game in which results seem at times to be totally unrelated to method or logic? A man on good terms with his putter can defy the professors of science and golf and still collect the money.

Yet the motion of the ball across the green is not at all too difficult to analyse. The trouble is that it is a very human golfer who has to start the process off; and, no matter how familiar he may be with Newton's Laws of Motion, he may find it difficult to set the ball rolling on the course they would predict.

The knowledge that the task requires negligible physical effort, and indeed is absurdly simple on the face of it, is no help at all either.

Nevertheless there are several things which science can say about putting which will, at least, sweep away some of the complicated misconceptions that clutter up the minds of many golfers. By leaving them free to concentrate on the essentials, this may help their putting.

Three parts to the mechanics of putting
As with the drive, or any other golf shot, there are three separate mechanical processes to be considered. There's the whole business of getting the right part of the clubface to the ball, moving in the right direction and at the right speed; there's the actual impact between putter and ball; and finally there's the roll of the ball across the green.

The first process, the technique of putting, is, of course, only partly determined by mechanical considerations; it has physiological, anatomical and—perhaps most important of all—mental aspects as well.

Let's deal first with the pure mechanics, starting with impact. What happens at impact very obviously affects the way the ball will roll across the green. But it also decides the best way to hit any putt: technique is not an end in itself, but merely a way of achieving the mechanical requirements of the sort of impact you want. This is true of all golf shots: to have a clear idea of what is desirable and what undesirable, what is possible and what impossible, in the actual contact between clubhead and ball, makes it much easier to devise and understand the best ways of swinging the club.

Split second impact
The most important thing to realize about impact in a putt is

that it is basically just like impact in a drive; it lasts a very short time indeed, from which it follows (see Chapter 22) that the putter head, while actually in contact with the ball, behaves almost as though it were disconnected from the shaft. The time of contact varies from half a millisecond (the same as for a drive) in a long putt to about three-quarters of a millisecond in a short tap-in putt. This means, for example, that on a putt of six feet, the head of the putter will travel only about a fortieth of an inch while in contact with the ball.

These figures are theoretical predictions; but the team verified them experimentally. The time of contact between ball and clubface was checked by recording the times of making and breaking an electric current between the putter and a specially prepared ball. The distance of travel was measured by stopping the follow-through of a machine-swung putter, by means of solidly fixed wooden blocks, a very short distance after first contact with the ball, and finding out how much the putt was affected.

For example, with the putter head moving into impact at about twelve feet per second, as it would for a twenty-foot putt on greens of average speed, the time of contact between putter and ball turned out to be 0·6 millisecond. The distance the putter head travelled in this time was 0·07 inch.

The putting machine used in this, and in other experiments described in this chapter, was constructed by an enthusiastic West of England amateur golfer, Trevor Schofield. In essence, it swings the putter pendulum-fashion, in a plane adjusted to the lie of the putter. By drawing it back to the same point each time and releasing it, the putter can be made to strike the ball very consistently.

Putts skid first, then roll
Another point in the mechanics of putting impact which has an important bearing on the technique of putting is that, for all practical purposes, it is impossible with a normal putter to put any useful spin on the ball. Putters often have a few degrees of loft, which can impart a very small amount of backspin; but it cannot amount to more than one or two revolutions per second, and it will make little or no difference to the putt.

The reason for this lies in the way the ball moves across the green immediately after being struck with a putter. At first it doesn't roll at all, but slides. As it does so, friction between its cover and the grass begins at once to slow it down; and since

21:1 *The putting machine used in the tests. Trevor Schofield, who constructed it, is seen demonstrating how hitting the ball off the toe or heel of the putter leaves the putt short and to one side or other of the intended line.*

this friction is acting upon the circumference of the ball, it also makes the ball start to spin. At first, nevertheless, it continues to slide because it is not yet spinning fast enough to keep up with its forward speed across the green.

The frictional force is continuously increasing the spin rate and reducing the forward speed, though; and so there soon comes a time when the two speeds 'match'; with the ball now spinning at just the right speed to roll, instead of slide.

From this point on, there is no further slipping at the point of contact between ball and ground, friction ceases, and the ball rolls the rest of the way till it stops. Generally speaking, there is much less resistance to a rolling ball than there is by frictional resistance to a sliding one; so from now on the ball slows up much more gradually than it did while it was still sliding. This is all shown diagrammatically in Fig. 21:2.

It is worth noting here that the speed of rotation of the ball reaches its greatest at the moment when sliding stops. (This point, which is obvious and of no great consequence in the context of the putt, will be an extremely important one to bear in mind when we talk, in Chapter 23, about the application of spin to the ball in a full shot.)

How far any putt skids before it starts to roll will, of course, depend on what the surface of the green is like; but, for a ball set off without spin, a liberal estimate of the skidding phase would be 20% of the total length of the putt: say four feet in a twenty-foot putt. Even a five-foot putt will skid for about its first foot of travel.

Obviously, for any given strength of hit, the *distance* travelled before rolling starts depends on the roughness of the grass; but the *speed* at which the ball is moving when it starts to roll does not. It is the same for any level surface. For example, a ball leaving the clubface at twenty feet per second would start true rolling when it slowed down to about 14·6 feet per second, whether the putt was struck across a green as rough as a fairway, or one as smooth as a billiard table.

The main point to appreciate in all this is that, on any sort of putt, and however it is struck, the ball will simply be rolling —just rolling—after quite a small fraction of its total travel— certainly long before it reaches the hole. Therefore, any slight topspin, backspin or sidespin which can be applied to it by the putter will have no effect at all on the major part of its path, nor on the likelihood of its diving into the hole.

This is shown in Fig. 21:3 for three putts which all set off at seventeen feet per second but with different spins imparted to

129

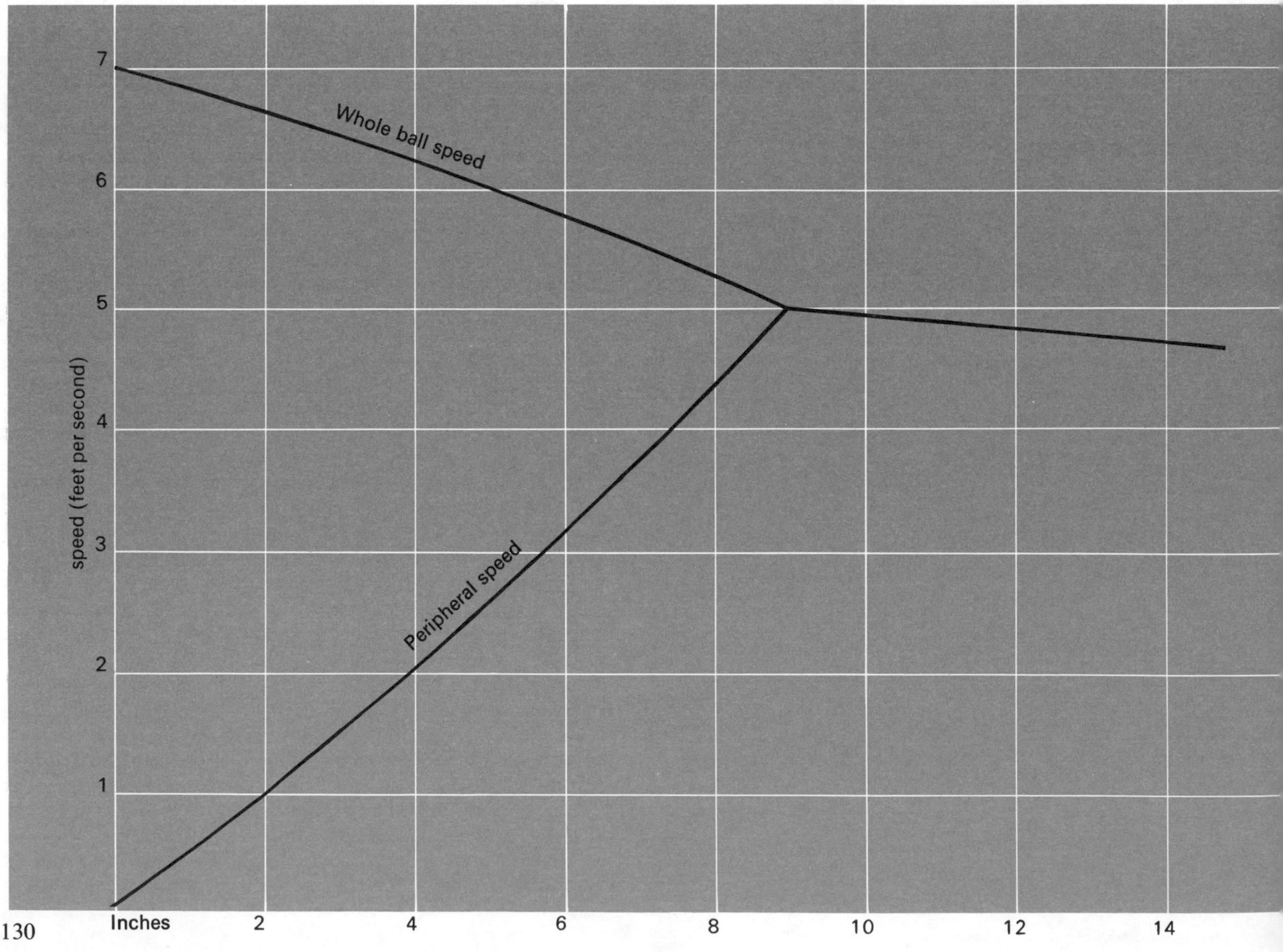

speed (feet per second)

Whole ball speed

Peripheral speed

7

6

5

4

3

2

1

130   Inches   2   4   6   8   10   12   14

them—no spin, 2·2 revolutions per second backspin, and 2·2 revolutions per second topspin. These are roughly the speed and the rates of spin which would be produced by a loftless putter, travelling at eleven or twelve feet per second: first horizontally (no spin), second downward at about 5° to the horizontal, but with the face pointing horizontally (backspin), and third upwards at about 5° to the horizontal, but with the face pointing horizontally (topspin). These spins are, in fact, about as great as could be expected on any properly struck putt (i.e. not topped).

For all practical purposes, as the diagram shows, the three end-results are the same.

On the course, things might not work out quite like this. In all but the last few inches of an actual putt on a golf green, the ball tends to ride along the top of the grass, or even move in a series of shallow bounces; and it rises to this slightly elevated level from its rest position, nestling down in the grass, within a few inches of leaving the face of the putter.* This inevitably makes it bounce a little at first; and it is to minimize the effect of the bouncing that most putters have a few degrees of loft.

The direction in which the putter head is travelling may also affect things a little in this way. In particular, any putt hit downwards will tend to jump more than usual; and thus may be more liable to behave unpredictably, before it settles down to rolling. By striking a ball well above its middle (about two-thirds of the way up) it is theoretically possible to start it rolling from the moment it leaves the putter face; but this would be a half top, which, however effective on the hard surface of the billiard table, is no good on the softer golf green. On a green, here again, the ball will set off with a jump.

The conclusion must therefore be that deliberate efforts to impart topspin—or backspin—to a putt are not worth while: at least not for the effect spin has on the motion of the ball. To

21:2 Profile of a five-foot putt on a very true green. The ball sets off without spin at a speed of 7 ft per sec and slides at first. While it does so, friction both slows it up, and imparts forward spin. Thus the 'whole ball speed' drops and the 'peripheral speed'—the speed at which the circumference of the ball is turning around its centre—rises. (A peripheral speed of 5 ft per sec corresponds to a speed of rotation of just under 12 revs per sec.) When the whole ball speed and the peripheral speed eventually become equal, then there is no relative movement between the ball and the green at the point of contact, sliding friction stops, and the ball simply rolls. The (usually) considerably smaller rolling resistance then slows the ball down more gradually. This particular putt would come to rest in just under 5 feet.

* See article by R. D. Smyth in *Golf World,* June 1967.

the extent that attempting to put spin on the ball can change any player's putting stroke, there is, of course, the possibility that it will improve his putting; but this is a change in technique (to which we return later) not an effect of spin.

You can't slice or hook a putt

Sidespin on a putt comes into much the same category as topspin or backspin. We can put a bit more of it on, since the blade of the club can be drawn across the ball at quite a sharp angle; but its effect is still negligible. Once again, after a short distance, the ball will simply be rolling across the green.

In theory, it is possible to make the ball curve in the early sliding part of its path; but even then only by the simultaneous application of sidespin together with *appreciable* topspin or backspin, so as to make the ball spin about a horizontal axis along the line of play, in the same sort of way as a rifle bullet does. But it is almost impossible to do this with a putter. It seems, at least, extremely unlikely that by applying ordinary sidespin to the ball we can ever hook or slice a putt; that is, actually make it bend effectively and to order, relative to its free-rolling path.

If we think about it for a moment we soon realize that there is absolutely no reason for ever believing we could. The fact that clockwise spin (looking down on the ball) causes a slice (a curve to the right) in a drive whistling at high speed through the air has no relevance at all to the effect of spin on a ball rolling slowly across a green. In the drive the motion of the ball is determined by aerodynamic forces; in the putt we can completely ignore them.

Returning to the statement made above, that, coupled with appreciable backspin or topspin, sidespin can cause the ball to curve whilst sliding, you will see that even then precisely the opposite may happen on the ground to what happens in the air. Perhaps the most familiar example of this is to be found on the billiard table, where a ball hit with what the golfer would regard as slicing spin may curve not to the right, but to the left. Here the top of the ball is hit in a downward direction, as well as on the left side, and spin about the horizontal axis is therefore '*left-handed*' spin (with the top of the ball moving to the left). Even in this case, where, moreover, the amount of spin is much larger than the golfer could ever impart with his putter, the swerve takes place only in the first few inches of a path that would measure twenty feet or more.

We can sometimes see the exactly opposite effect of com-

131

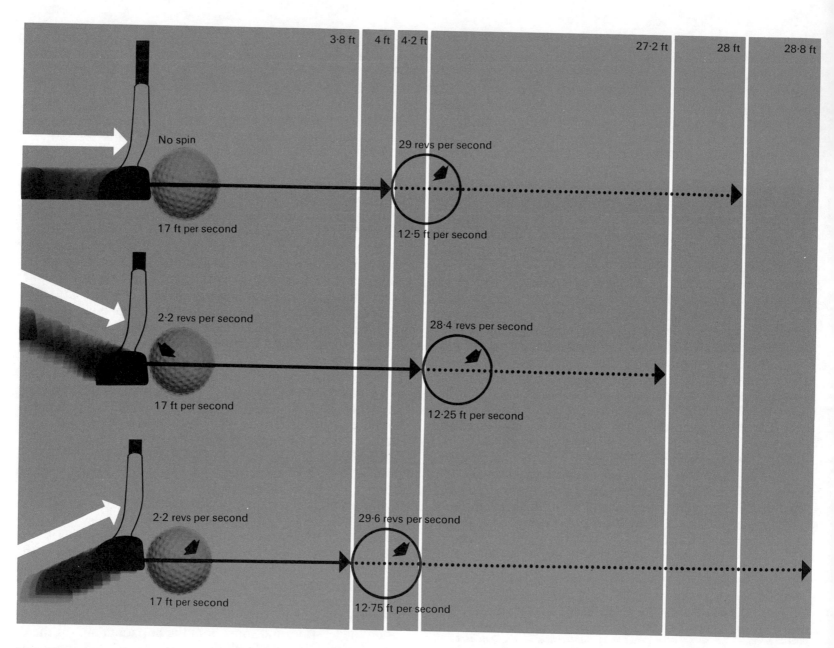

21:3 *The distance a putt travels is very little affected by spin. All three putts shown set off at the same speed (17 ft per sec) but with different spin—no spin (top), 2·2 revs per sec backspin (middle), and 2·2 revs per sec forward spin (bottom). The full lines—up to the first arrowhead—represent the sliding phase in each case: that part of the putt in which the ball is gradually changing from pure sliding at the beginning, through part sliding, part rolling, to pure rolling at the end. The dotted line represents the pure rolling part of the putt. The spin of 2·2 revs per sec is just about as much as it is possible to impart to a putt of this length in ordinary circumstances, and you can see that it doesn't have much effect on the distance the putt travels. The distances, speeds and spins in this diagram are all calculated ones, but would be typical of good putting surfaces. ·*

bining backspin and 'slicing spin' to form 'right-handed' rifle-bullet spin if we play a very cut-up shot from a greenside bunker. The ball curves sharply to the *right* on hitting the surface of the green.

To sum up: sidespin, when coupled with *considerable backspin*, can produce, in the initial stages of the ball's path across the green, a curve in the *same* direction as it does through the air; when coupled with *considerable topspin*, it can produce a curve in the *opposite* direction to that which it produces through the air. But without backspin or topspin, which is always approximately the case in a putt, sidespin produces no curve at all. We do not, let us repeat, hook or slice putts by applying sidespin.

Machine tests back up theory

The only effect we get when we pull or push the face of the putter across the line to the hole is to pull or push the ball's path a little way away from the direction in which the clubface is pointing, towards the direction in which the clubhead is moving. This is a result of friction between the ball and the clubface (see Chapter 23).

Putting-machine tests confirm the theory. For example, in one test the machine was set for a putt of about twenty feet, but set also to swing 20° to the left of the direction in which the face of the putter was pointing. The ball finished about fifteen inches to the left of the position it finished in when the putter was swung straight, and showed no sign at all of curving on its way. This would mean that the ball left the putter at about 4° to the direction in which the face was pointing—that is, much nearer this direction than the direction of swing. It also lost about a foot in length.

Table 21:1 How hitting the ball one inch on either side of the centre of the putter face affects two different lengths of putt. (Each figure is the average of 24 putts using one particular putter in the putting machine.)

Point of contact of ball on putter face	DISTANCE TRAVELLED		DEVIATION LEFT OR RIGHT	
	Putt strength (1)	Putt strength (2)	Putt strength (1)	Putt strength (2)
1″ towards toe	14·1 ft	9·0 ft	5″ R	8″ R
centre	20·4 ft	11·2 ft	0	0
1″ towards heel	17·4 ft	9·2 ft	8″ L	7″ L

Off-centre impact, and the design of putters

The effects of striking the ball badly off-centre with any club have been discussed in Chapter 19. The general conclusions described there hold for the putter also; badly off-centre impact loses distance, and pushes or pulls the ball, depending on whether the ball is struck from the toe or heel. The actual amount by which putts are affected depends on the type of putter, but the same general rules apply to any putter.

In a typical experiment, the putting machine was set to hit putts which travelled about twenty feet when hit in the centre of the putter face. When the ball position was moved one inch towards the heel or toe, the putts stopped four to six feet short of the central-hit distance, and about seven inches to one side —left if heeled, right if toed.

Hardly anyone ever hits a putt as far off-centre as this; and it is, in fact, unlikely that many *short* putts are missed through failure to hit the ball in the middle of the putter. But, on a long putt, where we are less likely to hit the ball right in the centre of the face, that loss of distance can be crucial. On a sixty-foot putt, for instance, that same one-inch error would lose about fifteen feet in length. A half-inch error, which is easily within the realms of possibility in a putt of this length, would leave the ball about five feet short—quite enough to make all the difference between two-putting and three-putting.

Here the designers of putters could help by marking clearly, on the top of the blade perhaps, the point on the face where the ball is supposed to be hit. Those centre-shafted putters in which the shaft comes in slightly heelward of the centre of the head can be particularly awkward in this respect; we are left in some doubt whether to strike the ball off the centre of the blade or off the bottom of the shaft.

It would also help considerably if some of the weight of the head could be shifted to the heel and some to the toe, still leaving the centre of gravity in the middle. For example, if the rectangular putter head (*a*) in Fig. 21:5 were chopped up into pieces (*b*), and these were re-allocated as in (*c*), the redesigned head would reduce, by almost half, the distance lost by an off-centre hit: simply because it would twist less easily through its greater concentration of weight at either end. (The whole question of distribution of weight in the clubhead is dealt with in Chapter 32.)

Very few putters at present on general sale satisfy this design feature—and, of those which do, we strongly suspect that some do so by accident!

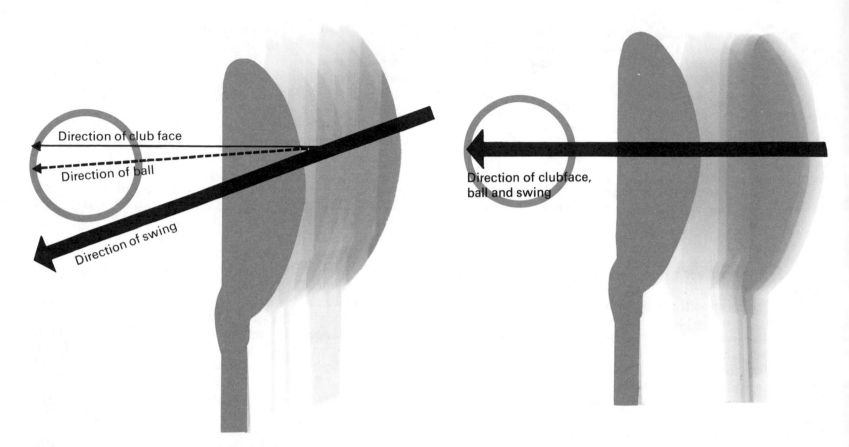

21:4 *The effect of 'coming across' a putt. Experiments show that the direction in which the ball sets off is governed very largely by where the face of the putter is pointing, and only a little by the direction in which the head of the putter is moving. Having the blade 'square' at impact is the most important single point to concentrate on in holing out.*

What we can forget about when putting

Now what do all these facts about impact have to do with finding a good technique for putting? They say one thing loud and clear: all we have to do is bring the putter head to the ball square to, and along, the intended line at the correct speed. We can forget all such complications as applying topspin, hooking or slicing, hitting on the upstroke, using a sharp tap or a smooth flowing stroke, accelerating the putter head through the ball and so on: at least in so far as none of these will make the slightest difference to the way the ball will behave.

134

The ball, if you like to think of it this way, is of strictly limited intelligence. It cannot tell whether it has been struck 'with authority', as one professional puts it, or tentatively; with an accelerating stroke or a slowing-down one; or even with a rhythmic sweep or a nervous stab. All it can do is to set off at a speed determined entirely by the weight and speed of the putter head, and in a direction determined jointly by the direction in which the head is swung and the direction in which the face is pointing—and nearer the latter if they differ.

This does not mean that for any individual the feeling of using a smooth flowing stroke, or a short sharp tap, or an accelerating clubhead, or a slightly upward-travelling clubhead will serve no useful purpose. But if it does, it will merely be by helping to swing the putter blade square to, and along, the intended line. Let us repeat again: no method of striking the ball will make it dive into the hole more readily than any other method.

Techniques and 'twitches'

When we come to the problem of recommending a technique we must admit we cannot. The variety of methods which mechanical considerations allow is much greater than in a drive or any other full shot, for the simple reason that you don't need to hit a putt hard. In all drives, one of the conditions which severely restrict the possible methods of swinging is the need to channel energy from many parts of the body into the clubhead just in order to get it moving as fast as possible. In putting we don't need to do this; so basically the only demand is that the method shall be mechanically simple.

It should be noted, though, that a putt is just as much a pre-programmed event as a drive. The downswing usually takes less than a fifth of a second, a little shorter than most drives; and the whole swing takes about half a second compared with about a second for a drive. So there's no question of *guiding* the putter head back to the ball. Once the golfer has begun his downswing, he is just as totally committed to striking it in the way that his 'computer' has programmed things as he is in a drive or in any other golf stroke.

It may be partly because of this that some people have so much trouble in getting the whole swing started back on a very short putt. They stand transfixed, with the ball only a foot or two from the hole, and the putter head laid behind it, but for some reason cannot bring themselves to take the club back. Some actually have to stop, walk away and try again; even then they may only finally produce a nervous stab, or 'twitch', as likely to send the ball six feet past the hole, and crooked, as into it.

This affliction may well have its roots in the golfer's awareness that the task is a ridiculously simple one, yet that the consequences of failure, at least in his mind, are serious. He does not have to concentrate particularly on judging the line, or the strength; instead he may suddenly become acutely conscious of the movement he is about to make. What should be an automatic unified movement, becomes a complicated problem of consciously co-ordinating many separate small movements. He has all the time in the world to carry out the task, but, as we said earlier, he knows that once he starts doing it he cannot stop it or change it. In those circumstances his brain, dithering with doubts and apprehensions, may boggle at giving the order to get on with it.

If that is a fair description of the underlying mental processes, what is the remedy?

Essentially anyone afflicted like this has somehow to make the job of actually swinging the putter automatic again: to be done without thinking.

One way of doing this is to have a set drill for *all* putts—the sort of thing that Bobby Locke had: two practice swings, step up to the ball, putter head in front of ball, putter head behind ball, then strike. The details don't matter; the important thing is that the whole process should be a single unit, so that starting the backswing is not the first stage, but follows on without conscious effort from what went before.

Many a golfer is unable to form this sort of habit, though. The best chance of curing his 'twitch' is to get him to think of something else; either by making the putt appear more difficult, or at least different in some way, or by actually occupying his mind with some quite irrelevant problem. A

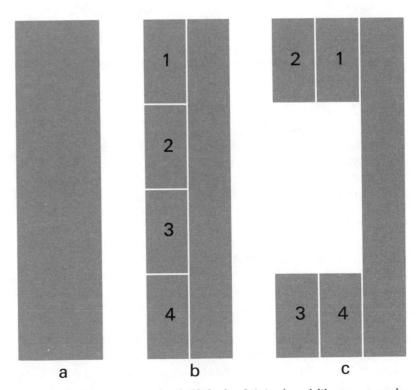

21:5 *Redesigning a putter head. If the head (a), shaped like a rectangular block (looking down on it), is cut up and fitted together as in (c), it will twist much less under an off-centre impact than the original. This makes for greater consistency both in direction and distance.*

135

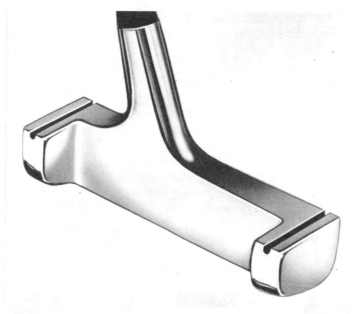

21:6 *Two putters with good weight distribution. The concentration of weight at the ends of the blade allows a wider margin of error in striking. The 'Ping' putter was certainly designed with this in mind.*

change in putting style can help; and perhaps most if it is a *complete* change—for example, to the 'croquet' style, where the player faces the hole and swings the putter between his legs like a croquet mallet. Alas, by the time you read this, this particular escape route for 'twitchers' will already be closed, if the ruling bodies implement their proposals to ban croquet putting.

Another possibility, not so commonly known, is sometimes surprisingly effective: shut your eyes after lining up. Many 'twitchers' then find it comparatively easy to swing the club-head quite smoothly and accurately enough to hole the nasty two- and three-footers which normally leave them paralysed with fear.

Both these 'cures' present the player with a set of rather novel problems, which occupy his mind and thereby relegate the business of actually moving the club to a lower level of consciousness.

As a last resort, any incurable 'twitcher' might try doing mental arithmetic or reciting poetry as he shapes up to his two-footer. Preferably not aloud, though.

136

How do the pros do it?

Returning to the general question of technique, the team did, of course, study the putting styles of professional golfers in the hope of finding common features. In particular they took high speed film of sixteen first-class players attempting putts of six feet, twenty feet and fifty feet. But analysis revealed more differences than similarities. They found wide stances (heels fourteen inches apart, Sewell), and narrow stances (heels one inch apart, Faulkner's then current method); they found the ball placed near the toes and far from the toes; they found long backswings and short backswings, long follow-throughs and short follow-throughs, and all combinations of length of backswing and length of follow-through; they found speeding up of the clubhead through the ball and also slowing down.

The only features of the set-up for the putt where the professionals showed a measure of constancy were the ball position, and the head position. Most of them had the ball placed opposite the left foot, and their eyes almost directly above the ball.

Simplicity and confidence

So we cannot say much about technique—beyond the simple mechanical demands already stated. Once a player has adopted any of the many possible *simple methods*, putting is largely a matter of confidence. Most of the gimmicks which help putting are probably just ways of bolstering confidence by giving him something positive to think about.

This is even more important in putting than in driving, where an all-out effort is being made. In putting, the clubhead momentum can give very little help in guiding the swing, so it helps all the more to have one simple objective in mind; and it matters little what that objective is so long as it doesn't complicate things. Thus two extreme opposites in technique, such as giving the ball a sharp tap, and giving it a smooth flowing stroke, may produce equally good effects in different players. Even the same player, should he lose his touch with one method, can often benefit by changing to the other. So long as it 'feels' right, it very likely is right. Confidence breeds success; and success breeds confidence.

Why we miss putts

Why do we miss putts? Not just short putts, but putts of any length. If we never ask ourselves this question we ought to. Not that there is any disgrace in failing to hole a thirty-foot putt—even the best golfers miss those regularly—but, since we are presumably trying to hole it, there must be *some* physical reason for failing to do so.

Indeed there will very likely be several reasons, whose relative importance may depend on the length of putt. To putt better, we need to identify them: to know how, and on what, to practise.

You can boil the reasons down to just four:
1. Failure to assess the correct line (i.e. an error of judgment).
2. Failure to set the ball off on the line selected (an error of execution).
3. Gross error in strength such that the ball does not reach the hole, or hits it so hard that it jumps over it (judgment and execution).
4. Random irregularities in the green which cannot be allowed for.

Of course we know that having 'this to win the Open'—or the club championship, or the monthly medal—will make some people miss a putt they might otherwise have holed—but only by doing one of the things listed above.

Reasons 1, 2 and 3 are completely separable only on a perfectly flat green. Otherwise they are to some extent interdependent. Nevertheless it is useful to think of two categories of error: namely, those made before we begin to swing the putter back, involving assessment of the putt, and those made during the stroke itself, involving perhaps a misalignment of the putter blade.

Bumps on the green ultimately limit putting

However, let's first look at that fourth reason, the one which is completely beyond the control of the player. It is a fact that even where several putts are hit in an identical way from the same spot and in the same direction, they will not finish up in exactly the same place. Random irregularities in the green ensure that.

The team investigated the size of this effect with the putting machine already described. To avoid wearing 'tracks' on the green they didn't actually putt the ball at a hole; but the results they obtained have been converted, in the table, into terms of holing or missing putts of various lengths, and then compared with the performance of professional golfers.

Table 21:2 *How a pro's putting compares with a machine's, on good greens.*

Length of putt	Missed by 'perfect' machine	Missed by professional golfers
6 feet	2%	45%
20 feet	50%	88%
60 feet	80%	97%

The figures refer to a green in fairly good condition. The machine would certainly perform worse on a poor green, as the professional in all probability would too. On a billiard table, on the other hand, the machine would hole almost every single putt.

What do the figures signify?

For a start, if we miss a putt of six feet or less, it is hardly ever the fault of the green; and since it is unlikely to be error 3 above (wrong strength) it will nearly always be a combination of errors 1 and 2, wrong judgment of line, or faulty execution. We'll discuss the question of which is the more likely to be the cause in a moment.

From long distances on the green, a lot of putts are going to miss anyhow, whether we make errors 1, 2 or 3 or not. In fact, if a long putt goes in, it's a fluke. That's not to deny that some people will consistently average more long putts holed per ten rounds, say, than others; they will, through being less liable to make errors 1, 2 and 3. But it remains true that, however well it is judged and struck, to hole any one specific long putt is largely a matter of chance.

On intermediate-length putts the moral from the figures is: don't expect miracles. Except on very good greens indeed, we are going to miss half the putts we strike from twenty feet however perfectly we putt; and so is everyone else.

Errors of judgment or execution?

Is it possible to tell whether errors of judgment or execution are more important in missing the shorter putts?

The team carried out tests on golfers to try to find this out for a six-foot putt. Many hundreds of golfers were given several attempts at the same six-foot putt. If the *only* cause of missing were misjudgment of the line, you could expect a lot more of the second putts to be holed than of the first putts, since each golfer would have learned quite a lot about the line from the first putt. You could also expect similar, though successively smaller, improvements going to the third, fourth, fifth putt etc.

On the other hand, if the *only* cause of missing were errors in executing the stroke, little or no improvement would be expected in successive putts.

These two alternatives, of course, over-simplify the situation. Subtle psychological considerations can also affect the result. A man may not approach the fifth putt in the same way as he approaches the first; he may have lost interest, or conversely he may be under considerable accumulating tension, especially if he has holed all his previous attempts.

In the event, there *was* an improvement in the results of successive putts, but not a very marked one. For example, of the four thousand or so golfing spectators who took part in a test carried out at Muirfield at the 1966 Open Championship, only 33% holed their first attempt at a curly six-footer, but this rose to 38% at the second attempt, and continued to rise rather more slowly, finally reaching 43% at the fifth attempt. The team concluded that both the simple sorts of error contribute to missing six-foot putts. This they found a little surprising, having suspected that not hitting the ball on the line chosen was the main cause of missed short putts. (Surely no one misses one of eighteen inches by misjudging the line?)

However, it may be that in the player's mind it is not possible to separate the two kinds of error. For example, a man may miss a three-foot putt, ostensibly by pulling it to the left of the hole (an error of execution); but the real reason for his doing so may have been uncertainty in his own mind as to whether he had correctly assessed the line in the first place (a suspected error of judgment).

Despite these complications, it is probably worth the trouble for any keen golfer to make some effort to discover why he misses putts; perhaps by testing himself in the way described. If he does no better on his second attempt at a putt than on his first, it might well be that he should be practising his putting stroke, without bothering too much about aiming at a hole, or allowing for borrows. If he shows a marked improvement on his second attempts, he needs to check his methods of gauging borrows and judging the pace of the greens.

For a start, on putts with a definite borrow, he might note whether he tends to miss on the high side or the low side of the hole. The golfers in the Muirfield putting experiment missed far more putts on the low side than on the high side—twice as many in fact. All classes of golfer tended to underestimate the borrow in this way, though the low-handicap players were less guilty of it than the high-handicap players; so, although it seems there is something in the traditional distinction between missing on the 'amateur' and on the 'professional' side, it is a distinction in degree only.

Building up experience

Assessment of a putt is a very complex skill; but basically what it amounts to is drawing on a vast store of experience, built up from previous practice, play and analogous situations. If you like (and the analogy is a good one), the memory part of the golfer's computer stores away records of previous putts, and, when faced with a new putt, uses data from these records in making the necessary calculations to set his putting mechanism going.

It isn't just as cut and dried as that, of course, because even when faced with a completely new situation his brain will use its reasoning powers to make some sort of shot at coping with it. Even in that case, though, the reasoning will usually be by way of some similar situation, probably not a golfing one, with which he is familiar.

For example, if a player came to a green where the hole was

cut on the top of a three-foot-square, foot-high stone slab, with vertical sides, his brain would quickly come to the conclusion, 'this is impossible'—even though no such putt existed in its memory. It would draw on its experience of analogous situations and decide which, if any, of them applied.

Part of learning to putt, then, is simply building up experience; and it can very plausibly be argued, to say the least, that we should practise in such a way as to make that experience as wide as possible. That is to say, we should not simply practise with normal golf balls and normal putters on normal golf greens; but that we should practise on a wide variety of slopes, including very steep ones; on a variety of surfaces, from very true to very rough; and even use a variety of different balls—tennis balls, cricket balls, glass marbles. Just before starting a medal round, would, of course, not be a good time for this sort of experiment.

All this may sound a little frivolous; but it represents an application to golf of a general view held by many experts in physical education. It has never been properly tested in putting; but it would certainly make an interesting experiment to carry out on two groups of complete beginners—one to learn putting by this method, the other by conventional methods.

Spirit levels, plumb-lines and croquet mallets

The whole business of assessing the line is a complex psychological problem; and, at least in the outward manifestations, good players do not conform closely to any set pattern.

Some do it while addressing the ball just before striking the putt, though undoubtedly they have been gathering information beforehand when walking up to, and on to the green. Many crouch down behind the ball and look from ball to hole, while others look from hole to ball. Occasionally they do this while lying full length on the green and with their eyes almost at ground level. Some stand back some distance from the midpoint of their putt and view it at right angles to the line; and others try to get information from the lie of the surrounding land. Some walk alongside the line of the putt and peer downwards at the surface of the green particularly near the hole.

Artificial aids such as spirit levels are illegal; but some golfers claim that it helps to dangle their putters from thumb and forefinger, as a plumb-line, while looking along the putt from ball to hole, though this can hardly tell them anything they did not already know. Some do pretty well everything— and take a long time about it too.

Precisely how a man uses his eyes in studying the line may very well be important. It is quite possible that outstanding 'readers of the green' do it differently from the ordinary man; and perhaps even that day-to-day variations in the performance of an individual may be attributable to variations in how well his eyes are serving him. It is undoubtedly true that most golfers have days when they 'read the greens' well, and others when they cannot see the line at all.

The team were unable to carry out any experiments on this; but for any future researcher the problem of exactly how a man uses his eyes in putting would make an interesting and rewarding study. Special apparatus exists which continuously records where the eyes are directed; but it is very expensive.

Lining up the blade

In this context, it is worth mentioning one fairly recent development of special interest—the 'croquet mallet' style of putting—even though it will be banned by the Rules of Golf by the time you read this. There are a number of variations of this style, but basically the player squarely faces the hole and swings the putter between his legs.

An advantage claimed by the designer of one particular 'croquet mallet' putter is that the method helps the eyes to do their part of the job more accurately. He calls his putter the 'Berkhamsted *Binocular*' to underline the point.

The team were not, in fact, able to determine whether by

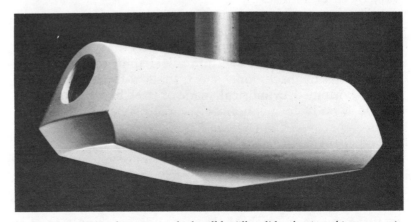

21:7 *A 'croquet' style putter—which will be 'illegal' by the time this appears in print. Quite apart from the different technique in swinging this type of putter, the designer of this particular model claims that standing behind the ball and looking with both eyes along the line of the putt gives the golfer an advantage in lining up the putt. Hence the name, 'Binocular' putter.*

looking directly along the line of the putt with both eyes square to the line a golfer is more likely to assess the line correctly. But they were able to test the claim that the blade of this putter can be more accurately and consistently lined up towards the hole than the blade of a conventional putter.

They found that there probably was some substance to this claim, although errors in lining up the blade at address were in general so small as to be only a minor cause of missing putts. In any case the superior performance of the Binocular putter, in this respect, might well have been due to other design features, notably the sharp straight-edge striking surface as seen by the eye. (In the model tested, the head is actually cylindrical, almost, and the front surface appears as a straight line when looking down on it.) Surprisingly enough, with most conventional putters, not only could the golfer see something of the bottom edge of the clubface as well as the top edge when he addressed the ball, but the face itself was very slightly convex (bulged)—for what reason we cannot imagine.

Centre-shafted, or blade, or what?

This brings us to the subject of putters. There is far more variety in this one club than in any other. Even among the sixteen professionals, whose putting styles were filmed, there were differences of up to four ounces in the weights of their putters; and the lengths of shaft of putters in fairly general use vary by several inches.

It is when we come to the head, though, that designers really let their imaginations run riot. For a start, the shaft comes in at every conceivable position from the heel to the centre of the head; and heads themselves are thick, thin, rounded at the back, flat at the back, long, short, shallow-faced, deep-faced, round-bottomed, cylindrical, made of steel, brass, aluminium, plastic, wood—to mention only some of the possible variations.

The team has carried out many tests to try to find out whether players using any one type of putter get better results with it than those using any other. For example, at the Schweppes P.G.A. Championship, held at Princes, Sandwich, in April 1965, the putting of all the competitors was recorded at three greens on each of three rounds—making a total of 1122 'man-greens', and 2049 putts. The putters were divided into three main types, blade, centre-shafted and mallet. About equal numbers of professionals used the first two types, and

140

Table 21:3 *Comparison of three types of putter at a professional tournament.*

Length of putt	PERCENTAGE HOLED		
	Blade	Centre shafted	Mallet
0–3 feet	97%	97%	97%
3–6 feet	65%	66%	64%
6–9 feet	37%	40%	37%
Average distance long putts from over 30 feet finished from hole	3·0 ft	3·3 ft	3·1 ft
Average number of putts per green	1·82	1·81	1·88

a slightly smaller number the third. The results of the comparison between putters is shown in Table 21:3.

Golfers may like to imagine that the figures prove something; but in fact none of the differences is statistically significant. (That means that if we did the experiment again we should probably get some of the differences reversed.) So as far as this test goes, no one type of putter showed itself better for golfers in general than any other.

This confirms the results of another test carried out on ordinary golfers and non-golfers, in which about 4000 six-foot putts on an artificial surface were recorded.

One thing which this series of tests did tentatively suggest was that the best *weight* of a putter probably depends on the speed of the greens. There was some evidence that on the fast artificial surfaces the heavy putters did not do too well.

It would, of course, be going too far to say that science had proved this, but it may well be that a golfer would gain by carrying two putters, a fairly heavy one with a little loft, for use on slow greens, or on very long putts, and a light one with virtually no loft, for very fast greens and for holing out short putts. It is not such a ridiculous idea to carry two putters, since anything from a third to a half of any golfer's strokes are played on the green.

At the time of writing, analysis of the 1966 Muirfield experiment involving over 18,000 six-foot putts is going on, and some conclusions have emerged on the comparison between putters.

If we broadly classify the dozen or so putters used as blade, centre-shafted or mallet, this latest experiment confirms the conclusions of the previous ones: no one of these types came out better than the others. But again there was the suggestion that heavy putters were at a disadvantage on the fast artificial surfaces; for example, the putter that was clearly worst (with 33% of putts holed, against an average for all putters of 39%) was heavy and, by common consent, rather clumsy.

The one very definite and surprising result, however, was that the grotesque-looking putter shown in the photograph (Fig. 21:8) performed quite significantly better than any of the others. In this test, which, let us remember, involved only six-foot putts on true, fast and sloping surfaces, 49% of all the putts struck with it went in, compared with the next best putter's 41%, and the overall average of 39%.

Before readers rush out to order one we should perhaps add that the design is illegal—at least in the form tested.

21:8 Grotesque but effective. This (illegal) putter came out best in extensive tests of different putters in which golfers of all abilities tried to hole six-foot putts.

How can all this help us in choosing a putter for ourselves?

To have the weight right for the sort of green we usually putt on, to have the weight well distributed as described earlier, to have a straight, clear front edge to the blade; all these are likely to help a little. But the most sensible single piece of advice a scientist, or a professional, or anyone else can give a golfer is to putt with the club he likes best. Confidence in his choice of club is likely to be more important than anything else.

Make putting easier?

Before leaving putting, let's look at an idea which is put forward from time to time; that a hole larger than the present $4\frac{1}{4}$-inch diameter one would reduce the importance of putting, and make for a better balance between long shots played through the green and those played on the green.

Naturally the most ardent supporters of the suggestion are those who putt badly; equally well the most violent opponents are those who putt well. As with the big ball *v.* small ball controversy (see Chapter 26), neither argument is notable for being based on hard fact. So perhaps an objective look would do no harm. The increase in size suggested is usually a small one but to get a clearer idea of how things would be affected let us see how a hole $8\frac{1}{2}$ inches across—twice the present diameter—would change the game.

Besides doubling the width of the target, this also doubles the depth from back to front; and this means that a ball travelling at a speed that would take it twenty to twenty-five feet past the hole on an average green will just about fall back in if it hits this double-size hole bang in the middle. For a normal hole the just-fall-back-in speed corresponds to an overshoot distance of only five or six feet. Gauging borrows is therefore not so important with the $8\frac{1}{2}$-inch hole; you can just hit the putt hard.

The effect this will have on the likelihood of holing a putt depends, of course, on its length. Putts of a foot or less should go in every time with either hole; but really long putts (twenty yards or more) might be expected to go in six to eight times as often.

The results of an experiment to test the effect of the $8\frac{1}{2}$-inch hole are shown in Table 21:4. Fifty shots (not really enough statistically) were putted or pitched at both an $8\frac{1}{2}$-inch hole and a normal $4\frac{1}{4}$-inch hole similarly situated.

The reader can draw his own conclusions about the big hole

Table 21:4 *How doubling the diameter of the hole would affect the game: the results of 50 shots hit at 4¼″ and 8½″ holes from a variety of distances.*

	6-ft PUTT		15-ft PUTT		45-ft PUTT		50-yd PITCH	
	4¼″ hole	8½″ hole	4¼″ hole	8½″ hole	4¼″ hole	8½″ hole	4¼″ hole	8½″ hole
Down in one shot	22	44	9	20	2	9	–	2
Down in two shots	28	6	38	30	41	40	18	36
Down in three shots	–	–	3	–	7	1	32	12
Average number to get down	1·56	1·12	1·88	1·60	2·10	1·84	2·64	2·20

21:9 *As big as a bucket. But this 8½-inch hole (twice normal diameter) will knock off only about six shots per round, and you* can *miss six footers with it.*

from the figures; but the most noteworthy points seem to be (i) the near certainty of holing from six feet, (ii) the virtual elimination of three-putting, and (iii) the very good chance of getting down in two shots from fifty yards, which is considerably more than edge-of-the-green distance.

If readers care to try this experiment themselves, it will provide them with an afternoon's instructive amusement. An 8½-inch hole may not sound all that big, but when you see it on the green it looks like a small quarry. You get the feeling that it is quite impossible to miss from five yards, and you will probably try to crash the ball straight at the hole without bothering about trivialities like borrows. But this is false confidence and you will soon discover that you *can* and *do* miss if you seriously misjudge the borrow.

Now what does all this mean in terms of strokes saved in a round of golf? It is possible to use the figures in a rough calculation; and the conclusion is that a scratch golfer would save something like six shots. Remember, that is for our 8½-inch hole; for the sizes suggested by the reformers, which vary from 4½ inches to 6 inches, the saving would be correspondingly less.

Whether or not it would reduce the importance of putting is another matter. Certainly it would reduce the total number, but the man who was putting well would still take fewer putts than the man who was putting badly. The latter would merely be 'twitching' on the six- to eight-footers instead of on the two- to three-footers as he does now; or not holing his share

of the fifteen-footers instead of not holing his share of the six-footers.

Anyhow, even if it did reduce the importance of putting, would it make golf a better game? That can only be answered by trying it, but we are inclined to doubt it—for the simple reason that it is the one part of the game where the average golfer feels that, on his day, he could see the pants off Messrs Nicklaus, Palmer and Player.

Section 6

What Happens when a Ball is Struck

Chapter 22

The Ballistics of Golf: Free–wheeling through the Ball

Ballistics is the study of the behaviour of projectiles. In flight, a golf ball is just as much a projectile as a shell is; and there are a number of obvious similarities between the golf shot and the long-range artillery shot. Both the golfer and the gunner are trying to land a missile upon a target whose range and direction are estimated in some way. The distance to which either a shell or a ball flies depends upon the speed with which it is projected and the angle of elevation at which it is sent off.

Both gunner and golfer are aware of the likely effects of any wind, and allow for it in line and angle. Neither gunner nor golfer, once the missile is sent off, can do anything further to affect its flight—though the golfer often reacts as if he could, with body twisting, club waving or impassioned invocations. All he's really doing, of course, is expressing his own feelings. Once the stroke is played, the ball's course is built into it.

The actual technique and types of flight used are very different from each other—notably in the shell being aerodynamically shaped and spinning on the axis of its own line of flight, whereas the golf ball is round and spins—or at least is usually meant to spin—on a horizontal axis at right angles to its line of flight.

The distinction, though, which the gunner makes between 'external ballistics', which deals with the flight of the shell through the air from the moment it leaves the gun, and 'internal ballistics', which deals with the reactions inside the gun from the moment the charge is fired, can quite usefully be applied to the study of golf as well. In golf we can call the latter side of things 'impact ballistics', taking place during the very short but finite period of time during which clubface and ball are in contact with each other.

A shot is settled in half a millisecond

We called the duration of impact 'finite': in that it is a definitely measurable period of time, long enough for a very great deal of action and reaction to take place between its beginning and its end. A lot can happen during this impact-time, simply because it happens so very fast.

For almost all golf shots, the time between a point on the clubface first striking against the ball and the time when the ball springs completely clear of it and away into flight is about half a millisecond (0·0005 second). Even the slow-moving, gentle impact of a putt lasts less than one millisecond.

It is perhaps one of the most arresting basic facts about the game of golf that everything which happens to the ensuing

144

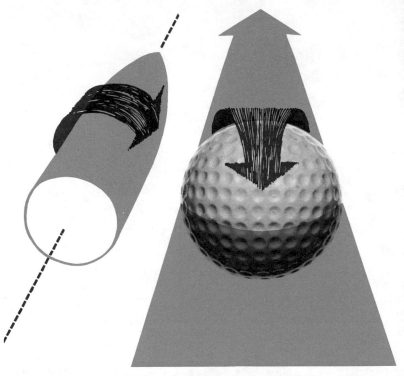

22:1 *Two different sorts of spin which aid the flight of projectiles. An artillery shell, or a bullet, is made to spin around an axis lying along its line of flight. The gyroscopic effect keeps its nose pointing forward and so stabilizes its flight. An accurately struck golf ball spins around a horizontal axis lying across the line of flight. In that case, the spin affects the flow of air past the ball in such a way as to create a 'lifting' force which, by partially counteracting gravity, prolongs the time of flight of the ball.*

shot—whether it be long, short, sliced, fanned, or even perfect —is decided in that very short space of time.

Impact=three-quarters of an inch at 100 m.p.h.

A golf stroke is not just a very short-impact blow, however. It is also a very high-speed one. In a full drive the clubhead will swing through the ball at about 100 miles per hour.

Even at this speed, though, in 0·0005 second it will travel barely an inch between first touching the ball and losing contact with it. In fact the forces at impact slow down the clubhead; so that the actual distance the clubhead travels while in contact with the ball is even less: more like three-quarters of an inch.

In a putt, although impact-time is a little longer, distance travelled in contact is very much shorter on account of the much lower speed of the clubhead: only about one twenty-fifth of an inch for a six-foot putt struck at around five miles per hour.

Nothing the golfer can do can extend this distance through which the clubhead remains in contact with the ball. It is very much the same, incidentally, for the American-sized 1·68-inch ball as it is for the British 1·62-inch ball.

One crucial result of the very short impact-time in golf is the lightning rise of the force applied between the clubhead and the ball from zero at first touch to a very high rating indeed. The average force applied to the ball during the total impact-time on a full drive, for instance, works out at about 1400 pounds. As the force increases from zero at the beginning of impact, and falls off again to zero at the end of it, to achieve such a high *average* rating, the *peak* force must be around 2000 pounds, perhaps even a full ton.

The ton at the end of the club

The way the clubhead behaves during this almost explosive high-speed application of huge force reveals one very important fact about the conditions under which it hits the ball, and one which contradicts the playing beliefs of many an experienced golfer.

Most of us have a strong subjective feeling that we are, in some way, pressing the clubhead through the ball by the action of our hands at impact; and that we are sensing in our fingers the power of the blow imparted to the ball.

This is a complete illusion, however much we 'feel' it to be true. We do, of course, feel the impact at our hands, but it is delayed by the flexibility of the shaft, so that the ball has left the clubface before we feel any reaction. The flexibility in the shaft also spreads out the rapid rise and fall of the force and softens it, which perhaps explains the sensation that some people have of holding the ball on the clubface for a considerable time. But whatever the reaction we feel through our hands on hitting the ball, it is still quite irrelevant to any study of what happens between club and ball.

Hand reaction to impact can't affect the shot

Let us put some figures to the delays involved in the golfer sensing the reaction at his hands. It takes slightly longer than the total time of impact—two-thirds of a millisecond as against impact's half-millisecond—for any reaction to travel up the metal of the shaft from shank to top. By the time this affects the golfer's fingers through the grip, which both damps and slows it further, the ball will already be in clear flight.

Even then, it will take at least another ten milliseconds (a hundredth of a second) for the message to travel from his fingers to his brain. Thus the ball will be more than a foot clear of the clubhead before the golfer can even be aware of the impact, far less do anything about it. For his brain to react to the message, and send orders back to the hands, and for them then to begin to carry them out, would take a whole fifth of a second—no less than four hundred times as long as impact actually lasted. The ball will then be fifteen yards away.

So far as he is concerned with being able to do anything consciously to the ball during impact, therefore, the player might just as well be swinging the clubhead on the end of a piece of string.

We can arrive at the same conclusion by putting the argument in a slightly different way. Impact with the ball pushes the clubhead back on the shaft by only a few tenths of an inch. To bend the shaft by this amount requires a force of only a few pounds; and conversely in this bent-back condition the shaft applies only a few pounds' force to the clubhead. So this is all that the shaft (and with it the player's hands) can apply to the clubhead during impact—quite negligible compared with the force approaching one ton which the clubhead applies to the ball—and the ball to the clubhead. It means that virtually all the resistance to impact, during actual contact, is borne by the inertia of the clubhead. That is to say, at that moment it might just as well not be connected to the player.

This is such a vital point, in its effect both on the golf swing and on club design, that the team felt it really ought to be confirmed by a direct practical test: by actually 'disconnecting' the head of the club from the shaft at impact.

This they did, using a specially made two-wood with a hinge in the shaft just above the head. At impact the hinge can give way completely, and the ball is hit only by the clubhead.

In the test, this club was used to hit thirty shots, which were then compared in length with thirty hit by a similar two-wood with a normal shaft. The shots hit by the hinged club averaged at 215 yards—only five yards shorter than the average with the ordinary club.

Even that small difference is hardly likely to have arisen from any basic change, on account of the hinge, in what goes on at impact. It is much more likely simply to be the result of a

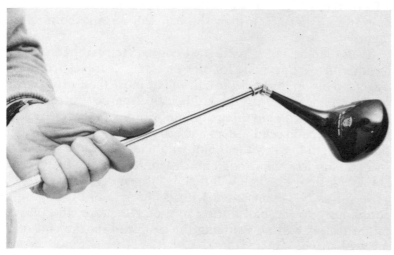

22:2 *No, nothing has broken here. The club merely has a very free hinge in the shaft just above the head. In driving tests the negligible difference between distances achieved with this club and a similar ordinary club confirmed the theory that during impact the clubhead behaves as a freely moving object— that is as though it were not connected to the shaft.*

reduction in clubhead speed; caused either by the extra 'useless' weight in the hinge, or by the rather wobbly feel to the club which may well have made the golfers who tested it 'go easy' when swinging.

At any rate the experiment proved, to the satisfaction of the scientists, the point which theory had strongly suggested: during impact the clubhead acts as though quite disconnected from the player.

Free-wheeling through impact

An important consequence of the inability of the player to

exert any positive influence on the ball during impact, is this: the only dynamic factor that matters in producing distance is clubhead speed. A given clubhead making square contact with the ball at 100 miles per hour will send it the same distance whether it is accelerating, slowing down, or moving at constant speed.

It may conceivably help your game to feel you are accelerating through impact, in so far as it may prevent the common fault of reaching maximum clubhead speed too soon; it may also be true that, in certain shots, particularly short putts, an actual acceleration of the clubhead will reduce the tendency to turn the blade off-line. These things *may* be true; we do not intend to argue the point here. But what is certainly not true is that acceleration of the clubhead into impact will produce any effect whatsoever on the ball beyond that produced by the pure speed at which it is travelling; and furthermore, in any full shot, acceleration through impact is a sure sign of wasted effort which could have been used to produce greater speed at impact if it had been applied earlier. By and large, all the major effort should have expended itself by the time the clubhead reaches the ball.

We are left with the inescapable conclusion that, from all points of view having any bearing upon the ballistics of impact, once the player has swung his clubhead through the forward swing to within a few inches of impact, the clubhead might as well be a separate projectile, flying freely under its own momentum along its own predetermined path, for all the further relevance either the player or his grip upon the club can have to what happens next.

The player has, in effect, put the clubhead into orbit around his hub; and by the time it meets the ball, it is on its own.

When R. T. Jones Jnr. said in the 1920's that he always felt

− 2 msec	0 (impact)	+ $\frac{1}{4}$ msec

 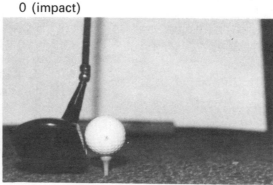 

that he himself was 'free-wheeling' through impact, he could hardly have summed up better the true situation for the player. The whole effective part of any man or woman's stroke at any golf ball is completed before he or she actually hits it; and thus any energy not already by then slung out into the clubhead is powerless to affect the shot in any way whatsoever.

Letting the club do the work

Bobby Jones's feeling of 'free-wheeling' through impact suggests that he was one of the few golfers who instinctively realized this, and that he succeeded in discharging all his effort into the clubhead before he came into impact, then left the clubhead to get on with the stroke on its own. Which is

what it is going to do anyway, whatever any player may feel or think.

In a golf swing, there are thus two entirely separate actions. The golfer himself just gets the clubhead swinging as fast and as truly as he can before impact, and then can affect the stroke no more. The clubhead, travelling at the speed and direction already given to it by the player's swing, then hits the ball on its own, according to the laws governing its movement as a free body.

Isn't one of golf's oldest cries, repeated by thousands of professionals almost every week all round the world: 'Just swing, and then let the club do the work'?

How right they are.

22:3 *The hinged club through impact. Despite being completely free, the hinge is hardly bent back at all and the shot flies just as well as one hit with a normal club. Readers should not be misled by the kink in the shaft even before the clubhead strikes the ball. The club is a 'Crookshank' wood whose design, even without the hinge, features a built-in kink in the shaft.*

+ 1 msec

+ 3 msec

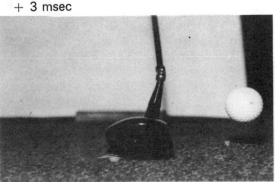

+ 5 msec

Chapter 23

The Ballistics of Golf: How Spin and Flight Begin

When a clubhead flies into the ball at 100 miles per hour in a full drive, it imparts two main kinds of motion to it: travel through the air and spin while it travels.

The way it actually puts the spin on the ball is the more complicated reaction of the two; so first we'll look at the simplest of all ways of starting a ball into flight: square impact with a loftless club. Although this is unlike any normal golf shot, it enables us to look at the origin of the ball's speed through the air with the greatest simplicity, but no loss of accuracy. As we said in Chapter 20, it makes perfectly good sense to think of a driver as having no loft when we are considering only the forward speed imparted to the ball.

A golf stroke is a collision

The first thing to get clear is that the ball is not 'thrown' in any way by the clubhead. On the contrary, it is projected into flight by a straightforward collision.

Three stages in a typical collision of this sort are shown in Fig. 23:1. Between Stages 1 and 2, part of the energy of motion of the clubhead goes into flattening out the ball and is stored as elastic energy within the ball. When the ball is as flat as it will go, it has to move at the same speed as the clubface; and so, for an instant of time, forms a combined single mass with it.

How fast clubhead and ball move together for this split second will depend upon their relative weights and speeds before impact. In the simple case we have here, the 100 miles per hour, seven-ounce clubhead loses 19 miles per hour, so that both move at 81 miles per hour.

After Stage 2 the elastic energy in the ball is released as it begins to round itself out again, and it 'pushes itself off' from the clubface, simultaneously pushing the clubhead back a bit. The extra speed so gained by the ball is greater than the speed lost by the clubhead simply because the ball is lighter than the clubhead.

Thus, by the time Stage 3 of the diagram has been reached and the ball is just clear of the clubface, its speed has been increased by 54 miles per hour, and the clubhead speed reduced by 12 miles per hour; giving final speeds of 135 miles per hour for the ball, and 69 miles per hour for the clubhead.

A critical factor: the energy of the bounce

The exact measure of the final speeds arising out of the basic 100 miles per hour collision depends largely upon what proportion of the original energy of motion ('kinetic energy') of the clubhead is lost. In every impact between clubhead and

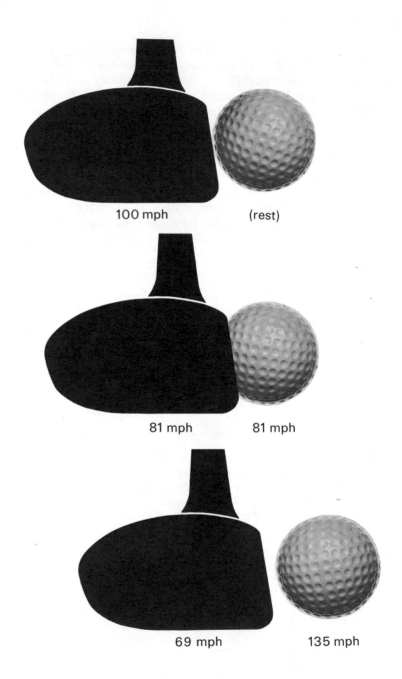

100 mph   (rest)

81 mph   81 mph

69 mph   135 mph

23:1 *Three stages near impact in a drive. From top to bottom: the instant of first contact, about midway through impact, and finally just after the ball leaves the clubface.*

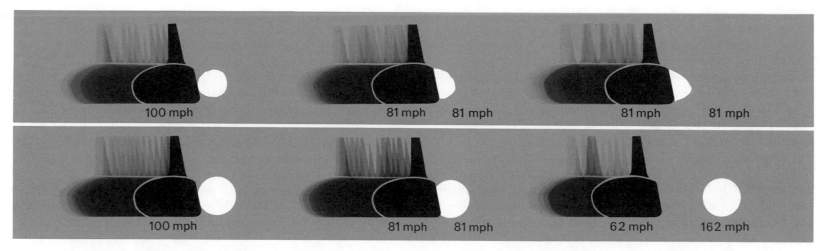

23:2 *Completely inelastic, and perfectly elastic collisions. The upper drawing shows three stages near impact with a golf ball made of putty (coefficient of restitution=0). The lower one shows the same impact with a perfectly elastic ball (coefficient of restitution=1).*

ball some of this energy is lost in the process of being turned into compression energy (elastic energy) and then released into kinetic energy again as impact ends.

In golf, thus, the ball will never fly away as fast as it would from a 'perfectly elastic' impact with the clubface. If such an impact were possible, the difference would show in the second stage of the operation, not the first.

The first is dependent only on masses and speeds. If a seven-ounce clubhead hits a 1·62-ounce ball of firm putty at 100 miles per hour, they both travel at 81 miles per hour at Stage 2, and continue at that speed (so long as all the putty sticks to the clubface).

Exactly the same first-stage effect would apply in a perfectly elastic impact. But in this case the final speeds would be less in the case of the club, and more in the case of the ball: through the increased energy of the springing-apart reaction between them.

Both examples are shown in Fig. 23:2.

It will be clear to the reader at once how important for the length of his drive is the degree of elasticity of the collision between clubface and ball; and this very largely depends, of course, upon the degree of elasticity of the ball's behaviour, rather than the club's. The face of a club is so hard compared with the ball, that there is virtually no deformation of the clubhead, and consequently little energy loss in it.

Bounce = 'coefficient of restitution'

The actual equation which governs the various speeds produced in different circumstances of elasticity is given, for those who may be interested, in Appendix I at the end of the book. In essence, it amounts to saying that the speed at which the ball flies off is X times the speed at which the clubhead struck it, and that the size of X depends on the relative weights of the two and upon a factor called the 'coefficient of restitution', which is merely a way of putting mathematically how closely the collision comes to being a perfectly elastic one.

A high coefficient of restitution is not, on its own, enough when you come to the practical business of making a golf ball. The ball must not shatter under the impact of the club; that is to say, it must deform elastically to a large enough extent to keep the internal stresses within reasonable limits.

For instance, a glass marble dropped on a stone floor has a higher coefficient of restitution than a golf ball, and will spring away more sharply. It's still no good trying to hit it with a golf club; it will just shatter.

Why a ball needs to flatten out on the club

The internal stresses produced in any substance at impact are inversely proportional to the extent to which it is prepared to be knocked out of shape. Half the deformation, twice the force generated in the material—very roughly. A marble gives to a blow possibly only to one ten-thousandth the extent of a golf ball. If the blow is anything more than a very gentle one, huge internal stresses are produced, which shatter the marble.

A golf ball thus needs to give to the bang from the club—to

149

be very 'elastic' in the everyday-speech sense—and thereby keep the internal stresses generated by the blow within non-destructive limits. At the same time it must have a very high ability to spring forcefully back into its original shape.

How makers seek to achieve this, we needn't go into in detail here (see Chapter 26). But readers will see from the photographs in the present chapter how much a golf ball flattens out against the surface of the club and how forcefully it springs away again.

The high figure of 135 miles per hour, out of a theoretical maximum of 162 miles per hour in the square-impact illustrations we gave earlier in this chapter, show how successful makers have been in combining these two essential qualities in a golf ball.

The clubhead factor
We deal with this subject at some length in Chapter 32. In the meantime the reader may look again at the paragraph headed 'Weight' in Chapter 1, where he will easily spot that the heavier the clubhead the faster the ball will fly away.

This is true, though, only so long as the heavier club can still be swung at the same speed; and in fact clubhead weight and swinging speed seem to affect each other in such good balance around the customary seven-ounce weight of a clubhead that in practice a man changing the weight of his club by anything up to three ounces plus or minus of the seven-ounce norm makes surprisingly little difference to the distance he can send the ball with it. Why this is so is taken up in Chapter 32.

How loft affects the collision
Having discussed idealized square-on impact with a clubhead, let's now look at the actual impact situation in a golf shot and see exactly how the ball is given its 'angle of projection'—that is, the point in the sky towards which it starts off—and the backspin which will make it 'hold up' in the air as it flies, and carry anything from two to six times as far as it would if it was driven off without any spin at all.

As soon as you use a lofted club in golf, you are no longer hitting the ball a square blow, but instead are hitting it an oblique one.

We talk in golf all the time—as indeed we already have in earlier chapters—about the importance of hitting the ball 'square'; but all we mean most of the time is square as seen

from above the clubhead as it flies through the ball: square, that is, either to the line of aim or to the direction of swing, or —preferably, indeed, as we have seen—both.

In this chapter we have talked so far about a 'perfectly square' impact, that is, one with the face at right angles to its direction of travel, no matter from what angle you look at it. In normal golf, though, the blow is never square if you look at it from ground level at one side or the other. The loft on the club lays the face back so that it points well above the forward direction in which it is travelling.

When a ball is struck with a face laid back at an angle like this, three things happen which do not happen in the perfectly square blow we have been looking at in this chapter so far.

23:3 *Splitting the clubhead speed into two 'components'. We can think of a clubhead whose loft is 30° (five-iron or so) and which is travelling horizontally at 100 m.p.h., as having the two simultaneous speeds shown. The 87 m.p.h. component at right angles to the clubface chiefly governs the speed at which the ball will set off; the 50 m.p.h. component parallel to the clubface governs the amount of backspin imparted to the ball, and also affects the angle it flies off at (see Fig. 23:4). The length of the lines—the two sides and diagonal of the rectangle —represent the speeds.*

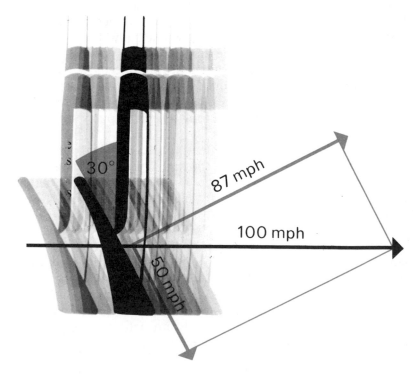

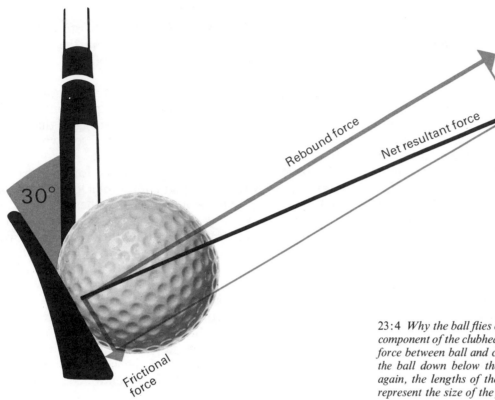

23:4 Why the ball flies off lower than the loft angle of the club. The 'tangential' component of the clubhead speed (50 m.p.h. in Fig. 23:3) gives rise to a frictional force between ball and clubface. This puts backspin on the ball and also forces the ball down below the line of a straight rebound from the clubface. Here again, the lengths of the lines—the two sides and diagonal of the rectangle—represent the size of the forces.

1. The blow imparts backspin to the ball. The more the loft, the more the backspin.
2. The obliqueness of the blow, as explained in Chapter 20, leaves only a component of the clubhead momentum available to drive the ball forward, and thus reduces the speed at which it flies off. The more the loft, the lower the starting speed.
3. It makes the ball set off in a different and higher-aimed direction from that in which the clubhead is travelling. The more the loft, the higher the angle.

What determines a lofted shot's speed and spin?

This time there is not just one simple force of impact, square between clubface and ball, and thus operating entirely at right angles to the clubface. Instead there is a force acting obliquely between ball and clubface. In practical effect, we can regard it as having two components acting at right angles to each other during impact.

You can regard the velocity of the clubhead flying towards the ball as consisting of two parts: a 'perpendicular compon-

ent' at right angles to the face of the club, and a 'tangential component' parallel to the face.

In the diagram the clubhead speed is supposed to be 100 miles per hour; if the loft is 30° then the two components of the ball's velocity are roughly 87 miles per hour (perpendicular) and 50 miles per hour (tangential).

At impact the elastic processes of compression and rebound, already described for the square contact, go on as before, but are governed by the size of the perpendicular component of clubhead velocity; and since this is reduced in comparison with the absolutely square blow, it follows that the ball will be set off at a lower speed.

If the clubface and ball were in the scientific sense perfectly smooth this would be the only effect of loft. That is, the ball would go off at reduced speed, with no spin, and exactly at right angles to the face: 30° of loft, so 30° of elevation in the case illustrated (Fig. 23:3).

Because both ball and clubface are rough, however, there is a frictional force between them, acting parallel to the face of the club. This has two effects on the ball: it starts it spinning,

151

and it pushes it down a bit below the perpendicular to the clubface (Fig. 23:4). Thus the ball always leaves the clubface at an angle of elevation somewhere between the direction in which the clubhead is travelling and that in which its face is pointing, but usually a good deal nearer the latter.

In short, speed, spin and angle of projection are related to one another in a fairly straightforward way; and it is not difficult to see that for any given blow, the greater the loft on the club, the less will be the velocity of the ball, the greater will be the spin, and the higher will be the angle of projection, though it will never reach the angle of loft of the club itself.

These effects are illustrated in Fig. 23:5, where the ball is struck by seven-ounce clubheads of different degrees of loft, travelling at 100 miles per hour. Of course, the whole argument applies equally well to an oblique blow producing sidespin; the diagram could, for instance, represent a view looking down on a driver hitting the ball with the face becoming progressively more closed to the line of swing. In that case the ball will start off nearer to the direction in which the face is pointing than that in which the clubhead is travelling. The figures are just examples, and will depend on a number of other factors as well as those already mentioned.

A closer look at the application of spin

One of these factors is the roughness of the surfaces of ball and club. The rougher the face of the club, the more it will pull the starting direction of the ball down towards the approximately horizontal line on which the clubhead is travelling. It is not true, though—and this goes against much long-established lore of golf—that the rougher the surface of the club the more backspin it will necessarily impart to the ball.

Why this is so takes a little explaining; but it follows from the way spin is produced by the impact of the clubface.

When a lofted club hits a ball, the impact has at least two separate stages, so far as loft is concerned—sliding and rolling. The sequence goes something like this:

1. *Slide turning into roll*
   The ball slides upwards across the clubface, squashing out against it at the same time. From the moment it starts to do so, friction between the dimpled ball and the roughened or grooved clubface surface begins to turn this slide into a roll.
2. *Pure rolling*
   The ball reaches its maximum speed of spinning at the

split second at which it completely stops sliding and begins to do nothing but roll. From then on until the moment it springs clear of the clubface, its speed of roll slows down.

Not too much is known about the ball's resistance to rolling when in a very squashed state; but experiments which the team did on this at low speeds of rolling suggest that it may be very large. In that case slowing down of roll would be very rapid.

We have already seen these stages of lofted-impact spin-reaction at work in the simpler context of a long putt (Chapter 21). First it mainly slides over the grass; then it begins to turn as well as slide; then its slip-rolling speed catches up with the speed at which it is travelling across the green, and it rolls at its fastest; then it begins to slow down. You get a similar effect visible on a billiard ball, hit exactly halfway up by the cue, and sent skidding across the table.

In an impact with a lofted club at golf, these four stages all take place within the compass of less than a quarter of a single revolution of the ball; but this does not affect the fact that they do happen, and in the same sequence. In fact there may be other stages, on account of the large changes in shape undergone by the ball, but the two mentioned are sufficient to carry on with the argument.

Backspin does not depend on roughening the clubface

In all this, there is one rather odd thing about the whole relationship between the ball and the clubface, though.

Against a perfectly smooth clubface, the ball would slide all the way and never begin to roll at all. And, as you might expect, the rougher you make the clubface, the more quickly the ball will stop sliding up it, start rolling up it as well, and finally begin wholly to roll.

But its speed of rolling at this instant (after which it will begin to slow down) is not affected by how long it has taken to reach it. It is exactly like the putt moving across the green in this respect (Chapter 21). A rougher clubface gets it to the point of pure rolling more quickly, but adds nothing to its

23:5 *How different degrees of loft affect the way a clubhead of fixed weight (7 ounces) travelling at a fixed speed (100 m.p.h.) sets the ball off into flight. The clubs corresponding to the various lofts are shown, but the figures will not apply exactly to actual shots hit with these clubs, since only the driver among them has a seven-ounce clubhead and can be swung at 100 m.p.h.*

Angle of club face	Corresponding club	Trajectory	Speed	Spin (revs per second)
0°	Driver with vertical face		135 mph	Zero
10°	Driver	8°	134 mph	60
30°	Five iron	23°	105 mph	120
45°	Nine iron	29°	90 mph	180

maximum speed of rolling, and thus only leaves it a longer opportunity to slow down again before it leaves the clubface.

This carries an implication which may surprise many golfers. Although the time taken for the ball to stop sliding is not yet known for certain, it is likely—at least on long and medium irons—to be less than the total time it takes for the ball to be compressed and then spring clear of the clubface again into flight. What this means, in simple terms, is that by making the faces of these iron clubs rougher, a golfer may well only reduce the final backspin he puts on the ball with them.

Probably there is an ideal roughness of surface for each club according to its loft and how hard the player using it hits the ball.

An experiment in spin

This the team does not yet know. And the basic measurement of speeds of sliding, spinning and rolling during the half-millisecond contact between ball and clubface, which would be necessary to establish a detailed model of what happens, poses technical problems of extreme difficulty. However, the final outcome of the complicated interplay of these factors is not too difficult to measure.

What the team could do then was to check the effects on any one shot of varying the roughness of the surface of the club used to strike the ball; and this they did, filming each impact as the stroke was played.

The results largely bear out their other conclusions, reached mathematically from the theory of physics and mechanics.

Clubfaces: smooth and rough—a slightly puzzling experiment

To test the effect upon flight and backspin of the degree of roughness of the clubface, you need pairs of clubs, identical in every respect except that one has a normal grooved and sand-blasted clubface, whereas the other's face is smooth. Dunlop kindly manufactured three pairs like this, a pair of five-irons, a pair of seven-irons and a pair of nine-irons.

There were two separate experiments. First a professional, Norman Quigley, then at Princes, Sandwich, hit shots into an indoor net while the speed and spin of the ball and the angle to the horizontal at which it set off were measured for each stroke. About fifty shots were hit with each club (twenty-five with the smooth and twenty-five with the grooved) in this test.

Then outdoor measurements were made on the carry, run

23:6 *How speed and spin are measured. Two flashes of very short duration (1/100 of a millisecond or less) are set off, usually by the clubhead touching two wires together. The camera shutter is held open throughout most of the swing, in a semi-darkened room, and so the positions of ball and clubhead at the instant of both flashes are recorded on the one picture. The time between the flashes is measured electronically, and distances and angles are measured directly from the photograph. In this particular shot with a five-iron, in a measured time of 3·2 milliseconds, the ball has moved 5¾ inches and turned through an angle of 140°; from which we calculate its velocity as 150 ft per sec (or 102 m.p.h.) and its spin rate as 122 revs per sec.*

and total range of another series of strokes struck by Quigley, and also two series struck by low-handicap amateurs as well. Each player hit about a hundred shots with each club (fifty with the smooth and fifty with the grooved) in this test.

Tables 23:1 and 23:2 set out the results of these tests.

The reader should guard against drawing too many conclusions from the table of results. Many of the differences between the smooth and grooved clubs, including those in the amount of spin applied, are not significant—that is to say they are of a size which could have arisen by chance if, for example, two identical grooved clubs had been used.

Nevertheless, it does appear that the smooth-faced clubs send the ball a little further; both in carry and run, and *possibly* with a little less backspin.

None of these differences seem such as to make any practical difference in actual play; especially as any player adjusts his

Table 23:1 Smooth and grooved clubs: starting speed, spin and angle of shots hit by a professional.

	FIVE-IRON		SEVEN-IRON	
	Smooth	Grooved	Smooth	Grooved
Average speed (feet per second)	144·7	144·8	132·7	133·1
Average spin (revs per second)	77	84	121	123
Average angle of projection	12·8°	12·6°	20·0°	20·0°

game to the ranges he gets with his own swing from whatever set of irons he uses, and the broad general conclusion is that grooves make very little difference to the contact between ball and clubface.

These results are consistent with some obtained in experiments carried out for the United States Golf Association by the Arthur D. Little research company. They concluded that smooth clubfaces *could* impart as much backspin as ordinary grooved faces, but were less consistent in doing so. Their experiments, which included both laboratory and field tests, also suggested that a small degree of roughness (e.g. very shallow grooving) would consistently impart just as much backspin as normal, or for that matter, extra-deep grooves.

At the same time, the universal practice of grooving and roughening the surface of iron clubs has long been given so much weight by players—even to the point of appeals against illegal roughening in Ryder Cup matches—that one must look for some useful purpose—or at least the origin of this practice.

Several possibilities arise. First: that it began with gutty balls, which flew better when abraded all the time by roughened clubfaces—a consideration which would be irrelevant with the modern ball.

Second: grooves look attractive, and give the player an illusion of control. This is not a facetious comment, because how a golfer feels about a shot can have quite an effect on how he plays it.

Third: the roughening might be expected to send the ball off on a slightly lower trajectory, which top-class players might prefer. The laboratory test on shots hit by Norman Quigley did not substantiate this; but the American tests did. Of course, *perfectly* smooth clubfaces (in the scientific sense) would produce quite appreciably higher trajectories.

Fourth: the tests were all on full shots with medium and short irons. Might the grooved clubs give some additional spin in a short pitch which would be of vital importance if a quick stop were required?

Table 23:2 Smooth and grooved clubs: carry, run and total length of experimental shots.

	Distance (yards)	PROFESSIONAL		AMATEUR A		AMATEUR B	
		Smooth	Grooved	Smooth	Grooved	Smooth	Grooved
Five-iron	Average carry	155	154	139	138	173	165
	Average run	31	27	35	29	16	15
	Average overall distance	186	181	174	167	189	180
Seven-iron	Average carry	138	137	126	123	136	126
	Average run	19	17	22	20	Ground frozen, run meaningless	
	Average overall distance	157	154	148	143	Ground frozen, run meaningless	
Nine-iron	Average carry	111	109	99	98	107	104
	Average run	16	15	16	15	As for seven-iron	
	Average overall distance	127	124	115	113	As for seven-iron	

23:7 *The smooth-faced nine-iron used in the tests described in this chapter.*

Well, they *might*—but they don't—at least not so far as further tests could tell. The amount of run obtained on forty-yard pitches to a green with the rough and smooth nine-irons —averaged over fifty shots with each club—was virtually identical—36·7 feet with the smooth and 37·9 feet with the grooved club.

Fifth: grooves may preserve the effective roughness of the clubface when water or grass juices get smeared on to the clubface.

What happens out of juicy grass?
It is certainly worth looking at what happens if the face of the club is wet.

For a start it depends what you mean by wet. When violently compressed between ball and club at impact, liquids can do peculiar things. Undoubtedly in some conditions a lubricating film can be formed between ball and clubface; and this can apparently make the contact almost a pure sliding one, with the result that very little backspin is applied.

This does not seem to happen with pure water. But it does with soapy water, and might perhaps also happen with grass juice, which would account for the 'flier' the pros get out of very lush rough or even grassy fairways. This is a shot in which the ball shoots out a bit faster and higher than might be expected and which does not 'bite' when it lands. All of those phenomena would be expected if an efficient lubricating film were present between clubface and ball. In those circumstances, it is just possible that the grooved face might retain a little more grip.

The only evidence we have, though—a very high speed film of a couple of shots—suggests that, with a soap film at any rate, neither the rough-faced nor the smooth-faced club can apply much backspin to the shot; in both cases the ball is still sliding up the face when it springs away from it again. Whether a roughened face can put more spin on the ball than a smooth one when some less efficient lubricating film like grass juice is present, is something which has yet to show up in any experiment the team has made.

Most of this, though, is supposition, and the main conclusion stands: that it is certainly not self-evident in what way, if at all, artificial roughening of the faces of iron clubs will affect the shot, and that experiments rather suggest, that, in most circumstances, and for all practical purposes, they produce no effect at all.

This was exactly how it seemed, indeed, to the golfers who carried out the tests. To them the shots felt the same and the results looked the same.

How much difference does a warm ball make?
Many golfers believe that on cold days they can add a few yards to the length of their drives by using two balls at alternate holes, keeping the one not in use meanwhile in the warmest pocket available. There may well be something in this, though the denser cold air will always prevent them from achieving summer-day distances.

A ball's coefficient of restitution—the liveliness, that is, with which it springs away again after being flattened against the clubface—is directly affected by its temperature; and keeping it warm can make it start off quite a bit faster from impact and thus fly quite a bit further from the tee. A drive which will carry 200 yards with the ball at 70°F (21°C) will carry only 185 yards when the ball is at freezing point.

The effect upon a ball's temperature of keeping it in your trouser pocket for ten minutes on a cold day, though, is very much less than the optimist may believe. Rubber is a poor conductor of heat, and it may take several hours for a ball to heat up all the way through, however warm it feels on its surface.

But it also loses heat only very slowly too; and it will thus have quite an effect on the length of a player's drive on a cold day for him to store a few golf balls in the boiler-house the night before, and then to use a different one every three or four holes, keeping the others in his trouser pockets.

Chapter 24

The Flight of the Ball: Spin, Lift and Drag

The calculated use of air-resistance effects upon the flight of a ball, or indeed upon anything kicked, hit, thrown or slung, is common to many games and sports; and often the missile is specially shaped and adapted to make special use of these effects.

In cricket, bowlers can position the raised seam of the ball so as to make it curve in flight. In baseball, tennis or football, the ball is often made to spin by the manner in which it is thrown, struck or kicked, again with the object of making it curve deceptively in flight or become otherwise more difficult to catch or play back accurately. In a different way, the rugby touch-kicker or the discus thrower may also use spin as a direct aid to their own specially shaped projectiles' most effective trajectories in flight.

In no game, though, are the effects of aerodynamic forces more fundamental than they are in golf. The major fascinations of the game as we know it entirely depend upon them.

Golf's three aerodynamic forces

In any typical trajectory of a golf ball through the air, from impact until the moment when it hits the ground again, you can most conveniently look at the aerodynamic forces acting upon it if you separate them into three component parts.

1. *Drag,* what we loosely call 'air resistance', acting in directly the opposite direction to that in which the ball is flying at any moment.

2. *Lift,* acting upwards (in the vertical plane) at right angles to the ball's direction of travel.

3. *Yaw,* or 'sideways force', acting at right angles to both the other two forces.

There is, of course, another force acting all the time: the force of the ball's weight under gravity, acting always vertically downwards, no matter in what direction the ball is travelling.

Yaw, of course, is not present in a straight golf shot, and we can leave it aside for the moment, while we examine the exact way in which drag and lift go to work during a ball's flight.

We are all familiar with *drag.* Stand on a windy hill, put a hand out of a speeding car, stir the water in a bath, and you experience drag directly. It works in exactly the same way when air is flowing past a stationary object as it does when the object is itself moving through still air.

Though few of us directly experience *lift,* it can be seen in operation when a boy throws a thin flat stone, or in flying a kite, or in a 'chopped' shot at table tennis.

24:1 *The forces acting on a golf ball in flight. Drag depends mainly on the speed of the ball; lift and yaw depend, as well, on its spin—lift on backspin, and yaw on (usually) unwanted sidespin. The three aerodynamic forces all get smaller as the ball slows down in flight; and since its weight, acting vertically downwards, remains the same the ball eventually returns to earth, however wayward any particular combination of the aerodynamic forces may have made its flight.*

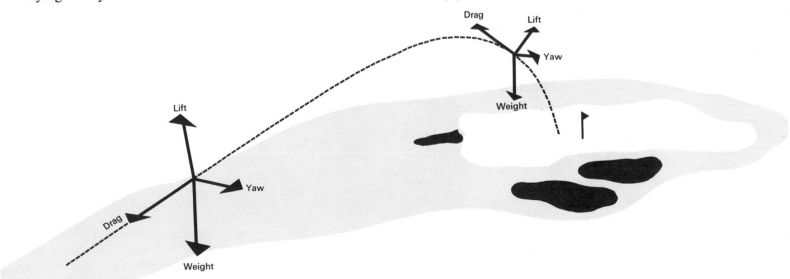

To the non-golfer, lift's effect in golf is startlingly obvious. To his eye, the long boring drives which the golfer's senses are conditioned to accept as normal appear to stay up in the air almost miraculously longer than they should, and finally to fall much more slowly than his eye would expect them to.

Any reader can quickly check for himself how marked this effect really is. Throw a ball sixty feet up into the air and it will hit the ground in less than four seconds. But send off a full drive, in which the ball goes sixty feet up at its highest point, and it will take more like six seconds—50% longer—before it pitches. As the non-golfer could see at once, 'something is keeping it up in the air longer'; and the force doing this comes, of course, as we have already remarked in Chapter 20, from backspin.

Before this was understood, golf was something of a puzzle to the scientist. The first to realize the full significance of backspin was Professor Tait of Edinburgh University, around 1890. The story goes that on more than one occasion the Professor calculated that a golf ball could not be hit more than *X* yards through the air—only to have his own son, Freddie, sending one ten yards further the following morning! There may well be a moral in that for present-day golf research scientists.

There had to be an explanation; and thus the Professor came in the end to perceive the significance of backspin in producing lift in a shot and thereby making the ball carry further through the air than had seemed mathematically possible without it.

Air-flow, wake and eddies

How does lift work?

The effect may be simple; but the forces behind it are quite complicated and interesting; and even drag is by no means as simple as everyday experience might suggest.

Let's start with what happens when a fluid like air flows around a stationary ball. Fig. 24:2 shows this situation. The air at the 'front' of the ball is slowed down, and indeed brought to rest at the exact point where the flow divides. In contrast the air near (but not hard against) the 'sides' of the ball is speeded up relative to the general speed of flow. You can see this happening in the photograph, with the 'streamlines' bunched together (implying faster flow) at the top and bottom of the ball.

When any fluid flows faster, it exerts less pressure on what-

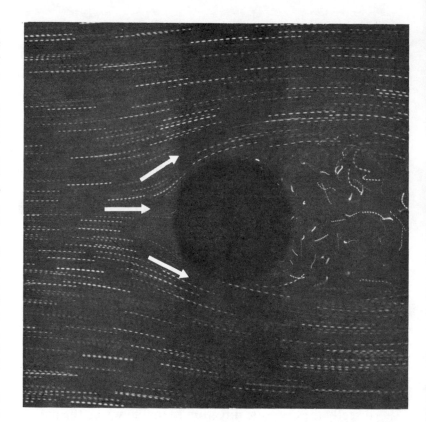

24:2 *How air flows past a non-spinning ball. In fact, this is neither a ball, nor is it air; it is a photograph of water, with a large number of minute polystyrene beads suspended in it, flowing past a cylinder. In essence, though, the air-flow past a ball, is similar. The photograph is taken by leaving the camera shutter open while illuminating the flow area with 10 rapid flashes (at 1/100 second intervals). Each bead therefore appears 10 times in the photograph as part of a 10-dot streak, whose length gives an indication of the speed of flow. Short streaks mean low speed; long streaks, high speed. You can see that, relative to the undisturbed flow far away from the ball, the fluid slows down at the front of the ball, and speeds up as it goes past the top and bottom. These correspond to areas of high pressure at the front and low pressure at the top and bottom. You can also see how the smooth flow breaks away from the surface of the ball at top and bottom, leaving an area of irregular eddies—the wake—behind the ball.*

ever is around it. This is why, for example, hurricane force winds can lift the roofs off houses; the static air inside exerts a greater pressure than the air moving swiftly over the roof, and literally pushes the roof off. Readers can demonstrate the effect to themselves in a rather less drastic way by hanging two sheets of paper parallel to each other two or three inches apart and blowing down between them. The sheets move closer together, not further apart as you might think.

Returning to the ball in the illustration then, the higher speeds at the top and bottom—and indeed all round the sides of the ball—represent areas of low pressure, and the almost static air at the front an area of high pressure.

The next thing to notice is that the air, having speeded up as it flows past the outer rim of the ball, does not flow on closely round to the back of it. Instead, it flows onwards roughly in the direction in which it was going in the first place, while the area behind the ball fills up instead with eddies.

These eddies are formed by the behaviour of the layer of air very close to the surface of the ball. As this 'boundary layer' moves over the surface of the ball, it experiences a frictional resistance which slows it up; so instead of 'climbing' the gradient of increasing pressure round towards the back of the ball, it is brought to a halt and then breaks away from the surface of the ball while still in the low-pressure region. Of course it does this all round the ball, not just at the top and bottom as the photograph might suggest; and as it trails away, it defines a region, circular in section, within which eddies form, instead of a simple flow pattern. The eddies in turn break away, and trail off into a turbulent 'wake'; just like the wake behind a ship.

The extent to which the wake affects the movement of a ball through a fluid depends upon the exact point at which the boundary layer breaks away from the surface. This, in turn, depends upon how fast the fluid is moving past the ball and upon how rough the ball's surface is. But for a very wide range of speeds, certainly those with which we are here concerned, the boundary layer breaks away just ahead of the point exactly halfway through the low-pressure region, where the fluid passes the ball at its full diameter. Thus the size of the ball determines the width of the wake, which stays much the same over a wide range of speeds.

The wake causes drag

The effect of this pattern—high pressure in front of the ball, lower pressure at the sides as the air flows past it, and then an eddying area of wake behind it—is to produce resistance to the flow. We can look at the origin of the drag either as the difference in pressure between the slow-moving high-pressure zone at the front and the faster-moving eddying zone at the rear; or as a measure of the energy used in churning up these eddies; or both. It's the same sort of resistance that we feel if we try to move a flat stick (like a ruler) broadside on rapidly through water.

This 'pressure drag', as it is called is strong enough to make any direct friction between the air and the ball's surface (or the water and the stick's surface) relatively insignificant, and thus forgettable. In golf, friction contributes little to total drag.

Spin brings in lift

Let's now see what happens when the ball is made to spin as the air flows past it. The effect is the same whichever direction and angle the ball is spinning in, so we can imagine that we are looking at the picture along a horizontal line of sight, and the ball has backspin on it (Fig. 24:3).

The spin of the surface drags a certain amount of the nearest air round with it. The effect of this is to make the general airstream move more freely, and faster, over the top of the ball, thus lowering the pressure there. At the same time the flow past the bottom of the ball is obstructed and slowed up, thus raising the pressure compared with the pressure at the same place in the non-spinning ball. It is still, of course, lower than the pressure at the front of the ball, where the air is almost stationary.

Lower pressure above the ball than beneath it creates one thing—lift: a force acting upwards towards the low-pressure area. The wings of an aeroplane achieve the same effect by their special 'aerofoil' shape, and by being angled slightly to the airstream.

The strength of the lift force obviously depends upon the difference in pressure below and above the ball; and this in turn will depend upon how efficiently the air is dragged around with the spinning surface of the ball; and *this*, in turn, can depend largely upon the roughness of the ball's surface.

This is the principal reason for golf balls having 'dimples'. As the first users of the old 'gutties' found, no matter how much backspin you put on a smooth ball, you can get comparatively little lift with it, and can hardly make it fly even seventy yards through the air, compared with the 220 yards or so of carry achieved nowadays by good players.

Another effect of the spin dragging more air round with the ball is to widen the wake slightly, increase the area and energy of the eddies and thus increase drag, simultaneously with inducing lift.

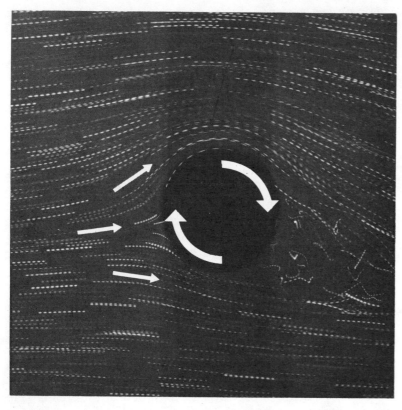

24:3 *How air flows past a backspinning ball. Here again what we see is water rather than air, and a cylinder instead of a ball—but again most of the essential features of the flow are similar. As with the non-spinning ball, the flow is slowed down at the front (short streaks); but this time you can see quite clearly that the flow over the top of the ball, which is moving in the same direction as the air, is faster (long streaks) than that over the bottom, which is moving in the opposite direction. The pressure is therefore lower above the ball than below it; and this means a net upwards force is acting on the ball—lift.*

Spin affects both lift and drag

If we are to predict the effect of drag and lift in actual play, we have first to answer a few questions about the way these forces operate. For example, how do drag and lift compare with the weight of the ball? How quickly do they increase with greater speeds through the air, or greater speeds of spin, or both together?

To answer questions like these involves quite difficult and complicated science: both in the mathematical theory of flow past a spinning rough-surfaced sphere, and in setting up

reliable experiments to tell you more about it. But broadly what happens is that the faster a ball is flying, the greater will be the drag, with drag increasing a little faster than speed. For instance, as a ball's speed doubles from, say, 100 to 200 feet per second, the drag generated goes up about two and a half times.

A faster rate of spin also adds to drag, but only comparatively mildly. The drag at 100 revolutions per second is only about 20% greater than that at sixty revolutions per second.

Lift also increases along with air-speed and spin-speed, reacting, not unexpectedly, quite rapidly to extra spin as well as—like drag—to extra speed.

Both drag and lift, in sum, increase quickly as a ball's *speed* through the air is increased, but as its *rate of spin* is increased lift increases much more quickly than drag.

Drag and lift shape a basic trajectory

During the flight of a single shot, say a long drive, these changes will obviously be important. For instance, as the ball flies away from the tee, drag may be at three to four ounces, and lift at about two and a half ounces. By the time the ball falls towards the ground, drag will have dropped to around one ounce, and lift right down to only a quarter of an ounce or so, both operating throughout together with the golf ball's weight of 1·62 ounces.

At the beginning of the drive, lift can thus actually be greater than the ball's weight. The ball's flight path will, in that case, actually begin to curve upwards from the moment it settles into flight. Not very much, though; for even at that stage the extra ounce or so of lift will shift its path above a bee-line by only about a foot in every hundred feet: a rate of climb imperceptible to the eye of the striker. (Though, for instance, a four-wood struck very hard off a downslope from a bit of high ground against a breeze may have enough backspin to start off below the horizontal and curve up again into a fairly normal-looking trajectory before falling to the ground at the end of its flight.)

Drag, meanwhile, is resisting the ball's motion through the air right from the split second it takes off, thus steadily reducing both its speed and its rate of spin, and with them the strength of the lift force being applied to it. In a very little time, lift is reduced in this way to less than the ball's 1·62 ounce weight; so that its flight path begins to curve downwards—albeit still nothing like so quickly as that of a completely

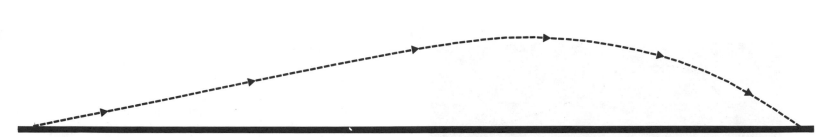

24:4 *The asymmetric trajectory of a drive. A large lift force at the beginning of the ball's flight counteracts gravity to a great extent and enables the ball to move almost in a straight line. Later, with spin and speed dropping, the lift force gets smaller and the trajectory becomes more like that of a thrown stone.*

smooth ball, or one sent off without any backspin at all.

A ball's forward speed through the air drops off much more quickly than its rate of spin. Even at the end of a full drive, a ball can still be spinning at around 75% of the rate given to it at impact.

Drives themselves vary considerably, even when they feel exactly the same to the player striking them. A good player's drive may actually set off curving slightly upwards, or only just about holding its own in a straight line—and the latter will be much more the impression the player gets of it as he watches it go away.

It is this near-bee-line first flight which gives the good golf shot its characteristic trajectory, with the highest point about two-thirds of the way towards its forward end, where the ball pitches. The further the ball goes, the smaller lift becomes as both air-speed and spin decrease, and the more the ball's trajectory begins to look like that of a thrown stone or a ball hit without backspin.

The practical science of dimpling
We mentioned earlier that for a ball to be able to be given lift, through backspin, it must have a fairly rough surface. More or less any sort of roughness of surface will enable a ball to lift. But in golf other factors come into it too: appearance, for instance, and ease of manufacture.

All manner of markings have been tried since it was first discovered that the gutty ball needed to be roughened before it would fly well, but in the end the simple circular dimple has proved most successful.

The science of what size, shape and depth the dimples should best be given is quite complicated. The best answer has to balance a number of different effects. The shallower you make

the dimples, for instance, the less lift they will give. But the deeper you make them, the more drag you get as well, to mention only one factor in the reckoning.

The forces involved, moreover, do not vary in any simple way with changes in the design of the surface markings. The interior shape of each dimple, and the sharpness of its edge, as well as its depth, all have fairly complicated effects upon how the ball is likely to react to spin. It would take quite a thick treatise on aerodynamics to do the subject justice; and, even then, there would still be details which we could not honestly say were completely understood.

For quite a wide variety of these other factors, though, it is found in practice, that a dimple depth of around 0·013 inch gives the best result.

How marked the effects of varying the depth of the dimple can be, is shown in the graph (Fig. 24:5). These results were recorded by Dunlop when they were experimenting with square mesh markings for which the maximum carry proved to be that obtained with a slightly smaller depth, of 0·010 inch.

No particular depth or design will, of course, be best for every shot any golfer plays; and the chosen design and depth is always a calculated compromise.

If anyone insisted on extracting the very last yard or two from any shot, he would need almost as many types or depths of indentation as there are shots in golf. For a start, there would be differences for long, medium and short hitting, and for playing into or with the wind. And there would really also need to be a different ball for use with each club.

Fortunately, though, the distance lost by using a standard ball for all shots can only be a matter of a yard or two in the worst circumstances; and as the only stroke in the game for which maximum distance is essential is the long shot, the standard dimple is designed to give the longest carry on a good golfer's drive. This is something we go into in Chapter 26. But as far as flight and spin are concerned, the standard dimple suits the size and weight of the standard ball well enough; and that is all we are concerned with here.

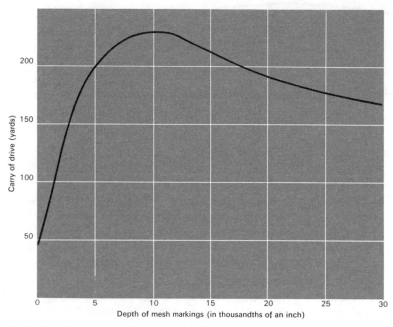

24:5 *How depth of marking on the ball affects a good drive. The graph summarizes results obtained by the Dunlop Sports Company using their driving machine to hit balls with different depths of marking. They used balls with square mesh markings in this experiment. The results of similar studies on the more common round dimple markings are more complicated to interpret (and to present graphically), since you cannot change the depth of a round dimple without also changing its shape or area. Square mesh markings can be cut shallower or deeper without changing anything else.*

24:6 *Two unusual drives. This shows what would happen to a 'normal' drive if it were hit, first without any backspin, and second in a vacuum. Notice how much shorter and lower are the 'no spin' and 'vacuum' trajectories. The times of flight, 2·1 seconds (no spin) and 2·2 seconds (vacuum), are also much less than the 5·5 seconds of the normal drive.*

A bit of moonshine

We mentioned earlier that a smooth ball will give little lift. In fact, it can actually experience negative lift at certain combinations of speed and spin, and so, in practice, carry an even shorter distance than an ordinary dimpled ball hit without spin. Fig. 24:6 shows the trajectory of the non-spinning ball, compared with an otherwise identical shot hit with normal spin. It shows also what the shot would look like if there were no air at all.

The surprising thing here is that the shot in a vacuum would not carry anything like so far as the normal shot. In other words, the lift produced by spin through the air much more than compensates for the disadvantage of the air resistance.

Notice also how low both the spinless and airless shots fly. The normal shot reaches a maximum height of about seventy feet, but the other two do not even reach twenty feet.

Things would be different, of course, if these two could be projected at 45°. At that angle, the vacuum shot would carry 430 yards. There is no prospect of our playing golf in a vacuum—at least not on earth. But it is perhaps amusing to speculate how the game of golf might develop on the moon, where there is no atmosphere, and the force of gravity is only about one-sixth of that on earth.

, Some future astronaut with a golf club would find that a drive would carry over one and a half miles, if sent off at 45°. Par fives would all need to be well over three miles in length; and thirty square miles would be needed for an eighteen-hole course. There would be other attractions: slicing and hooking would, for instance, be impossible. Besides the long driving, there might be some interesting hazards to surmount; but that one-and-a-half-mile drive could be hit clean over an 1800-foot moon-hill with something to spare; so recovery play might prove to have spectacular possibilities as well.

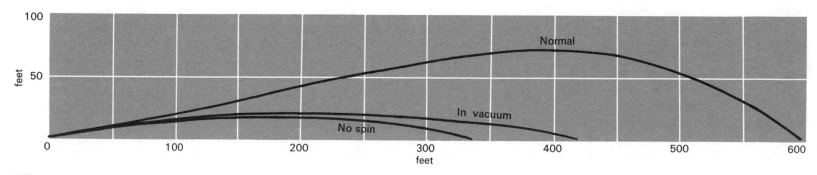

Chapter 25

The Flight of the Ball: Applying Theory to Play

Even in a standard shot like a drive from a level tee, considerable variations can and do arise—not only from one player to the next, but also from one shot to the next by the same player. Everything affecting spin, lift, drag, carry and run can vary—not to mention atmospheric conditions, such as wind, humidity and temperature.

The team studied some of these effects upon trajectory experimentally, by using a driving machine, and others theoretically, by calculating trajectories with a computer.

The advantage of using a computer is that you can carry out complicated experiments without having to set up complicated equipment (provided you have a computer, of course!). You can investigate the effects of playing with balls of any weight, size or resilience you choose, without having to have them manufactured. You can test the effects upon a ball's trajectory of winds of any strength you wish, including a hurricane.

You can even indulge in flights of fancy quite impossible to test out experimentally: such as what would happen if you drove a ball in a vacuum, or in water, or treacle, or on some planet with a much smaller force of gravity than ours, or a thinner atmosphere, or even in a topsy-turvy universe where the ball had negative mass, and responded to a blow by moving off smartly in the opposite direction. Some of these are a very long way from the game as we know it, but they can be none the less fascinating—and instructive—for that.

The disadvantage of computer 'experiments' is that you can never be 100% certain that you have got the basic theories exactly right. For this reason alone, you have to use practical tests to check that the computer is giving sensible results. A driving machine, sending ball after ball whistling down the range, can demonstrate an effect in a much more graphic way than a computer, even though—or perhaps because—you may have to spend several hours hitting and measuring dozens of shots, as against the few seconds required by the computer.

The team accordingly collected results from both sorts of test. The driving machine used belonged to the Dunlop Sports Company, who supplied many of their own results as well.

A formula for a drive's length
One of the more arresting findings from all this work was the simplicity of the relationship between the length of a drive and the speed at which the ball left the clubhead. To get the carry in yards of drives with the British-size ball going off at about the usual 10° above the horizontal, multiply the speed (in feet per second) by one and a half, and subtract 103. Or, in brief mathematics:

$$\text{Carry} = 1\cdot5v - 103$$

Although this formula results from a complex interplay of the aerodynamic forces we talked about earlier and is by no means exactly right for all circumstances all the time, it is valid for quite a wide range of normally hit drives in still air.

If you assume an average amount of run, there is a similar formula for the overall length of drive:

$$\text{Overall range} = 1\cdot25v - 27$$

Thus a good drive sent off at 200 feet per second (which is 136 miles per hour and which would require a clubhead speed of about 100 miles per hour) will carry, under the first formula, 197 yards and run to a total length, under the second formula, of 223 yards. Both formulae, in fact, work well for any well-hit drive sent off at anything between 100 and 170 miles per hour and thus carrying anything from 120 to 270 yards.

In this, both computer and driving machine agree: a welcome confirmation of the soundness of the theoretical basis of the computations, and one which enabled the team to apply the same method to wider problems later.

The best angle to hit a drive at?
One problem the team tackled in this work on trajectories was of direct practical interest for all golfers: what is the best angle of elevation at which to send off the ball in order to make it go as far as possible?

In the simplest trajectory of all, that of a ball sent off in a vacuum where there would be neither lift nor drag, the angle of 45°, halfway between horizontal and vertical, always gives the longest carry. Even in air, the best angle for a non-spinning ball (upon which drag will operate, but not lift), is still nearly 45°; although the range will be very much reduced for the same speed of sending-off, and the calculation of effects of air resistance is fairly complicated.

For a simple illustration of why 45° or so is the most effective angle, watch a child squirting water out of a garden hose and seeing how far the jet can be made to fly before it hits the ground. As the nozzle is raised towards 45°, the fall-point creeps forward along the ground. At 45° it stops; and beyond that angle it begins to come back again towards the nozzle.

At 45° half the energy with which the water is sent off is used in keeping it up in the air long enough for the other half to send it to its maximum possible range. If you try to improve on this by raising the spout, you reduce the forward-going velocity too much; if you try to improve on it by lowering the spout the water doesn't stay in the air long enough for the increased forward velocity to be effective.

Exactly the same goes for a ball or stone thrown without spin; but the creation of a lift force by means of spin in a golf shot drastically changes this situation. Straightaway the ball can be kept in the air for long enough without having to use a lot of its initial energy out of impact in climbing high. In a manner of speaking, lift gives the ball a bit of 'glide' in its path through the air. The ball can therefore be set off at a shallower angle; or, to use the technical terminology introduced in Chapter 23, the horizontal component of velocity can be increased.

When you remember that lift always works at right angles to the direction of flight at any moment, another advantage of the lower angle at which you can send the ball off is soon obvious. All the time the ball is climbing to the highest point in its trajectory, lift will, to some extent, be working against the ball's forward movement, as in Fig. 25:1, as well as doing its main work of keeping it up in the air; but the shallower the angle at which the ball is climbing, the less lift will work against forward flight.

Aiming for the longest carry

The team's tests showed that, for maximum carry, the most effective send-off angle for a good drive hit at usual speed and spin rate is, in fact, about 20° above the horizontal. Yet we have already been talking freely of a good drive going off at about 10°, not 20°.

In this contrast lies the whole key to the effort some professionals make to tee the ball high and forward, and hit it slightly on the upswing, in the belief that thereby they send it further.

They are right. This can send it further. But the reason is nothing to do with 'imparting topspin to the ball'. No golfer ever hit a good drive—or any drive at all, other than a complete top—with 'topspin'. The real reason is simply to add a few degrees to the 10° above horizontal at which a driver sends the ball off if swung horizontally through the ball; and thus to send it off nearer the best possible starting angle—for the

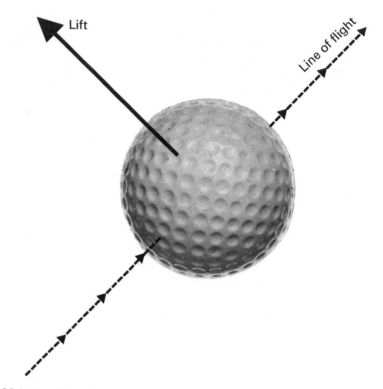

25:1 *How lift can hold the ball back. In a steeply rising trajectory the lift force is to some extent directed backwards.*

speed and rate of spin a driver gives the ball—of 20°.

Why not just file back the face of the driver another 12° or 13° and then hit the ball normally, leaving the extra loft to raise the send-off angle to 20°? Because it won't work out the way you mean it to. Add 12° of loft to the face of a driver, for instance, and, because you make the blow more oblique, you cut by 6% the speed with which it sends the ball away *and* you double the backspin. The result is a weaker, and considerably more soaring shot, which falls shorter than your original drive instead of going further.

Increasing the angle at which you drive the ball off will add to the distance it goes only if you do it without either reducing the ball's speed off the clubface or increasing its spin. This a player can only do by timing and positioning his whole swing so as to hit the ball with normal impact action, but slightly on the upswing, instead of at the horizontal.

To send a ball off at 20°, a driver with 10° of loft on its face would have to be swung at about 13° above the horizontal as it hits the ball. This is very nearly impossible; but, if it were, a blow like this would give a strong player's ball the longest possible carry from the tee.

Aiming for total length

So far we have been talking only about aiming for the longest carry. Usually what we actually want from a drive is the longest total distance: carry plus run.

How far a ball runs on landing depends on a lot of fairly obvious factors like the speed and angle with which it touches down, the nature, length, wetness of the turf and how hard or soft the ground is.

These all vary widely, but however they stand for any shot, one fact is constant: that the faster the ball is travelling forward as it lands, the further it will run. Thus even if a lower-flying drive loses quite a bit on carry, it may more than make up for that in run. So although 20° may still be the best angle at which to send off a full drive towards a marshy inland February fairway, something nearer 10° will give the longest drive on dry summer seaside turf.

In most combinations of conditions, the longest drive will often be the one that goes off at 12° or 13°—a little higher than the starting angle of most people's drives, most of the time, but not very much so.

In general, in fact, comparatively little may be gained in total distance off the tee even by the most strenuous and drastic attempts to alter the trajectory. For the vast majority of golfers, especially upon British Isles fairways, hitting the ball true and in good timing will thus prove much more important to good driving than 'flying this one a bit higher'.

A two-wood from the tee?

As we've said, the best angle at which to send a drive off from the tee still depends, amongst other things, upon how fast it is going to set off: that is, how hard you are going to hit it.

For the average good golfer 20° and 13° are likely to give the longest carry and total length respectively. For a very big hitter, 18° and 11° might be more effective angles. For the shorter hitter, though, who gives the ball a gentler blow, the corresponding angles will most certainly be higher: more like 25° and 18°.

The reason for this, of course, is that the weaker hitter needs a bit more backspin on his shot in order to give it his greatest length. This is why many older players and lady golfers—as well as beginners and children—often seem to drive better with a spoon than a driver.

How anyone actually makes contact with the ball, of course, affects this as well as how hard he hits it; but certainly only the really big hitter can get any advantage out of using a very straight-faced driver. Club makers nowadays, knowing this, tend to make drivers with more loft than in the past—especially when they are designed for general sale to week-end players.

Here again, though, any player may be a rule unto himself. A short-hitting slicer, for instance, may manage best with a straight-faced driver simply because his habitual slight slice puts abnormal loft on the ball. Conversely, of course, he may have developed his slice through trying to get the ball to fly with a driver too straight-faced for him; and like the man who hits the ball straight but not far, might do much better in the long run with a two- or even a three-wood.

How wind affects a ball's flight

From what we have already seen about the relationship of spin, drag, carry and lift, the effects of wind blowing with or against the shot will be fairly obvious.

A wind behind will, in effect, reduce the speed at which the ball sets off through the air; so that although the player sends it off at the usual speed from the tee and with the usual rate of backspin, once it is in flight both drag and lift will be less than usual. To make up for this drop in lift, the ball thus needs to be sent off at a higher angle of projection, or with more backspin than usual, or both.

With the wind blowing dead against the shot, equally clearly, both drag and lift will be increased, so that unless the drive is sent off lower than usual or with reduced backspin, or both, the ball will tend to soar above its customary trajectory, and drop short.

The fact that for any wind, there will be a best angle for any drive to be sent off at suggests that the reverse might also be true: that for any particular angle of projection of a drive, there would be one strength of wind which would send the ball further than all others. Although this is not true of a drive's total length, for which—as every golfer knows—the bigger the wind, the longer the run, it is true for carry, as many professional golfers know too.

An example can most easily make this clear. Table 25:1 shows the effect of different winds on the same drive.

Table 25:1 *The computed effect of wind on a well-hit drive.*

Wind speed (feet/second)	Carry of shot (yards)	Total length of shot (yards)*	Time of flight (seconds)
40 (against)	160	165	7·3
20 (against)	190	207	6·5
0 (calm)	202	232	5·8
20 (behind)	208	253	5·1
40 (behind)	204	266	4·4

* The run included in this column is an estimate based on the forward speed of the ball when it first hits the ground. It will in any event depend on ground conditions.

As can be seen, although the total length of the drive steadily increases as headwind drops and following wind swells, the same is not true for carry. As the strength of a following wind increases from 20 feet per second to 40 feet per second, carry begins to drop again. The actual turning point, when you work out all the figures, proves to be a wind speed of 25 feet per second.

The figures in the table are computed ones; there is an element of doubt in their absolute values. The point being made though, is not in doubt, namely that the carry of any given drive will not increase indefinitely with a stronger and stronger following wind. Because the reduction in lift tends to cancel out the reduction in drag, the carry will reach a maximum, which in this particular case is calculated to occur at a wind speed of 25 feet per second and will thereafter begin to drop again.

The more lofted the shot, the higher will be the wind speed for maximum carry; and, in anything short of a hurricane, it would be safe to assume that the carry of medium and short irons will increase with the strength of the following wind.

A following wind can never, of course, make a ball accelerate forward (failing a gust of over 140 miles per hour). It merely reduces drag and thus slows the ball down from its initial 135 miles per hour or so more gradually than usual.

The reduction in carry of a drive can obviously be quite important to a player if he stands on a tee in a strong following wind, and decides to try to fly the ball over a distant bunker. If he really knows his game, he may decide that he'll be more sure of achieving the carry with a two- or three-wood than a

driver. He'll need more backspin than usual in order to keep the ball in the air long enough to drop beyond the bunker; and he will need this more critically than the greater speed off the clubface he gets from a driver.

In practice, most competent golfers instinctively make corrections to the angles at which they send the ball off when playing against or downwind, either by adjusting their method of striking, or by changing their club: higher and a shorter club downwind, lower and a longer club against the wind.

A strong headwind doubles the width of hooks and slices

The table also shows how the time of flight of the ball can vary according to the strength of the wind blowing behind it or against it.

Downwind shots, despite travelling further, come down again more quickly: only five seconds for a full drive with a strong breeze behind, for instance, compared to six and a half for a similar stroke into a similar breeze. This, of course, radically affects the amount of damage unintentional sidespin can do to where the ball lands up. The factors involved here can be stated fairly simply.

When a sidespun ball is flying through the air, the amount by which it will deviate to right or left is proportional to the square of the time during which the sidespin force operates.

Quite apart from the strength of the force itself, therefore, the amount the 40-feet-per-second wind against would make the ball deviate compared to the same wind behind would be —from the table—as $7·3^2$ is to $4·4^2$. That is, the headwind shot would go about 2·7 times more crooked than the downwind one.

But that is only part of the story. The force causing hooks and slices is basically the same as that causing lift. In fact, it is just lift with the axis of spin slightly tilted (see Chapter 20). The hooking or slicing force will thus similarly vary rapidly with the speed of air-flow past the ball, just as the lift force does.

It works out that the sidespin force at the start-off of a hooked or sliced drive, against that same 40-feet-per-second wind, is more than twice the sidespin force from the same stroke with the same wind behind.

The difference lessens as the ball flies; but taking the whole flight of the ball, there's still, on average, about twice as much sidespin force acting on it throughout its flight against the wind as there is for the same shot downwind.

Thus, reckoning sidespin force and time of flight together,

any hooked or sliced shot is likely to curve during its flight over five times more (2×2·7) into such a headwind than it would downwind.

What this boils down to is that the golfer can expect that a shot, which would hook or slice ten yards off the line in calm air, will curve only five yards off-line in a strong downwind, but no less than twenty-five yards off-line when struck into a strong headwind.

Nearly every golfer, of course, is aware of how this works in practice. But the mathematical size of the effect, in terms of comparison upwind and downwind, may still be new to him; and it is always worth remembering when trying to score as well as possible on a windy day, in face of the hazards as they present themselves hole by hole.

Using a crosswind

Most good golfers know they can gain extra distance on a drive by fading it in a left to right wind, or hooking it in a right to left wind. They may not appreciate the reason for this. It isn't just that the wind is then partially assisting the ball as it nears the end of its flight; but that, in a crosswind, sidespin can actually reduce the drag.

Fig. 25:2 shows how this works, looking down on a ball hit with pure slicing spin through a left to right crosswind. Since the spin makes the front of the ball move in the same direction as the wind, the air flows faster across the front than across the back—exactly as we saw in Chapter 24. And high velocity in front of the ball means low pressure there; low velocity at the back of the ball means high pressure *there*. On its own, this effect would produce a forward force urging the ball on, but it is, of course, combined with all the other effects of drag, lift and sideways force we have already described. The result is that it merely reduces the drag.

Conversely if the ball is spinning in the opposite direction, with its front surface moving against the wind, the drag is increased. This is what happens when we 'hold one up against the wind'.

Possible golfs

In all this and the previous chapter we have been dealing only with the ballistics of golf as it actually affects the man or woman playing the game with the clubs and balls we now use for it.

There is still nothing whatsoever scientifically sacred or

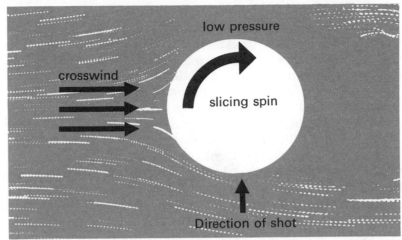

25:2 *Using a cross-wind to gain distance. In this view, looking down on a ball hit with slicing spin, the cross-wind is blowing from left to right. By virtue of its spin, the front of the ball is moving in the same direction as the wind. The air flows faster across the front than across the back; and the pressure is thus lower at the front than at the back as explained in Chapter 24. The situation is complicated by the drag due to the general forward movement of the ball, and the ball is not actually 'sucked' forward as the diagram might suggest. But the drag is reduced and extra distance will be gained as compared with a similar shot hit without slicing spin. It must be aimed off well to the left, of course.*

immutable about those. If one were inventing golf from scratch and wanted to make the best use of the scientific possibilities, there would be no particular reason to light upon the present conventional design of clubs, nor of the way they make up a set. There would perhaps be even less reason to decide on the present size and weight of the ball.

Who is to say that a 7000-yard walk and a three-and-a-half-hour round (or up to six hours in the United States) with all that it involves in land and maintenance costs, makes for the best way of playing the game? Even the hole size of $4\frac{1}{4}$ inches is without real justification other than custom fossilizing historic accident.

It could well be that a change in any or all of the basic equipment rules of the game would make it an even more enjoyable and fascinating test of skill or convenient form of recreation for the majority of those who play it, or both.

This is not just a wide topic but a perfectly legitimate one. We have looked at the question of hole size in Chapter 21 and in Chapters 26 and 32 we take a look here and there at what would happen if we changed some of the game's basic equipment.

Chapter 26

As we said in the last chapter, there is nothing scientifically sacred about the size and weight of the ball used for golf, whether in its British or American version. Before we look into this more closely, a word or two about how the present ball has evolved and how it is made.

As most people know, the golf ball has developed through a number of distinct stages since the game began. As far as we can now find out, the original balls used for the game were shaped out of the most obvious material then available: wood. Next, from the fourteenth or fifteenth century onwards, came the 'feathery' ball: a leather casing stuffed tight with a whole top-hatful of feathers. Making this was a tough, laborious and tricky craft, which put the price of them outside the range of any but Scottish nobles and other comparatively prosperous golfers, while the ordinary working Scot went on playing with wood.

Understandably, nobody was more scathing about the heretical 'gutty', when it first came in about 1848, than those professionals who had the strongest vested interest in the skills of feathery ball making. The gutty—moulded directly out of a lump of the gutta-percha used as packing for imports from the East—completely undermined their craft and trade.

Resilient feathery v. tough gutty v. resilient Haskell

For a time they made as much as they could out of the fact that it felt harder on the clubface, which thus had to be made of softer wood; and freshly moulded gutties, smooth as a billiard ball, did not fly so well as the feathery—with which, after all, the St Andrean Frenchman M. Messieux had once hit the Long Hole In in two shots.

It was found, though, that as the gutty became scuffed in play, it flew better; that it was wholly undamaged by being used in the rain; and that if the worst came to the worst, it could always be hammered or remoulded into shape again. These advantages won the day.

The decisive blow to the feathery came when one of the makers, Gourlay, began to turn out gutties at about a shilling each where the feathery then cost up to four shillings. At a stroke, a good ball came within the pockets of the ordinary golfer, and the gate was opened to the great expansion of the game over the next fifty years amongst all kinds and classes in England as well as Scotland. Even the club-makers found some compensation in the speed with which the hard gutty cracked clubheads or wore them out.

The coming of the modern ball began around 1900 when an American golfer, Dr Haskell, realized the possibilities of winding rubber thread tightly into a ball and then putting a cover on it: thus giving the ball some of the resilience and softness off the club of the old feathery again.

The 'Haskell' was an altogether more lively and pleasanter ball to hit; it got up more readily and it flew further; and this, despite its cost, again proved decisive. When Alexander Herd found the amateur John Ball outdriving him with one of these new-fangled balls during a practice round for the 1902 Open at Hoylake, he bought some himself, won the Championship with them, and that about settled the issue for good.

The criteria of the modern ball

Out of the Haskell has evolved the modern ball. Manufacturers' attempts to make better and better versions of it have focused mainly on the three key playing properties: durability, stability in flight, and, most of all, resilience.

The kind of resilience needed, as we saw in Chapter 23, is that which combines the ability in a ball to 'give' to the club's blow, by flattening out, with the highest possible liveliness in springing forcefully back into shape again: a high 'coefficient of restitution'. The two together have decisive effects upon how well a ball will last, upon what it feels like to hit, and upon how far it will go.

An ordinary unstressed lump of rubber, of course, will fill the bill for 'give'; but it takes the modern ball's twenty-five to thirty yards of rubber windings—stretched to almost ten times that length around a central core—to give enough resilience to offer the best combination so far achieved of a large range of 'give', or deformation, and a high coefficient of restitution. The central core is necessary in order to bring the ball's weight up to 1·62 ounces. Usually it consists of a sac filled with heavy paste, but some makers use steel centres.

Various factors limit how far the makers can go. If they try to give a ball an even higher coefficient of restitution by winding the thread too tightly, it only snaps, either straightaway or as soon as the ball is knocked about a bit. However, makers can, if they want, produce balls with the thread wound more tightly than it is for the standard balls sold to week-end golfers. Indeed, a small proportion of balls produced by the standard manufacturing process turn out to be over-tightly wound, and may be rejected for general sale. These hard balls are sometimes supplied to professionals; and in America they are

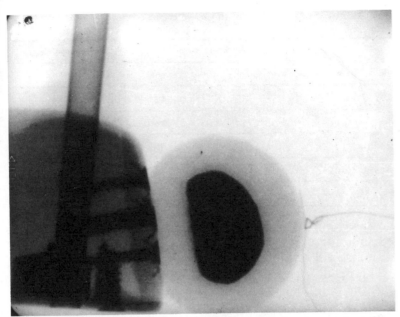

26:1 *An X-ray flash picture of the ball and clubhead at impact in a drive. The elastic windings of the ball show up as a grey outer shell, and the central sac of heavy paste appears very dark. You can see how much the centre is deformed by the blow. For this reason the material used for the centre must be carefully chosen, otherwise too much energy may be lost in deforming it.*

Table 26:1 *How ball 'compression' affects the length of a drive.*

'Compression' of ball	CARRY OF DRIVES (YARDS)		
	Short drive	Medium drive	Long drive
Hard	173	216	257
Medium	166	207	242
Soft	162	201	232

offered for general sale as 'high compression' balls.

Their coefficient of restitution is higher than that of the standard sale ball, and they fly further when hit by any kind of golfer. They stay in contact with the clubface for a slightly shorter time; and although this should not affect the 'control' a player has over the shot, it *does* mean that the force between ball and clubface rises more sharply and to a higher value than with the standard ball. This is transmitted up the shaft as a 'harder feel' to the hands, which the average player usually dislikes; and he is quite happy to accept the makers' implied assurances that the softer ball is best for him.

Harder balls go further

On this point, we are grateful for the results of tests made by Dunlop. Their driving machine had been set to hit balls of different compressions at three speeds of swing, chosen to represent the drives of long, medium and short hitters. The results shown in Table 26:1 speak for themselves. Even for the ladies, a 'high compression' ball goes further—if they hit it as well.

Has the best possible resilience already been reached in the manufacture of golf balls? There is certainly still considerable background research going on into materials or treatment for the centre round which the thread is wound, for the thread itself, and for making the cover. Another development is in methods of 'lubricating' the threads so as to cut down the energy lost in squashing the ball. Possibly most significant of all, experiments are being made with new materials, from which a homogeneous ball (made in one piece, of one material, like the gutty) can be made.

There may be difficult technical problems to overcome in this last development, but it is not impossible that, twenty years from now, all golf balls will be of this type. Being much less complicated to manufacture than the present ball, they ought to be cheaper, they ought to be virtually indestructible, and they may even be considerably more lively.

Whether there would be any point in any maker producing a substantially more resilient ball, though, is doubtful. Both in Britain and America the ruling bodies of golf, the Royal and Ancient Golf Club of St Andrews and the United States Golf Association, have been concerned for some time at the greater and greater distances professionals have been able to hit better and better balls.

Does the ball already go too far?

The U.S.G.A. already limit resilience by means of a testing machine of their own, from which no ball may exceed a certain speed out of impact from a set strength of the machine's striking. The U.S.G.A. in 1965 went so far as to declare a number of latest models of American balls illegal; and thus compel the makers to withdraw all offending stocks of them.

The R. and A. as yet enforce no such limitation on a British ball's liveliness though they have been looking into the possibilities. Their caution in the matter should not be taken for any conservative obstinacy, but more an appreciation of the many unsatisfactory features, both in principle and in practical operation, of velocity testing as a means of limiting the distance a golf ball can be driven.

There can be little doubt, though, that if some makers suddenly produced a ball with a coefficient of restitution substantially improving on the current top-class ball's 0·68 to 0·70, thus perhaps adding anything up to 40 yards to the carry of a good drive, the issue would become—to say the least of it— a live one.

There has been, for a long time, a strong school of thought amongst experienced British golfers which holds that the modern ball already goes too far for the good of the game. During the last forty years it has reduced the championship playing value of many famous courses, and enforced the provision of new back tees everywhere, thus incidentally adding to the total land needed for a course and to the time taken to play a round. All of these make good arguments, they say, not just for setting a limit to the distance the ball will go, but —better still—for reducing it again to below its present formidable power of carry.

How to limit the ball by weight: 'A golf ball should float'?

Limiting the distance the ball can be driven could, of course, be done quite easily without making any specific rules for speed off impact. It could be done by limiting its weight to something less than the present 1·62 ounces; perhaps by a simple rule saying: A golf ball shall float in water.

This would, in effect, reduce a ball's maximum weight by just over 0·3 ounce to about 1·3 ounces, assuming the diameter remained at 1·62 inches. (A 1·68-inch 'floater' would weigh about 1·45 ounces.)

What effect would such a ball have upon the game?

Although externally it could be identical to the present ball, it would have to differ a bit internally. No heavy central core would be required; or alternatively the central sac could be filled with water. In either event the ball would be slightly more resilient than the present 1·62-ounce ball, and thus even livelier off the clubface. It would, in fact, leave the clubhead between 5% and 7% faster, instead of just the 2½% you would expect as a direct result of being lighter.

On the face of it, this would seem to make a 1·3-ounce ball fly even further than the average 1·62-ounce present production ball. But this effect is more than counterbalanced by the

170

Table 26:2 *The computed effect on various drives of using a lighter ball (all distances in yards).*

Kind of drive	1·62-OUNCE BALL		1·3-OUNCE BALL		DIFFERENCES	
	Carry	Total	Carry	Total	Carry	Total
Very short	145	177	143	167	2	10
Medium short	174	205	166	189	8	16
Medium	202	232	189	210	13	22
Medium long	230	258	210	230	20	28
Very long	257	284	228	248	29	36

increased effects upon the ball, once in flight, of the aerodynamic forces working upon a smaller weight of ball. The net effect will be an apparent increase in lift and drag.

The result of all this will be a higher, shorter trajectory, with the ball finally falling to the ground at a steeper angle, and thus running less than a 1·62-ounce ball, too.

Table 26:2 shows what a computer predicted about the way different strengths of drives would fly with 1·62-ounce and 1·3-ounce balls.

These figures the team were able to check against some kindly supplied by Dunlop, who had carried out a similar experiment with their driving machine. The practical figures tally very well with the computed ones. For instance, Dunlop found that the 1·3-ounce ball cut the carry of a short drive from 169 yards to 164, and of a longer drive from 220 yards to 204.

A gain for the average player—and the average golf club

Both these approaches therefore agree that when playing a 1·3-ounce ball the long hitter loses very much more distance from the tee than the weaker player. For instance, the shorter hitter who needs two of his very best shots to reach the green at a 410-yard hole, would still get within twenty yards of the green with the 1·3-ounce ball. But the tiger accustomed to reaching 500-yard par-five holes in two shots, would find himself with a seventy-yard pitch to play with the 1·3-ounce ball.

Look at it another way. Where either player normally needs a drive and a five-iron, the short hitter would still only need a drive and a three-iron, whereas the long hitter would now need two of his best woods.

All this could make the short hitter—the great majority of

golfers—look with some favour upon the idea of a switch to 1·3 ounces.

Until that is, he also heard that the 1·3-ounce ball tends to hook and slice more violently than the 1·62-ounce one—and that into a strong wind it soars to vast heights and loses a lot of distance. But even this could be partly overcome, in all probability, by reducing the depth of the dimpling, thus reducing both drag and lift together.

Here again, the better player might welcome the remaining increased spin effects in that they would enable him to move the ball in the air more easily, and to make it sit down on a green much more firmly (chiefly through its steeper angle of descent).

In its general effects a 1·3-ounce 'floater' would, at one blow, restore many an old course, which had become little more than a drive-and-pitch track for the tigers, to something like its original value, when any hole over 400 yards meant a hard-won 4 at the best.

Even if it achieved nothing else, it would enable clubs to abandon—at least for ordinary play—all the modern-age back tees which have added anything from 200 to 800 yards to the walks between green and tee at hundreds of courses. Except on special occasions of tiger events, if even then, there'd be an end to those long treks back to tees never envisaged when the course was originally laid out.

The time, effort and fatigue saved would be considerable. The more, in fact, you think about the 1·3-ounce ball, and the more you look at it with some detachment, purely for its effects upon the game, the more there seems to be to recommend it.

Mr Average Golfer would almost certainly gain most by its introduction; but whether he would ever be persuaded of this is far less certain. His greatest pleasure lies in 'hitting a snifter' as Wodehouse once put it; and snifters apparently satisfy him more for size than quality.

It is possible that the 1·3-ounce ball would pose some problems on wind-swept seaside putting greens; and in general 1·3-ounces might prove to be just *too* light. But this is something which can only be found out by trying it. In fact, a tournament or two played with 1·3-ounce balls would be very instructive in many ways; and probably—in the increased spin effects offered to the professionals—much more entertaining and technically interesting than any played nowadays with present balls.

What about the American ball?

Before leaving the general subject of ballistics of golf, we should mention the Big Ball *v.* Small Ball controversy.

It has long been alleged—and is still argued determinedly by many very experienced players, golf writers and pundits in general—that the 1·68-inch American-size ball is a better ball for golf than the 1·62-inch size ball. It is argued that it requires the player to strike it more accurately to get the best results, that it sits up better on the fairway for the average golfer to hit, that it enables a skilled player to make it curve intentionally in the air more surely, that it can be made to sit down more securely when pitching into a green, and that owing to its larger diameter it holds its line slightly more truly when rolling over the surface irregularities which exist even in the best greens in the world.

Against this, its detractors allege that, even if its aerodynamic effects enable any intentional spin to be applied to it more effectively, the same goes for unintentional spin, which is far more to the point for the average golfer. In particular they have said that, when struck by a less-skilled player, it tends to soar altogether too easily, and is much more affected by wind. Above all, they say, the lesser distance it flies from the tee would spoil the game for the week-end golfer.

Its enthusiasts counter-argue that the average golfer can't judge it quickly by switching to it from the 1·62-inch ball, because his whole game has been founded and adjusted to the requirements and reactions of the smaller ball, that his swing is accordingly biased in favour of the small one, and that immediately unfavourable reactions to it are thus largely unreliable.

Some even go so far as to claim that the size of the ball is in part responsible for American teams consistently beating the British at their own national game; and for the almost complete eclipse of British professional golf by American upon the tournament stages of the world.

What do we mean by a 'better ball' anyway?

The complete conviction with which these arguments—even the last one—are usually presented may well lead the fair-minded reader to imagine that the facts of the controversy are known; and that only the deductions from the facts are in dispute. But if he tries to find these facts for himself he will soon be disillusioned.

Professional A will claim he loses twenty yards from his

drives with the big ball, while professional B will say there is no difference; golf writer X will knowledgeably estimate a saving of two strokes per round on the putting green by the use of the big ball, while golf writer Y will equally knowledgeably say there is no difference. If he is in an uncharitable mood, the fair-minded reader could be forgiven for supposing that those whose support for one ball or the other is most violent, are just those whose knowledge of the facts is most wanting.

Not that facts are the whole story. The criteria which make one ball preferable to another in the fullest sense are, for the most part outside the scope of physical science. Even if one ball could be shown conclusively to produce lower scores than the other, it would not automatically be a 'better' ball for golf (although it would be the one golfers would use so long as the rules permitted it). Golfers have first to agree upon what they mean by better—and that is really what the whole argument is about. Or rather that is what it *should* be about; but uncertainty, or worse, assumed knowledge, of the actual differences between the two balls has tended to obscure the main issues.

So what we want first of all are facts. In some cases these are simple to discover; in others more difficult. Effects on drive length fall into the first category; effect on overall putting performance into the second. But they are all questions which can, at least in principle, be answered by measurement of some sort.

Factual comparisons: 1·62 versus 1·68

The major part of the research into this was carried out at the Royal Military College of Science, Shrivenham, and at Loughborough University of Technology. The experiments themselves concerned what differences in behaviour and re-action there might be at impact, in flight and on the putting green.

To a large extent they were unable to take account of two important factors in the controversy: the effect of the big ball upon a player's confidence, together with any effects playing consistently with it may eventually have upon his manner of striking a golf ball, and as a result, upon the general calibre of his game.

As the diagram shows, the difference in size between the two balls is small, so however much greater the difference may seem to the golfer addressing the ball, we can expect that any differences in practical behaviour will also be small. The

172

26:2 *The difference in size between the American (1·68 inch) and British (1·62 inch) balls. The silhouettes are actual size.*

experiments, therefore, had to be as accurate as possible, and to be subjected to careful statistical analysis.

For practical reasons the tests were confined to balls made by two leading British manufacturers. There is, of course, the possibility that the ballistic characteristics of British-made American-size balls are not entirely the same as those of American-made ones; but, even so, it seems very unlikely that the conclusions reached would be drastically altered by a wider survey covering all makes of ball.

1·632 versus 1·692

The first thing the team did was to check the actual dimensions of the balls supplied for the experiments. Both were found to vary quite a bit in size, but generally to keep well within the legal limits, the '1·62-inch' balls averaging at 1·632 inches and the '1·68-inch' at 1·692 inches. Both were thus an average 0·012 inch larger than the official minimum size: representing, in fact, a fairly wide 'tolerance' in manufacture.

At the same time the sizes were quite constant enough, in relation to the size of the difference between them, to confirm that ballistically the experiments would be dealing with two quite distinct and different balls. The same went for a quantity called the 'figure of merit' (mass divided by diameter squared), which gives a rough guide to any projectile's ballistic perform-ance. This averaged 17·01 for the British size, 15·83 for the American.

Differences are unpredictable

It is perhaps worth pointing out at this stage that the 1·68-inch ball is not, and cannot be, just a slightly scaled-up version of the 1·62-inch ball. For one thing, if it were, it would weigh not 1·62 ounces (nominal) but about 1·8 ounces; so even if the effect of a simple change of scale were predictable, it might not have much bearing on the actual difference between the two golf balls.

Take the central core, round which the elastic thread is wound. In the 1·68-inch ball it will certainly be lighter and possibly also smaller than in the 1·62-inch ball. In any event there will be more elastic thread wound round the core, so that the resilience and hence the speed off the clubhead may differ in an unexpected way.

The situation is further complicated by makers' tendency to wind the thread more tightly in the 1·68-inch ball. This would make it 'harder'; but, being bigger, it may still deform under impact just as much as the 1·62-inch ball. In fact, it is virtually impossible to predict whether one ball will leave the clubhead faster than the other.

Or take spin. Among the factors on which the amount of spin imparted depends, is the moment of inertia of the ball; and since less of the weight of the larger ball is concentrated at the centre, its moment of inertia is disproportionately larger than the small ball's. The spin will also depend on the amount of compression, the duration of contact and a number of other factors which are not simply related to size, so here again you have to measure it to be sure.

Finally in its flight through the air the ball experiences aerodynamic forces which depend in a fairly simple way on its size; roughly speaking we should expect them to be proportional to the area, or, specifically, to be about 7½% larger on the 1·68-inch ball than on the 1·62-inch ball. But, at least in the case of lift, the depth and shape of the dimples is a critical factor, and most manufacturers adjust these to give trajectories of about the same height with both ball sizes.

Since sidespin is just lift applied at an angle, it follows from this that the difference in the effect of a slice or hook will also be reduced, if not eliminated. Here again, then, it is impossible to make theoretical predictions with any confidence. The effect may vary from one make of ball to another. We must actually make measurements.

Remarkable identity out of impact

Figures supplied by Dunlop, based on driving-machine tests, suggest that, at least in a drive, the two sizes of ball leave the clubhead in almost identical fashion; almost, but not quite,

for in their tests the big ball took nearly 10% less spin than the small ball, and went off about 1% faster. Angles of elevation were not significantly different.

The G.S.G.B. team repeated and extended these experiments to cover five-iron and seven-iron shots as well as drives, and the balls were struck by a professional golfer. They found no differences in speed, spin or angle of elevation with any of the three clubs; or more strictly, the extremely small differences they did find could have easily arisen by random effects. Some of the results of these tests are shown in Figs. 26:3 and 26:4.

Taking due account of the fact that some measurements were more reliable and constant than others, the team's overall assessment of the way the large and small ball respond to the same impact is:

1. The angle of elevation is the same.
2. The spin imparted is probably about the same, and certainly any difference is no bigger than the rather large variations in spin you get from shot to shot anyway.
3. The speed of the big ball could be very marginally greater than that of the small ball, due in part to the increased tension and greater volume of elastic thread; but here again, if there is a difference, it is smaller than shot-to-shot variations in speed.

In sum: the same swing with the same club sends either size of ball off in very much the same way.

Flight variations

The next thing was to test the flight characteristics of each ball. Again figures were already available from Dunlop, and again shots hit by a professional golfer (Norman Quigley) were measured. In addition, the team actually used the Dunlop driving machine for their own tests, and finally tested both balls in a wind-tunnel to obtain basic information on the aerodynamic forces.

The out-of-doors tests with the professional showed up no significant difference between the two ball sizes in the length (carry) obtained with any of the three clubs, driver, five-iron and seven-iron.

On the other hand in the driving-machine test the big ball suffered a small loss of length: ranging from about eight yards in the carry of a long drive (230 yards to 222 yards), down to four or five yards in the carry of a short drive (180 yards to 176 yards). The big ball comes to earth rather more steeply—

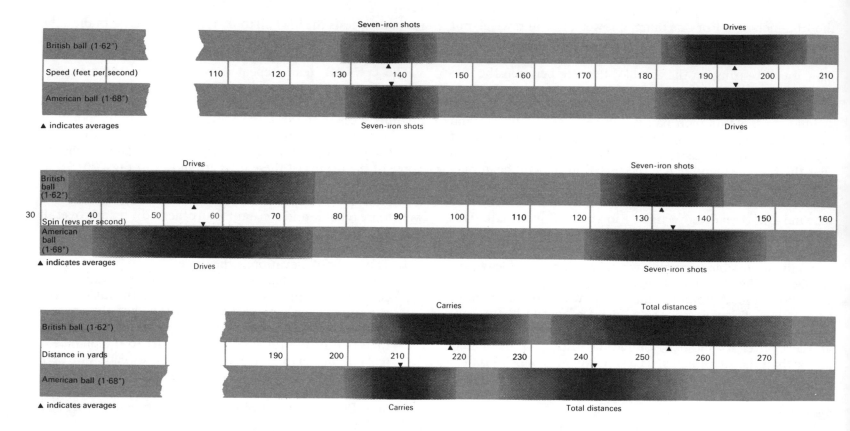

								Seven-iron shots										Drives		
British ball (1·62″)																				
Speed (feet per second)			110	120	130	140	150	160	170	180	190	200	210				
American ball (1·68″)																				

▲ indicates averages

Seven-iron shots   Drives

		Drives												Seven-iron shots						
British ball (1·62″)																				
Spin (revs per second)	40	50	60	70	80	90	100	110	120	130	140	150	160				
American ball (1·68″)																				

▲ indicates averages   Drives   Seven-iron shots

					Carries			Total distances							
British ball (1·62″)															
Distance in yards		190	200	210	220	230	240	250	260	270					
American ball (1·68″)															

▲ indicates averages   Carries   Total distances

or if you prefer it, with less forward speed—than the small ball, and thus does not run so far. In this way it may lose a further three to five yards in average ground conditions.

The height of the trajectories turned out to be much the same. This may surprise some readers; but it shouldn't really do so, because the dimples on the larger ball are usually designed to give it roughly the same height of trajectory as the small ball. It does, however, cast serious doubts on one of the favourite arguments advanced by supporters of the big ball: that it encourages the development of a swing which will drive the ball forward and not scoop it up.

As we said earlier, the reduction in lift, produced by adjustments to the dimples of the big ball, will also tend to reduce the effects of sidespin and, so to some extent at least, compensate for the extra area of the big ball. This too was borne out by tests: in producing hooks and slices some forty yards off-line from a given setting of the driving machine, the two balls were indistinguishable.

174

26:3 *The speed at which British size (1·62-inch) and American size (1·68-inch) balls leave the clubhead of a seven-iron and a driver. The diagrams represent the results of many shots hit by a professional golfer. You can see that in this test the two sizes of ball behaved almost identically—both in average speed imparted and in the 'spread' of observed speed around the average, as represented by the shading. (For technically minded readers the shading in the diagrams covers two standard deviations on either side of the average.)*

26:4 *The spin imparted to the British size (1·62-inch) and the American size (1·68-inch) ball by a driver and a seven-iron. The diagram represents the results of many shots hit by a professional golfer. You can see that in this test the two sizes of ball took on almost the same amount of spin on average. Notice the large 'spread' in the observed spins, as indicated by the shading; some drives, for example, took on nearly twice as much spin as others.*

26:5 *The length of drives hit by a machine using the two sizes of ball. The 'spread', as represented by the shading, of a large number of shots, even when hit by a machine at a fixed setting, puts a different perspective on the bald statement that 'on average the British ball carried 8 yards further, and ran an overall distance of 12 yards further than the American'. The spread would be greater for a good golfer; greater still for the average club golfer. In fact, the lengths of his drives with the two sizes of ball would overlap so much that he could not distinguish between them on the basis of distance alone.*

The effect of a crosswind was also studied. This is fundamentally not a process depending on spin; it is rather just drag operating sideways. The dimples which give less lift to the big ball would not be expected to reduce the drag correspondingly (which, of course, is why the big ball loses distance) and the big ball might well be more affected by crosswinds.

This expectation was again borne out by experiment, though the difference observed is greater than would be expected on theoretical grounds. On drives averaging 240 yards or so, a strong crosswind blew the American-size balls about fifteen yards off course, as against only nine yards for the British.

What theory says about it

Many of these results may surprise readers: particularly those who have been swayed by the more persuasive supporters of one ball or the other; and there are a few more surprises to come. Meantime it is worth looking a bit more deeply at the reasons for some of the differences in flight—or, in some cases, the absence of differences where they might have been expected.

Other things being equal, the very simplest considerations, as we said, suggest that both the lift and the drag forces would depend on the area of the ball: that the forces acting upon the big ball would thus be $7\frac{1}{2}\%$ greater than those upon the small ball. But by altering the dimples the manufacturers can change that a little; and it really requires direct measurement of these two forces in a wind-tunnel to find out exactly what the differences are.

The team did this, and confirmed, in general, that drag on the American ball was approximately $7\frac{1}{2}\%$ greater than on the British ball. Lift was also greater, but it was not possible to say by how much, since it fluctuated in an irregular way over the observed range of velocities which were, in any case, owing to limitations in the wind-tunnel, lower than the velocities actually produced in play.

It was decided, therefore, that in computing theoretical trajectories, both drag and lift should be assumed to be $7\frac{1}{2}\%$ greater on the American ball for the same combination of spin and speed.

On this basis, computed ranges confirmed, in general terms, the driving-machine results. Table 26:3 shows this for three lengths of drive. The amount of run is, of course, something that will vary a lot, and therefore figures for overall distance

Table 26:3 *Computed differences in range between British (1·62″) and American (1·68″) balls. (All distances in yards.)*

Kind of drive	BRITISH BALL		AMERICAN BALL		DIFFERENCE	
	Carry	Total	Carry	Total	Carry	Total
Short	145	177	143	173	2	4
Medium	202	232	198	226	4	6
Long	257	284	250	274	7	10

must be viewed with some reservation. Nevertheless, in almost any ground conditions the small ball will run a little further than the big ball. In short, we can be confident that the *differences* in carry are reasonably accurate and that the differences in overall range will be slightly greater, approximating to the figures in the table for some particular near-average ground conditions.

The computed effect of head and tail winds on the 'Medium drive' of Table 26:3 is shown in Table 26:4. With the same reservations about run as in Table 26:3, you can see that the six-yard difference in overall range is almost doubled when the drive is played into a strong wind, and halved when the wind is helping. The differences would, of course, be greater for the 'Long drive' of Table 26:3 and less for the 'Short drive'.

One slightly surprising result of the calculations was that despite the assumed difference of $7\frac{1}{2}\%$ in lift the height of the computed trajectories was only 5% greater for the big ball than for the small one (three feet in sixty feet) and the time of flight only $2\frac{1}{2}\%$ greater. As we observed earlier, in practice the lift may not differ by as much as $7\frac{1}{2}\%$, so even these small differences probably exaggerate the true situation. Incidentally, the slightly longer time of flight of the 1·68-inch ball

Table 26:4 *Comparison of wind effect on the British (1·62″) and American (1·68″) balls: computed trajectories for a well-hit drive. (All distances in yards.)*

Wind condition	BRITISH BALL		AMERICAN BALL		DIFFERENCE	
	Carry	Total	Carry	Total	Carry	Total
40 feet per sec against	160	165	151	154	9	11
Calm	202	232	198	226	4	6
40 feet per sec behind	204	267	204	264	0	3

accounts for the surprisingly small loss in carry in a drive—surprising that is, in view of the greater drag. A $2\frac{1}{2}\%$ increase in time of flight would mean roughly five yards 'won back' from the loss in carry suffered through the greater drag on the big ball.

Pitching to the green—nothing in it

The team carried out tests to try to answer two questions: first, does one ball stop more quickly than the other on a short pitch to the green; second, and equally important, is the amount of run on a short pitch more consistent (and so more predictable) with one ball than with the other?

In neither case did they find any significant difference between the two balls. For example, on a nine-iron pitch carrying thirty yards through the air to a fast, but not bone-hard green, tests showed that the big ball ran, on average, 36·5 feet, and the small ball 36·7 feet—virtually identical.

The consistency of run, represented by a statistical quantity called the 'standard deviation', was also very much the same for both sizes of ball.

Of course, indistinguishable behaviour on the short pitches will not necessarily carry over to full iron shots to the green. The team did not test the run on these; but it is plausible to argue that owing to the big ball's slightly steeper descent, long approach shots with it will run a little less than those with the small ball, at least on some types of green.

Even in that case, though, the difference in run is unlikely to amount to more than 10% of the total run—about what it is in a drive.

The overall conclusion then is that, though the bigger ball may stop marginally more quickly from a full iron shot, on short pitches neither ball has any advantage over the other—either in quickness or consistency of stop.

Putting differences—also non-existent

The team's experiments on putting were very comprehensive. They included machine tests of consistency of behaviour, on good greens, bad greens and on laboratory test surfaces; and, in addition, thousands of putts struck by hundreds of golfers on both real greens and artificial surfaces were measured and recorded.

The results of these experiments are too numerous to detail here, but one example fairly represents the essence of them. Well over a hundred golfers took part in a putting competition

Table 26:5 *British (1·62″) ball v. American (1·68″) ball on the greens: results of a putting competition.*

	British ball (1·62″)	American ball (1·68″)
Holes played	1017	1017
Total putts	2046	2037
Average score for a nine-hole round	18·11	18·03
Number of holes in one	132	133

in which each had to play two rounds on a putting green, whose nine holes varied from 10 feet to 36 feet in length. They played in pairs, each pair being given one British-size and one American-size ball, which they exchanged after every hole. Thus every hole was played an equal number of times with both sizes of ball.

The results are summarized in Table 26:5. The small differences are not statistically significant. In other words the experiment failed to establish that golfers putt any better with one ball than with the other.

With two unimportant exceptions, that has been the conclusion reached in all the tests so far carried out.

We'd better just mention these exceptions, however. The first is that on an exceedingly rough artificial surface (much rougher than any green is likely to be) there was some suggestion, and no more than that, that the 1·68-inch ball was less easily knocked off its line.

The other exception is just the converse of the first: on the very true, almost billiard table surfaces used in the Muirfield putting experiments (see Chapter 21) the British ball was holed slightly more often than the American (40% of putts holed as against 38%). It is not certain that this was entirely an effect of ball size. Other factors may have had a slight effect; for example, some putters were used predominantly with one ball or the other. Nevertheless, even allowing for this sort of effect, there was at least a suggestion that the British ball was a little more likely to go in. When you think about it, this is what you would expect on a 100% true surface—simply *because* of its smaller size; going to extremes, a marble would go in more easily than a tennis ball. Calculations show that the speed at which a golf ball must be travelling in order just to fall back in when it hits the centre of the hole is about 2% greater for the British ball than for the American.

Of course, greens on all golf courses have surfaces somewhere between billiard table smoothness and doormat roughness; so that the slight advantages of one ball or the other will tend to cancel each other.

Thus even the experiments which did produce a difference in putting performance between the two sizes of ball, when taken together are consistent with the conclusion of all the other putting tests: that is, *on the green neither ball has any practical advantages over the other*.

The differences summarized

As far as the effects on playing golf are concerned, the experiments and calculations seem to establish the following physical differences in behaviour between the two ball sizes, when struck in exactly the same way:

A. *Areas where differences almost certainly exist*
1. Carry through the air (1·68-inch loses 2% to 4%).
2. Amount of run on a drive or other full shot (1·68-inch runs up to 10% less).
3. Sideways deviation in a crosswind (1·68-inch deviates 20% to 30% more).
4. Loss of length in a strong headwind (1·68-inch loses more).

B. *Areas where differences probably do not exist, or are so small as to be negligible*
1. Initial velocity, spin and angle of projection of the ball.
2. General performance on and around the green.

C. *Areas where differences depend on dimpling as well as on size (and which may therefore vary from one make to another)*
1. Height of trajectory (1·68-inch may fly up to 5% higher).
2. Amount of deviation in a sliced or hooked shot (1·68-inch may deviate up to 5% more).

The psychology of the matter

So much for the physical factors in the matter—the factors which determine how the two sizes of ball will fly and roll, if struck in precisely the same way. The psychological factors are obviously of equal importance since they can affect how well any player strikes the ball, and thus perhaps modify some of the findings quoted above from straightforward physical investigation. There seems reason to believe that one

critically important difference between the two balls is in the simple and obvious one that the American ball looks bigger—surprisingly much bigger—to the player addressing the ball.

This has two effects. It *looks* easier to hit. And since its centre of gravity is usually 0·05 to 0·06 inch higher above the ground on account both of its larger radius and of its tendency to rest higher on the grass, it must actually *be* easier to hit too—especially for the weaker player, whose dominant problem in the game is getting the ball to fly well at all. To this extent there may be substance in the argument that the player feels he has to 'scoop' or 'flick' at the small ball. The main gain here, though, is still likely to be the one of confidence.

The second effect is that of any individual player's preconceived ideas—be they even wholly erroneous ones—about the ball he is playing with. If, for instance, he expects he is going to be able to pick up the big ball more easily from a tight lie with a two-wood, most likely that's exactly what he will do. If, on the other hand, he is afraid that his drive into the teeth of the wind with the big ball will slice more viciously than usual, then very likely *that* will happen. In all points in golf involving methods and results, confidence promotes success, and lack of confidence disaster. Believing is more than halfway towards achieving.

Not least important, in this context, may be the repeated superstitions associated with putting and the big ball: it will hold its line better, it will dive into the hole more readily, and the like. A man with years of agonized jitters behind him will snatch at any straw of hope, and desperately want it to work. The chances are that it will—at least for a time—so long as he holes the first few he tries. He has eyes only for the thing he seeks. Fortune-tellers and tipsters alike make their livelihood out of this almost universal human weakness.

A recommendation—and the next step?

From the rather heavy cautiousness of much of the above, it might seem as if the team formed no strong general conclusions of their own.

This would not be true at all. Physical differences *have* been established: but neither in number, nor in size, are they so great as many golfers have believed. Indeed the differences that do exist are smaller than the shot-to-shot variations of even the best of golfers, and would probably remain undetected in play. In other words, if a man did not know he was playing with a big ball instead of a small one, it is very unlikely

177

that anything in the results of his shots in the course of a round of golf would make him suspect it.

The logical conclusion from this is that, for the sake of uniformity throughout the world, it is probably worth while our adopting the 1·68-inch ball used in America. It will make virtually no difference to anybody's golf; and golfers will have forgotten all about the controversy a few months after its introduction. In particular, we should not expect to win the Walker Cup, Ryder Cup, or Curtis Cup by virtue of developing super-swings to cope with it. Swings, we strongly suspect, will remain exactly as they were; except those belonging to people who devoutly believe they will have to change.

Let's go a step further, though. If uniformity were established throughout the world, it would then be much easier for the Royal and Ancient Golf Club and the United States Golf Association to get together and give serious consideration to reduction in weight, or possibly increase in size, as a better way of limiting or even reducing the distance a golf ball can be hit. We could even finish up with the rule suggested earlier in this chapter: A golf ball shall float in water.

Section 7

Analysing a Tournament

Chapter 27

Analysing a Tournament: Why Bother?

'You drive for show and putt for dough', is a well-known saying of American professional golf: meaning that, however glorious the professional golfer's long shots, putting is the part of the game which finally and decisively determines his score, and thus his income.

At the same time many ordinary golfers over the last fifty years must have thought, 'If only I could drive like Harry Vardon, or Henry Cotton, or Ben Hogan, or Jack Nicklaus...' (or whoever his current idol happened to be), his idea being that long, straight driving is all-important.

Behind sentiments like these must lie a rough-and-ready mental analysis of the professional golfer's play, dividing the game into a few departments, weighing up variations in performance in these departments, and perhaps comparing the professional's standard of performance with the average golfer's.

These comparisons are nearly always matters of opinion. But they need not be. By making enough of the right kind of observations it is quite possible to analyse in detail exactly how well professional golfers—or, for that matter, ordinary club golfers—do play the game, and to make valid comparisons between the various departments of their games.

Furthermore, establishing exactly how good the leading players are makes it possible to set standards both for learning the game, and for improving in it.

Of course, we know the overall standards, in terms of scores for eighteen holes. But what about the separate components which contribute to the overall standard? How far do they drive? How accurately? How close do they put the ball to the hole when playing from 150 yards? How close from thirty yards? How are these affected by playing from bunkers or rough?

Perhaps it's worth putting the reason for studying all this in another way; as it was put, in fact, by the member of the scientific team who suggested it. He said, roughly: 'We are supposed to be carrying out a study of the golf swing. To do so we want, among other things, to know just how effective a good swing is; and what are the size and frequency of the errors which arise in it. A few members of the panel have some idea of these things, but no one seems to be able to say anything very precise. Cannot we make some basic measurements of the accuracy and effectiveness of good swings in action—preferably under realistic conditions such as at a tournament?'

Naturally it took a non-golfing member of the G.S.G.B.

team of scientists to make such a childishly obvious suggestion!

To answer these questions, then, they organized a team of observers to make a detailed study of play in the Dunlop Masters Tournament at Royal Birkdale in June 1964. In this tournament forty invited players, the leading professional golfers in the British Isles plus a few selected overseas golfers, played four rounds of stroke play: one round on each of the first two days and two rounds on the last day. There was an added interest in it, in that the whole tournament was played exclusively with the 1·68-inch American-size ball.

Analysing the play in this tournament could not, of course, provide any comparison between the performances of professionals and of average golfers. Since then, however, the team have made similar studies of amateur golfers and of lady golfers. At the time of writing these have been only partially analysed; so we are going to concentrate here on the professionals; but we'll make interim comparisons with the amateurs and the ladies where possible.

Besides just measuring the general standard of professional play, we can make two interesting direct comparisons within it. First, we can examine the likely effect of similar improvements (or deteriorations) in different departments of the game, and so get some idea of their relative importance in scoring. Second, we can compare the all-round performance of those who did well in the tournament with that of those who did badly. Thus we may be able to say exactly how many strokes the leading prizewinners gained by dint of their putting, or their long approaches, or their driving.

Many a golfer might have guessed that the main difference between the top nine players in a professional tournament and the bottom nine would prove to be somewhere in the putting. This was duly proved. Obvious, you might say; but what would come next in effect? Chipping? Bunker shots? Driving? Short pitches?

In fact: none of these. The next big difference came in the medium and long iron shots. They and putting between them accounted for *over* 80% of the difference between the scores of the top nine and the bottom nine.

A challenge from the findings

Another arresting result which came out of the main analysis of the play was the tremendous difference it would make to a run-of-the-mill tournament professional's scoring if he were to be able to add twenty yards to the length of his drive, keep them all on the fairway, and then halve the usual inaccuracy of his strokes from there to the hole.

That would certainly be a pretty tall order in the way of self-improvement! But the difference it would make in his scoring is really remarkable. For a player whose scores at Birkdale averaged at *two strokes over par* per round, an improvement like this would knock his average score down to *twelve strokes under par*!

It could, in fact, knock a customary score of 74 to a customary 62. A wholly outlandish round, that might seem—yet the following year Gary Player did, in fact, reel off two 62's in one tournament over a championship course in Australia.

The real interest in all this lies in the implication that 25% of such an improvement might not, really, be an impossible target for a tournament professional to aim at. Yet it would cut his scores by three or four strokes a round—enough to lift an unknown young assistant into the Ryder Cup level in a single season!

What they looked for, where, and how

The team set itself the following specific aims:
1. To measure the performance of first-class professional golfers in the different departments of the game, with a view to setting standards.
2. To determine the importance of each of these departments in professional golf.
3. To determine in what aspects of the game the leading professionals are superior to the others.
4. After a similar study of amateur and lady golfers, to determine where they have most scope for improvement in comparison with the professional.

How to set about this?

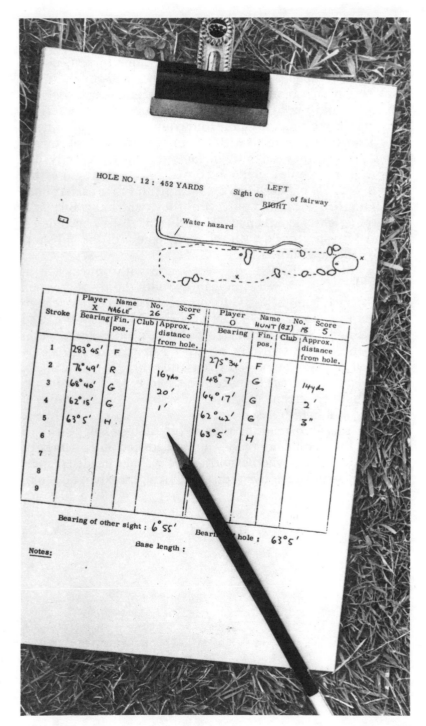

27:1 *A specimen of data sheet for the Birkdale study. Observers, in this case on the left-hand side of the twelfth fairway near the green, recorded angular bearings for every shot played at this hole. Combination of these records with similar ones obtained from the right-hand side of the fairway gave the exact position of every shot to within a few inches. Visual estimates ('Approximate distance from hole' column) served as a check on gross errors in reading the instruments. For example, had the angular bearing of Nagle's third shot been misread as 63° 40' instead of 68° 40', then its distance from the hole would have been calculated as 6·1 feet. Comparison of this with the estimate of 20 feet on the data sheet illustrated (and of 18 feet by the observer on the other side of the fairway) would have indicated an error, and the observation would have been rejected or re-examined.*

Ideally, of course, they would have liked to record the exact point from which every stroke in the whole tournament was struck and precisely where and how it came to rest, noting whether it stopped on the fairway, in the semi-rough, in the thick rough, in a bunker or ditch, in the hole—or anywhere! This could have been done with a hundred trained observers working throughout the whole four rounds of the tournament.

To keep the experiment within comfortable limits of control and statistics, they set out, in fact, to analyse exactly one thousand 'man-holes'. They recorded how every man of the forty in the field played holes 2, 4, 7, 8, 12 and 13 in each round; plus hole 16 in one round only. (For those who know Birkdale, holes 12 (slightly lengthened), 13 and 16 have now become 13, 14 and 17 respectively, with the replacement of the old short 17th by the new short 12th.)

Most of the observations were made with optical instruments, though some were made by eye with the aid of a system of markers (distance posts, for example). The team went to considerable trouble to ensure accuracy of observation and also to eliminate accidental errors. All we need say here is that at the end of the tournament, they had recorded precisely where each shot was played from and where it ended up, in terms of both distance from the hole and type of lie (fairway, rough, bunker, green etc.), for every stroke on every one of the thousand man-holes.

From this information, plus a bit of checking with the P.G.A., they could in theory have deduced all manner of information—even whether short, stocky, bald-headed players over forty struck their five-iron shots straighter than tall, thin,

bespectacled players under thirty!

The most useful thing to do, though, seemed to be to break up the game into four simple compartments: Driving; Long approaches; Short approaches; and Putting. This they did.

The reader should remember here, perhaps, that since the field for the Dunlop Masters Tournament consists only of forty players, each one invited because of some special distinction in the game, the standard of play tends to be higher and more uniform from top to bottom than in most other tournaments. This may well mean that the differences discovered between the play of the leading nine and the trailing nine in this tournament, taking them on the final scores, were less than they would have been for the first two rounds of a run-of-the-mill tournament, in which up to 140 players of all abilities, ages and degrees of experience would be competing.

For their first experiment of this kind, though, the team needed a tournament in which a small field all played the complete four rounds. The whole work of research would then be manageable in size, and no special allowances would be needed for the removal of all the least successful players from the final two rounds, as they would be in an ordinary tournament.

In the Masters, in fact, the team analysed the play of the best of the professionals in that British season, during an event which meant a lot to them both in direct prize money and in the professional value of the title to the winner, and during which each man played to the finish.

What they found out about their play in each of the selected departments of the game, and what the results seemed to signify, are the subjects of the next four chapters.

Chapter 28

Analysing a Tournament: Driving – Length Counts for Most

One of the simplest questions to answer was how far and how straight did the professionals drive.

On holes 2, 8 and 12 in all four rounds, and on 16 in one round, the team recorded 515 drives, both for length and for where the ball finished up. (The recorders watched 520 drives in all, but five were either unobserved or wrongly recorded.)

They had arranged beforehand for a nearby weather station to record the strength and direction of the wind every two hours on each day of the tournament. In the event, it varied only slightly each day. The average wind speeds for the four rounds respectively were 8, 9, 14 and 16 miles per hour. At the second hole it blew against and from the right on the first two rounds, and dead against on the third and fourth. At the 8th and 12th it was more or less dead behind all the time. At the 16th it was behind and from the left during the single round in which observations were made there.

A breeze is worth twenty yards

Even this wind, never more than a breeze and averaging at only 12 miles per hour, considerably affected the driving; as the hole-by-hole table of all the drives recorded shows very clearly.

The wind seems to have made, in fact, about 45 yards' difference in the distance the pros hit the ball between the 2nd, where it was mainly against, and the 8th and 16th, where it was behind.

Although it was also behind at the 12th, the drives here averaged twenty yards less than those at the 8th and 16th. The reason for this was almost certainly the existence of a bunker covering half the width of the fairway, on the left side, at about 270 yards from the tee. This meant that, with the wind

behind them and a firm iron shot still required to reach the green after the drive, the professionals either drove with a spoon instead of a driver in order to make sure of stopping short of the bunker; or else, in an effort to keep to the right of it they tended to drive into the rough, thus losing distance. This presumably also accounted for the lower fraction on the fairway at this hole.

These points aside, the table shows that using the 1·68-inch diameter ball on a seaside course with about average amount of run in the ground, the first-class professional drives the ball about 250 yards from the tee, and hits fairways thirty to forty yards wide about seven times in every ten drives. Not surprisingly, drives which stayed on the fairway averaged a little longer (258 yards) than the overall average. This is partly a reflection of the greater run on the fairway than in the rough and partly also of loss of carry suffered by badly mishit shots.

How wind can affect driving was well illustrated by the difference it made at the second hole when it doubled in strength from 8 to 15 miles per hour and moved from the 'two o'clock' direction (i.e. against and from the right) to dead against. The change in headwind from 4 miles per hour (the headwind component of 8 miles per hour from two o'clock) to 15 miles per hour did two things to the drives. First, the average length dropped from 242 yards to 213 yards; and secondly, the percentage of drives finishing on the fairway there dropped from 76% to 72%—although this difference in accuracy is not big enough to be 'significant' in scientific terms.

Comparing the most and least successful

The longest driver in the tournament turned out, not very surprisingly, to be Roberto de Vicenzo, whose fairway drives averaged 291 yards, including one whopper of 345 yards. Remember though, that 70% of the drives recorded—including this one—were hit downwind. The shortest was Harry Bradshaw whose fairway drives averaged 219 yards.

When the team compared the driving of the nine players who came top in the tournament with that of the nine players who came bottom, they found that the players more successful in this event drove only slightly further than the bottom nine —the average lengths of drive being 255 and 248 yards respectively. Their accuracy was much the same.

It is possible to calculate what these seven extra yards mean in terms of strokes gained by the top players. The calculation

Table 28:1 *Driving: Length and accuracy of the pros at Birkdale.*

Hole	Average wind angle	Width of fairway (yards)	Proportion of drives finding the fairway	Average length of drives (yards)
2	Against and from right	40	75% (of 156)	228
8	Behind	33	71% (of 160)	272
12	Behind	20–40	61% (of 159)	253
16	Behind and from left	30–35	68% (of 40)	276
	Overall average	30–35	69% (of 515)	253

has to run right through the game, of course, from tee to hole. But by taking into account calculations made for the other types of strokes involved (which we'll look at in the next three chapters), the team were able to show that by their slightly longer driving alone the top nine players gained half a stroke per round over the bottom nine.

What is an extra twenty yards from the tee worth?

We can carry this sort of calculation a bit further and look at the difference it might be expected to make to a man's scoring if he added twenty yards to the length of his drives, and put them all on the fairway, instead of missing the fairway with three out of every ten.

It turns out that the extra straightness would gain him a stroke a round, the extra length 1·2 strokes per round.

The implications of this may surprise readers. For one thing, it seems that a first-class professional could gain more by driving the ball twenty yards further, than he could gain by cutting out the three loose drives in every ten (which he had at Birkdale), and thus becoming that idol of golf writers and followers alike—the hundred-per-cent-straight man. It's less surprising, perhaps, when you remember the often erratic routes to the hole taken by such highly successful players as Joe Carr, Harry Weetman and Arnold Palmer; and, of course, it would almost certainly not apply in the same way over a course beset with tough heather, tiger country and close-to-the-fairway boundary fences where even a slightly wayward shot could finish up lost, unplayable or out of bounds. Some of this country does indeed exist in Birkdale's notorious willow scrub; but in most of Birkdale's rough, as it was in June 1964, so long as the ball was not too far from the fairway, a strong player could often still aim for a par with the next stroke.

Even at Birkdale, tee-distance counts for more than straightness

Put it another way, and you can deduce the equally arresting probability that, had any professional in the Masters decided to go all out for distance, so long as he consequently managed to add five yards to the average length of his drives, he would still have gained in his score over the whole tournament—even if, by thus going for length, he had missed one extra fairway in every round. (This assumes, of course, that those shots which missed the fairway would not have gone into much wilder country than before.)

In fact, putting it rather loosely, distance from the tee seems

Table 28:2 *Who drove how far at Birkdale? The average length of drives finishing on the fairway for a few selected players.*

	Average length of drive on fairway (yards)	Position in order of length
de Vicenzo	291	1
Will	279	2
Phillips	274	3
Weetman	273	4
Alliss	265	8
Gregson	260	15
Huggett	257	22
Hunt (B. J.)	252	27
Faulkner	248	33
Haliburton	240	38
Locke	238	39
Bradshaw	219	40

to count for more than accuracy—at least for first-class professionals over a course like Birkdale. Whatever course is played on, though, the balance between the advantages of length and of straightness in driving will depend very much upon the severity of the rough and the chances of longer, wilder shots ending up unplayable or lost.

The same research carried out on a more open course could be expected to show even greater advantage to be gained from long driving at the expense of straightness. On a course on which the ball was lost every time it went off the fairway the balance would swing very much in favour of straightness.

At the very least, the Birkdale experiment offers encouragement to the ambitious young amateur who decides to go all out to develop length from the tee, and not to worry too much about consistent straightness until he has first given his game the power that appeals to him most. He may well be working on very sensible lines after all.

Remember, though, that the conclusion reached applied to

first-class professionals; it may or may not apply to club golfers.

How do amateurs and ladies compare with pros?
More recent results have been worked out on the driving of good amateurs at the Berkshire Trophy (handicaps two or better) and good lady golfers at the English Ladies' Championship (average handicap three). The table shows how they compared with the driving of the specially invited professionals at Birkdale, and also with that of the entire field (including pre-qualifiers) in an ordinary run-of-the-mill professional tournament, held at Little Aston, an inland course.

The Birkdale professionals played the 1·68-inch ball but any loss of length they suffered on that account (ten yards, say) would be roughly balanced by their average being taken over three holes downwind and one against. The amateurs', ladies' and Little Aston professionals' drives were measured at two

Table 28:3 *Driving: How the amateurs and ladies compare with the pros.*

	Birkdale pros	Little Aston pros	Men amateurs	Lady amateurs
Average length of drives on fairway	258 yds	242 yds	239 yds	190 yds
Accuracy	69% on fairways 35 yds wide	66% on fairways 45 yds wide	59% on fairways 45 yds wide	71% on fairways 40 yds wide

holes running in opposite directions, so wind effects would cancel out.

On the basis of their longer and straighter driving one can estimate that the Birkdale professionals would gain about two strokes per round over first-class amateurs.

Chapter 29

Analysing a Tournament: Putting

Let's turn now to the only other fixed point in the game, the hole in the green, and see what happens there.

For the professionals, strokes from tee to green involve rather less wide a variety of golf than they do for the rest of us. Once on the green, though, the game is almost exactly the same for the pros as it is for every other golfer. There is nothing at all any of them can do there with a putter which any other player, no matter what his handicap, is not capable of doing also.

However hard a professional may work at his putting, in fact, he cannot make the ball roll in any way the ordinary golfer cannot. All he can do is to practise and practise away until he has schooled himself, physically, mechanically and mentally, to produce the best putting stroke possible, to read the green accurately, and to strike the ball precisely on the line he chooses at the strength he needs.

Even this won't hole every putt, because of the effects of irregularities of surface. Putting, in fact, is the one part of the game where the pro's whole game is most vulnerable. He is unlikely to have an air-shot on the tee or through the green, or even to duff a stroke completely; but he can miss a short putt just like any other golfer—and that adds just as much to his score for the hole as does the beginner's complete foozle with any other club.

How many from how far

The interest in analysing the pros' putting at Birkdale was not, of course, primarily to check how many putts they took on each green; simply because this is often more a measure of how well a man is striking his shots into the greens than of how well he is putting. For example, the more times he misses the green with his iron shot and leaves himself a chip, the more often he is likely to get down in only one putt. Similarly, a handicap golfer missing most of his second shots will tend to be pitching into a lot of greens from short range, and may thus need fewer putts in the round than a professional playing perfect golf through the green.

What the team was looking for, on the contrary, was not so much 'how many' as 'how accurately': how close to the hole the professionals left putts of different distances, and what proportion of them they holed.

The number of putts taken per green can be considerably affected by characteristics of the course: how large the greens are, how fast and how true their surface, how difficult their

Table 29:1 *Numbers of putts on 1000 'man-greens' at Birkdale.*

	No. of times	No. of putts
Ball holed from off the green	6	0
First putt holed (1 putt)	315	315
Second putt holed (2 putts)	636	1272
Third putt holed (3 putts)	43	129
Total	1000	1716

contours are to judge, and even where the holes are placed.

The team did nevertheless record the numbers of putts taken; and Table 29:1 sets out the results for the thousand times a player was observed putting on a green.

This gives an average number of putts per green of just under $1\frac{3}{4}$ and an average number of putts per round of just under 31.

The irrelevancy of counting the number of putts taken per round (except of course when related to all the other actual strokes taken during the round), is well illustrated by the next table (29:2) which shows how the average number of putts taken at the sixteenth hole was substantially less than at the others. This was almost certainly because, where the players were normally approaching all the other greens from between 200 and 150 yards, the long 16th was only just out of

Table 29:2 *Green by green breakdown of total putts at Birkdale.*

Hole	Length (yards)	Total number of putts taken in four rounds	Average no. per player per green
2	427	281	1·756
4	201	271	1·694
7	143	272	1·700
8	459	274	1·713
12	452	279	1·744
13	199	278	1·738
16	510	61 (one round only)	1·525
	Total	1716	1·716

Table 29:3 *Complete putting performance of the pros at Birkdale. The figures in the main part of the table are the numbers of putts played from the ranges given along the top, and finishing at distances from the hole given down the side.*

		STARTING DISTANCE FROM HOLE (YARDS)										
		0–1	1–2	2–3	3–4	4–6	6–8	8–10	10–12	12–14	14–16	over 16
	Holed	683 (99%)	152 (74%)	58 (48%)	30 (38%)	35 (23%)	13 (12%)	10 (11%)	3 (4%)	3 (4%)	2 (4%)	5 (8%)
FINISHING DISTANCE FROM HOLE (YARDS)	0–½	8	46	51	37	87	56	43	34	19	18	16
	½–1	1	6	9	11	28	33	32	24	25	13	15
	1–1½		1	2	1	2	8	5	15	13	8	10
	1½–2						1	1	4	6	5	4
	2–2½				1			1	2	3	4	7
	2½–3							1		1	1	
	3–3½									1		1
	over 3½										1	
Total		692	205	120	80	152	111	93	83	70	52	58
STROKES TO HOLE OUT	1	683	152	58	30	35	13	10	3	3	2	5
	2	9	53	62	48	115	95	79	77	56	40	45
	3				2	2	3	4	3	11	10	8
Average number of strokes to hole out		1·013	1·259	1·517	1·62	1·78	1·91	1·94	2·00	2·11	2·15	2·05

range in two shots for most of them. The majority, therefore, were pitching their third shot into it from less than fifty yards; which, of course, offered them every time a chance of leaving the ball close enough to hole the first putt.

Table 29:3 sets out how well the players putted from various distances at all holes, including both how many putts they holed and how close to the hole they left the putts they missed.

The first figures worked out, for each separate hole, showed that the standard of putting was very much the same on all the greens recorded. This was to be expected, since no green appeared to offer any special difficulties which the others did not. Running the results from all the greens together, to give an accurate general picture of how the professionals putted, produced the figures in Table 29:3.

An example will probably help the reader to understand it. Suppose you want to know how good the pros were on putts of five yards. Look along the 'starting distance from hole' row of figures at the top, and you will come to the heading '4–6' (yards). The column of figures below this gives the performance when the pros were putting from this distance. Thus a total of 152 putts between four and six yards in length were observed, of which 35 (or 23%) were holed. Of those which missed, 87 finished less than half a yard from the hole, 28 finished between half a yard and a yard away, and 2 finished between a yard and a yard and a half away. If you want to know how many putts the pros took to get down rather than how close to the hole they left them, the figures near the foot of the column tell you. Out of the total of 152, only one putt

187

was needed 35 times, two putts 115 times, and three putts twice, making an average of 1·78 putts.

These professionals didn't 'twitch'

Some interesting points stand out in the table. The number of short putts missed was very small indeed: from three feet or less only 9 in 683. This almost certainly represents a substantially higher standard of reliability in holing the short ones than that of most club golfers. It would represent almost heaven on earth to those lower-handicap amateurs afflicted for years with the 'yips' or the 'twitch', and who can—and do —at times miss anything up to two in every three from three feet.

That this reliability in holing out is consistent for the top-class professionals shows clearly in the figures for increasing lengths of putt. From three feet to six feet, they still holed three in four; from six feet to nine feet, nearly one in every two; and from nine feet to twelve feet, they were still getting in more than one in three.

Light on an old controversy

Only from twelve feet did the professionals' chances of holing drop to below one in four. This figure, incidentally seems to offer fairly strong confirmation of the small likelihood of their gaining a reward, in the shape of a birdie, from an iron shot laid between twelve and fifteen feet from the hole—the sort of length of putt often left after an excellently judged and executed stroke. This is one issue upon which the veteran American Champion, Gene Sarazen, has long based his belief that to put a proper premium upon good stroke-making, golf needs a 6-inch hole, and that the $4\frac{1}{4}$-inch diameter we use now is too small for the game to work at its best. We discussed this in Chapter 21.

Another interesting point which emerges, is that it is only when the length of his putt is ten yards or more that the top-class professional begins to leave one in four of them more than three feet from the hole; and that only from about twelve yards outwards does he begin to become even 10% liable to take three putts.

Putting probabilities

Another way of stating the results from the table is to show them in the form of a 'probability of holing out' curve, plotted against different lengths of putts as in Fig. 29:1.

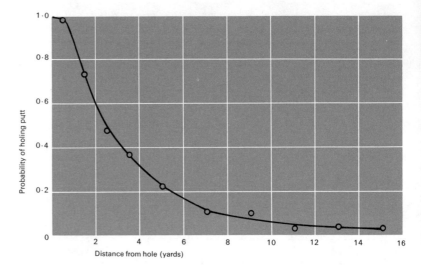

29:1 *The odds on holing out from different distances on the green. The circles are the observed probabilities at Birkdale; the graph is drawn as a smooth curve to smooth out random fluctuations in the observations. It shows that the pros at Birkdale had a 9 in 10 chance of holing from 1 yard, and a better than 2 in 10 chance of holing from 5 yards.*

Even for those into whom the mere sight of a graph like this strikes immediate terror, it works quite simply really. Look along the scale at the bottom to any length of putt you have in mind; then look at the point on the curve immediately above it, and you can at once read off at that level up the graph, in the scale on the left, the chance which the average professional at Birkdale had of holing any one putt from that distance. The circles merely show where the particular points taken directly from the table were 'plotted', after which the curve itself was drawn as a smooth combination of their slight variations.

For instance, for a putt of four yards, the chance of holing it was just over 0·3, or nearly one chance in three.

The second graph (Fig. 29:2) takes in as well the chance of holing the second putt after missing the first, from any range. You read it in exactly the same way. For instance, from four yards the professionals at Birkdale were likely, on average, to need 1·7 putts.

The critical factor of gauging the strength

The team also checked the comparative importance, in holing out, of direction and strength. By means of a mathematical study of results, they were able to show that up to a distance of

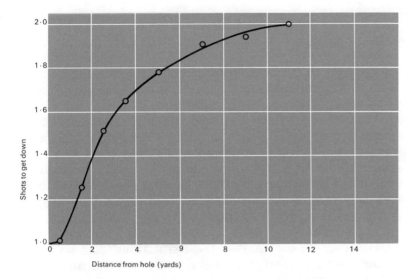

29:2 *The average number of putts the pros at Birkdale needed to hole out from different distances. For example, from 3 yards they averaged about 1·6 putts— or roughly speaking two putts three times out of five, and one putt twice out of five.*

four yards from the hole the professionals hardly ever missed a putt through leaving it short of the hole, or hitting it too hard to drop.

Above that length of putt, though, it appears—as indeed one might have expected—that gauging the strength of the putt becomes progressively more important, until from about ten yards outwards it is just as important a factor in holing out as is hitting the putt on the correct line.

The importance of getting strength right in *laying a long putt dead* is common knowledge amongst golfers; and, of course, on a sloping green, strength and direction are mutually dependent on each other. It's still of interest, though, to see how increasingly important strength of putt is in determining the putt's chances of *dropping into the hole* as the distance from which it is struck increases.

British pros don't putt worse than Americans

Another comparison of some interest which the team were able to make was between the standard of putting at Birkdale and the standard of putting in four United States Open Championships from 1963 to 1966.

These were recorded and analysed by Jack Reddy, and published in the U.S.G.A. *Golf Journal* of November 1964,

November 1965, and November 1966. The distances Reddy worked from were different from the G.S.G.B. team's, and along with differences in the method of observation between the two studies, this might conceivably produce small distortions in comparing their results. The team nevertheless adjusted their figures to compare directly with Reddy's (Table 29:4). From the comparison there can be little doubt that the players at Birkdale putted just as well as the fifty or so qualifiers for the last day's play in each of the U.S. Opens, and considerably better in the four to twelve foot range, than the whole American field of 150.

Since most of the players at Birkdale were British, this seems to contradict the accepted belief that American professionals putt more consistently than ours do. We cannot be certain about generalizations like this however, because the precise state and nature of the greens affects performance markedly. The difficulties of the greens during the 1963 U.S. Open were widely reported at the time; and indeed the fluctuation from year to year of the American results underlines the dependence on the greens themselves. For example, in the four to seven foot range the proportions of putts holed varied from as low as 48% (in 1963) to as high as 64% (in 1965), averaging at 58% over the four years.

The G.S.G.B. team experienced the same effect when they repeated their study of putting during the Schweppes P.G.A. Championship held at Princes, Sandwich, in April 1965. Many players complained of difficulties on the greens and this was duly reflected in their results, which were poorer than in any of the other studies.

Table 29:4 *Do American pros putt better than British? Putts holed in four U.S. Opens compared with the performance of the pros at Birkdale and Sandwich.*

	BRITISH TOURNAMENTS		U.S. OPEN RESULTS (averaged 1963 to 1966)	
Distance	Birkdale	Sandwich	All players	Qualifiers
0–2 feet	99%	99%	99%	99%
2–4 feet	89%	83%	87%	89%
4–7 feet	65%	54%	58%	64%
7–12 feet	38%	32%	34%	38%
12–30 feet	16%	12%	14%	15%

Table 29:5 *Putting: Comparison of professionals, amateurs and ladies.*

Length of putt	PROPORTION OF PUTTS HOLED		
	Birkdale professionals	Berkshire amateurs	Ladies
Up to 3 feet	99%	99%	98%
3–6 feet	74%	73%	68%
6–9 feet	48%	48%	47%
9–12 feet	38%	42%	23%*
12–30 feet	16%	8%	11%
Fraction of greens requiring three putts	1 in 23	1 in 20	1 in 10
How close, on average, did they put their long† putts?	2·4 feet	2·5 feet	4·4 feet

* This figure unreliable: not enough observations.
† Putts of 30 feet or more.

Amateurs sometimes putt as well as pros

A similar study of putting at the Berkshire Tournament for amateurs of handicaps two or better revealed the surprising result that their standard was almost identical with the professionals at Birkdale. The comparison is summarized in Table 29:5. You would not expect amateurs, even county-class ones, to putt as well as the best professionals and we can only suppose that the state of the greens must have been partially responsible for this result. The greens certainly looked very true to the observers recording the data.

Ladies' putting: not so good as you might think

Expert opinion has never been unanimous on how the putting (and short game generally) of the best lady golfers compares with that of first-class men.

The last column of Table 29:5 summarizes putting at the 1966 English Ladies' Championship, held at Hayling Golf Club; and suggests that the ladies were not so good as the men, particularly on the long putts.

It may not be quite fair to draw this conclusion with absolute firmness on the basis of this one set of results. For one thing,

the field in the English Ladies' Championships, with handicaps ranging up to nine, could not be regarded as truly representative of 'the best lady golfers'; at least not in the sense that the players in the Dunlop Masters, or the Berkshire Trophy (handicap limit two) were representative respectively of the best men professionals and amateurs.

Furthermore when you compare putting in stroke-play events (as were all the men's tournaments analysed) with putting in a match-play tournament (as was the Ladies') you must always be a little uncertain of the validity of the comparison. For instance, a player may not try to hole a putt of ten feet or so if she has 'two for it' in match-play; or from twenty or thirty feet with 'this for the half' she may hit the ball hard at the hole regardless of how far past it will run.

However, in the analysis these situations were noted and some allowances and adjustments made for them, and also for conceded short putts; so it does seem that the ladies in this tournament did putt worse than the best men golfers—at least in three-putting twice as often, and leaving their long putts twice as far from the hole.

Seven strokes a tournament: the difference between good putters and very good putters

A telling comparison is made in Table 29:6, between the putting of those who finished in the first nine places at Birkdale

Table 29:6 *Putting at Birkdale: how the leaders and the tail-enders compared with the field as a whole.*

Length of putt	PROPORTION OF PUTTS HOLED		
	Top nine players	Bottom nine players	All players
Up to 3 feet	99%	98%	99%
3–6 feet	77%	73%	74%
6–9 feet	67%	43%	48%
9–12 feet	48%	35%	38%
Fraction of greens requiring three putts	1 in 32	1 in 16	1 in 23
How close, on average, did they put their long* putts?	2 feet	2·8 feet	2·4 feet

* Putts of 30 feet or more.

and that of those who finished in the bottom nine places.

From these tables, together with some calculations about the length of the first putt, it is possible to work out *exactly* how many strokes the top nine gained over the bottom nine *by better putting alone*—that is to say, assuming that their play up to the green had been the same (which, of course, it wasn't).

It comes out as just about a tenth of a stroke per hole, which adds up to 1·8 strokes per round.

This may seem a small difference, until you set it in the context of actual scoring. The difference in average score per round between the top nine and the bottom nine was, in fact, only just about four strokes—the difference between 72·6 and 76·7 strokes. Very nearly half of this difference was thus the result of putting.

If, for instance, the winner, Le Grange, had putted to the same standard as those who finished in the last nine places, we could expect him to have taken seven strokes more for the whole tournament than he did, in which case he would have finished fourteenth equal, and have won only about £40 instead of £2000!

The huge gains from better putting

The survey of the Masters Tournament at Birkdale thus confirmed most emphatically the importance to a professional's scoring of how well he can putt—however well he may play the rest of the game.

The next step seemed to be to assess how big a difference to his scoring it would make if, without any change in the rest of his game, he was able to make a really substantial improvement in his putting standard.

Suppose, for instance, that he could train himself to double his accuracy from any distance: that is, to hole out from any distance as well as he previously did from half that distance.

In other words, from six yards, he would hole out as often as he previously did from three, and would leave those he missed as close to the hole as he previously left those he missed from three yards.

From the results, tables and other calculations, you can get a straight answer to this. For the average professional at Birkdale, such an improvement would have cut 4·2 strokes from his average score per round—enough to have lifted the man who finished thirty-fifth out of forty into first place.

Obviously an improvement of this kind, worth seventeen strokes over seventy-two holes, would be a wholly staggering achievement for a professional, whose putting is already of a higher standard than that of the vast majority of golfers. Yet it is only just over twice the actual difference in putting standard between the top nine and the bottom nine during the actual play in the Masters, which included only professionals of the highest standing.

If a man, setting out to achieve such an improvement could actually achieve only 25% success in doing so, he could still cut his average score for a four-round tournament by four strokes. And as every golfer knows, differences in the standard of his putting from week to week or even from round to round, can quite easily make, in actual experience, six strokes difference—or more—to his score over eighteen holes!

Perhaps, as most professionals know, the key to it is the very substantial improvement a golfer can make to his game, simply by cutting out the days when he putts badly: that is, by making his best putting consistent enough to avoid rounds in which he throws away a fistful of strokes through putting badly. For the low-handicap week-end golfer of variable putting standard, the scope the Birkdale experiment reveals for improving his score on the greens is—to say the least—challenging.

Chapter 30

Analysing a Tournament: Short Approaches

In their analysis of the data collected at Birkdale, the team studied how well the professionals played their short approach shots. Here they included all shots played with a club other than a putter from any distance between ten and seventy yards from the hole.

The first surprise was that professionals, even of the Masters standard, play far more strokes from this range than the week-end golfer might expect them to. The average handicap amateur himself, of course, is likely to play anything up to one —or even two—on every hole; and many a low-handicap player manages to get round in the seventies by good chipping rather than by hitting the greens in the right number of shots. Both know that, for them, the short approach shot is an essential scoring stroke.

One at every second hole

Both, though, might expect top-class professionals to hit at least three greens in four in the right number of shots. Yet, even though the holes studied were all ones where the green was in range of a normal first or second shot, the professionals had to play one of these short approach shots at, on average, just about every second hole.

Table 30:1 shows how these shots were played.

For this exercise, scrub, bushes and very long grass, were counted as 'heavy rough'. There were only a small number of strokes which came into this category. They are included in the table, but, for simplicity of analysis, left out of all further work on this part of the Birkdale study.

How close from how far away?

Table 30:2 shows how close to the hole, on average, the professionals placed the ball with their short approach shots from different distances, playing from the fairway. This gives a basic picture of their standard, unhampered by the bad lies experienced in rough and bunkers.

The next table (30:3) shows how much less accurate were the shots played from the rough, but not 'heavy rough'. As the reader can see, playing them from off-the-fairway lies made quite a difference to how close the pros put them.

Those played from bunkers were even more erratic, as Table 30:4 shows. At Birkdale, professional bunker play seems to have proved by no means as easy as some have claimed it is.

In fact, as can be seen from the tables, the professionals did

Table 30:1 *Number of short approaches (from 10 to 70 yards) played by the professionals in 1000 holes at Birkdale.*

	From fairway	From rough	From heavy rough	From bunkers	Total
Number in 1000 holes	166	149	17	126	458
Equivalent number per 18-hole round	3	3—	0+	2+	8+

Table 30:2 *How the pros played the short approach shots at Birkdale: from the fairway. The figures in the main part of the table are the number of shots played from the ranges given along the top, and finishing at distances from the hole given down the side.*

Finishing distance from hole (yards)	DISTANCE FROM HOLE FROM WHICH SHOT PLAYED (YARDS)				
	10–20	20–30	30–40	40–50	50–70
Holed		1			
0–1	33	8	2		
1–2	23	15	4	3	1
2–3	13	11	3	5	1
3–4	4	9	3	1	2
4–6	2	3	3	4	2
6–8			1	2	3
8–10			1		1
10–12					
12–14		1			
Total number from each range	75	48	17	15	11
Average finishing distance from the hole (yards)	1·4	2·4	3·3	3·6	4·7
*Median finishing distance from the hole (yards)	1·2	2·0	2·8	3·0	5·0

* See text for explanation of 'median'.

Table 30:3 *How the pros played the short approach shots at Birkdale: from the rough.*

Finishing distance from hole (yards)	DISTANCE FROM HOLE FROM WHICH SHOT PLAYED (YARDS)				
	10–20	20–30	30–40	40–50	50–70
Holed	2	1			
0–1	12	6	1		
1–2	15	14	5		
2–3	8	5	6	3	1
3–4	4	4	3	1	
4–6	8	8	7	2	
6–8	2	2	5		
8–10	1	1	1		1
10–12		1	3		
12–14		2	1	1	1
14–16		1	1		1
16–18					
18–20		2		1	
over 20		1	3	1	
Total number from each range	52	48	36	9	4
Average finishing distance from the hole (yards)	2·4	4·7	6·7	8·3	10*
†Median finishing distance from the hole (yards)	1·8	2·6	4·9	5·0	11*

* These figures unreliable: not enough observations.
† See text for explanation of 'median'.

Table 30:4 *How the pros played bunker shots around the greens at Birkdale.*

Finishing distance from hole (yards)	DISTANCE FROM HOLE FROM WHICH SHOT PLAYED (YARDS)			
	10–20	20–30	30–40	40–50
Holed	1	1		
0–1	4	2	2	
1–2	6	9	2	1
2–3	3	17	2	1
3–4	3	6	2	1
4–6	3	9	7	
6–8	2	6	4	1
8–10	2	4	1	
10–12		3		
12–14	1	7		1
14–16	1			
16–18	1	1		1
18–20		1		
over 20		4	2	1
Total number from each range	27	70	22	7
Average finishing distance from the hole (yards)	4·5	6·4	6·0	9·5*
Median finishing distance from the hole (yards)	2·8	4·0	4·9	7·0*

* These figures unreliable: not enough observations.
See text for explanation of 'median'.

better out of rough than they did out of sand. From bunkers within thirty yards, they left the ball, on average, over fifteen feet from the hole: nowhere near enough for a probable chance of holing the putt. They got down in two strokes from within this range, in fact, only about once in every three tries. They left the ball dead—within a yard of the hole—only once in every twelve tries, whereas playing from the same distance on a fairway lie, they put the ball within a yard, on average, better than once in every three shots.

This contradicts a fairly widely held belief that professional golfers are almost as good out of greenside bunkers as they are off grass. A lot must obviously depend on the nature of the bunkers: not just the condition of the sand, but their placing, design and construction.

A few 'median' comparisons

The percentages below illustrate all this rather more vividly. They were worked out by taking the distances compared with which half the shots played from various distances lay further away and half nearer. This is known as a 'median' finishing distance, and it may differ a little from the usual 'average'. For example, if we look, in Table 30:2, at the 48 approaches played from a distance of twenty to thirty yards, we see that half (24 of them) finished within two yards of the hole, and the other half finished further away; so the median finishing distance in that case is 2·0 yards.

The 'median' can be a useful figure whenever the 'average' is unduly affected by one or two freak results at one extreme: in this case a few very bad shots. The same column in the table gives an example of this; one freak bad shot raises the average finishing distance from 2·14 to 2·36 yards, but raises the median finishing distance only from 1·97 yards to 2·00 yards.

It turns out that from each type of lie, the median finishing distance from the hole is a fairly constant proportion of the length of the shot, regardless of what that length is; and the short approaching of the professionals at Birkdale can therefore be summed up very briefly.

The median finishing distance, expressed as a percentage of the starting distance was:

From fairway	7·8%
From rough	12·3%
From bunkers	15·8%

Table 30:5 shows how these figures (fairway and rough only) compare with the same quantity worked out at the Schweppes Tournament at Sandwich, for the amateurs at Berkshire and for the ladies at Hayling.

The figures in the table should be interpreted in the light of quite marked differences in difficulty. This must always be, to some extent, a matter of opinion but the team judged the greens at Sandwich (in April) to be considerably more difficult to approach than those at Birkdale or Berkshire (in June), with Hayling (in May) intermediate.

The rough near the greens at Sandwich was almost indistinguishable from fairway; at Berkshire it was mostly heather, from which it is notoriously difficult to judge a shot; and at Birkdale it was intermediate between the other two.

As in putting, the short approaching of the ladies appears to be considerably poorer than that of the men, even allowing for differences in conditions. A specific example will highlight the meaning of the figures in the table: from 40 yards range, playing off fairway lies, the ladies left half their shots more than 7½ yards from the hole, whereas, from the same distance, the Birkdale pros put half *their* shots within 3 yards of the hole. To put it another way, the Birkdale pros did nearly as well from 100 yards as the ladies did from 40 yards.

In contrast, on the long shots to the green, the analysis in the next chapter shows the ladies to be only a little less accurate than the men. In fact—and for aspiring lady champions this may be the most significant single conclusion in the whole book—relatively speaking, *short approaches are the shots that good lady golfers play worst*. This is true at least in so far as the play of the competitors in the English Ladies Championship at Hayling represented first-class ladies' golf.

Reve.ting to the play of the professionals at Birkdale, and still using the idea of 'medians' instead of averages, the performance of the top nine and the bottom nine players can be compared; and the result is that the study revealed no significant differences in their standards of short approach play from any of the three types of lie. In other words, as far as you can tell, the top nine gained nothing over the bottom nine in this department of the game.

The value of short-game practice: less than you'd think?

How much effect on scoring does the short game have? Or, as the scientists put it themselves: 'If the professionals could raise the standard of their short approach play, without any change in other parts of their game, how would this affect their scoring'?

They decided to take, as an example here, the same sort of drastic improvement they assessed for putting: an ability to put the ball as close to the hole, from any distance, as they now

Table 30:5 *Short approach shots: summary of the standard achieved by professionals, amateurs and ladies.*

	PERCENTAGE INACCURACY			
	Birkdale pros	Sandwich pros	Berkshire amateurs	Ladies
From fairway	7·8%	10·4%	10·0%	18·6%
From rough	12·3%	11·6%	19·5%	24%*

The figures express median finishing distance as a percentage of starting distance, and apply to shots played from distances of 20 to 70 yards.
* This figure unreliable: not enough observations.

put it from half that distance. If a professional could achieve such an improvement, he would save:

In short approaches from fairway and rough: 1·2 strokes per round.

In bunker shots within the same range: half a stroke per round.

The two together: 1·7 strokes per round.

This perhaps understates how much he would gain, because of the 1000 'man-holes' observed in this study, 960 were on holes where the second shot was easily in range of the green. Only forty were on the par five sixteenth, where the green is out of range in two shots, and thus calls for a short approach almost every time.

The gain could still hardly be more than two strokes per round, and the improvement in standard of performance to achieve that would be a staggering one for any man to manage, not least because the standard of the tournament profes-

sional's short game, is, in general, very good already.

It seems pretty clear, then, that intensive practice at short approaching is not going to do a very great deal to reduce a top-class professional's scoring, partly because his standard is high already, and partly because he plays less than nine short approaches per round.

On the other hand, it might be a wholly different story for the amateur, who takes three shots to get down from twenty yards more often than he takes two, and who plays more short approaches in every round than the professional normally does.

This is, of course, only assumption. All that the scientists can say for certain is that, for the professionals playing at Birkdale, the study there seems to suggest that time spent practising putting looks, on the face of it, likely to save them more strokes a round—on their game as it was then—than time spent practising short approaches.

Chapter 31

Analysing a Tournament: Long Approach Shots – Where Tournaments are Won

When professionals play on a course like Birkdale, which has only one drive-and-pitch hole, shots in the 50 to 130 yard range do not occur often enough to enable statistically reliable observations of them to be made; and, by the same token, good or bad playing of them does not much affect scoring.

There is therefore a gap in the analysis here, and we jump on to the 130 to 220 yard range, for which the professional will nearly always take a full shot with some club or other. To all of them we give here the label 'long approaches'.

These strokes were obviously particularly telling ones at Birkdale, because, allowing for an average drive of 250 yards, on all but three or possibly four holes of the course (the long 1st, 14th and 16th, and the drive-and-short-pitch 5th) a shot of this kind is needed. This is fairly typical of championship courses; although shorter courses call for fewer long approaches, and instead more second shots of under 130 yards.

The results recorded at Birkdale may not necessarily be characteristic of the same professionals' playing shots of these lengths on another course. Some strokes on any layout—and not necessarily the longest ones—are more difficult than others, in relation to the club called for. The general pattern of the results though, does give an accurate enough picture of the play of the professionals at Birkdale for the analysis of them to offer firm conclusions.

How close from how far

The first thing the team did was to work out how accurate the professionals had proved themselves to be from different distances. With the results set into columns applying to each ten-yard range-bracket out from the hole. Table 31:1 shows the pattern which emerged. As you'd expect, the results show, apart from a few statistical fluctuations, a steady decrease in

Table 31:1 *How the pros played the long approaches at Birkdale: from the fairway. The figures in the main part of the table are the numbers of shots played from the ranges given along the top, and finishing at distances from the hole given down the side.*

Finishing distance from hole (yards)	DISTANCE FROM WHICH SHOT PLAYED (YARDS)								
	130–140	140–150	150–160	160–170	170–180	180–190	190–200	200–210	210–220
0–5	3	2	4	9	11	5	5	2	2
5–10	4	4	8	13	14	17	10	10	8
10–15	1	2	6	11	8	18	7	7	3
15–20	2	2	4	7	8	5	18	5	3
20–25			2	7	2	2	8	8	3
25–30				1		6	11	6	5
30–35					1		6		4
35–40							1	5	
40–45						1		2	
45–50			1					1	
Total number	10	10	25	48	44	54	66	46	28
*Median finishing distance from hole (yards)	7·5	8·8	10·4	10·9	8·9	11·4	18·1	19·0	16·3
Fraction reaching green	0·9	0·9	0·72	0·81	0·80	0·76	0·44	0·52	0·43

* See Chapter 30 for explanation of 'median'.

accuracy as the range of the stroke increased. (The appearance of a grouping in the 5 to 10 yard range is just the result of the 0 to 5 yard 'bull' being only one-third the area of the 5 to 10 yard 'inner'.)

Readers will no doubt find their own 'most interesting' observation from the table, depending perhaps on their own strengths and weaknesses. To the many golfers who find the short irons the least difficult part of the game it may seem surprising that, even when playing only an eight- or nine-iron from the fairway, the professionals missed the fairly generous greens with one shot in every ten; and that when they got out to about five-iron length, they missed the green with one shot in five.

Those same readers will, on the other hand, be quite impressed by the fact that about half of the pros' long irons and fairway woods found the greens—though in fact this represents quite a uniform progression upwards from the pitching irons.

Short-hole tee shots

Table 31:1 includes only the strokes played from the fairways. The three par-three holes on which play was recorded, the 4th, 7th and 13th, involving a stroke from a peg tee, in each case from a high tee to a green lying like a target on a lower level, were treated separately. The results are shown in Table 31:2.

The thirteenth green lies on a slight plateau, with slopes in front and on either side tending to turn away a marginal ball. The fourth green is flat. On the other hand it is smaller in area than the thirteenth green, and was played for the most part across a left to right wind, which most golfers regard as more difficult than the right to left wind experienced at the 13th.

In the event, the professionals found the 4th more difficult. They missed the fourth green with well over half their tee shots to it; yet held the 13th with three out of every five shots —only slightly fewer than they held the fifty-yard shorter 7th with.

You might rather expect a teed stroke to be more accurate than one from the fairway. In fact this was not the case at Birkdale; tee shots at par-three holes, and second shots at par-four holes were, length-for-length, of practically equal accuracy. As there were no obvious extra difficulties in the short-hole green contours, it seems that from well-kept, level fairways (Birkdale's *are* for the most part) professionals are just as accurate as from a tee.

Table 31:2 *How close the pros put their tee shots at Birkdale's short holes.*

Finishing distance from hole (yards)	HOLE NO. 7 143 yards	HOLE NO. 13 199 yards	HOLE NO. 4 201 yards
0–2	6	3	1
2–4	10	4	9
4–6	19	10	4
6–8	22	11	4
8–10	20	13	12
10–12	30	17	11
12–14	13	15	26
14–16	12	20	13
16–18	14	7	16
18–20	8	3	15
20–25	4	29	26
25–30		10	6
30–35	2	13	11
35–40		2	2
40–45		3	2
45–50			2
Total number	160	160	160
*Median distance from hole (yards)	10·2	14·7	16·0
Fraction reaching green	0·675	0·619	0·438
Approximate area of green (sq ft)	4300	5700	4500

* See Chapter 30 for explanation of 'median'.

For every yard a constant fraction of a stroke

The team went on to discover something else unexpected, but of firm interest. As with the short approaches, there proved to be a constant relationship between the range of the stroke (whether from fairway or from tee) and how close to the hole the player put the ball. Moreover, and surprisingly, this was the self-same relationship as that which applied to short approaches.

Put another way, it means that, whether they were playing a run-up from twenty yards, or a full two-wood from 220 yards, or anything in between, the professionals at Birkdale hit half their shots to within a distance from the hole which was a constant fraction, $7\frac{1}{2}\%$ to 8%, of the range from which each stroke was played. That the wide applicability of this simple relationship was not a 'fluke' of the Birkdale results was confirmed by further studies on first-class amateurs at Berkshire and on professionals at Little Aston. Here again the same relation held for long shots to the green as for short approaches from fairway—the constant fraction being once more around 8% for the professionals, but rising to 10% for the amateurs.

The curious thing is that this simple relationship did not hold for the ladies. The median accuracy of the long approach shots of the competitors in the English Ladies Championship at Hayling was 12%: for example, from 150 yards they put half their shots within 18 yards of the hole. For short approaches the figure was 18%. Thus on their long approaches the ladies were only a little less accurate than the men; on short approaches they were *much* less accurate. Why the gap between lady golfers and men golfers should be widest in the department of the game where ladies are at no physical disadvantage remains a mystery, but the implications for lady golfers are obvious.

Even for men, there is, of course, a limit to how far any such constant fraction can apply. Above a range of about 220 yards, as the green becomes out of range to an increasing proportion of players, the fraction begins to increase sharply, and the general relationship runs out.

For the rest, though, it applies. From 200 yards, for example, half of the Birkdale professionals' shots would finish within fifteen yards of the hole; and half the Berkshire first-class amateurs' within twenty yards. From twenty yards half the pros' shots would finish within one and a half yards; and half the amateurs' within two yards.

This, in itself, was remarkable for its stark simplicity. Perhaps the most fascinating part of the study, though, followed on from it.

The team checked the numbers of strokes it took the professionals to get down from different ranges. These were calculated, where necessary, by combining ranges from the hole for long shots with the number taken to get down from different distances around the putting green. On doing this, they discovered an equally simple continuous relationship between the range from which a stroke was played and the number of strokes taken to get down.

This relation can be summarized in a simple formula, which proved to apply to all approaches of more than thirty yards from the hole:

$$\text{Number of shots to get down} = 0.0044x + 2.35$$
$$\text{(where } x \text{ is the distance in yards)}$$

There seemed no reason to expect such a simple relationship as this.

Curious, then, they took the analysis further. They found the relationship to be a basic truth of the whole game of golf. For when they applied the formula to distances beyond approach range, i.e. over 220 yards, it predicted with quite surprising accuracy how many strokes the players would have taken to get down, right from the tee, on all four of the longer holes recorded.

Some allowance had to be made, of course, for the effect the wind has on the playing length of the hole. Since the wind, as was during the tournament, seemed to be worth about twenty yards on a drive when dead against (see Chapter 28), the lengths of the 8th, 12th and 16th were reduced and that of the 2nd increased by that amount. With these corrections the predictions of the simple formula are compared, in Table 31:3, with the actual average scores at these holes.

'S.S.S.-by-length' is valid—and accurate

Continuing with the simple formula you can find other curious coincidences, one of which is that the pros at Birkdale on average played exactly to a handicap of scratch!

Table 31:3 *How the scores predicted by the formula on this page compare with actual scores at four of Birkdale's longer holes.*

Hole	Effective playing length (yards)	Score predicted by formula	Actual average score
2	450	4·33	4·40
8	440	4·29	4·30
12	430	4·24	4·26
16	490	4·51	4·58

One way, used in America, of reckoning the par of a course is to allot fractional par scores to every hole based on its length. For example:

A hole of 200 yards is given a fractional par of 3·20 strokes.
A hole of 300 yards is given a fractional par of 3·65 strokes.
A hole of 400 yards is given a fractional par of 4·10 strokes.
A hole of 500 yards is given a fractional par of 4·57 strokes.
—and so on; for every distance there is an exact fractional par.

Now apply our formula. Take 200 yards first, and we get:

$$0{\cdot}0044 \times 200 + 2{\cdot}35 = 0{\cdot}88 + 2{\cdot}35 = 3{\cdot}23$$

This is very close to the fractional par figure of 3·20.

It proves to work just as well for each and every one. For 300 yards it gives 3·67; for 400 yards it gives 4·11, and for 500 yards it gives 4·55. It almost seems like magic.

And that's not all. In the British Isles, Standard Scratch Scores are now based on total yardage of the course. For example:

A course of 6900 yards is given S.S.S. 73.
A course of 6300 yards is given S.S.S. 70.
A course of 5700 yards is given S.S.S. 67.

Our formula has to be slightly modified to cope with a whole course. There are eighteen holes, so you need to add $18 \times 2{\cdot}35$ (i.e. 42·3) to the $0{\cdot}0044x$. Doing this, take 6300 yards, and you get:

$$6300 \times 0{\cdot}0044 + 42{\cdot}3 = 27{\cdot}7 + 42{\cdot}3 = 70{\cdot}0$$

—dead right again! Similarly for 6900 yards you get 72·6, and for 5700 yards 67·3.

This means not only that the average pro at Birkdale played to about scratch; but more significant, that the system for fixing the par or S.S.S. in both America and in this country seems to have got the relationship between S.S.S. and distance exactly right—almost certainly by inspired guesswork! (Though analysis of a few more tournaments on a variety of courses would be required to confirm this once for all.)

Rough costs a quarter of a stroke more

Table 31:4 summarizes the observations on long approaches from the rough, comparing them with fairway results.

There are two points to note. First, that the results are worse than those from the fairway by about the same amount as in short approaches; and second, that at extreme range the figure increases sharply—due obviously to the players' diffi-

Table 31:4 *How playing from the rough affected the long approaches at Birkdale.*

		DISTANCE FROM WHICH SHOT PLAYED (YARDS)			
		140–160	160–180	180–200	200–220
*Median finishing distance from hole (yards)	Played from fairway	9·0 (35)	10·0 (92)	14·6 (120)	18·2 (74)
	Played from rough	15·0 (8)	22·5 (9)	24·2 (29)	36·2 (45)

Figures in brackets are numbers of observations; the fewer the observations, the less reliable the median value.
* See Chapter 30 for explanation of 'median'.

culty in reaching the green at all from a lie in the rough more than 200 yards away.

From the observations the team were able to conclude that, for the players concerned there, playing long approaches from Birkdale's rough, as it then was, increased the inaccuracy of strokes by between 60% and 65%. As a result, for a wide range of strokes—from about fifty yards up to about 200 yards—it added, on average, about a quarter of a stroke to the player's score for the hole.

Wind

Another factor the team looked into was the effect wind had on the accuracy of long approaches. They did this by comparing the results from different distances at the 2nd, where the wind, averaging at 12 miles per hour, blew more or less against, and at the 8th and 12th, where it blew more or less behind. In general, wind seemed to have made little difference to the iron shots to the green, except of course, to the extreme-length ones through putting the green out of range.

Thus from 140 to 200 yards the performance of the pros when playing into the wind (at the second hole) and playing with it (at the 8th) was virtually the same. This is probably the result of two balancing effects. It is undoubtedly more difficult to hit the ball straight against the wind (see Chapter 25); on the other hand it is easier to hit it the correct distance chiefly because it stops almost dead on landing.

Beyond 200 yards, in fact in the 200 to 220 yard range, the difficulty in reaching the green into wind is reflected in a 50% greater median finishing distance than downwind (twenty-three yards, as against sixteen).

Table 31:5 *How far the pros hit the American (1·68″) ball with each club at Birkdale.*

CLUB	WOODS				IRONS								
	Driver	2	3	4	2	3	4	5	6	7	8	9	10
Distance (yards)	250	236	222	208	208	!96	184	172	160	148	136	124	112

How far with each club?

From information gathered on clubs used for different shots, particularly at the par-three holes, the next table (31:5) was compiled, showing the average distances obtained by the professionals at Birkdale with each club. Readers should remember that the American-size ball was used; to convert to British size, add ten yards at the top of the scale and practically nothing at the bottom. The lengths, particularly with the longer clubs, depend on the state of the ground, of course, and windless conditions are assumed.

What is good iron play worth?

How far did different players' standards of long approaches affect the result of the tournament? This, again, was calculated. Table 31:6 shows how the comparison worked out, for all the holes examined, including the three short holes.

The overall superiority of the top nine players is clear. Though the differences are small, their effect on overall performance is quite significant. Taking all eighteen of the players concerned to have hit the average drive for the whole field, and to have played their short approaches and putted to the average standard too, the team were able to show that the difference in standard of strokes from 140 to 220 yards gave the top nine an advantage of about one and a quarter strokes per round over the bottom nine; that is, five strokes in the whole tournament.

The team then went on to analyse the difference which could be made to a man's score by doubling the accuracy of his iron play—the same improvement already examined for putting and short approaching. They found that it would amount to over four times the difference between the top nine and the bottom nine: an improvement of five and a half strokes per round or twenty-two in the whole tournament.

Table 31:7 shows how this would have worked out round Birkdale hole by hole (assuming, for the sake of the illustration, that the player hits every drive 250 yards), and by how much the player would cut his score at each hole.

The table suggests, thus, that the amount of improvement to be gained by doubling the accuracy of his long game is—for a professional of the class playing at Birkdale—greater even than that he could achieve by a similar improvement in his putting (4·2 strokes per round), and much greater than that he could achieve by a similar improvement in short approaching (1·7 strokes per round).

Of course, when we talk of 'similar' improvements in several departments of the game, we are not implying any certainty that these improvements are all equally easy to achieve.

It's worth comment in this connection that, unlike putting, long-iron play in general is not affected by any irregularities of the greens. An accurately judged and well-struck full iron shot will end up closer to the hole than a poorly executed one nearly every time; whereas a perfectly struck and perfectly aimed putt is always liable to be thrown off-line by irregularities on the green, and to finish up no better than a badly struck putt.

Iron play will, of course, have less effect on shorter courses. But it would not be going too far to conclude that it is in full-

Table 31:6 *Long approaches at Birkdale: how the leaders compared with the tail-enders.*

		DISTANCE FROM WHICH SHOT PLAYED (YARDS)			
		140–160*	160–180	180–200*	200–220*
†Median finishing distance from hole (yards)	Top nine players	9·8 (46)	9·0 (22)	13·6 (63)	14·5 (50)
	Bottom nine players	12·0 (42)	10·8 (17)	13·8 (64)	17·7 (54)

Figures in brackets are numbers of observations; the fewer the observations, the less reliable the median value.
* Short hole tee shots included in these ranges.
† See Chapter 30 for explanation of 'median'.

200

shot iron play as well as in putting that the main difference in calibre makes itself felt between different levels of top-class professional golfers, and the degree of success they have in tournaments.

The reader may feel, the more he thinks about it, that it coincides with his own impression of any tournaments he has watched. It certainly looks as if the old saying about 'Driving for show and putting for dough' misses an essential point.

Table 31:7 *The benefits of improved long approaches: an estimate of the strokes gained by halving their inaccuracy.*

| Hole | Length of hole remaining after 250 yard drive | SHOTS TO GET DOWN FROM THIS DISTANCE | |
		Normal standard	Improved standard
1	243	No long approach required	
2	177	3·13	2·74
3	166	3·08	2·71
4*	201	3·23	2·79
5	70	No long approach required	
6	218	3·30	2·82
7*	143	2·98	2·67
8	209	3·26	2·81
9	160	3·05	2·71
10	143	2·98	2·67
11	162	3·06	2·71
12	202	3·23	2·79
13*	199	3·23	2·79
14	286	No long approach required	
15	131	2·92	2·64
16	260	No long approach required	
17*	186	3·16	2·76
18	200	3·23	2·79
	Total	43·84	38·39

* Par three hole: no drive required.   Difference = 5·45 strokes per round

Table 31:8 *How much the pros at Birkdale would have gained by drastic improvements in their game.*

	Gain in strokes per round
By 'doubling' accuracy of putting	4·2
By 'doubling' accuracy of short approaches	1·7
By 'doubling' accuracy of long approaches	5·5
By 100% accuracy and extra 20 yards on drives	2·2
Total	1·6

How all this can help the week-end golfer

There may be a useful precept in all this for the week-end golfer seeking the most effective way to improve his golf. When he can afford the time, he should go and practise his iron shots, and leave the putting to odd moments. His putting is probably of a far higher comparative calibre than the rest of his game anyway. After all, nearly every long-handicap man at times putts well enough to be scratch.

31:1 *They all seem the same when you are cold and wet. Recording lengths of drives at a professional tournament is not always as enjoyable or interesting a way of spending three days as you might think.*

It is dangerous, though, to try to draw too many conclusions about the club golfer from this study. Strictly it applies only to a selected group of professionals, playing at Birkdale in certain wind and ground conditions.

What can be of use to the club golfer, particularly the low-handicap man aspiring to greater things, are the yard-sticks it sets up. When he's practising five-iron shots from 160 yards he can have in mind the professional's standard of hitting half the shots to within twelve yards of the hole ($7\frac{1}{2}\%$ of 160 yards); when he's pitching his practice balls to a hole forty yards away, he can be thinking in terms of half within three yards; and when he is on the practice putting green he can be aiming at holing nine out of ten from three feet, five out of ten from seven feet and two out of ten from fifteen feet.

This about sums up those main features of the Birkdale study which are of interest to the golfing reader. For its thoroughness, scientific method, and comprehensive curiosity about the meanings hidden behind the five thousand odd strokes witnessed and recorded in detail, it undoubtedly set an entirely new standard in golf analysis.

Section 8   Wider Aspects of Research

Chapter 32

Possibilities for the Design of Clubs

'The club shall not be substantially different from the traditional and customary form and make.' This Rule of Golf is capable of being used with equal facility to welcome or to ban almost any doubtful innovation in clubs; and it seems to sum up the right philosophy of what, in principle, is or is not to be allowed in the way of improvements in club design.

Few golfers would think it unfair to improve the design of clubs so long as golf were left essentially the same game as before. On the other hand, few would defend any new design which made the game too easy altogether, or even equally easy for all golfers.

To do so might be no pipe dream. It may be quite possible to make a tee which will virtually guarantee a straight-flying drive and even have the effect of making the ball travel some fifty yards further (see Appendix II). It might even turn out that one way in which scientific research may ultimately serve golf may be in predicting some obviously undesirable ingenuities in time to forewarn the rulemakers about them.

In general, though, it is obviously healthy for any game to welcome improvements in design which help the player to enjoy his recreation at it, so long as nothing is allowed to undermine its essential problems and necessary skills. That surely goes as validly for golf as for any other artificial challenge devised by man for his own amusement or satisfaction, making use of recognized difficulties, rules and equipment.

How much basic design?

To what extent clubmakers have already turned science to the service of the golfer in the design of the clubs they offer him seems, at the least, doubtful. Clubmakers, in general, seem to be just beginning to take the possibilities seriously.

Through most of golf's history, however, the vast majority of clubs have never been really 'designed' at all. Great craftsmen, like Philp, have produced better clubs than their fellows, but almost entirely through art, instinct, feel and touch. Since clubs began to be generally mass produced in the 1920's, almost every new model has been produced more by making slight rule of thumb changes—suggested perhaps by professionals, or by clubmakers' own intuition, or even largely for reasons of appearance—than from any basic investigations of the best design for the job. Fashion seems to play a very big part in club marketing too; and fashions in clubs change almost as rapidly as those in women's clothes.

Table 32:1 *Dimensions, weights and other properties of two typical clubs.*

	DRIVER	FIVE-IRON
Loft	10°	31°
Lie	54°	60°
Length of shaft	43″	37″
Weight of head	7·25 oz	9·50 oz
Weight of shaft	4·25 oz	4·25 oz
Weight of grip, underpacking etc.	2·00 oz	2·00 oz
Total weight	13·50 oz	15·75 oz
Distance from top of grip to centre of gravity of club (balance point)	30″	27·5″
Distance between centre of gravity of clubhead and direction-line of shaft	1·375″	1·5″
Moment of weight about a point 12″ from the top of the grip	243 oz ins	244 oz ins
Corresponding reading on manufacturers' 'swing-weight' scale	D2	D2
Moment of inertia about a point 4″ from top of grip (i.e. where left hand goes)	5·65 lbs ft²	5·21 lbs ft²
Whippiness: frequency of vibration when clamped at grip and allowed to vibrate freely (cycles per sec)	4·9	6·2

In fact, despite one or two near misses, it is doubtful if any manufacturer has yet asked himself, scientifically, the questions:

What exactly does a club have to do?

and:

What design will enable it to do it best?

The sections which follow report the team's preliminary attempt to find out the right questions to ask, and, in some cases, to suggest the answers.

Questions about clubs

First, what precisely are we talking about? Let's look closely at the modern club. Table 32:1 gives some dimensions and weights of a typical driver and a typical five-iron.

Most of this is self-explanatory. 'Lie' is the angle the shaft makes with the ground when the clubhead is fairly grounded. And we should also explain 'moment of the club's weight' and 'moment of inertia'. Both are, in effect, measures of the combined effect of a club's weight and length.

The first is simple: hold a club out horizontally in front of you in one hand, and what you feel is the moment—that is the 'pull' of the club's weight about the point you are holding. If you hold it twelve inches from the end, then you feel what the manufacturers call 'swing weight'.

The second is a little more complicated. If you swing a club by wrist movement alone, it is the club's moment of inertia which you feel and which governs how fast you can swing the head around your hands for any force you apply through your fingers.

One, in fact, measures the club's static 'pull' in your hand when you hold it out; the other the inertial resistance when you swing it around your hand.

Both of these qualities, together with the whippiness and a number of other minor factors, determine a club's 'feel' when you swing it; and that is one of the reasons why clubs of different length—say a three- and an eight-iron from a 'matched set'—can never feel exactly the same when you swing them.

We go into the whole question of feel, matching and swing-weighting of sets in the next chapter. Before we do that, though, let's take a critical look over some of the more obvious and straightforward characteristics of clubs.

What does a clubhead need?

If you consider for a moment how varied are the possibilities open to any man making a clubhead, obvious questions he needs to ask himself first are:

What is the best shape for the clubhead?
What is the best size for it: how deep, how long, how thick?
What is the best weight?
What is the best way to distribute and balance that weight?
How long should the face be and where and how marked and prepared?
And so on; and there can obviously be no immediate end to the questions which follow each other in endless sequence, each arising out of those before.

Not a single one of them can really be answered at all until you have an absolutely clear picture of what a clubhead has to do in a swing.

It's very much easier than it might be to assess this because of that basic fact about impact explained in Chapter 22: that impact is short enough and club shafts flexible enough for the clubhead and ball to react during impact as if the clubhead was in free flight under the effect of its own momentum and nothing else.

This will be true, at least, for all shots except those where the ball is hit badly off-centre and where the club has a high resistance to torsion, which all steel shafts do. Even in this case, the lack of torsion in the shaft will twist the handle in the player's hands far more than it will affect the impact between clubhead and ball.

What this amounts to, for all practical purposes, is that you can design a clubhead for its specific job of sending the ball off into flight in the way you want it to, without having to complicate things by taking account of what sort of shaft is fitted to it.

A wide choice of weight in a driver

A driver's job is to hit the ball as far as possible. Leaving aside all the human and design variables in golf for the time being (such as angle of blow, shape of clubhead etc.), and looking just at clubhead weight, Table 32:2 shows how *for a given clubhead speed* different weights of clubhead will affect the speed at which the ball is sent off. (The formula relating clubhead weight and ball speed is given in Appendix I.)

Table 32:2 How clubhead weight affects the speed of a typical first-class ball in a drive.

WEIGHT OF HEAD	BALL SPEEDS
1·6 oz	0·84 times the speed of the clubhead
4·8 oz	1·26 times the speed of the clubhead
8·0 oz	1·40 times the speed of the clubhead
1 lb	1·53 times the speed of the clubhead
16 lb	1·67 times the speed of the clubhead

The rate of increase in ball speed gets less and less the heavier you make the clubhead; and in reality, of course, the heavier the clubhead the less fast the player can swing it. If you take this into consideration, together with the human factors involved in golf (such as that the body, arms and clubshaft are moving at impact and thus absorbing a proportion of the energy generated in the swing), for quite a variety of reasonable assumptions the best practical headweight for a conventional driver (43 inches long) turns out to be not far from the seven ounces or so of the modern driver.

Arrestingly, it also emerges that the 'optimum' clubhead weight is a very 'flat' one: i.e. that any clubhead weight between about five ounces and about ten ounces would seem to make comparatively little practical difference in golf to how far any golfer can drive the ball.

Table 32:3, which is based on a formula (given graphically in Appendix I) derived using reasonable but not wholly verifiable assumptions, shows this in detail, for a goodish golfer swinging each clubhead as fast as he can.

This seems so startling, especially in view of most golfers' feeling that even quarter-ounce differences in weight make a lot of difference to power, that the team then checked it by

Table 32:3 The overall effect of different clubhead weight on a good drive—allowing for the slower speed at which a heavy head can be swung.

Clubhead weight (ounces)	Clubhead speed (feet/second)	Ball speed (feet/second)	Length of carry (yards)
0	203	0	0
1	193	125	Less than 100
2	185	173	156
4	172	206	206
6	162	214	218
8	153	215	219
10	147	213	216
12	141	209	210
16	132	202	200
24	119	187	178

practical experiment. They asked several golfers to swing a club whose weight of head varied from 3·5 ounces to 12·3 ounces and measured the clubhead speeds produced with each. From this, they calculated how far each blow would send the ball.

Again, it seemed that the combined effects of clubhead weight and clubhead speed came to very much the same for a wide range of clubhead weights from 5·7 ounces up to 12·3 ounces.

Trying the same test with golfers actually driving balls proved more difficult, since no player finds it easy to hit a ball well with a clubhead weight very different from the one he is used to. But for square-hit shots it still seemed true that varying the clubhead weight, from six to ten ounces (that is, total club weight, including shaft and grip, from twelve to sixteen ounces) produced no significant difference in the distance the players tested could drive the ball.

Further, and more sophisticated, calculations on a computer then confirmed this basic finding a second time.

Thus, within these limits, changing the weight of a clubhead is important far more for getting the best out of any player's swing—particularly his rhythm and timing—than for any other reason; and any golfer can feel free to use a driver weighing, in all, anything from eleven ounces to sixteen ounces, so long as it suits his strength, swing and timing.

Within that range of weight, he is unlikely to be sacrificing anything in the length of shot he can achieve with the club, so long as it really does suit him and his swing, and helps to make it accurate and consistent.

The lighter the club, though, the faster he will have to swing it; and the heavier the club, the slower his swing can and will become. It should perhaps be mentioned that most of the golfers tested tended to slice with the very heavy club; but not all did.

Weights of clubs in general

One other basic point about the golfer's relationship with the weight of clubs he uses should be mentioned here. This is the fact that any clubhead weight is a very rough compromise, in any case, between two opposing mechanical needs in his swing.

The method by which the energy in a golf swing is transmitted from its main source (the body and the legs) to the ball involves two quite serious 'mismatches', as an engineer would call them. To get the greatest amount of *clubhead* energy transferred to the *ball* both clubhead and ball should weigh the same. But at the same time, to get the greatest amount of energy out of the *man* into the *clubhead*, the clubhead should weigh several pounds at least.

For example, the amount of energy an expert hammer thrower is able to put into the 'head' of his sixteen-pound missile is about ten times that which a golfer is able to impart to his clubhead. Because of that other mismatch, though, the hammer (were it shaped to hit a golf ball) would send it off only at 130 feet per second or so, compared with the 210 feet per second at which a clubhead sends it off. Whereas about 42% of a clubhead's energy is transferred to the ball, less than 2% of the energy of the sixteen-pound hammer would be.

The best weight for any clubhead, then, always involves a compromise between the best weight for transferring energy from man to clubhead, and that for transferring energy from clubhead to ball.

It would seem that the more efficiently a man swings, the more that compromise can lean towards getting the greatest amount of energy transferred from clubhead to ball. Translated into simple golfing terms, this would mean that to get maximum distance the better the player the lighter his driver should be. We certainly cannot say it has been proved, but theory and reasonable argument suggest it.

Incidentally, the long driving tee mentioned earlier (and described in Appendix II) works by improving the energy transfer from clubhead to ball, without reducing the clubhead weight.

Apart from the driver, and perhaps the fairway woods and long irons, all of which may be needed to send the ball as far as possible from the lies available, most of the clubs in a set need to be designed for accurate, predictable and consistent striking and ball-control; not primarily for maximum range for the loft involved. Many other factors may thus affect the best weight and design for them. How these factors may apply will be shown in the rest of the chapter.

Where should the weight be?

So far we have thought in terms only of what happens when a ball is struck squarely by a point on the clubface in line with the club's centre of gravity. But in practice it may easily not be, and, as we explained in detail in Chapter 19, blows struck away from this 'sweet spot' spoil the shot, through the club-face, as a result, twisting one way or another during contact with the ball.

Golfers are always going to hit a proportion of shots slightly off-centre, instead of 'bang on the button' every time. Clubheads need to be designed, therefore, to twist as little as possible whenever this happens.

In practice, this means that the moment of inertia of the clubhead should be as large as possible. As we saw earlier in this chapter, the moment of inertia is a measure of any object's inertial resistance to turning. A large flywheel has a high moment of inertia—it is difficult to get going, but once it does it is difficult to stop.

Heaviness thus helps towards having a large moment of inertia; but it is not the whole story. The way the weight is distributed is important too. The further the bulk of its weight can be placed from the axis of rotation, the greater becomes the moment of inertia. Thus a bicycle wheel, with most of its weight at the rim, will have a higher moment of inertia than a simple solid flat disc of the same size and total weight.

The centre of rotation in the golf club, at least during the brief period of contact with the ball, is the centre of gravity of the clubhead. So to make sure the clubhead is twisted as little as possible by an off-centre blow, the clubhead should be as heavy as possible, and the weight should be distributed as far from the centre of gravity as possible (both, of course, within the limits set by other needs in design—like optimum weight, for instance). It is just this consideration which leads to the putter head design suggested in Chapter 21 (Fig. 21:5).

From this point of view, iron club design that, as one advertisement has it, 'scientifically places the weight behind the ball for greater distance on every shot', has got things exactly the wrong way round. In theory, at least, the golfer would hit the ball straighter and better with a club shaped like (*b*) in Fig. 32:1 than with one shaped like (*a*). These have the same weight and the centre of gravity in the same place, and therefore will hit the ball the same distance from the centre of the clubface; but (*b*) has a very much higher moment of inertia, would thus twist much less readily when the ball was hit off-centre and so lose less in distance and accuracy.

What other effects such a design as (*b*) might have cannot properly be found out without controlled testing in a machine swinging the club as a golfer does. Such a machine does not exist in this country. If the middle section of the shape of (*b*) were too thin, for instance, it might 'give' under impact enough

207

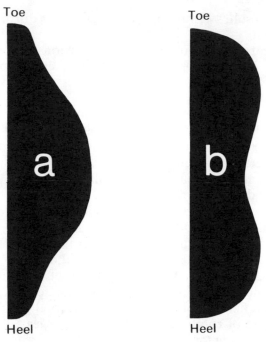

Toe

a

Heel

Toe

b

Heel

32:1 *Bad clubhead weight distribution (a) and good weight distribution (b). Shots hit slightly off-centre will twist a clubhead whose weight is concentrated near the middle more than one whose weight lies mainly at the heel and toe; and will thus be less powerful and perhaps more crooked.*

32:2 *A clubhead with variable weight distribution. This experimental five-iron has two weights which slide along a groove on the back of the club.*

to lessen the length of the shot. There might also be other effects involved, of subjective importance to the golfer—in the 'feel' of the shot off the clubface, for instance. These could only be tested by playing experience.

Critical weighting in wooden clubs

When you come to consider the shape and weight distribution of the heads of wooden clubs, far wider possibilities emerge, simply because the customarily large size of a wooden clubhead offers more scope for adjusting its weight distribution. You could even build into it a tendency to hit its own special variety of shot.

For instance, by making the face of the club plane-straight instead of convex-curved (see Chapter 19), and then by concentrating the weight far back and near the heel, as in Fig. 32:3, you could bias it heavily towards producing a hook: and a hook, moreover, which would set off to the right and curve back towards or even across the centre of the fairway.

Such a club might prove able to alleviate the troubles of fairly wild slicers—though only, of course, at the expense of adding a contrary correction to whatever was wrong with the sufferer's swing in the first place. Similarly, by concentrating the weight high behind the face of an iron club, you could build into it a tendency to produce low-flying shots.

In both these cases, the clubs would lose something in range and in sweetness of feel, since their working would depend upon there being a twist of the whole clubhead at impact.

Golfers who enjoy tinkering with the weights of their clubs should therefore be doubly careful about precisely what they are doing. It may be a clubhead's total weight which affects the feel of the club to the player—especially without a ball. But it will be the precise location of any weight added or removed, and its effects upon the balance of the clubhead as a whole, which will prove decisive in governing the club's future reactions and performance.

Alter the position of the clubhead's centre of gravity, for

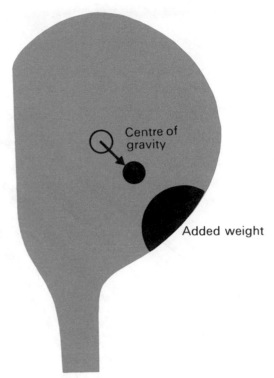

32:3 A hooking driver. Adding weight at the back, near the heel, pulls the centre of gravity in that direction. The 'gear effect' (Chapter 19) will then impart hooking spin to a shot hit from the centre of the clubface.

instance, and you at once need to alter the curvature of the face—unless you wish to change its gear-effect for balls hit anywhere other than the sweet spot. For example, if you add weight very near the face, then toed shots will tend to stay more out to the right, instead of curving in through the previous gear-effect. Shots hit off the heel will tend similarly to stay left.

There is another point, too. Very pronounced shifting of the weight could possibly make the clubhead react differently to the swing. Thus, although concentration of the weight at the toe of an iron will produce a hook if the ball is struck squarely off the centre of the face, it is conceivable that it will also tend to make the toe lag behind in the latter stages of the downswing and so leave the face open at impact, thus tending to cause a slice. We cannot be more certain than that at present, because it would require exhaustive experiments to reach any conclusions; and again, a proper club-testing machine would be needed to carry them out. There seems unfortunately,

little evidence to suggest that many manufacturers have done any properly controlled tests either.

Varying the length of the shaft

How long should a golf club be? Looking at the driver first of all, the conflict between the demands of distance and control are obvious. It is fairly clear that, for a variety of reasons, the longer a club is, the more difficult it will be to bring the centre of the clubface squarely to the ball. It is, at least at first sight, almost equally clear that one ought to be able to move a clubhead on the end of a six-foot shaft faster than one on the end of a three-foot shaft.

There are, however, some reservations about any such supposed increase in speed. A six-foot shaft will weigh more than twice as much as a three-foot shaft, and so a lot of energy will be wasted swinging the extra amount of shaft; and not just in swinging it, because the aerodynamic drag—air resistance—of any shaft is quite appreciable, particularly near impact, and the longer the shaft the greater this will be. Because of its increased distance from the grip, the moment of inertia of the head will also increase; and how this will affect the way the two-lever model swing works is by no means obvious.

Some work was done, therefore, upon what effect varying the length of the shaft might have: firstly by computer calculations on the two-lever model, using clubs of different lengths, and second by making a driver of length 55 inches (twelve inches longer than usual) and getting golfers to hit shots with it.

The results of both the calculations and the practical tests suggest about four feet as the length which potentially gives greatest range from the tee. Above that length, increased resistances of one sort or another more than cancel out any advantages. At the time of writing, a 47-inch driver has just been made, and preliminary tests seem to confirm this length as being near optimum for long driving.

In the practical tests, the 55-inch driver produced trajectories much higher than normal, probably through effects of shaft flexibility (see below). The result was that the average carry obtained with the 55-inch driver was longer than with a conventional club, even though the overall length of shot (carry and run) was not.

Although most of the golfers found it more difficult to strike the ball square and true with the long club (about one in three of all shots were mishits, compared with one in seven

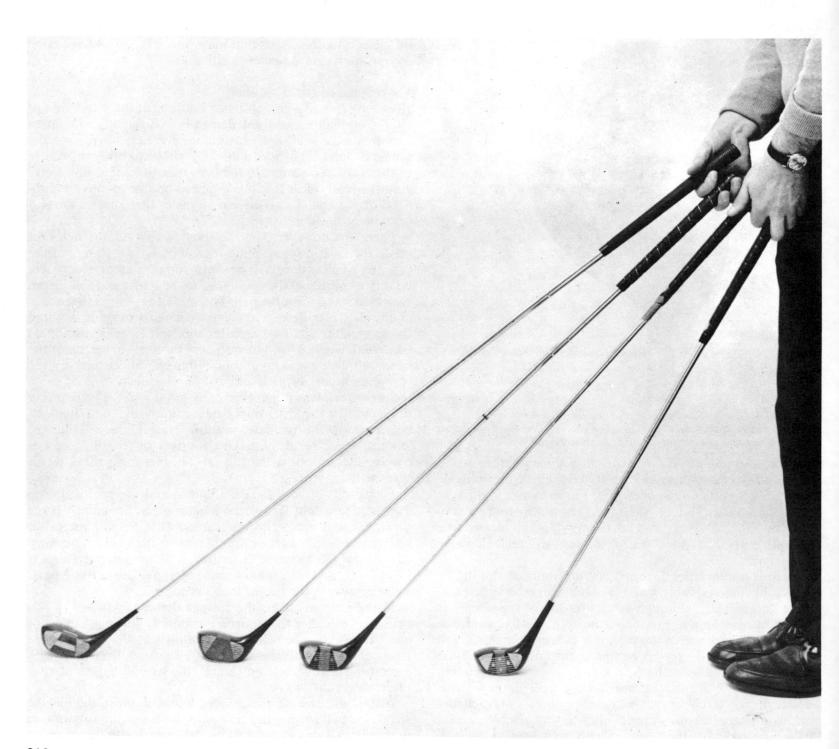

with an ordinary driver), some did not; and some even hit the ball straighter than with their own club. The last peculiarity could probably be put down to the fact that it was virtually impossible to swing the 55-inch driver jerkily; its very inertia ensured a smooth unhurried swing.

Tests using a very short driver (37-inches, i.e. normal five-iron length) corroborated the above results. The golfers trying it produced very short carries and low trajectories.

What kind of shaft—distance and direction effects

Any shaft vibrates during the swing at a variety of angles and to an extent that depends on how the player is applying himself to the shot. It's probably true that each individual golfer generates vibration patterns in the shaft that are highly characteristic of him (see Chapter 35) and different from those even of players with very similar swings. It is certainly possible that correct timing of these vibrations could increase clubhead speed at impact, and conversely that mistiming could lose clubhead speed, and also cause loss of accuracy.

The question is: how big are these effects likely to be in practice?

You can answer this question by experiment, or by theoretical calculation. Let's take experiment first, where one definite finding was that different degrees of whippiness do not very much affect the distance the ball can be sent with any club. In a test using three drivers with different degrees of whip (X, R and L shafts), golfers of all abilities hit their best drives with each club almost exactly the same distance. This confirms theoretical predictions that variations in shaft flexibility can make only about five yards difference to the best possible drive any golfer can hit.

Even this is probably an overestimate, because it assumes that the clubhead is 'springing forward' on the shaft as it strikes the ball. In fact there is ample photographic evidence to suggest that—for good players and bad, for whippy shafts and stiff—the clubhead has already sprung forward to the limit of its travel by the time it strikes the ball. You can see this in Figs. 8:2 and 8:8 in Chapter 8. In that case clubhead

32:4 *Experimental drivers. Their lengths are respectively 55 inches, 47 inches, 43 inches (normal) and 37 inches. Golfers who tested them found the 47-inch club hit the longest drives—about 10 yards longer than the normal (43-inch) one, with the 55-inch club somewhere in between. The 37-inch driver hit very short low drives. All the golfers had great difficulty in controlling both the longest and the shortest club.*

speed at impact would not depend on the type of shaft at all, and the distance obtained would not vary.

The same consideration, however, can lead to up to twenty yards variation in the line of a drive. This is because bending the shaft forward (or back) closes (or opens) the face—by about $2\frac{1}{2}°$ for every inch deflection of the clubhead. Variation between these extremes could therefore produce hooks or slices well into the rough. This only confirms the well-known suspicion many players hold that whippier shafts tend to make it more difficult to hit the ball consistently.

Flexibility, feel and timing

If this were the whole story, it would strongly suggest that there is nothing to be gained by flexibility in the shaft. But it can't be; clubs were never made with completely rigid shafts. Even the very stiff shafts used by some professionals bend and vibrate quite considerably during their swing at a drive.

We can suggest a few plausible reasons for this. For one thing, there is the 'feel' of the club. The stiffer any shaft, the more harshly it will transmit the shock of impact to the hands, and the more 'dead' and unresponsive the club will feel to waggle and to swing.

Some flexibility of shaft can thus be psychologically important for the golfer, and—in the way it can affect his reactions during the swing—mechanically important to his hitting of the ball. Too stiff a shaft, for him, may even make it more difficult for him both to swing the clubhead smoothly and to get the feel of timing it into impact.

How flexibility may help timing

Early in this book we discussed the possibility of adding an extra hinge to the model, and said that if it could be applied accurately within the model action and timing needed, it could add a little extra to the power of the stroke. In this way some flexibility in the shaft, by automatically adding some of the effect of an extra hinge-and-hinge-back effect spread over the lower part of the shaft, but without giving the difficulty that an extra hinge would give, may indeed add a little to the efficiency of the basic two-lever action in discharging energy into the clubhead.

The chief effect, in practice, of variations in shaft flexibility is probably to vary the precise point in the swing at which greatest clubhead speed is achieved, rather than to vary the greatest clubhead speed itself.

32:5 *How bending the shaft forward, as it always is just before impact, closes the face of the club. The bigger the bend the more the face is closed. This might be one reason why whippy shafts help weaker players.*

Thus, for any given player, flexibility (or whippiness) of shaft and timing of action go together and are mutually interdependent. A whippier shaft may well need a slightly slower swing, since the whip will delay the action; and on the face of it people with fast swings will do better with stiff shafts. But so long as both types of shaft are properly timed, the distance achieved will be about the same.

Does the whip square up the face?
With nearly all golfers, good and bad, the shaft is bent forward at impact by an inch or so and consequently the clubface is closed (relative to the straight-shafted position) by about $2\frac{1}{2}°$. This happens even in straight shots, which suggests that, with a rigid shaft the face would have been slightly open, producing a slice. Might it be possible that the whip in the shaft is a means of counteracting a general inability to bring the clubface back square to the ball?

It is a question we cannot conclusively answer; but it may be relevant that golfers with weak hands usually benefit from using whippy shafts—which bend forward more, therefore giving more help in squaring up the clubface than stiffer shafts.

The bent-forward position of the shaft at impact also increases the loft of the club, and for this reason a whippy club will usually give the ball a higher flight than a stiff one. This is probably also why the long driver mentioned earlier produced high trajectories.

Personal preference is paramount
The reader may already feel slightly bewildered by all this; and we haven't yet discussed the vibrations of clubs in the heel to toe direction, which also affects the timing of the stroke. However, it isn't really difficult to sum up the question of shaft flexibility.

It is one part of golf in which the player's own needs and preferences in feel and timing must be paramount. For any golfer, a more flexible shaft will give a 'softer' feel to the shock of impact, a more responsive feel to the club against his hands, and a timing reaction which he can sense more clearly during the swing. Against this, it may also tend to make it more difficult for him, at least on full strokes, to bring the clubhead consistently through each successive shot.

Flexibility and 'torsion'
We haven't yet mentioned the factor of twisting upon its own

32:6 A club with a tennis racquet grip. The weight is the same as a normal golf club so the 'balance' is the same; but because of the way it affects the golfer's grip, it restricts his wrist movement and produces wild slices nearly all the time.

axis, which a shaft may or may not do. The more easily it does this—and one main difference between steel and hickory shafts is in the greatly increased torsional rigidity of steel—again the softer the feel to the swing, but the more chance is simultaneously offered to the clubhead to come in slightly on the twist.

The modern steel shaft allows very little twisting of this

kind: an aid to straight hitting on the face of it. But it also means that any twist given to the clubhead at impact, by a stroke hit off-centre, imparts a 'stinging' shock to the hands, by sending that twist sharply up the shaft, instead of cushioning it in the torsional springiness of the shaft.

The capacity of hickory shafts to absorb shocks from off-centre blows was, in fact, one of the assets lost to the game with the introduction of steel. It's interesting to see that a British manufacturer* has now found a way of putting back some of this torsional flexibility by bonding the grip to the unyielding steel shaft underneath by means of a pneumatic elastic layer. The effect is to give a softer feel to any shot, and less 'stinging' of the hands from bad ones.

Thin grips to cure a slice?

Grip thickness is another factor which contributes to the feel of a club, and to the way it is swung. A thick grip restricts movement at the wrist; and, in terms of the two-lever model of the swing, this means that the hinge between the two levers will experience difficulty in straightening out. The clubhead will lag behind the hands at impact, and the face will probably be 'open' since the forearm roll necessary to square it up tends to go automatically with the wrist action.

In theory then, a thick grip should cause a slice; and in practice that is exactly how it works out. Tests in which golfers used a driver with a grip like a tennis racquet's, but of the same weight as a normal golf grip, produced huge slices averaging at thirty-five yards.

The converse experiment, with an abnormally thin grip, was not carried out; but it is reasonable to suppose that by virtue of freer wrist action a thin grip will tend to produce hooks—or cure slices—at least for a time.

The beginning of a big subject

These are, of course, only some of the factors in design and function which manufacturers fifty years from now will have investigated scientifically. There are an almost limitless number of minor design features possible in the making of golf clubs which all affect each other and react upon the golfer using them.

We are by no means in a position yet to lay down any hard or fast rules. At the same time it does seem possible to make some tentative suggestions of future lines of development; and in the next chapter we are going to attempt them.

* J. H. Onions Limited. 'Crookshank' clubs.   213

Chapter 33

Questions on the Matching of Clubs

Most golfers have an intuitive idea of what they mean by a 'matched' set of clubs. The clubs must look alike, and they must in some way feel alike. Manufacturers tend to give the impression that every club of their matched set 'feels' and swings identically. Golfers often have a strong impression that they don't.

Would it be a good thing, in any case, for all clubs in a set to feel identical when swung? So long as they are all of different lengths, and designed to send the ball different distances, this is rather unlikely, to start with; and there certainly *is* something to be said for having clubs of different lengths, giving greatest distance with longest clubs and greatest control with shortest clubs.

Being of different lengths, they demand different ball positions—nearer to the feet with short irons—and therefore different planes of swing; for the short irons are thus swung in a more upright plane, and this generally means a somewhat shorter swing as well.

The type of shot to be played is different, too. The short irons have to toss the ball up in the air with as much backspin as possible; and this demands a more definitely downward sweep of the clubhead through the ball than for the long irons or woods, which sweep the ball off the turf with a more nearly horizontally travelling clubhead.

All these differences in turn lead, with many players, to others in width and openness of stance, in grip, in general body posture—and not least in what goes on in the player's mind. All in all then, it is certainly not self-evident that a set of clubs should all 'feel' the same. It might rather be argued that they should all feel different—to cater in some way for the differences already noted.

The difficulty here lies in the phrase, 'in some way'. The point is: in what way? The factors involved are so complicated and interdependent that it would be virtually impossible to say precisely how each club should differ from the others. The right answer would, in any case, probably vary from person to person.

We therefore need to look for some rather simple method of matching clubs in a set, so that the feel at least varies in a uniform way from the longest to the shortest club.

It has, incidentally, never really been properly demonstrated that a set of completely unmatched clubs (for instance, different appearances, different shafts, different weights, different feels from club to club) makes for less consistent

golf than a matched set. But it is at least a plausible assumption that it is likely to. Most people, at all events, believe it does.

'Feel' is a complicated property of a club

How then should a set be matched? We must first ask what is involved in 'feel'. In golf clubs, it depends mainly on the size, and direction, and variation with time, of the forces and torques acting between the club and the hands. These forces in turn depend not just on how the club is swung, but on a number of mechanical properties of the club itself.

Ignoring shaft flexibility for the moment, the forces reacting upon the hands when the club is waggled or swung depend on the weight of the club, the moment of its weight about the place where you grip, and the moment of inertia about the same point—probably in ascending order of importance. The two 'moments' are explained in Chapter 32, page 205.

The point to note here, though, is that with clubs of different lengths, all three quantities cannot remain constant. How they should vary is more than half the problem in 'matching' clubs.

'Swing-weighting': a compromise rule of thumb?

The process known as 'swing-weighting', which most manufacturers use, appears to bring some sort of methodical basis to this aspect of club-matching. What exactly it is that swing-weighting is supposed to be measuring remains by no means clear, even perhaps to the makers themselves. To the professional who is selling the clubs and the golfer who is buying them, the whole thing is something of a mystery, though it is assumed to be a lot more scientific than, in fact, it appears to be when you look into it.

Swing-weighting actually works like this. The manufacturer puts the club in an expensive swing-weight balance (usually made by a firm in the U.S.), and reads off a number like C6 or D2, or possibly 19·65 or 20·6, depending on whether he is using the 'lorythmic' or 'official' scales (whatever either really means).

Any golfer can measure this same quantity himself with kitchen scales and a ruler. Swing-weight is simply the moment of the club's weight about a point twelve inches from the grip end of the club. To measure it, all you need to know is what the club weighs, and where its centre of gravity or balance point is.

You can find the centre of gravity, usually a foot or so

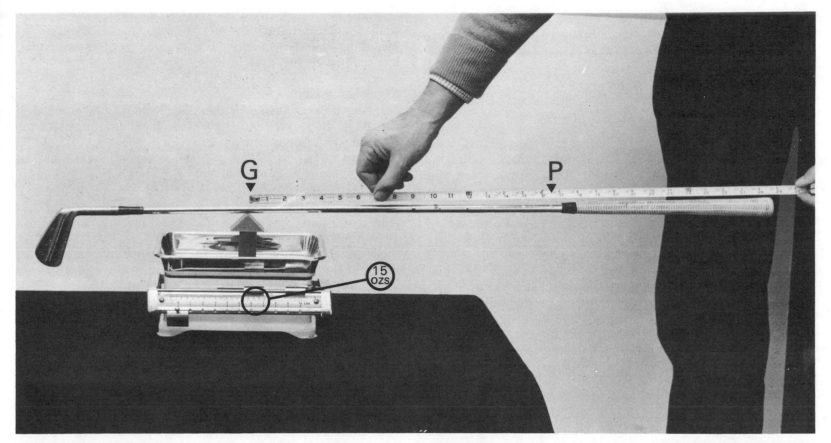

33:1 *The things which determine the swing weight of a typical two-iron. Its weight is 15 ounces and its centre of gravity G is 28½ inches from the top end of the grip—or 16½ inches from a point, P, 12 inches from the top of the grip. The swing weight is found simply by multiplying 15×16½=247½ ounce-inches, which corresponds to D4 on the lorythmic scale (see Fig. 33:2).*

from the head, by balancing the club across any sharp edge (a wooden chair back, or even a finger). A typical two-iron weighs fifteen ounces and the balance point (G, in Fig. 33:1) is 28½ inches from the top end of the shaft.

You get the swing-weight by simply multiplying the weight by the distance PG, which is 16½ inches in this case. Thus:

$$15 \times 16\tfrac{1}{2} = 247\tfrac{1}{2}$$

which corresponds to about D4 on the mysterious 'lorythmic' scale. For the benefit of sticklers for scientific accuracy, the units in which we ought to express this quantity are 'ounce-inches'; but in what follows we shall refer only to the number.

If half an ounce were removed from the head it would reduce this moment by 13—making it 234½ (or C7). Similarly half an ounce added would give 260½ (or E0). By moving the centre of gravity nearer to the grip, weight added to the grip actually reduces the swing-weight.

For anyone interested in carrying out this test on his own clubs, Fig. 33:2 shows corresponding values. Roughly speaking, increments of two on the ounces×inches scale correspond to one point on the 'lorythmic' swing-weight scale; so that, for instance, 246 would be D3, or 238 would be C9. You need a kitchen scale good enough to detect differences of a quarter of an ounce, since this corresponds to about two points on the 'lorythmic' scale (though such small differences probably don't matter in actual play).

Now how useful really is this form of swing-weighting as

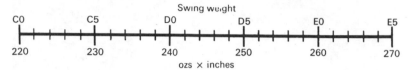

33:2 *How to convert 'do-it-yourself' swing weights as described in the text and in Fig.* 33:1 *to manufacturers' ('lorythmic') swing weights.*

a method of matching clubs? The answer is that, if you have a set of clubs of roughly the same swing-weight, then you can be pretty sure that you will get a *smooth variation* in 'swing-feel' as you go through the set.

What you will not get is identical 'swing-feel', nor necessarily the best sort of variation for practical golf. There may very well be potentially better ways of matching clubs.

You could, for instance, try matching clubs by their moment of inertia, since this should affect the feel of a club pivoting about the wrists far more than the moment (or swing-weight) does. If you matched the moments of inertia about the pivot point where the left hand grips the shaft, the general effect would be to make each shorter club progressively a little bit heavier than they are in existing sets matched by swing-weighting.

Swing-weighting, let us remember, measures instead the moment of the club's weight about a point *twelve inches* from the top of the club—i.e. down near the foot of the grip, well below where the hands go.

Why is this particular and apparently inappropriate point chosen? The answer, by deduction, seems to be that by choosing that particular point—twelve inches from the end—a compromise has been reached between matching by moment of inertia, and by moment of weight about the point of gripping. That is to say, in a set of irons of 'identical swing-weight', as you go from the two-iron to the nine-iron, the moment of inertia about the mean gripping point slowly *decreases*, while the moment of the club's weight about the same point slowly *increases*.

Swing-weighting, in fact, seems to balance two factors in a quite arbitrary way, and the effective 'swing-feel' of a club still depends very much on exactly where you grip it. If the two-iron we mentioned earlier, for instance, had half an inch taken off the top of the grip—little more than the depth of the cap at the top—its reading on a swing-weight balance would drop from D4 to D0.

It remains extremely doubtful whether this form of swing-weighting of clubs is really the best guide to what 'matching' sets really calls for, even in weight and balance alone.

Matching flexibility for feel

Nor may the matter of weight, balance and length, which is all swing-weighting covers, be even the most important factor in an ideal club-matching system.

Every golfer knows that you can get two drivers identical in length, weight, swing-weight, etc., but which feel quite different when you swing them because one of them has a more flexible type of shaft in it. Whatever the weight and length of a club, the nature of its shaft has a great effect on what it feels like to swing.

Shafts could be 'matched' for flexibility in a number of different ways. The effect is really a composite one. Inherent flexibility itself depends on the cross-section and material of the shaft. But the weight of the head and the length of the shaft also contribute to what golfers understand as 'whippiness'. This kind of combined flexibility effect very much influences the feel of a club. It would probably therefore be worth while trying to match the shafts for this combined effect, even if only for a smooth variation in effect from club to club.

To do this, two fairly obvious measures of the flexibility of shaft could be used. One would be the deflection produced by a standard force (say one pound) at the clubhead when the grip is clamped—this could be made uniform throughout the set. But that would not give much indication of the reactive forces on the hands. A better method would be to clamp the club at the grip, vibrate it, and match a set according to the frequency of vibrations, since this combines weight, length and stiffness.

At the time of writing, in fact, some manufacturers are considering this possibility. In the swing, the hands can never 'clamp' the club completely tight, and any club's frequency thus varies a bit. Nevertheless matching in this way would probably satisfy the minimum requirement that shaft characteristics shall vary smoothly throughout the set.

The science of shaft feel

Since shaft-frequency matching may be not only important, but also practicable, some explanation of how to set about it may be of interest. The basic scientific formulae which govern how much a shaft will bend and how rapidly it will vibrate are given in Appendix I. We can sum them up by saying that a club can be made to have a slower rate of vibration (i.e. appear whippier when handled) by at least four methods:

1. Making the head heavier (10% increase in mass means about 4% reduction in the frequency of vibration).
2. Making the shaft longer (10% increase in length means about 15% reduction in the frequency of vibration).
3. Making the shaft of an inherently less rigid material.
4. Constructing the shaft to be less rigid (i.e. reduced outside diameter, or wall thickness).

What you can do by Methods 3 and 4 is limited in one direction by the fact that you have to make the shaft to a certain strength to withstand impact (with the ground rather than the ball), and in the other direction by the need to avoid excessive air resistance. A shaft one inch in diameter, for example, would add a great deal to air resistance and cut down the speed at which the clubhead could be swung by 5% or more.

As we go from two-iron to nine-iron, the weight of the head increases from about nine ounces to eleven ounces (i.e. by 20%), while the length of the shaft from gripping point to head decreases from about $34\frac{1}{2}$ inches to 31 inches (i.e. by 10%). The increase in weight would, on its own, reduce the frequency of vibration by about 8%, while the decrease in length would, on its own, increase the frequency of vibration by about 15%. Together they cause an overall increase of 7% or so—giving a faster vibration that is, and a stiffer feel.

These figures apply to a shaft of constant cross-section. But they suggest that, given similar shafts, a nine-iron will feel appreciably stiffer than a two-iron. This difference could be adjusted by fitting a more flexible shaft to the nine-iron. But on the contrary, in almost all sets of clubs at present manufactured, the shafts get inherently *stiffer*—not more flexible—going from two-iron down to nine-iron. The result is that the nine-iron feels much stiffer than the two-iron. Check measurements of vibration of two such clubs gave the following results:

6·8 cycles per second for the nine-iron,
5·7 cycles per second for the two-iron,

and, incidentally, 4·2 cycles per second for the driver.

Thus, in this set, using frequency as a measure of effective stiffness, the nine-iron was almost 20% 'stiffer' than the two-iron—which is difficult to understand in a set supposed to be matched for 'feel'.

There may be a reason for this, but it is not obvious. We can only suggest that this is a point which some really enterprising club manufacturer might well look into.

Grips affect wrist action

As we saw in the last chapter, thickness of grip can affect the actual swing. Here again, though, it is not obvious that all clubs in any set should have the same grip thickness. The thinner the grip, the freer the wrist action. Some players might prefer thinner grips for freer wrist action on shorter clubs, some exactly the opposite.

A suggested approach to better matching of sets

We've said a lot about matching, and one of the main points to come out is that although there is no way of making clubs in a set feel *identical*, there are many ways of making 'swing-feel' vary smoothly from the longest to the shortest club.

One logical way might be as follows:

1. Loft, lies and lengths of clubs much as they are now.
2. Make the weight of a driver head around seven ounces, then vary the head weight down the set so as to give a constant moment of inertia about a mean gripping point (say four inches from the top of the shaft). This would make the more lofted clubs slightly heavier than they usually are.
3. Select the shafts to give each club, when clamped at the grip, a frequency of vibration which varies in some regular way from club to club down the set from driver to wedge. As a start, the same frequency for all clubs could be tried. This would, in general make lofted clubs whippier than they now usually are.

Here, at least, is a working theory upon which to design a set matched in a more thoroughgoing way than any set has been matched up to now. Whether better matching would produce significantly better results from the golfer is another question. But it can only be answered by trying it.

How many clubs?

The difference in range between successive clubs in a full set of nine irons (2, 3, 4, 5, 6, 7, 8, 9, wedge) is about twelve yards for a professional and perhaps nine yards for an ordinary club golfer.

217

To warrant such fine graduation in range the professional must be able both to judge his distances to better than twelve yards, and to strike his shots consistently with any club within that range. This he may well be able to do.

But the middle and long handicap golfer probably does not judge distances to better than nine yards, and certainly does not strike his shots consistently within a range of nine yards with any club. It follows that, if his set were reduced, for example, to six irons, equally spaced in loft, and corresponding to $2\frac{1}{2}$, 4, $5\frac{1}{2}$, 7, $8\frac{1}{2}$, wedge in a full set, the increase in the gap between clubs to thirteen or fourteen yards would be unlikely to make a scrap of difference to his game.

By the same token, two wooden clubs are enough for most golfers. Adding a putter makes a total of nine clubs, which would represent a saving of £25 to £30 on a new set. This number of clubs can, without much effort, be carried round in a small bag (saving £5 to £25 on a big one) without wheeling it on a trolley (saving £7 to £10); and also making for a quicker round of golf.

A specialist club nearly every handicap player could use

The ordinary golfer's set might also include, or have added to it, at least one club designed specially to get the ball as far as possible out of the thickish, but not knee-deep, rough: heavy and compact of head, the loft of about a six-iron in the present range, and with the weight biased near the heel to reduce the tendency of the clubface to close when forced through long grass and heather.

The need for design testing

How well and how far any of these ideas might work could only be found out by experiment. In this, work with a model-type testing machine would help enormously.

Even professionals cannot be sure of the effects of a new idea beforehand. Golf is a highly subjective game; and the player's reactions to anything can only be found out by experience. Even then they are very often coloured by preconceived ideas.

Experiments carried out at Portmarnock in 1965 in which spectators at the Dunlop Masters Tournament took part, showed that very few golfers could detect, by waggling and swinging, a quite markedly maverick club in a set otherwise 'matched' as the maker supplied it. This went both for weight of head ('wrong' by half an ounce) and shaft stiffness ('wrong' by two grades). Of course, this does not necessarily mean that, over a number of rounds, they would not have become distrustful—if only subconsciously—about the one maverick club in their bag; but it is still a little surprising how few could pick it out just by waggling.

In any serious attempt to produce clubs matched more ambitiously than they are at present, the maker will need to work through three stages:

1. Comprehensive tests on a machine made to swing a club as a human golfer does.
2. Practical testing by professionals.
3. Sample testing amongst ordinary golfers.

The second and third of these are, of course, just matters of proper organization, though, as we shall see in the next chapter, more effort and planning than you might think is required to get reliable results. Expert opinion is of some value, but is no substitute for controlled measurements.

The first stage, however, requires the construction of a suitable machine; and the team see this as an essential step, not just in matching clubs, but in the whole business of designing them. It is remarkable, to say the least, in this day and age when products much less complicated are scientifically designed and tested, that no means exists in this country for proper controlled testing of possible designs of golf clubs; the more so when you realize that a machine to do the job could probably be built for under £1000.

Chapter 34

The Complications of Finding out

We have said it elsewhere but let us emphasize it again: this is not a textbook on how to play golf.

It simply gives an account of the most searching analysis of the game ever undertaken, together with a provisional statement of some of the scientific principles of golf. It goes as far —and only as far—as the G.S.G.B. team have been able to bring them to light, on the basis of the facts they have so far been able to establish about the way the game is played.

What the reader can make of the basic principles set out in the book depends very much on himself. It may take him some effort to follow them in detail, and apply them intelligently to his own game, but if he can, he may well be able to use them to improve alike his golf and his enjoyment of the game, both at once and, perhaps even more so, in the long run. But it's only fair to say that if he doesn't quite get them clear in the way they apply to all golf, including his, he may only confuse himself and make an already difficult and complicated game even more difficult and complicated.

Using this book

This sort of danger is always present when you analyse, explain and consciously think of the details of any physical action which you normally carry out almost instinctively. The classic case usually quoted is of the centipede being brought to a grinding neurotic halt on being asked to describe how he walked.

As it applies to golf, though, the effect is not unlike driving a car. There's many a perfectly adequate driver who automatically moves the pedals, gear lever, and steering wheel, without the slightest idea of what goes on under the bonnet—or anywhere else, for that matter. If he then studies how a car actually works in detail, thinking in the broader practical mechanical terms may at first make him a slightly less confident driver, through making him more preoccupied with what he is doing. But in the longer run, knowing more fully how what he is doing affects the behaviour of the car will add to his confidence, his safety, and make him a better driver all round. The really skilled driver—a Grand Prix driver, for instance—knows exactly how his transmission, gear box, engine, steering and brakes work, and just what they are— and are not—capable of. That doesn't mean that at any specific time during a race he will be thinking in terms of their detailed working, but it does mean that his whole driving method is based on thorough understanding of them.

Analysing the golf swing works in much the same way. It won't achieve miracles. There's no question of any guarantee that studying this book will halve the reader's handicap. But there's no reason at all why he should not achieve just that— or even more—if he applies it all intelligently.

The book most certainly does offer to the golfer reliable guidance of a kind he's never had before. How he uses it is up to him. It can equally certainly greatly enrich and enlarge his interest and enjoyment in the game.

Proving anything in golf is less simple than it looks

Most experienced golfers have formed their own opinions about the game and the swing; and because of their experience, and probably ability too, their opinions undoubtedly count for something in golf.

Unverifiable opinions, though, however well informed, and well based on experience, do not constitute *proof*. And when you try to get proof, even simple-looking situations turn out to be unexpectedly complicated.

We can show what we mean by taking an apparently simple example. The opinion is widely held that clubs with whippy shafts are more suitable for elderly, high handicap golfers than for younger and stronger players; and stiff shafts vice versa. Circumstantial evidence supports this belief. We know that many pros use stiff shafts, and many ladies and older players use whippy shafts.

But this is not *proof*. How *would* you prove it—or disprove it?

Obviously you'd have to carry out tests. But just exactly what sort of test? Think about it for a while before reading on: what precisely are you trying to establish and how would you go about it?

For a start, are you trying to find out whether whippy shafts enable weaker golfers to hit the ball farther, or more accurately, or more consistently, or with less effort, or less shock, or what? Or is there some other less easily definable, but more basically important, way in which they are 'better'?

Let's just take one of these points—the distance different players can hit the ball with shafts of differing degrees of whip. It is in fact the easiest one to deal with. But it is still quite a complicated business to work out a way of testing it reliably.

Planning a test

You start by having three clubs made—one with a whippy

34:1

34:2

34:3

34:1–34:9 *Some of the G.S.G.B. experiments in progress. They include: putting tests at the 1966 Open Championship at Muirfield (34:3), in which 4000 golfers struck 20,000 six-foot putts on two artificial surfaces (one of which is also shown in 34:4 with the average number of putts out of ten which professionals would hole from various distances displayed); measurement of the speed of the ball in a drive, also at Muirfield, 1966 (34:5); weighing and measuring competitors in the 1966 Schweppes P.G.A. Championship at Saunton (34:2); electromyography (measuring muscular activity) on selected golfers (34:6); and studies on impact ballistics of the ball (34:7 and 34:9).*

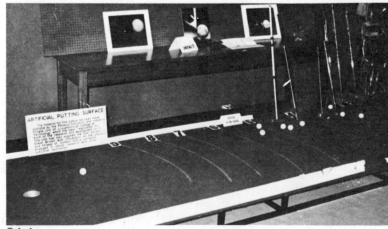
34:4

34:5

34:7

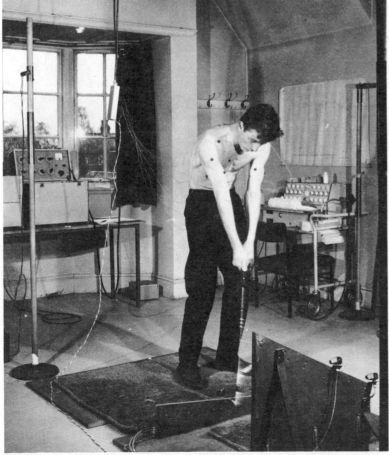

34:6

34:8

34:9

shaft (L), one with a medium shaft (R), and one with a stiff shaft (X)—then you want a number of golfers to test them. But straightaway the situation already bristles with decisions which have to be taken logically.

What sort of clubs? A driver probably, since in this test it is the effect on length of shot you are trying to establish. But perhaps many of your subjects don't normally use a driver, and will perform badly on that account? After all, ladies and elderly gentlemen often drive with a two- or even a three-wood. But then again, most of the stronger young players *do* use a driver; and you are going to need both age groups in your test. Would it perhaps be better to go to a club—say a three-wood or a long iron—which they can all use (*can* they all use long irons?) off the grass, but with which they also achieve reasonable distances?

Incidentally, might the time saved by hitting the ball off grass rather than teeing it up for a drive be a factor worth taking into consideration? With a supply of balls lying on the ground you can hit about five shots a minute off the grass, but only three if you have to tee up each time. These differences might be very important in a thorough test needing perhaps two thousand shots. On the other hand, especially with the older subjects, a pause to rest between shots may be necessary anyway.

How many golfers to hit how many shots?
Suppose, rightly or wrongly, you decide that a driver is the club to use. Three drivers then have to be made with shafts of different degrees of whip; in all other respects they have to be identical.

Or have they? In particular, should the clubhead weight be the same, since it is common practice among manufacturers to put lighter clubheads on the whippy shafts and heavier on the stiff? You decide, however, that weight can perhaps be examined later; in this test it is intrinsic shaft flexibility you are looking at. So: all clubs to have heads of the same weight.

What weight? You've got to make a start somewhere, so you decide to get an ordinary R (medium) shafted driver and ask the manufacturers to make two clubheads identical in weight to the one on the R shaft and fit them to a whippy shaft and a stiff one. You make a mental note that the whole experiment may have to be repeated with a different clubhead weight. (And perhaps a different design of club? No one club suits everyone, whatever shaft is in it.)

For the moment however, you've got your basic equipment to be tested. What about the golfers who are going to test it? How many golfers do you need and how many shots should they hit?

It really takes a statistician to answer this question. But in order to do so, he has to know what sort of difference in length of drive you are looking for. Thirty yards? Ten yards? Five yards? One yard, or what? And he has to know something about how the distance any given person hits the ball varies from shot to shot, and how the distance varies from person to person.

Then there is the question of mishits; not so much slices or hooks which could be considered in a test of *accuracy*, but complete mishits: topped and fluffed shots. If you are comparing the effectiveness of different shafts in getting maximum distance from the tee, you can hardly count mishits in a calculation of average distance. But since the likelihood of producing mishits *may* depend on the type of shaft, you cannot disregard them.

Perhaps you decide to count the fraction of shots which are mishit, using that as one indication of the suitability of the shaft to the player, then measure the average distance achieved by only the best 25% of shots hit by each player. Thus if each golfer hits twenty shots with a given club, you measure only the five longest, and that will give a fair indication of the *potential* of the club for that player.

But of course you miss something by doing that. How far the not quite perfectly hit shots go *is* of interest, so perhaps you ought to count *all* shots other than mishits. But here you run into another difficulty: how bad does a shot have to be to count as a 'mishit'? Many shots are clearly either good shots or complete fluffs. But, especially with higher handicap golfers, there are also plenty of shots which are neither. In these cases, how do you draw the line between a mishit and rather less than a perfect hit?

And *who* draws the line? The striker himself? He may have preconceived ideas about which club he thinks is best for him, and this will affect his judgment. An outside observer is not ideal either, because he cannot really tell how well a shot was struck without seeing the flight of the ball. And if the flight of the ball is brought in, you run the risk of making distance the criterion of an acceptable shot. If you do *that*, you complicate the working out of the significance of the results of your test; and maybe even invalidate it.

Perhaps we've already carried this far enough to illustrate the point: how careful and thorough your preliminary thinking and planning has to be.

Organizing an experiment: further practical considerations
We'd still only have gone about a quarter of the way to starting any actual test though.

We'll summarize some of the remaining considerations in the form of staccato questions:

What should be the balance of handicaps amongst your testing players?

When, where, how, and for how long can you get the players?

How many balls does each hit before a rest, or a change of club?

Do you measure results of each shot, or in batches?

What rate of measuring and checking will you have to work at?

Can the players keep up that speed? Should they?

Will it actually take weeks to get all the results you want?

Can you reasonably expect to occupy any part of a golf course for that amount of time? If not, where else can it be done?

Say you get all this planned. Then:

How do you allow for the need to adjust from one shaft to another? and to make sure the order doesn't affect the results?

How do you allow for better club-to-club adaptability of low handicap players? Do you *want* them to adapt? (A built-in tendency of a club to slice for example might show up better before the player adapts to it.)

How can you best allow for each player's good and bad patches?

Or wind changes, weather changes, during the tests?

Widening the scope of the test
Wouldn't it be saner just to give up the whole idea and go into a monastery?

On the other hand you have gone to a lot of trouble to organize your test; your volunteer golfers, your observers and your equipment are all going to be at the testing ground which you have arranged during a specified period of days. Far from giving up the whole idea, you may find the opposite temptation arising: to take this opportunity of testing a few more club

properties such as variations in weight and in length, or possibly in grip thickness or clubhead design or material.

The policy for dealing with temptation of this sort remains unchanged through the centuries: yield not. Your statistician has told you how many shots are required with each club to give results with a certain significance. If you reduce this number you jeopardize the whole test; at worst it could be a complete waste of time. The only way to fit more clubs into the test is by taking more time.

One final point. If you have thought of all these possible complications, and come to some decision as to how to cope with them *before* you actually carry out any tests, you are a genius.

What almost certainly happens in practice is that you think of a few of them, but only discover the others either as you carry out the test, or afterwards while analysing the results. The likelihood is that you'll have to repeat the whole operation—or at best make do with results which don't tell you as much as you hoped.

Is it all really necessary?
Have we made our point?

It really is difficult to carry out a test of this sort in such a way as to provide meaningful answers. Even these answers will often be qualified; to preserve scientific honesty we must at times say, '. . . it is likely that . . .', or '. . . provided that . . .'.

And of course, the example we have been considering is a relatively straightforward one. Here at least we are examining the effect of a difference (in shaft flexibility) which is clearly defined and measurable. When you come to differences in swing technique the picture is much more complicated.

Even, for example, the difference between 'squares' and 'rollers' is by no means cut and dried; and getting statistics to *prove* that one method was more reliable than the other would be quite unimaginably difficult and complicated—which is why, in Chapter 16, the G.S.G.B. team, having no access to the supernatural insight occasionally apparently accessible to some golf enthusiasts, could go only so far into the subject.

A check for the sceptic
If the down-to-earth, to-hell-with-scientific-nonsense reader is now feeling that we've made a huge mountain out of an insignificant molehill of a test, let him try a simple experiment —one in which the 'right' answer is known in advance.

Let him try to prove that he hits the ball a progressively decreasing distance as he goes, in sequence, through his irons from two-iron down to nine-iron. Do it the down-to-earth, to-hell-with-scientific-nonsense way by hitting a shot with each club. It's a fairly safe bet that he'll get one of them out of sequence somewhere and so 'prove' one or more of his clubs to be 'wrong' in some way. But they aren't; so let him do the test again, but think about it first. How many shots? What order? What about mishits? And so on. In fact go back to page 219.

How much does it all cost?

We conclude the episode of the club-testing experiment by making a rough assessment of what it might cost you. You may be lucky in being able to borrow equipment, or in persuading manufacturers to give you clubs and balls; but it still costs *somebody* something, so we'll include it. The total cost, then, of an experiment such as the one described might work out at £300 or so, as follows:

Three clubs and six dozen balls	£40
Labour during experiment (one scientist plus three assistants for seven days)	175
Labour for analysis (one scientist plus one assistant for five days)	75
Sundry expenses (to volunteers, marker posts, postage, fares)	10
	£300

This does not include any fees or expenses for the services of the players, for the use of sports grounds, or measuring equipment; nor does it allow for the possibility of having to repeat the test because you haven't thought of a lot of the snags the first time. Nevertheless it shows what even a simple test can cost if it is to be done properly.

No complicated apparatus is needed for a test like this. But as soon as electrical equipment is needed, experimental work can become very expensive—and most of the G.S.G.B. experimental programme did use such equipment. Indeed the whole investigation could never have been carried out as a properly costed programme. It would have been far too expensive. The G.S.G.B. were fortunate in finding scientists whose own research interests could be served by examining the golf swing, and whose services and equipment were thus available at little cost.

The £300 for the club test is, of course, chicken feed compared with the vast sums of money spent by people buying golf equipment, or by firms advertising it; which makes it all the more surprising how little effort manufacturers seem to make to test clubs systematically in this way, relying instead on experienced opinion—always liable to subjective bias. In fact only 1% of the estimated £5½ million spent annually on golf equipment in this country (not to mention the $200 million in U.S.A.) would finance a very comprehensive research programme. Some industries plough back 10% or more in research. Golf is no worse than other sports in this respect, and it is interesting to speculate on what improvements in standards and facilities could be achieved by a sports research centre financed to the tune of 1% of the annual turnover in all sports.

Chapter 35

Enough of the difficulties. What of the future?

If the scientific study of golf is thought, so far as it goes, to have provided useful information, where should it go from here? As a start let us look at some of the projects at present under discussion or early development by the G.S.G.B. team.

A model-like machine to test clubs

First of all, the one with the most immediate practical significance: a machine to test golf clubs. It cannot of course replace tests by human golfers, nor opinions of expert golfers; but it can do a very great deal to complement them. All three ways are necessary to test new ideas about golf clubs properly. The G.S.G.B. team has prepared a design for a machine which will swing a golf club by reproducing the main movements of the two-lever model. Besides its main purpose, such a machine will reveal something, perhaps a lot, about the golf swing itself.

An automatic learner-prompter

Secondly, there are all the possible devices which might help a golfer to learn more quickly; which will tell him when he has swung well, and when he has not, more reliably and possibly earlier than the result of the shot does. The ideal device, as we said in Chapter 18, would give him a signal of some kind the instant he went wrong on the backswing.

Strain gauge consistency patterns

The G.S.G.B. team haven't looked at that particular problem yet, but they have been investigating a method of testing the consistency of successive swings, by the use of strain gauges in the shaft of the club. These give a continuous record, during the swing, of the amount of bending of the shaft in any direction.

Although it is difficult to interpret this in terms of what the golfer is doing to the club at any moment, each trace is uniquely related to the way he swings. Thus identical swings produce identical traces; very inconsistent swings produce inconsistent traces. You can see this from Fig. 35:1.

More questions about the model

The mechanics of the two-lever model provides a wide-open field for further interesting and instructive study. It requires painstaking computation of swings incorporating variations in length, timing, applied forces, club and body masses. The team has begun to do this in a very limited way. For example the discussion in Chapter 32, of the effects of variation in the weight and length of the club, is based on a small-scale survey of this sort.

Another example of the sort of result you can get, from the computation already done, is that the ideal clubhead weight for a woman is about two-thirds of an ounce less than for a man. The sceptical reader is no doubt saying he could have told us that without expensive computer calculations. This does not, however, detract from their value. On the contrary, it is reassuring to know that calculations on the model give the 'right' answer; it gives confidence when we come to look at situations where the answer is not known in advance. And even in the case quoted, the computations can say a bit more than the sceptic; that the ideal clubhead weight *is* less for a woman more because her weight (particularly of her arms) is less than a man's than because her strength is less.

More work for the model

A wider survey on the same lines as these examples could perhaps answer questions like:

Should weight and length of clubs depend on the player's strength and stature?

How important is the hit with the hands?

Why do most golfers, even good ones, get the clubhead going at its greatest speed six inches or more before impact, rather than at impact?

How is clubhead speed at impact affected by shortening or lengthening the backswing, by speeding it up or slowing it down, by cocking the wrists more or less?

How are these interrelated?

Would a change in weight of the ball require a change in weight or length of the club for best results?

Calculations using the simple two-lever model of the swing will throw light on all of these; and the G.S.G.B. team have also begun to study more complicated models, which represent body movements by co-axial cylinders (as in Chapter 7).

More questions about flight and impact

In Chapters 22 to 26 we have discussed in some detail both the flight of a golf ball through the air and its behaviour at impact. There are still several things about them which the scientists only partially understand, or to which they would like to put more exact numerical values.

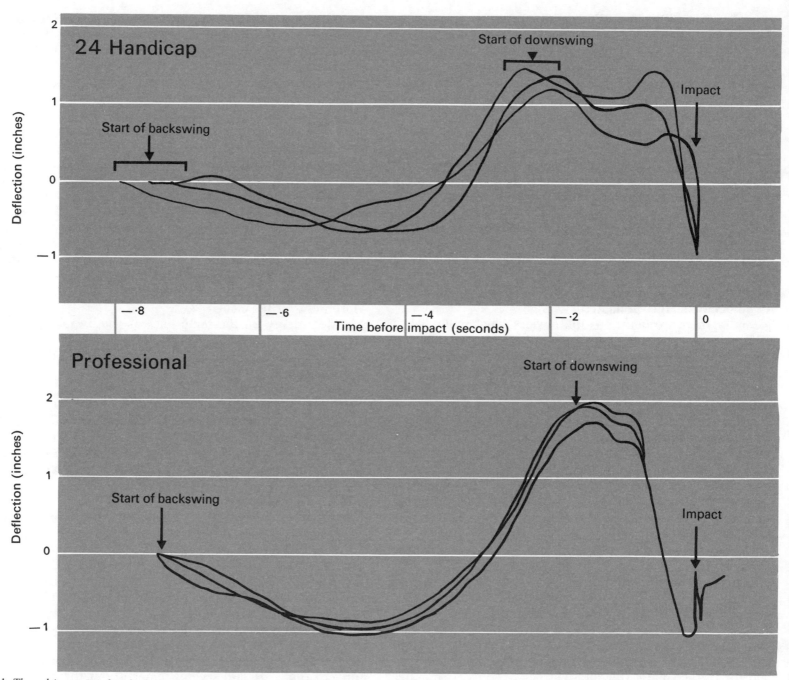

35:1 *Three driver swings by a high-handicap amateur and three by a professional. The traces record how much the shaft is bent back (positive deflection) or forward (negative deflection) at any time during the swing. You can see how much more consistent the professional's bending pattern is—in other words how much more consistently he has swung the club. This sort of record might form the basis of an automatic teaching device.*

They would like, for example, to be able to compute, more exactly than at present, the trajectory of any shot, given the speed, angle and spin with which it sets off, together with other relevant data like air temperature, pressure and humidity. They would like to know more about the spin left on the ball as it hits the ground at the end of its flight through the air, and about angles of descent for various kinds of shots, and for different sizes, weights and kinds of balls. They would also like to know very much more about the mechanism of energy loss which makes impact between clubhead and ball less than perfectly elastic; and to know how this is related to the way spin is imparted.

These may be primarily matters of scientific or technical interest, but until they are fully understood, no one can say for certain whether they may or may not have practical significance for the golfer.

More questions on teaching and learning

If we look even further ahead, at problems the team has only briefly touched on, there are a number of interesting and perhaps rewarding topics which some future investigator might tackle.

In Chapter 21, we mentioned one: the way the eyes are used in putting. We'll say no more here.

But in Chapter 18 we made tentative suggestions concerning methods of teaching and learning. Some of these could be tested by a sufficiently ambitious and well-organized programme of research. What is the best duration for a lesson or practice session; and what is the best interval of time between sessions? Is it best to learn basically by imitation or by instruction? Would it help beginners if the skills required were made less demanding at first, for example, by using a much bigger ball? Colleges of physical education are probably the best places to carry out investigations of that sort.

What makes a champion?

Another whole field of inquiry, which is so far almost untouched, concerns the personality of golfers, especially of good ones. Is it possible that the top players possess some quite definable innate qualities of character which could be measured in a test? If so, how does this affect their competitive ability psychologically? Through their swings? Through their golfing intelligence in general? Could young assistant professionals perhaps find out, by taking a test, how far they were

likely to succeed as tournament players? Or are any such qualities the kind which can be developed through competitive golf? Might any of them, perhaps, be very much more important than a simple ability to play to scratch at the age of 18? Would the sort of man who has them be likely to join a sponsored training scheme for young professionals? If not, does this doom such schemes to failure by their very nature?

All this is pure speculation; but, even in the present state of knowledge about these matters, personality tests might be able to provide interesting evidence.

Science in golf: possibilities unlimited

As you can see the possibilities for further research are limitless; and they are of interest not only to the golfer, but to the scientist as well. Many of the subjects we've just mentioned, and indeed much of the work on which this whole book is based, venture into territory largely unexplored so far in the scientific world.

The further, fully scientific book now being written goes into much more technical and scientific detail than this book. Although this scientific book is aimed primarily at other scientists, there should still be much in it for the keen student of golf.

Science is no sledge-hammer

Perhaps some readers are by now feeling slightly incredulous. Is this really *golf* we've been talking about? Is this the game based on the essentially simple idea of hitting a ball into a hole in the ground some distance away in as few hits as possible, and en route playing it as you find it? Isn't the charm and fascination of the game just its unpredictability? The never-really-knowing what's going to happen next, the frequent visitations by despair and frustration, the ever-present hope, and above all the inspiration from occasional fulfilment of that hope: these are surely the stuff of golf? Is some vast scientific sledge-hammer going to pulverize all that, and remove all the enjoyment from playing the game?

The short answer is: no. Not, at least, to any reader not already determined that it shall. We can allow a particular mental attitude to spoil any pleasure; but, on its own, understanding of how a thing works shouldn't have that effect. We do not appreciate a sunset any less for understanding the electromagnetic nature of light. Our enjoyment of Beethoven or the Beatles is in no way reduced by knowledge of the properties of sound waves, and the infinite combinations of harmonics which give each instrument its characteristic sound. And, in a sphere of aesthetic pleasure nearer the hearts of golfers, as we stride off the eighteenth green we do not head for the nineteenth with any less relish for knowing the chemical formula for alcohol.

If these pleasures were denied to scientists just because they could analyse some of the underlying physical and human processes, they would be a very unhappy species. And they are not.

In short, understanding in no way diminishes enjoyment. Certainly none of the golfers in the G.S.G.B. research team has in any way had his pleasure in playing the game dulled. Quite the reverse, in fact; deeper appreciation of its subtleties has made for even greater fascination. (Not to mention extra opportunities for gamesmanship during the game, and for one-up-manship in the bar afterwards!)

The idea of golf becoming completely predictable is, of course, absurd. Despite scientific analysis, despite mechanical or electronic aids which may be devised to perfect his swing, the shot still has to be played by a man who is aware of the possibilities and the consequences of success and failure. Golfers know that this situation will always give rise to unpredictability—good days and bad days. They have seen 'scientific' practice devices and 'infallible' new clubs come and go; and though the eagerness with which they clutch at these straws might suggest some perfectly conscious gullibility, deep down in their heart of hearts golfers are a sceptical and fatalistic breed. They know there is no easy way. Golfers were not meant to live happily ever after.

Appendix I

Some Formulae for Mathematically Minded Readers

It often helps the reader to understand a difficult subject, if he can get hold of some of the formulae involved and 'play about' with them: by inserting numbers in them and seeing how increasing this quantity, or reducing that one, affects the final outcome. In real-life situations, such as the golf swing, unfortunately, simple formulae don't often apply, or at least are only approximate.

Nevertheless we give below a few such formulae, which will enable readers who are so minded to work out for themselves, at least in a general way, how some of the simpler quantities in a golf swing can affect the result.

1. Units of speed
Throughout most of the book, *miles per hour* has been used as the unit of speed, mainly because most readers will be familiar with it. But *feet per second* is often more appropriate when referring to clubhead or ball speeds; and even *inches per millisecond* is sometimes useful when we are thinking of the speed of small movements around the short time of impact.

The diagrammatic scale will enable readers to convert speed from one set of units to the other.

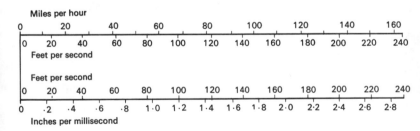

A:1 *Corresponding speeds expressed in different ways.*

2. Relation between range and ball velocity
For a ball velocity of v feet per second the carry and the overall range (carry plus run), in yards, of a drive are given approximately by:

$$\text{Carry} = 1 \cdot 5v - 103$$
$$\text{Overall range} = 1 \cdot 25v - 27$$

Limitations: These formulae are empirical fits to observed drives with British-size 1·62-inch balls. They apply only to squarely struck *drives* (i.e. not more-lofted shots) with velocities between 150 feet per second and 250 feet per second. The overall range assumes some sort of average ground conditions (see also Chapter 25).

3. The speed of the ball from impact
The velocity imparted to the ball by the head of a driver is given by:

$$v = U \times \frac{1+e}{1+(m/M)}$$

v = velocity of the ball immediately after impact.
U = velocity of the clubhead immediately before impact.
m = mass of the ball (1·62 ounces).
M = mass of the clubhead (usually 7 to 8 ounces).
e = the coefficient of restitution (the value of which varies slowly from about 0·67 in a hard hit drive to 0·80 in a putt).

Limitations: This formula applies only to square-on impacts —strictly speaking zero loft; but the error is negligible for the 10° or so of loft on a driver.

4. How the mass of the clubhead affects the speed at which it can be swung
The greatest speed a golfer can impart to the clubhead of a driver of conventional length depends on the mass of the clubhead in a way which is shown in the graph.

The separate curves for pro, good amateur, handicap golfer and duffer represent differences in the efficiency with which the golfer transfers the power he develops to the clubhead. They do not represent differences in basic muscular strength. The curves are drawn for men of average strength; variations in strength in any of the categories of golfer mentioned simply increase or decrease the clubhead speed. Thus a very strong man could produce about 10% more clubhead speed than the average shown on the graph; a woman would produce some 15% to 20% less.

Limitations: The theoretical basis of these curves is a little shaky: plausible but not verified. But they do fit such measurements as have been made. They say nothing, of course, about whether the clubhead is likely to be brought squarely to the ball.

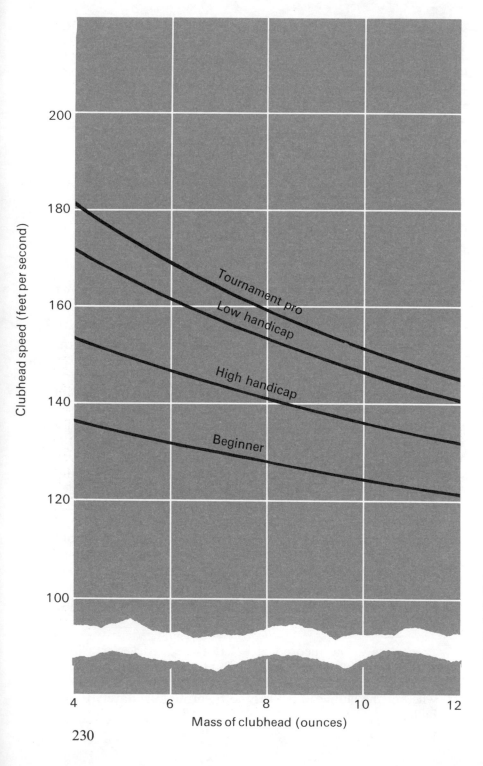

5. The rate of vibration of a golf shaft

A heavy head set at the end of a uniform flexible shaft, which is firmly clamped at the other end, will vibrate at a rate f times per second given by:

$$f = \frac{1}{2\pi}\sqrt{\frac{3EI}{(M+0\cdot24m)l^3}}$$

M = the mass of the head.
m = the mass of the shaft.
l = the length of the shaft from the point of clamping to the head.
E = an elastic property of the material of the shaft.
I = a quantity which depends on the precise cross-section of the shaft, and which represents its ability to resist bending.

In fact $I = (\pi/4)(a^4 - b^4)$ where a and b are the external and internal radii of the hollow shaft. In a normal golf shaft these vary along the length of the shaft, so the formula for frequency applies only if I is suitably averaged. If a and b are measured in inches, I varies from about $0\cdot001$ to about $0\cdot0002$ in an 'R' shaft for a driver.

A word of warning for readers who may like to put numbers in the formula and carry out their own calculation of frequency: be careful to express the quantities under the square root sign in a consistent set of units. Using inches as the unit of length, and ounces as the unit of mass, the quantity E has a value, for steel, of about $1\cdot9 \times 10^{11}$.

For example, if M = 7 ounces,
  m = 4 ounces,
  l = 39 inches (4 inches from end of shaft),
  and I = $0\cdot0006$ (rough average over whole shaft),
then f works out at $4\cdot3$ cycles per second.

Limitations: The formula for frequency applies to a *point* mass at the end of a shaft of *uniform* cross-section. A proper calculation of frequencies of a golf shaft, whose cross-section varies along its length is much more complicated. Nevertheless the simple formula gives a good idea of how the various quantities affect the frequency of vibration.

A:2 *Clubhead speeds generated by typical golfers of different abilities.*

Appendix II

A Device for Long Straight Shots

An excellent example of what might be achieved by artificial aids to the game is the hinge tee invented by D. H. Cockburn, of Iver, Bucks, and patented in U.K. and U.S.A.

This adapts the familiar principle of speeding the closing of a door by pushing it hard near the hinges. It works very simply as can be seen in the accompanying diagram (Fig. A:3). The base plate is laid on the ground, aimed on the required line. The other plate is set at about 45° to the base plate and hinges freely forward. The ball rests on a pin stuck into a shallow groove running up the length of the hinged plate.

As the clubhead is swung through the apparatus from the open end, the ball is projected into flight by the sharp forward swing of the hinged plate. As it goes, it flies up the groove, and takes on backspin.

The tee is still under development, and the trajectory it gives is too high; but you can still drive a little farther with it, than with an orthodox shot. With optimum design gains of up to fifty yards might well be possible; furthermore if the device were very accurately engineered, the high precision of striking required in a normal drive would be unnecessary.

By moving the pin up the hinged plate, you can vary the height of the 'shot'. The earlier it leaves the plate, the higher it flies. By having the pin right near the top and the ball overhanging the edge, you can get a high pitch which spins enough to bring the ball back on seaside greens.

The essential principle upon which the tee works concerns the mismatches mentioned in Chapter 32. When driven into the angle between the two plates, the clubhead experiences greater inertial resistance than the ball alone can provide; and more energy is transferred to the hinged plate (plus ball). If the device is correctly designed, a sufficiently large fraction of this is finally imparted to the ball to make it fly off faster than a direct impact with the club would.

Of course, it isn't really golf; for one thing you don't need a faced club to work it.

Even so, until recently it was by no means certain that its use, at least for driving, would have been technically illegal under the Rules of Golf. However, rewording of Rule 37–9 seems to remove any ambiguity by prohibiting 'any device which might assist the player in making a stroke . . .'

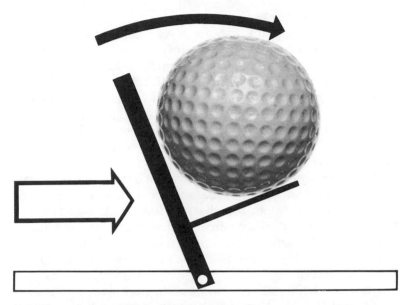

A:3 *The operation of the Cockburn tee.*

A:4 *The Cockburn tee in action. You can see the ball in three positions. First (and faintly) resting on the tee before impact; then just before leaving the tee; and finally in clear flight with the tee following through. By this stage backspin is clearly visible (about 70 revs per sec). The two clubhead positions, which are most clearly distinguished by looking at the 'neck' of the club, correspond to the last two ball positions.*

Appendix III

The Story of the G.S.G.B.'s Research Project

The man behind this book

Sir Aynsley Bridgland was born in Australia, graduated there as a civil engineer, and subsequently served in World War I on the Western Front. After the Armistice he was appointed Australian representative of John D. Rockefeller, and in 1929 came to England to set up his own business in the property market. With his background of civil engineering, mathematics and finance—and a full ration of confidence and enterprise—he did extremely well. His companies put up many large blocks in London.

He had many interests, which brought him into contact with a cross-section of equally successful people. For example, in the thirties he reorganized the London Clinic and thus entrained members of the medical profession. It was he who arranged for the safe and accurate transfer of the Mithraic Temple when it was exposed during excavations in Queen Victoria Street.

He was a keen golfer, who liked to play well, and a competent one too. His three ambitions as a young man were: to own a Rolls-Royce, to be a millionaire, and to be a scratch golfer. He achieved them all; and he always said that it was the last of the three which satisfied him most.

He was a great enthusiast for the game, and for all its interests; and he has left his mark in its history through his generous support of Princes, Sandwich, and Royal Cinque Ports, Deal; through his gifts towards the expenses of international teams; and perhaps above all through his founding and support of the Golf Society of Great Britain.

During a visit to the United States, in the early fifties he heard that championship golfers were co-operating with the scientists in Dr Edgerton's department at the Massachusetts Institute of Technology in high speed photographic studies of the way in which golf balls were deformed by impact with the clubhead.

Sir Aynsley saw the other side of the coin. To him it was an example of the way scientists could help sportsmen to improve their game. He believed that if there were any secrets, they would be discovered in terms of mechanical engineering principles. When he returned to Britain he sought out the equivalent of M.I.T., and was directed to the Imperial College of Science and Technology in London. He went to see Sir Patrick Linstead, the Rector, and asked him if he could suggest someone who might be interested in the idea of a scientific analysis of the game of golf.

It all began with baseball

It so happened that D. G. Christopherson, Professor of Applied Science, and a Fellow of the Royal Society, had some years previously written a paper for the Institute of Mechanical Engineers on the mathematical implications of the stroke in baseball. Sir Patrick, recognizing that Bridgland was serious about his request for scientific help, suggested that he meet Christopherson, who in due course was persuaded to write three articles in the *Bulletin* of the Golf Society of Great Britain on the 'Science of the Swing'. These were very well received and attracted a good deal of comment in the Press. The author admitted however, that he had barely scratched the surface of a very complicated process. It was as far as he could go on theoretical principles and with present knowledge. It was obvious too, he said, that any thorough study of the golf swing needed a large contribution by anatomists and physiologists.

Sir Aynsley, having made a successful foray into the area of the physical sciences, now turned his attention to the medical and biological fields. His friend Sir Arthur Porritt, President of the Royal College of Surgeons and a President of the British Olympics Committee, drew his attention to some work which had recently been done by Dr Harold Lewis in the Division of Human Physiology, National Institute for Medical Research in London; this was a study of the human power output in such sports as weight lifting and pole vaulting.

A challenge to research

Sir Aynsley wrote to Lewis, and asked him whether they could meet to discuss the possibility of research into golf. Lewis had a fully committed research programme and was initially rather sceptical of the value of golf research. However, thinking about it, he realized that a properly mounted project could throw light on some problems of neuro-muscular co-ordination.

He had another discussion with Sir Aynsley and told him that some of his fellow-scientists might be interested if the emphasis were primarily on this aspect using the golf stroke purely as an example.

The more he thought about it, the more interesting did the research challenge seem to him, and Lewis was encouraged to discuss the matter with members of the Physiological Society.

The team builds up

One of them was Professor Douglas Wilkie, who had collaborated with him on the work on human power output. Wilkie is a Professor of Physiology at University College, London, where he studies the function of muscles. In recent years he had become more and more interested in the applications of muscular activity and had made calculations about the feasibility of man-powered flight (it is just possible). Lewis's work with him was to provide some of the data about human power output in athletes, and Wilkie was receptive to the idea that golf might provide a useful 'laboratory' for further studies.

Lewis had also discussed the whole idea with another physiologist at the National Institute for Medical Research at Hampstead, London. He was Dr Reginald Whitney, Head of the Biomechanics Unit. This group does research into the ways in which the human body acts as a machine, and tries to answer basic questions such as, 'How does a man use his muscles to walk, to lift a weight, to jump?'

Lewis had a further discussion with Sir Aynsley and told him that he now knew that there was some interest among his colleagues. 'Well,' said Sir Aynsley, 'let's get together. Besides I want you to meet Professor Christopherson, and a young physicist, Cochran.'

The scientists meet each other

On 21st June 1961 the scientists sat down to lunch at the Savoy Hotel, London, with Sir Aynsley and Sir Geoffrey Howard (Chairman of the Golf Society of Great Britain). The scientists were Christopherson, Cochran, Lewis, Whitney and Wilkie.

Dr Alastair Cochran, then at the Atomic Energy Establishment, Winfrith, had been invited because he had shown interest in this work some years before when teaching at the Royal Military College of Science, Shrivenham. In May 1957, scheduled to give a 'popular lecture' (a tradition at Shrivenham), he chose to talk about the ballistic aspects of golf. There had not been many hard facts to go on, but he did get some basic data on golf balls by visiting Dunlop.

Cochran was then a handicap one golfer and played for Berkshire, Bucks and Oxford. It was at an inter-county match that he got talking to John Stobbs, his Herts opponent, who suggested that he expand his lecture into a series in *Golfing* magazine which Stobbs then edited. For the next year or so,

the manuscripts went backwards and forwards, while at Shrivenham Cochran devised some student experiments with golf balls in the wind tunnel; and with Bertie Daish, Head of the Ballistics Branch, set up teaching demonstrations showing the effects of impact on the ball.

In 1960, the series of articles appeared in *Golfing*, from February to August; and commanded wide interest as the most authoritative summary of the basic facts of impact and flight yet seen in a popular magazine.

Cochran also joined the recently formed Golf Society of Great Britain, and in its *Bulletin* for members, he read the third article by Professor Christopherson on the Science of the Swing in the issue of April 1961. He wrote to the editor for the two previous numbers and mentioned his own articles. Back came a letter from Sir Aynsley and thus in due course, Cochran arrived at the Savoy lunch.

The project begins to take shape

From then on, the group met for lunch discussions every two or three months, under Sir Aynsley's Chairmanship, choosing various topics for each meeting. One of the earliest was how to compare the 1·62-inch ball with the larger American 1·68-inch.

Lewis meanwhile had contacted Professor William Floyd, the country's first Professor of Ergonomics at Loughborough University of Technology. In 1961 Floyd was in the early stages of setting up his new department, and was interested in any ideas that might lead to useful research. Ergonomics is the science of fitting the job to the worker, so that his mental and physical comfort and capabilities are improved and his productivity is increased. It covers such fields as the control of noise in factories, the redesign of engineering equipment like crane cabs so that the worker can see what he is doing, and the design of car seats and controls so that all can be operated harmoniously without confusion, and thus with greater safety.

The application of such scientific methods to the game of golf intrigued Sir Aynsley, who reckoned that if it proved a success and a help towards improved performance at the sport, it would be a useful example to industry.

From Floyd's point of view, even coming right down to earth, the project was essentially in the spirit of Ergonomics. He realized that the answers to the questions simply didn't exist, and knew that it meant that research would have to be done to find the answers. No amount of talking, however erudite, could take the place of costly research which might take three to five years. If Sir Aynsley Bridgland undertook to find the money, and thus sponsor a scientist—if one could be found—Floyd was willing to direct this research in his department at Loughborough.

It soon became apparent that the group would have to be even further reinforced. First Bertie Daish, the ballistics expert from the Royal Military College of Science, was invited to join; then, to strengthen the aerodynamics side, Keith Legg, Professor of Aeronautical Engineering at Loughborough University, was invited.

By mid-1962 the Golf Society of Great Britain provided funds for a research fellow to work under Floyd at Loughborough, and Floyd invited David Noble, a physical education graduate of Loughborough College of Education. For his diploma Noble had conducted a research project on golf, making a series of measurements of strength of muscles and mobility of joints in a group of golfers and comparing it with a group of non-golfers.

Thus reinforced, the group met several times throughout 1962, and proposed a substantial research programme reflecting the specific interests of each member. By the end of the year a start had been made and a few research reports were beginning to appear. But it was obvious that, as the pace quickened, the developing work should be co-ordinated, and Cochran agreed to act as scientific chairman/secretary. It was apparent that there was too much work to do this part-time, and soon Sir Aynsley asked Cochran to accept a full-time appointment. It was an important decision for Cochran to make, but after careful deliberation he accepted.

The working party was further reinforced by Dr Donald Grieve, a physiologist and a colleague of Whitney's with a special background of physics and mathematics; and by Peter Sharman, an engineer in Legg's department at Loughborough. Anne Welford, who had been a scientific assistant with the Atomic Energy Authority, was appointed full-time scientific assistant and secretary to the project.

Cochran took up his full-time appointment in March 1963, and from then on the scientific working party met regularly, usually in the Golfer's Club at Whitehall Court, London.

The scope of the work
The method of working at these meetings was to work out the general approach to the problem and to suggest experiments and calculations, which individual members then undertook

to carry out. The results were always presented for discussion at subsequent meetings in the form of working party papers —of which well over a hundred were eventually produced. It is on these papers and the carefully recorded discussions on them that this book is based.

But that, of course, oversimplifies the picture. There were the countless discussions with professional golfers, which were not recorded in detail; there were the visits to tournaments usually for some specific purpose, but which, in addition, left general impressions that could not be put down on paper; there was the study of acres and acres of articles in golf books and magazines. Few of these things appear in working party documents, but much was absorbed from them.

The writing of the book
Sir Aynsley's idea in gathering the scientific working party together had been, from the first, to produce a scientific book about golf.

The further the research proceeded the more obvious it became that to produce a book of practical popular interest was going to be no easy task. When a team of ten scientists, all of different skills, attacks a project of this kind from their ten different points of view, the resulting series of reports, however individually fascinating are liable to have no obvious interconnection—at least to the layman.

Since co-ordinating the whole programme, and, in between times, carrying out some of the original research, was a full-time task for Cochran, it seemed best to bring in someone else to concentrate on the business of creating a coherent golf book from the tide of papers flowing in all the time.

At this stage therefore, the G.S.G.B. invited John Stobbs, Golf Correspondent of the (London) *Observer* for the previous ten years and author of several books about the game, to take on the job. As noted earlier, Stobbs and Cochran had already had dealings with each other. The respect they had for each other's abilities—both on and off the golf course—made a good basis for collaboration, and from the start they worked very closely together.

After much lengthy discussion, tape-recording, passing of notes and ideas—in which David Noble also played no small part—and drafting and redrafting of chapters (some up to five times), with each stage stimulating further discussion, rethinking, replanning and rewriting, the book took shape and most of it was typescript.

At this stage, Stobbs was put out of action for four months by illness. Cochran drafted the chapters not yet completed, revised the whole of the book in detail for balanced scientific accuracy, and laid the whole thing before the working party, for their detailed comments. These he incorporated in the text. He and Stobbs then went through the whole text again, chapter by chapter, preparing it finally for publication.

A further, scientific book

Early on it became clear that many of the detailed results of the investigation could not be presented or at best could be only briefly mentioned in a book like this one. Yet in many cases those were just the results which were of real scientific interest, and which should therefore see the light of day in some form. A second book was therefore suggested, to report the detailed results of the investigation and to survey other scientific work relating to it, for the benefit of other scientists— but also of interest to lay readers, whose appetites have been whetted by this book, and who wish to dig deeper into the subject.

This scientific volume is at present in preparation.

The place of the G.S.G.B.

Meantime, throughout all the planning, all the theorizing, and all the writing, the Golf Society of Great Britain had played its part. Although the moving spirit who started things going was one man—Sir Aynsley Bridgland—it is doubtful whether the investigation would ever have succeeded without the backing of the G.S.G.B.

The Society provided some of the money required (and scientific research costs a lot of money), but, much more important, the respect with which it was held in the golfing world added authority to the project and ensured the willing co-operation of professionals and equipment manufacturers. It is only right that this book should be thought of as the account of 'The Golf Society of Great Britain Scientific Study'.

Pen Portraits

ALASTAIR COCHRAN is Chairman of the Golf Society of Great Britain Scientific Working Party. He was born in Edinburgh in 1929 and was educated at George Heriot's School, and Edinburgh University where he took a B.Sc. in Physics in 1952 and subsequently did research in nuclear physics for his Ph.D. in 1955. He worked for a year on radar research with Ferranti in Edinburgh; then in 1956 became Senior lecturer in physics at the Royal Military College of Science, Shrivenham. It was there he first became interested in science applied to golf. In 1960 he joined the Atomic Energy Establishment at Winfrith Heath where he worked on nuclear power until 1963, when he took on the job of co-ordinating the G.S.G.B. scientific project. Naturally good at most ball games, he has 'always lacked the method and dedication to be first-class at any'. While at University he won blues in association football and golf, and captained the golf club. He retained a scratch handicap for a couple of years and, on moving to England, played county golf for Berks, Bucks and Oxon. He is a member of Woking Golf Club, the Royal and Ancient Golf Club of St Andrews and the Golf Society of Great Britain. He also played club rugby, and still plays cricket and badminton. He is married and lives at Woking, where he spends his spare time playing golf, amusing four children and just failing to cope with a large garden. Besides co-ordinating the whole project and sharing the writing of the book, he also carried out much of the theoretical work and mathematical analysis.

BERTIE DAISH is Principal Lecturer in Ballistics at the Royal Military College of Science, Shrivenham. He was born in 1913 in Plymouth and was educated at King Edward VI School, Totnes, Imperial College (University of London) and Exeter University. He holds an M.Sc. degree in Physics (London), and Associateship of the Royal College of Science (ARCS), the Diploma of Imperial College (DIC) and a Diploma in Education. Before the War, he schoolmastered in Peterborough, leaving to serve in the Army from 1940 to 1946. He was commissioned in the R.A.O.C. After the War he took up his present appointment at the Royal Military College of Science where he lectures to degree students in Physics and to Army Staff Officers in Ballistics. He is author or part-author of a number of textbooks on Physics; has produced sundry pamphlets on various ballistic techniques; and has recently published papers on certain aspects of Physics and games. He has lectured on this topic to physicists and engineers in various parts of the country as well as to a number of audiences of schoolchildren in the south and west of England, under the auspices of the Institute of Physics and the Physical Society. He is currently preparing a book on the subject. He was good at soccer, cricket and other games, and still plays a lot of golf and has retained a handicap of 5 in spite of this investigation, advancing years and the English Golf Union. He has played for his County's 'A' side ('presumably when they were short') and is a member of Frilford Heath Golf Club and the Golf Society of Great Britain. He spends his spare time with amateur dramatics, being a Governor of a local school, umpiring at cricket, playing darts at the local and encouraging his wife to cultivate the garden. Occasionally watches Rugby football and TV, and makes cine films. Loves the country and would hate to live in a big town. He has two daughters and (so far) two grandsons. He was responsible in the investigation for most of the high-speed cine-photography and subsequent analysis, for flash photographic studies of impact, for measurements of velocities and spins and generally for the application of ballistic techniques to the problem. He also helped with the observation of events at tournaments.

WILLIAM FLOYD is Professor of Ergonomics and Cybernetics at Loughborough University of Technology.

DONALD GRIEVE is a Senior Lecturer in the Anatomy Department of the Royal Free Hospital Medical School in London. He was born in 1931 in Woolwich, and educated at Eltham College, Woolwich Polytechnic and London University, where he read physics. While doing so he became interested in the application of his subject to biology and he went on to take an M.Sc. in physiology at University College, London. His National Service commission and secondment to the Ministry of Supply provided him with an interesting year of electronics applied to human physiology under field conditions. His interest in normal man as an 'experimental animal' has persisted. Some rather esoteric properties of muscle formed the subject of his Ph.D. when he returned to University. Since then, he has been interested in bridging the gap between the much-studied muscle cell in isolation and the normal behaviour of muscle tissues in the body. In 1961, he joined the Human Biomechanics Laboratory of the Medical Research Council and studied the development of walking in children. In his present position, to which he was appointed in 1967, he is continuing research into walking and also into problems of body rotation which are the 'fall-out' from the golf studies. His wife is an ergonomist and they have two of those rare children whose patterns of walking are described mathematically! His main hobby is oil painting. He found an attractive combination of physiology and physics in the golf problem. He developed some of the still camera techniques used, and was responsible for analysis and interpretation of the photographs in terms of models of the human golfer.

KEITH LEGG is Professor of Transport Technology at Loughborough University of Technology. He was born in 1924 in Kent and educated at Gillingham County Grammar School. He left school at the age of 15 and served a five-year apprenticeship with Short Brothers at Rochester, during which time he studied part-time for a London External B.Sc. in Engineering. Two years after receiving his degree he went to the College of Aeronautics at Cranfield to do a post-graduate course, specializing in Design and was awarded the Diploma of the College in 1949. He spent the next eight years with Short Brothers and Harland Limited in Belfast finishing up as Chief Structural Development Engineer. While there he pioneered integral construction and the use of the metal titanium in aircraft. In 1956 he went to South America as Chief Designer and Professor at the Brazilian Aeronautical Technical Centre; and four years later he returned to this country to take up his present appointment at Loughborough. His present interest is in promoting consciousness of the way that technology in transport is racing ahead with little regard to social and economic considerations or consequences. He is a Fellow of the Royal Aeronautical Society, and a Member of the Institution of Mechanical Engineers. He is married with two sons, one of whom has swum for Leicestershire. He himself is a keen follower of sport, and at present plays badminton and tennis. His other likes include music, especially opera, and reading autobiographies. He is very concerned about the welfare of spastics and is chairman of the Leicestershire County Spastic Society. He initiated and advised on the work done on the golf project in his department, both in the aerodynamics of golf balls and on the properties of golf clubs.

HAROLD LEWIS.is on the scientific staff of the Medical Research Council, and is also an Honorary Lecturer at University College, London. He was born in South Africa in 1921. He graduated in science and medicine at the University of Cape Town, and joined the South African Army. After the war he came to Britain as a post-graduate student at University College, and was subsequently appointed to the staff. He was a member of the British North Greenland Expedition (1952–1953) when he studied the medical reactions of the men to the Arctic environment. He was awarded the Polar Medal. He was Senior Visiting Fellow at Harvard University (1963–1964). and University of Illinois (1968). At the National Institute for Medical Research at Hampstead he has continued polar studies, particularly on the effects of isolation; he has studied the single handed transatlantic yachtsmen, and is at present mainly engaged on a continuing survey of the health of the Tristan da Cunha islanders. He is interested in scientific photography and has developed techniques for measuring human power output in such sports as weight lifting and pole vaulting. This is how he became interested in the science of golf. He played a leading part in the formation of the Scientific Working Party; he suggested the right scientists for the project, and later approached them. His interest in the mechanics of getting an inter-disciplinary project going is reflected in Appendix III which is largely his work. He is married with three children.

DAVID NOBLE carried out full-time research on the Golf Society of Great Britain project from 1962 until his untimely death, at the age of 28, in December 1967. During that time he was on the staff of the Department of Ergonomics and Cybernetics at Loughborough University of Technology. He was born in 1939 in Birmingham and educated at Moseley Grammar School and Loughborough Training College, where he graduated with first-class honours in Physical Education. It was here that he first became interested in research on golf and carried out some experiments on the strength and mobility of golfers. He was a very good all-round sportsman and obtained colours for rugby football and athletics—no mean feat at Loughborough. He also played golf, squash racquets and cricket. He represented the Midland Counties and the British Universities at athletics, and played first-class rugby for Leicester and Leicestershire. After spending a year teaching in a boys' grammar school in Birmingham, he returned, in 1962, to Loughborough, this time to the University of Technology, to take up the golf research post. At that time he began to play golf seriously, and reduced his handicap from 21 to 3, and played for Leicestershire, within three years. His work on golf was principally concerned with the physiology and psychology of skilled performance, as part of a larger programme of research on human skill at Loughborough. This and other aspects of the work involved direct contact with professional golfers, from which he derived much satisfaction and pleasure. Besides depriving the world of golf of a promising player and fine sportsman, his death has deprived Physical Education of the services of a young man who clearly had a great deal to contribute to the subject, possessing, as he did, a rare combination of qualifications: personal experience in physical education and sport at a high level of performance, coupled with insight and fundamental knowledge gained from research and theoretical study. He is survived by his wife and two young children.

PETER SHARMAN is a lecturer in the Department of Transport Technology at Loughborough University of Technology, where he teaches theory of structures and space dynamics. He was born in 1933 in Great Yarmouth. He left school at 15 and was apprenticed at Saunders-Roe Limited, Cowes, I.O.W. for five years gaining Higher National Certificate in Aeronautical Engineering. After an accelerated Mathematics course at Southampton University, he gained a Diploma in Aeronautical Engineering at the College of Aeronautics, Cranfield, and worked with Bristol Aircraft Limited on guided weapon design for three years. He was then appointed to his present position at Loughborough where he obtained an M.Sc. degree on plate theory. He is interested in the application of computer techniques to structural analysis and design, and is currently studying computer analysis of vehicle bodies. He is married with three young children, who occupy much of his spare time. His hobbies include swimming and natural history. He has strong views for freedom in education at all levels and unconventional teaching; and he is an active Christian worker. In the golf investigation he studied the properties of golf clubs, and has lectured to engineers all over the country on this.

REGINALD WHITNEY is head of the Laboratory of Human Biomechanics at the National Institute for Medical Research at Hampstead. He was born in 1914 in Birmingham, and was educated at King Edward Grammar School, Aston, and the University of Birmingham where he graduated in Zoology in 1936. He was engaged in zoological research and teaching until the outbreak of the 1939–1945 war, when he became a member of the scientific team engaged in the new field of Operational Research for the army. After the war, as a member of the Scientific Civil Service, he was involved in the emergence of another new subject—ergonomics, the scientific study of human work. In 1950 he joined the Medical Research Council's Unit for Research in Climate and Working Efficiency at Oxford University. During the following years, he became particularly interested in the application of new technical advances to a fresh study of human motion. In the golf investigation he was responsible for the analysis and interpretation of the forces acting at the golfer's feet. He is a widower with four children.

DOUGLAS WILKIE is Professor of Experimental Physiology at University College, London. He was born in 1922 in South London. He was educated at Bec School and, when evacuated in 1939, at Brighton Technical College; then, by means of scholarships, at University College, University College Hospital Medical School, and Yale University. His qualifications are all in clinical medicine: M.D. Yale 1943, M.B., B.S. London 1944, M.R.C.P. London 1945. He held a clinical appointment at University College Hospital which he enjoyed, but he wanted to continue some research in muscle physiology which he had started as a student, so he returned to the Department of Physiology, University College and has remained there, save for a period of National Service (1948–1950) at the Institute of Aviation Medicine, Farnborough. His original interest in the mechanical properties of muscle gradually got him involved with the energetics of the process by which muscle transforms chemical into mechanical energy. At present he studies this by a combination of chemical analysis with measurements of heat and work production. A sideline of this interest is the question of human power production, sparked off by the possibilities of man-powered flight. He has written many scientific articles on these subjects; also articles in Encyclopaedias (Britannica, Chambers, Dictionary of Physics) on Muscle. His wife is also a doctor doing research and they have one son. He likes travelling abroad, and cruising in his small sailing boat, and sometimes combines the two. He is 'no good at games', but has great respect and admiration for highly skilled games-players. His contribution to the golf investigation has been in calculation of power output and identification of possible sources of power.

*   *   *   *   *

JOHN STOBBS is a golf writer, until recently golf correspondent of the *Observer*. He was born in 1921 in Hertfordshire and educated at Berkhamsted and Oxford University where he read Philosophy, Politics and Economics. From 1949 he worked for *Leader, Picture Post, Lilliput* and other magazines, and finally in 1956 for the *Observer*. In addition, he edited *Golfing* from 1957 to 1962. He is the author or co-author of several books on golf, one of which had a go at the mysteries of golf ballistics. He is a low handicap golfer; he played for Oxford in 1948, and for Hertfordshire for some ten years until Saturday golf reporting prevented it. His fascination with the scientific theory of golf is a long-standing one, which was still further sharpened by five years practical ballistics of gunnery in the Royal Artillery; and of all golf writers he has shown the most maniacal interest in this side of the game. The task of digesting the scientific data from the Golf Society of Great Britain investigation, and helping to present it readably for the week-end golfer has been to him fascinating and tremendously worthwhile doing. He has been a member of Berkhamsted Golf Club continuously since 1930. He lives near Berkhamsted and loves the Chiltern countryside. His wife and three daughters share this, and golf too.

ANNE WELFORD, assistant to Dr Cochran in the golf research project, was born in Poole in 1941 of schoolteacher parents and brought up in Dorset. After leaving the County High School for Girls, Shaftesbury, in 1960, she worked as a scientific assistant at the Atomic Energy Establishment at Winfrith in a group largely concerned with compiling nuclear data. In 1963, after a short spell as a computer operator at the Agricultural Research Station at Harpenden, she did a 'crash' course in shorthand and typing and joined the golf research project in the dual role of scientific assistant and secretary. Since joining the group she has taken up golf and has the somewhat dubious distinction of being a member of a club some 500 miles away from where she lives! She is also a member of the Golf Society of Great Britain. Her family home is now on Skye in the Hebrides, and she spends a lot of time experiencing the delights of British Rail sleepers and travel by road in the Highlands in all weathers. Besides acting as scientific and secretarial assistant in the golf investigation, she organized several of the data-collecting expeditions such as the tournament analyses.

Most of the above Scientists are now members of the 'Sports Research Partnership', formed to undertake further research or consultancy in any field connected with sport or human movement.

Index